1989

The French and Spanish Popular Fronts

The French and Spanish Popular Fronts

Comparative Perspectives

Edited by

MARTIN S. ALEXANDER

Lecturer in the Department of History,
University of Southampton

HELEN GRAHAM

Lecturer in the Department of Spanish, Portuguese
and Latin American Studies, University of Southampton

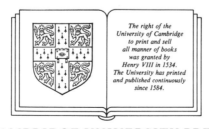

The right of the
University of Cambridge
to print and sell
all manner of books
was granted by
Henry VIII in 1534.
The University has printed
and published continuously
since 1584.

CAMBRIDGE UNIVERSITY PRESS
Cambridge
New York   New Rochelle   Melbourne   Sydney

Published by the Press Syndicate of the University of Cambridge
The Pitt Building, Trumpington Street, Cambridge CB2 1RP
32 East 57th Street, New York, NY 10022, USA
10 Stamford Road, Oakleigh, Melbourne, 3166, Australia

First published 1989

Printed in Great Britain at the University Press, Cambridge

British Library cataloguing in publication data

The French and Spanish popular fronts: comparative perspectives
1. Political movements: Popular fronts, to 1939
1. Alexander, Martin S.   11. Graham, Helen, *1959–*
324'.1

Library of Congress cataloguing in publication data

The French and Spanish popular fronts: comparative perspectives /
edited by Martin S. Alexander and Helen Graham
p.   cm.
Papers from the proceedings of an international conference held in
April 1986 at the University of Southampton
Includes index
ISBN 0 521 35081 6
1. Popular fronts – France – History – 20th century – Congresses
2. Popular fronts – Spain – History – 20th century – Congresses
3. France – Politics and government – 1914–1940 – Congresses
4. Spain – Politics and government – 1931–1939 – Congresses
1. Alexander, Martin S.   11. Graham, Helen, 1959–
DC396.F73   1989
944.08 – dc19   88-12299

ISBN 0 521 35081 6

CE

Contents

v

Contributors

Martin S. Alexander is Lecturer in modern French and British history at the University of Southampton. He wrote his DPhil on 'Maurice Gamelin and the defence of France' (1983). He contributed to Peter Paret's revised edition of *Makers of Modern Strategy: from Machiavelli to the nuclear age* (Princeton, 1986), and is joint General Editor of the Longman series 'The Post-War World: Studies in Contemporary History'.

Michael Alpert is Principal Lecturer at the Polytechnic of Central London. His publications include: *El ejército republicano en la guerra civil* (Paris, 1977); *La reforma militar de Azaña (1931–1933)* (Madrid, 1982) and numerous articles on various aspects of the Spanish Civil War and military politics in Spain.

David Berry is Lecturer in French in the Department of European Studies at the University of Loughborough. He is currently preparing a PhD on the French anarchist movement between the wars.

Christopher Cobb is Head of the School of Arts and Languages at Kingston Polytechnic. He is the author of *La cultura y el pueblo. España, 1930–1939* (Barcelona, 1981); 'El teatro de agitación y propaganda en España', *Literatura culta y literatura popular* (Seville, 1986); '*Mundo Obrero y la elaboración de una política de cultura popular (1931–39)*', *La Prensa de los Siglos XIX y XX* (Bilbao, 1986), and of numerous articles on the press, culture and policy in Spain.

Joel Colton is Professor of History and formerly Chairman of the Department of History at Duke University. A recipient of Guggenheim, Rockefeller and National Endowment for the Humanities fellowships, he was Director for Humanities at the Rockefeller Foundation, 1974–81, and is currently a co-president of the International Commission on the History of Social Movements and Social Structures. His books include *Léon Blum: humanist in politics* (New York, 1965 and 1974; Paris, 1968; and revised edition, Durham, North Carolina, 1987); *Compulsory Labor Arbitration in France 1936–1939* (New York, 1951) and, with R. R. Palmer, *A History of the Modern World* (New York, 1958; sixth edition 1984).

Alan Forrest is Senior Lecturer in French history at the University of Manchester. He has published *Society and Politics in Revolutionary Bordeaux* (Oxford, 1975); *The French Revolution and the Poor* (Oxford, 1981), translated as *La révolution française et les pauvres* (Paris, 1986).

Helen Graham is a Lecturer in the Department of Spanish, Portuguese and Latin American Studies at the University of Southampton. Among her recent publications are: 'The Spanish Popular Front and the Civil War' in H. Graham and P. Preston (eds.), *The Popular Front in Europe* (London, 1987) and 'The Socialist Youth in the JSU: the experience of organizational unity 1936–1938' in M. Blinkhorn (ed.), *Spain in Conflict 1931–1939* (London, 1987).

Paul Heywood is Lecturer in Politics, Queen Mary College, University of London. He is preparing a PhD entitled 'Deluded by theory: Marxism, the State and the failure of organized Socialism in Spain: 1879–1936'. He has published 'De las dificultades para ser marxista: el PSOE, 1879–1921', *Sistema*, 74 (1986) and 'Mirror-Images: the PCE and PSOE in the transition to democracy in Spain', *West European Politics*, 11.1 (1987).

Haywood Hunt is Lecturer with the European Division of the University of Maryland and holds a PhD from Case Western Reserve University, Cleveland, Ohio. He works on the French Radicals and has published 'Joining the Popular Front: Radical goals and objectives' and 'Edouard Daladier and French foreign policy in 1933: from the disarmament conference to the Four Power Pact', *Proceedings of the Western Society for French History* (1978, 1979 respectively).

Julian Jackson is a Lecturer in the Department of History at University College, Swansea. He is the author of *The Politics of Depression in France 1932–1936* (Cambridge, 1985) and *The Popular Front in France: defending democracy, 1934–1938* (Cambridge, 1988).

Contributors

Santos Juliá is a member of the Department of Political Science and Sociology at the Universidad Nacional de Educación a Distancia (UNED) (Madrid). He is the author of *Orígenes del Frente Popular en España (1934–1936)* (Madrid, 1979) and specializes in the political history of the Second Republic on which he has produced two monographical works and numerous articles.

Tom Kemp was Reader in Economic History at the University of Hull. He is the author of several books and articles on imperialism and industrialization. His books on France include *The French Economy 1913–1939, the history of a decline* (London, 1972) and *Stalinism in France* (London, 1984).

David A. L. Levy was formerly Lecturer in Politics and Contemporary History at Salford University and now works in current affairs radio. Among his recent publications are: 'The French Popular Front, 1936–37' in H. Graham and P. Preston (eds.), *The Popular Front in Europe* (London, 1987) and 'Mitterrand's foreign policy: business as usual?' in S. Maizey and M. Newman (eds.), *Mitterrand's France* (London, 1987).

José Manuel Macarro Vera is a member of the Department of Contemporary History at the University of Seville. He is the author of a monographical study of Seville during the Second Republic, *La utopia revolucionaria* (Seville, 1985) and numerous articles on the Spanish left and labour movement.

Siân Reynolds is Lecturer in French Politics and History at the University of Sussex. She has translated Fernand Braudel, *The Mediterranean* (London, 1972–3) and *Civilization and Capitalism* (London, 1981–4). She has edited and contributed to *Women, State and Revolution: essays on gender and power in Europe since 1789* (Brighton, 1986).

Adrian Rossiter was Research Fellow of Nuffield College, Oxford. He wrote his DPhil on 'Experiments with corporatist politics in Republican France, 1916–1939' and is the author of 'Popular Front economic policy and the Matignon negotiations', *Historical Journal*, July–September 1987.

Adrian Shubert is Canada Research Fellow in the Department of History at York University (Ontario). He is author of *The Road to Revolution in Spain: the coal miners of Asturias, 1860–1934* (Champaign-Urbana, 1987) and of several articles on modern Spanish social and political history.

Martin Stanton is a Lecturer and Director of Graduate Studies in European Studies at the University of Kent at Canterbury. He is the author of *Outside the Dream: Lacan and French styles of psychoanalysis* (London, 1983) and has published articles in the *Journal of Modern History* and *History Today*.

James Steel is a lecturer in the Department of French at the University of Glasgow.

Mary Vincent is a research student at St Antony's College, Oxford, and a recipient of a Vicente Cañada Blanch Junior Fellowship. She is preparing a DPhil on the Catholic church under the Second Spanish Republic.

Acknowledgements

This book stems from an international conference on the French and Spanish Popular Fronts which the editors convened at the University of Southampton in April 1986. For the success of that enterprise, which attracted over seventy scholars from Europe and America, the editors are pleased to acknowledge the valued financial assistance of the British Academy and the University of Southampton's Committee for Advanced Studies. They especially appreciate the support at the conference of Professor Paul Preston and Sir Raymond Carr. The editors are likewise grateful for the practical assistance and encouragement of the Departments of History and Spanish, Portuguese and Latin American Studies of the University of Southampton.

In the preparation of the manuscript the editors have contracted further debts and owe thanks to: Professor Joel Colton, Dr Adrian Shubert, Dr Adrian Rossiter and Dr Christopher Cobb for their essays which were specially written for this volume; to Professor Mike Kelly and Dr Bill Marshall of the Department of French, University of Southampton, for generously advising on specific contributions; to Dr Julian Jackson, University College Swansea, for locating a suitable jacket illustration; to Mrs Kathleen Sharpe and Mrs Alison Hamlin for their speedy and careful retyping of contributors' essays and to Kevin Taylor of Cambridge University Press for his interest, patience and support throughout the project.

Abbreviations

FRENCH

AEAR   Association des Ecrivains et Artistes Révolutionnaires
AIL   Amis d'Instruction Laique
AS   Amicales Socialistes
CFTC   Confédération Française de Travailleurs Chrétiens
CGPF   Confédération Générale de la Production Française
CGT   Confédération Générale du Travail
CGTU   Confédération Générale du Travail Unitaire
CLAJ   Centre Laique des Auberges de Jeunesse
CNE   Conseil National Economique
CSAR   Comité Secret d'Action Révolutionnaire
CVIA   Comité de Vigilance des Intellectuels Antifascistes
FAF   Fédération Anarchiste de Langue Française
FC   Front Commun contre le Fascisme
FCL   Fédération Communiste Libertaire
JAC   Jeunesses Anarchistes Communistes
MAP   Mouvement Amsterdam-Pleyel contre la Guerre et le Fascisme
PCF   Parti Communiste Français
POI   Parti Ouvrier Internationale
PPF   Parti Populaire Français
PSF   Parti Social Français

SIA	Solidarité Internationale Antifasciste
SFIO	Section Française de l'Internationale Ouvrière
UA	Union Anarchiste

SPANISH

AIT	Asociación Internacional de Trabajadores (First International)
AP	Acción Popular
BOC	Bloc Obrer i Camperol
CEDA	Confederación Española de Derechas Autónomas
CNT	Confederación Nacional de Trabajo
FAI	Federación Anarquista Ibéria
FETE	Federación Española de Trabajadores de la Enseñanza
FJS	Federación de Juventudes Socialistas
IR	Izquierda Republicana
PCE	Partido Comunista de España
POUM	Partido Obrero de Unificación Marxista
PSOE	Partido Socialista Obrero Español
UCT	Unión Generál de Trabajadores
UJC	Unión de Juventudes Comunistas
UR	Unión Republicana

Introduction

MARTIN S. ALEXANDER AND HELEN GRAHAM

Fifty years ago the vicious manifestations of fascism spawned by the severity of economic depression created the conditions for the birth of Popular Front coalitions in both Spain and France.[1] The dynamic of the electoral pacts which triumphed at the polls, in February and May 1936 respectively, lay in the pressing need to bar the way to political reaction in the domestic arena. Across two decades the left and labour in Europe had been in retreat. This was true irrespective of the level of socio-economic development, from heavily industrialized societies to argrarian economies. From Saxony to Seville, political and economic conservatism by the early 1930s, imbibing deeply of the new aggressive ideologies of fascism, was embarked upon an assault on workers' interests as ruthless and premeditated as the reduction of the red forty-eighters' barricades. An integral part of the left's strategy in both countries constituted a drive for social and economic improvements. By these the left sought to advance and entrench the bounds of a reformist consensus. In an age where fascist and quasi-fascist leaders claimed to oppose the excesses of incipient revolution, whilst in fact setting about the destruction both of social and economic reforms and the parliamentary systems via which they had been hard won, the reforming content of Popular Frontism signified the left's

---

[1] An examination of Popular Frontism as a political initiative in a European context lies beyond the scope of this volume: for this see H. Graham and P. Preston (eds.), *The Popular Front in Europe* (London, 1987).

I

move onto the offensive as its best means of defence – even of self-preservation.

Yet the mass mobilization which characterized both sides of the political divide in 1930s Europe highlights the uniqueness of the Popular Front experience in both Spain and France. It was far more than a narrow political initiative agreed between the hierarchies of the constituent parties – Socialists, Communists and Republicans. In an age of mass politicization, the Popular Front electoral initiatives were born of pressure from the grass roots, just as that same pressure radicalized the nature of the subsequent parliamentary projects. Once electoral victory had been secured, popular aspirations overflowed the barriers of the Fronts as vehicles for parliamentary action. Factory and land occupations in France and Spain ensured that fundamental items of social and economic reform remained at the head of the moderate parliamentarians' political agenda. Indeed in France the claims of the rank and file expanded the agenda, obtaining for workers the forty-hour week and paid holidays which had never featured in the electoral programme.

In attempting to recoup and assess the Popular Front experience at a distance of half a century, one must seek to understand the way in which it qualitatively transformed political life.[2] Taken in its broadest sense, as a social movement, the Popular Front widened the dimensions of political action. This crucial point is brought out in a variety of ways by several authors. In the Spanish coalmining region of Asturias – which was so central to the creation of the electoral alliance's dynamic – the ideal of mass mobilization enshrined in the Popular Front lived on after the national victory at the polls. Reaching beyond narrow electoral concerns, the Popular Front committees, established to coordinate the electoral campaign, became a vehicle for pressing local, working-class demands.[3] In France, too, there are striking examples of how the Popular Front transformed the politics of labour. In Marseille, where labour organization had previously functioned on the basis of clientelism and patronage – support being mobilized via appeals to race or nationality rather than class loyalty – there occurred a large-scale mobilization of industrial workers around specifically class-based issues. A significant number of French anarchists, inspired to some degree by their Spanish counterparts, drew close to the Front. They accepted the notion of an alliance with other

[2] L. Bodin and J. Touchard, *Front Populaire 1936: l'histoire par la presse* (Paris, 1985).
[3] For October 1934, see also special edition of *Estudios de Historia Social*, 31 (October–December 1984).

left-wing forces, not only because of the overwhelming need to oppose the advance of fascism by any means possible, but also because, as an unparalleled embodiment of working-class unity, they hoped to build upon its extra-parliamentary aspect. The Popular Front brought onto the political stage many more protagonists, who, by thus engaging, redefined the nature of political action. Not the least of these redefinitions concerned the impact of women's experience. It was in 'underdeveloped' Spain, ironically, that the franchise was procured and where the *force majeure* of military *pronunciamiento* and civil war perforce produced a dislocation of gender roles – if sadly a transient one. But within the French strike movement, too, the distinctive perspective of women workers sheds new light on the variations and indeed the limitations of the Popular Front experience. Culture and the media too, taken in their fullest senses, were at once instruments of political change and themselves transformed by the Popular Front experience.[4]

This collection of essays sets out to explore the multi-dimensional reality of Popular Front in both Spain and France. From the genesis of the Popular Front idea, through victory at the polls for inter-class electoral pacts, the volume charts the vexed course of reformist legislation as the frontist governments sought to accommodate – when not to forestall – the reactions of the institutional heavyweights: Church and army.[5] At the same time, in both national arenas, there emerged hostile conservative and radical critiques of the Fronts which respectively considered them to be anarchic and disintegrative of national economic strength or mere confidence tricks whereby the proletarian parties 'managed' the recession for capitalism in crisis.

Joel Colton's introductory essay on the origins of the French front synthesizes current historiography while opening up the debate towards consideration of the dynamic of political power and the balance of economic forces which underpinned the period of Popular Front government.[6] Santos Juliá, writing on the genesis of the Popular Front in Spain, highlights what is, at first sight, an important qualitative difference between the French and Spanish experiences which was to have profound

[4] See also G. Leroy and A. Roche, *Les écrivains et le Front Populaire* (Paris, 1986); P. Ory and J. F. Sirinelli, *Les intellectuels en France, de l'affaire Dreyfus à nos jours* (Paris, 1986).

[5] For the Catholic Church in France and Spain in the 1930s, see R. Rémond, *Les catholiques dans la France des années 30* (Paris, 1979); F. Lannon, *Privilege, Persecution and Prophecy: the Catholic Church in Spain 1875–1975* (Oxford, 1987).

[6] For a recent survey of the French Popular Front, see J. Kergoat, *La France du front populaire* (Paris, 1986).

consequences for the left in Spain during the Civil War: namely that the political influence wielded by the trade unions in Spain far outweighed that of either proletarian or bourgeois parties. So much so in fact that the author argues against the use of the term 'Popular Front' in the Spanish context until the formation of Juan Negrín's government in May 1937.[7] This signified that political hegemony had been recouped by the parties of Republican Spain as the unions were politically demobilized, subjected once again to the will of the central state and returned to the factories as the 'managers of production' whose task it was to meet production targets decided elsewhere. But in France too, as David Levy indicates, the Socialists in government had to face the 'newly politicized concept of industrial action' being advocated to some extent by all trade union leaders. In both cases increased union strength was a spin off of the massive worker mobilization itself. The Popular Front era saw a massive influx of members into the industrial unions. This unleashed a fierce organizational battle – in France between Socialists and Communists and in Spain a downright vicious one between Socialists, Communists and Anarchists – for bodies as well as minds in an age of mass politicization. Indeed in both countries it was the Popular Front elections which made the fortunes of the Communist parties, opening up unparalleled opportunities for expanding their memberships. The difference between the two national experiences here then is, though substantial, a question of degree rather than a qualitative one.

The notion of comparative perspectives which underscores the volume remains valid insofar as it relates to the underlying dynamic of the initiative and the unfavourable balance of socio-economic power which both the Popular Fronts had to confront. The political mandate invested in the frontist governments came up against *de facto* economic powers – albeit that these differed from France and Spain, reflecting the different levels of national socio-economic development.[8] Equally, the fact of civil war in Spain should not blind one to the essential similarity of the defeat suffered by both Popular Fronts. In ultra-polarized Spain the army, in its time-honoured role as the preserver of conservative interests, intervened to prevent the enactment of reform via the legislature once it became clear

---

[7] For the Popular Front in Spain, see also special edition of *Estudios de Historia Social*, 16–17 (January–June 1981); also H. Graham, 'The Spanish Popular Front and the Civil War' in *The Popular Front in Europe*, pp. 106–30.

[8] For Spain, see for example, J. M. Macarro Vera, *La utopia revolucionaria. Sevilla en la Segunda República* (Seville, 1985); S. Juliá, *Madrid 1931–1934. De la fiesta popular a la lucha de clases* (Madrid, 1984).

that parliamentary obstruction was insufficient as a barrier against it. In France the 'true' Popular Front government (May 1936 – June 1937) was subjected to a process of political erosion which in the end achieved the same effect: the halting of reform and the recouping of ground taken by urban and rural workers riding high on the euphoria of electoral victory. A common objective thus bound the conservative opponents of Popular Front in Spain and France, just as the will to reform united the frontists in both countries. Military rebellion and the ensuing conflict increased the stakes in Spain: it did not change them. The Civil War was literally the continuation of politics by other means: the issues – reform versus reaction – remained the same and with it the fundamental affinity with the French experience.

Nevertheless, the contrasts between the French and Spanish experiences are sufficiently striking when they occur to make clear the very different levels of socio-economic and political development on which the Popular Front reformers sought to build. The progressive Republicans and Socialists in Spain who had laid the foundations of Popular Front reformism between 1931 and 1933 were, of necessity, faced with the daunting task of enacting far more fundamental reforms than were their French counterparts.[9] As Paul Heywood underlines, the gargantuan practical problems of structural modernization confronting the Spanish reformers were compounded by the left's own faulty theoretical analysis of Spanish historical development. It would be these same errors of analysis that left the Spanish Socialists unprepared for the serious political contradictions inherent in the Popular Front which were to burst forth with such devastating consequences for the Republican cause during the Civil War. As Tom Kemp illustrates in his essay on the dissident French left, a profound awareness of precisely these contradictions had formed the basis of their Cassandra-like criticisms of the entire Popular Front strategy. Both their scepticism regarding the feasibility of bourgeois–proletarian alliances nationally and their distrust of Stalin's motives in promoting a frontist line internationally via the Comintern would be tragically vindicated by developments in the Republican zone during the Spanish Civil War.[10]

The political vision of the French front incorporated an ambitious and

[9] P. Preston, 'The creation of the Popular Front in Spain' in *The Popular Front in Europe*, pp. 84–105.

[10] For an illustration of bitter socialist–communist organizational rivalries during the Civil War in Spain, see H. Graham, 'The Socialist Youth in the JSU: the experience of organizational unity, 1936–8' in M. Blinkhorn (ed.), *Spain in Conflict* (London, 1986), pp. 83–102; see also 'Socialismo y Guerra Civil', *Anales de Historia*, vol. 2 (Madrid, 1987).

exhilarating sortie into the politics of leisure. Whilst paid holidays were enshrined at the heart of the first wave of French frontist legislation in June 1936, in Spain a majority of the proletariat – the starving rural landless – suffered long periods of chronic seasonal unemployment without even the benefit of parish relief. They were trapped in a network of social relations with landlords and estate stewards that can only be described as feudal. This disparity of social and economic development is perhaps most starkly reflected in the primacy of a basic literacy campaign and the emphasis placed on extra-mural education in the cultural policy of Spanish Popular Front strategists.

But while starting from distinctive base lines, both the Spanish and French fronts failed to match programme with practice. An enormous gap remained between the aspirations to reform of the social base and the economic possibilities perceived by moderate frontist politicians. The latter, fighting to preserve the political centre, sought to reverse or at least slow down the polarization process. Their problems were undoubtedly compounded by the constraints of economic crisis. But, as Macarro Vera indicates, the Spanish reformers were equally hamstrung by their total lack of any hard fiscal strategy with which to finance their package of social reforms. In attempting to present the latter before elaborating the former they courted disaster – not least in the withering parliamentary interventions of the Spanish right. Ironically, these conservatives made a hero of the French popular-frontist premier, Léon Blum, precisely because of the 'moderation' of his economic strategy and his attempts to reconcile the interests of labour and capital in a plan of national reconstruction. Yet these same restraints, informed by Blum's legalistic constitutionalism, served only to draw the fire of the more radical French left, notably Marceau Pivert and the Gauche Révolutionnaire.[11] Moreover, it was this very moderation, expressed in the prime minister's formula, 'ni déflation ni dévaluation' which precluded early use of the exchange rate to assist export-led economic recovery. The absence of a business boom led rapidly to bitterness and disillusion among Blum's erstwhile working-class supporters, who, by September 1936, were experiencing the damaging effects of this moderation with little sign of compensatory improvements day by day.

Popular Front politicians in France were, from the outset, acutely conscious of the responsibility placed on them by their electoral mandate.

[11] 'Il se veut un gouvernement social plus qu'un gouvernement socialiste . . .', S. Berstein, 'La chute du premier gouvernement de Front Populaire', *Le Monde*, 21–2 June 1987.

Introduction

Throughout July and August 1936 they plunged into legislation designed to turn their programme into policies. Drafting bills, facing amendments in committee and enacting laws like that of 11 August nationalizing selected armaments industries, the left's deputies and senators worked through the usual weeks of summer parliamentary recess.

Such intensive activity by the professional politicians inspired self-congratulation, a sense of achievement for the Popular Front as a national political force. For Radical *rapporteurs*, as for socialist senators, unprecedented quantities of legislation were tabled and enacted with quite unusual despatch. But parliamentary paperwork of this kind made little impression on militants and Popular Front voters. For industrial workers, the rank and file of Blum's support, the newly-won paid holidays remained, as Julian Jackson shows, a summer privilege of the few. Moreover, the early autumn hints of price inflation to erode the Matignon wage rises, together with scant sign of improving employment prospects, aroused disenchantment and social radicalization by September 1936. The slowness of Blum's policies to procure tangible material improvement for workers was met with incomprehension and suspicion: from the fringes of the leftist alliance, and by 1937 from outside it, PCF and CGT activists stood poised to profit, as self-proclaimed 'ministers of the masses', from these embittered social positions.

Thus the gear-change which disengaged the engine of frontist reform in France occurred not in February 1937 but as far back as the autumn of 1936. The hard facts of economic expenditure reveal that the Popular Front did more for guns than for butter. If public works was the image, rearmament was the reality. In France the budgetary allocation for public works was projected as 20 billion francs by the law of August 1936. Yet, in fact only *one* billion francs were spent over the next five years. By contrast, expenditure on the rearmament programme of 7 September 1936 amounted to 14 billion francs over a four-year period. In the final analysis, both the French and Spanish Popular Fronts as experiments in social and economic reform were 'disarmed' by the diversion of resources for the purposes of war, national defence and rearmament. In France the prioritization of the rearmament programme was presented as essential to the defence of the Republic from external aggressors, whilst in Spain the savage civil war unleashed by the military rebels deprived the Popular Front reformers of any choice in the matter.

With the passage of generations since the frustration of Popular Frontism, a sufficient perspective, along with a widening range of archival

7

sources, has enabled a comparative reappraisal of both the French and Spanish experiments. The present volume pursues such a reassessment by transcending the more orthodox but narrow boundaries of political analysis. Through contributions by leading scholars of the 1930s the phenomena of leftist mobilization and aspiration are seen to have encompassed ambitions for education, leisure and culture as well as initiatives in economic and social transformation. Diverse in their objectives, heterogenous in their support, both Popular Fronts were all along weakened by hidden cracks. Ironically, these resulted from the very pluralism which the architects of the Popular Fronts considered at the outset as their underlying strength.

The formation of the French Popular Front, 1934–6

JOEL COLTON

'With an unprecedented violence and rapidity the events of these past few days place us brutally in the presence of immediate fascist danger' read an appeal issued on 10 February 1934 by thirty-two French writers, artists, and other left-wing intellectuals aroused by the stormy events of 6 February – the *émeutes fascistes* – and their aftermath. Citing the 'terrible experience' of Germany as 'a lesson', the statement described working-class unity as indispensable to 'bar the route to fascism' and asked the old fratricidal enemies, the Socialists (SFIO) and Communists (PCF), to draw together in 'a spirit of conciliation'. Here was the Popular Front in embryo, built first on working-class unity of action and then broadened into a wider alliance of the political parties of the left, organized labour and intellectuals against the threat of fascism.[1] One of the most striking political phenomena to emerge from the social politics of the 1930s, the Popular Front opened the way for Socialists, reform-minded liberals, civil libertarians, and a

---

[1] For a recent listing of works on the French Popular Front see my *Léon Blum: humanist in politics* (New York, 1965; new edition, Durham, North Carolina, 1987), 1987 edition, pp. 495–521. The most detailed history remains Georges Lefranc, *Histoire du Front Populaire, 1934–1938* (Paris, 1965), with many key documents reproduced in the appendices. Useful for a sampling of the press during these years and for its bibliography is Louis Bodin and Jean Touchard, *Front Populaire 1936* (Paris, 1961; 4th edition, 1986). Archival materials for Léon Blum, Edouard Daladier, Vincent Auriol, Pierre Cot, and other participants in the Popular Front years are now available in Paris under the auspices of the Fondation Nationale des Sciences Politiques; the materials include manuscripts (some later published) and some unpublished correspondence. The appeal of the intellectuals cited in the text is reproduced in Lefranc, *Front Populaire*, Annexes, pp. 430–1.

broad range of intellectuals to submerge or suspend their mistrust of the Communists as an alien party serving the interests of the Soviet Union and to unite with them against the threat of domestic fascism and international fascist aggression. The object of this chapter is to reconstruct the climate that made the French Popular Front possible.

The Socialist leader Léon Blum, looking back upon the French Popular Front in later years, called it 'an instinctive defence reflex' against two sources of danger – first, 'the dangers that threatened the Republic, of which the most striking sign was the agitation of the paramilitary leagues and the uprising of 6 February 1934', and second, 'the economic depression which was crushing the working masses, the rural population and the middle class'.[2] In both respects his analysis was correct. A child of the depression, the Popular Front grew out of the deep malaise and loss of faith that the world economic crisis had generated. That the depression came later to France – towards the end of 1933, when many countries were showing signs of recovery, and when many in France thought they might escape its ravages – made the crisis even more resented. Political leaders in office applied only the received wisdom of the times – retrenchment to restore business confidence regardless of the cost to other social classes. The depression reinforced an atmosphere of political and social unease. How many, as in Germany, would abandon traditional political channels, lose faith in the parliamentary system itself, and listen to the siren call of the extremists, with their vaguely-defined but clearly authoritarian solutions?

On the eve of 6 February 1934, a year and nine months after the elections of May 1932 had returned the Radical Party as the leading party in the Chamber, the political situation in France was particularly muddled. The Radicals could govern with a left-wing majority only with Socialist votes. But the SFIO did not favour the deflationary policies of the Radicals and intermittently withdrew their support, leading to more than the usual cabinet instability. In eighteen months five Radical cabinets succeeded one another. One month after Camille Chautemps formed a fifth Radical cabinet in November 1933, a financial scandal, the notorious Stavisky affair, broke, implicating members of the cabinet itself. When Chautemps refused to permit a thorough independent investigation, and Stavisky was found dead, Chautemps was forced to resign.

Edouard Daladier, emerging as leader of the progressive younger wing of the Radical Party to challenge the leadership of Edouard Herriot, formed

[2] Testimony at Riom trial in 1942, *L'oeuvre de Léon Blum*, vol. 5, *1940–1945* (Paris, 1955), p. 233.

a new Radical government. He included conservative ministers in his cabinet, and at the same time, to please the SFIO and to affirm his identification with the left, he dismissed Jean Chiappe, known for his rightist and league sympathies, as prefect of police. On 6 February, the day that Daladier was to seek his first vote of confidence in the Chamber, the word went out to the right-wing leagues to demonstrate against the new cabinet. The Stavisky affair, the continuation in office of the Radicals, Daladier's dismissal of Chiappe to woo the left – all within the larger framework of the economic depression and nagging political instability – provided ready ammunition for the vitriolic press of the extreme right and the leagues. These groups vented their wrath on the system, bringing France closer to the threat of fascism than at any other time in the interwar years, and hence indirectly helping to create the anti-fascist Popular Front.

In the context of France in the 1930s the term 'fascism' is elusive because no homogeneous fascist movement existed, only a cluster of competing 'leagues'. Although the leagues were a peculiarly French phenomenon, they represented a close equivalent to fascist organizations flourishing elsewhere in the interwar years. Noisy and militant pressure groups, paramilitary in nature, operating outside parliament but with spokesmen within, and supported by a scurrilous press, the leagues were France's special contribution to European fascism.[3] They had a long earlier history, forming part of the French anti-republican tradition. Some, like the royalist Action Française and its affiliate the Camelots du Roi, went back to the anti-republican agitation of the Dreyfus affair. They enjoyed a renaissance in the 1920s because of widespread disillusionment with the peace and the postwar era and developed added strength and militancy in the depression years. Their members read the inflammatory rightist press – *Action Française, Gringoire, Je Suis Partout* – which dripped with anti-republican, anti-parliamentary and anti-semitic venom and called for physical action against political leaders of the left, even for assassination. Blum, who headed the Socialists, by virtue of also being Jewish, was a special target.

In 1934 no single leader or group was prepared to organize a 'march on Rome' or foment plans for a generals' revolt. But on 6 February 1934 when the word went out, members of the leagues were determined to show what they could do: demonstrate, flex their muscles, agitate in the streets,

---

[3] For interesting recent analyses of fascism in France see Zeev Sternhell, *Ni droite ni gauche: l'idéologie fasciste en France* (Paris, 1983; English translation, Berkeley, California, 1986), and Robert Soucy, *Fascism in France: the first wave, 1924–1933* (New Haven, Connecticut, 1986).

threaten the Chamber, perhaps prevent Daladier's vote of confidence, force the Chamber to adjourn, then who knew? In the light of the Stavisky scandal they wrapped themselves in the mantle of self-righteous indignation against the system and demonstrated with the old cry – *A bas les voleurs!* The afternoon of the Chamber debate they gathered by the thousands in the Place de la Concorde, just across the bridge from the Palais Bourbon where the Chamber sat. (Colonel de la Rocque assembled his group, the Croix de Feu, on the left bank, close to the Chamber, thus keeping his supporters aloof from the others.) As the demonstrations grew nastier and more violent, many deputies abandoned the Chamber and Daladier could scarcely complete his speech outlining his government's programme. For his part Blum defiantly called not only for a vote of confidence but for 'a vote of combat in defence of republican legality'. The forces of reaction, he said, were 'attemping a coup de force ... a brutal assault (*mainmise*) on public liberties'. 'La réaction fasciste,' he concluded, 'ne passera pas!'[4] Whatever his later hesitations in response to communist initiatives, Blum was the first to call for a militant stand in defence of the Republic. After nightfall, the police, under orders to restrain the demonstrators, twice opened fire. Before the night was over about twenty lay dead; hundreds were wounded or injured. The next day brought the startling news that Daladier had resigned despite the substantial vote of confidence he had received. It was the first time in the history of the Third Republic that a cabinet had fallen in response to pressure from the street. Gaston Doumergue, former president of the Republic from 1924–31, formed a so-called 'national union' government which included several ex-premiers and ranged from conservatives to Herriot and the Radicals. Some on the left, alarmed by the presence of the conservatives and by talk of constitutional reform, unjustifiably described it as 'pre-fascist'.

What did the leagues intend to do that night? Was there a concerted effort to overthrow the regime? Was there indeed 'a sixth of February'?[5] The question has never been resolved. A parliamentary investigation at the time and a postwar investigation each supported the interpretation that the demonstrators intended to invade the Chamber, intimidate those who had not fled, and proclaim a new provisional government. The postwar inquiry declared unequivocally that it was a 'veritable insurrection, minutely prepared'. Others have argued more cautiously that 6 February repre-

---

[4] The speech is reproduced in *L'oeuvre de Léon Blum*, vol. 4, part 1, *1934–1937* (Paris, 1964), pp. 8–10.

[5] This is the formulation of Max Beloff in 'The sixth of February' in James Joll (ed.), *The Decline of the Third Republic* (London, 1955), pp. 9–35; see especially p. 9.

sented no more than a right-wing street demonstration against the left-wing politicians, not an attempted *Putsch* or uprising.[6] In any event 6 February marked a decisive turning point. Whether or not a coup was possible, the perceived threat of a fascist insurrection served as a catalyst for the emergence of the Popular Front.

Where were the Communists at the time? The question is no idle one because as events unfolded no development was more important than the change in line of the French Communist Party after February 1934, a change that was at the heart of the worldwide Popular Front phenomenon. On 6 February, it is clear that the PCF, or at least members of the communist-led veterans' association, were also in the streets demonstrating against the Republic, even if, to be sure, at a reasonable distance from the rightist leagues. At the time they were still following a sectarian class-struggle line, denouncing the corrupt bourgeois republic and its defenders, the Socialists. From the 1920s on the PCF had supported the Republic, in Lenin's old phrase, as a rope supports a hanging man; and they worked with the Socialists, in another old communist formula, only 'to pluck the feathers from the socialist goose'. Even after the coming to power of Adolf Hitler in Germany in January 1933, the *front unique*, or united front of the working classes, meant in communist theory and practice a united front at the base, reaching out to the rank-and-file Socialists over the heads of their leaders, like appealing to soldiers in enemy trenches to desert and cross over.

L'Humanité had reminded its followers that one could not fight against the 'fascist bands' without simultaneously fighting against two other enemies – the government, led by the Radicals, which had allowed the leagues to flourish, and the Socialists, the principal supporters of the government. In the Chamber the ten PCF deputies voted against the motion of confidence. In the aftermath of the bloodshed the PCF denounced the government-ordered police violence directed against working-class Paris (*Paris ouvrier*), and denounced the treacherous Socialists. Hardly a word was said about the anti-republican agitation of the fascist leagues that had precipitated the events. Rejecting overtures from militant socialist leaders of the Seine federation for a joint demonstration against the leagues, the PCF chose to hold its own demonstrations on the night of 9

---

[6] The conclusions of the parliamentary investigation of the 1930s is summarized by the commission's chairman in Laurent Bonnevay, *Les journées sanglantes de février 1934* (Paris, 1935). For the statement by Charles Serre, who chaired the postwar inquiry, see Lefranc, *Front Populaire*, p. 18. For a more cautious interpretation of the events see René Rémond, *La droite en France de 1815 à nos jours: continuité et diversité d'une tradition* (Paris, 1954, 1963), p. 19.

February. When the government forbade them, clashes occurred; four demonstrators were killed, several were wounded, and some later died of their injuries, for a total of nine victims. For the PCF, and for others, the victims were working-class martyrs, even if the communist actions had been deliberately provocative.

Meanwhile other groups on the left, in addition to the militant Socialists of the Seine federation, had been galvanized into action by the events of 6 February. The CGT, its old syndicalist militancy reawakened, dramatically called for a nationwide general protest strike for Monday, 12 February. The SFIO leaders, even though making their own plans, quickly announced their support and called for simultaneous peaceful demonstrations in Paris and throughout the nation. The government, unwilling to see more bloodshed, and recognizing the determination of the left, raised no objections. But the attitude of the Communists, still reeling from the police action on 9 February, remained equivocal. As late as 11 February, *L'Humanité* was still attacking the Socialists and labour reformists who 'were pretending to lead the workers in the struggle against fascism'. Nonetheless intense debate was going on within the party. Jacques Doriot, in spite of the objections of Maurice Thorez and other party leaders, demanded joint action on a broad front against fascism. The issue was not fully resolved, but at the last moment a decision was reached to participate in the general strike and demonstrations.

12 February 1934 proved to be one of the *grandes journées* in the history of the French working class. The success of both the nationwide general strike and the demonstrations exceeded expectations. At the government's orders, the mounted police remained discreet, out of sight. Spectators lined the pavements as demonstrators marched from the Cours de Vincennes to the Place de la Nation. And in an incident long remembered in working-class legend, what might have developed into a last-minute confrontation between demonstrators led by the Socialists and the CGT and a separate group led by PCF militants turned not into a 'collision' but 'fraternization' – handshakes, songs, and cries of 'unity'.[7]

The events of that momentous week heightened the emotional appeal of unity but served only as a prologue to agreement on working-class unity of action. Despite the initial euphoria, mistrust and suspicion persisted on both sides. Negotiations initiated between the two parties had little

---

[7] For Blum's recollection of that day sixteen years later, see 'Il y a seize ans', *Le Populaire–Dimanche*, 12 February 1950, reproduced in *L'oeuvre de Léon Blum*, vol. 4, part I, *1934–1937*, pp. 13–17.

success. The SFIO leadership, for its part, despite pressure from its militants and rank and file, remained suspicious. The PCF, continuing in its sectarian class-struggle line, resumed its attacks on the Socialists and overrode those in their own party like Doriot who championed unity of action. But that spring the Comintern itself was winning Stalin's approval for a profound change in policy, largely under the influence of Georgii Dimitrov (the hero of the Reichstag fire trial and now a key figure on the Comintern's executive committee), who had been observing the events in France closely. In April he called for an end to attacks on the Socialists and proclaimed the need for a united front with the SFIO and its leaders in the interests of working-class unity for the struggle against fascism. Late that May an article in *Pravda* confirmed the new line. For a time, Thorez seems to have resisted, even after a visit to Moscow, but he finally rallied to the new policy and championed it at the PCF conference at Ivry, held between 23 and 26 June.[8]

Negotiations with the Socialists, broken off at one point, were now resumed in an entirely different spirit. Thorez accepted what *Le Populaire* called 'a non-aggression pact' – an initial pledge that both parties in their joint activities would desist from mutual recriminations and insults. A month later, on 27 July 1934, the two parties concluded a unity of action pact.[9] On 29 July, for the first time since their separation in December 1920, they jointly commemorated the twentieth anniversary of the assassination of Jean Jaurès.

A year after the events of February 1934, the nation as a whole remembered its dead. On 6 February 1935 Cardinal Verdier presided over a solemn mass held at Notre Dame in the presence of government officials. A few days later, on 10 February, a joint socialist–communist memorial procession marched to the Place de La République to honour the working-class victims. One remembered 6 February in different ways in a divided nation.

The unity of action pact was not many months old when in October a new communist initiative to transform the pact into a broader coalition once again took the Socialists by surprise. At a meeting of the fourteen

[8] See Irwin M. Wall, *French Communism in the Era of Stalin: the quest for unity and integration, 1945–1962* (Westport, Connecticut, 1983), pp. 13–16, which cites published Comintern sources and relevant Soviet studies; and John Santore, 'The Comintern's united front initiative of May 1934: French or Soviet inspiration?', *Canadian Journal of History*, 16 (December 1981), 405–23.

[9] The pact, along with the later 'platform of common action' of 22 September 1935, is reproduced in *L'oeuvre de Léon Blum*, vol. 4, part 1, *1934–1937*, pp. 222–5.

socialist and communist delegates appointed to coordinate the unity of action pact, Thorez with no preliminary notification came forward with the proposal that socialist–communist cooperation be widened to ensure 'the alliance of the middle classes'. At a public meeting the next day he called for a vast 'rassemblement populaire' – the first time the term was used. *L'Humanité* picked up the appeal and called for a 'Popular Front against fascism'. From that time on the two terms 'Rassemblement Populaire' (technically the correct name for the coalition that came into being) and 'Front Populaire' were used interchangeably, but the more militant sound of 'Popular Front', with its connotation of popular mobilization for action, prevailed.

When the Socialists embarked on the unity of action negotiations, there was no indication that the Comintern envisaged a broader coalition to reach out to the Radicals and others. There is evidence that in this instance Thorez and the PCF anticipated the Comintern – apparently confident that such a broad coalition was the logical consequence of the earlier decision for unity against fascism.[10] The initiative found favour in Moscow because the Radicals were likely to champion a firmer foreign policy against Nazi aggression than the traditionally pacifist and anti-militarist Socialists, and negotiations for a Franco-Soviet pact were already under way.

The Communist appeal fell on receptive ears. There was already a precedent for broad-based action. In March 1934 a group of left-wing intellectuals had created the Comité de Vigilance des Intellectuels Anti-fascistes (CVIA). The independent-minded Radical Gaston Bergéry had even earlier called for a broad coalition. Popular mass rallies reiterated the anti-fascist theme. No matter what the PCF's ulterior motives, it seemed important to many non-communists to heed the PCF's appeal for a coalition to include anti-fascist and reform-minded Radicals, the smaller parties of the left (many the products of schisms and secessions within the working-class parties over the years), the trade union confederations, civil liberties organizations like the League of the Rights of Man, and all others who would rally to the anti-fascist cause – a popular coalition to be drawn from *le pays républicain* to work together for 'jobs, liberty, and peace'.

Despite socialist suspicions – especially when the PCF proposed local Popular Front committees – the movement acquired a momentum of its own. In November 1934, at communist instigation, a 'central committee of anti-fascist unity of action' was formed. On 18 January 1935 a mass

[10] Wall, *French Communism*, pp. 15–16.

meeting was held in the Salle Bullier in Paris chaired by Victor Basch, president of the League of the Rights of Man, himself a Socialist. In May the signing of the Franco-Soviet mutual assistance pact made it possible for the PCF to put another segment of its sectarian past behind it. The party had Stalin's approval for giving national defence a high priority. The French Communists could now exploit patriotic memories of 1789 and 1792, project themselves as the 'new Jacobins' and continue in their efforts to win over the Radicals. In these months Blum, still apprehensive over PCF efforts to outmanoeuvre his party, seemed to think that reunification ('organic unity') under the aegis of the much larger SFIO would thwart such designs, but little came of the reunification negotiations that the Socialists initiated.

The militants of all camps serving on the 'central committee of anti-fascist unity of action' now laid plans for a great joint celebration of Bastille Day in July 1935, 'an assembly (*rassemblement*) of all citizens for the defence of democratic liberties, bread . . . and peace'. Invitations were issued to the three major political parties of the left (the Socialists, Communists, and Radicals), the smaller parties of the left, the two labour confederations (now in the midst of their own reunification negotiations), and other organizations such as the League of the Rights of Man, leftist veterans' groups, youth organizations, the Mouvement des Femmes. On a seniority basis Victor Basch took over the chairmanship of the organizing committee.

Meanwhile, with patriotism and the traditions of the Great Revolution being evoked as never before, the Radicals, too, were caught up in the tide even though the party was still represented in the Laval cabinet, which was committed to retrenchment and at best an ambivalent foreign policy. Setbacks in recent municipal elections also induced the Radicals to read the writing on the wall and to worry about their waning electoral support. Under pressure from Daladier and other Young Turks in the party, the Radicals accepted the invitation.

There was a sense of historic importance to the giant celebrations of 14 July 1935. Participants felt a *frisson* of pride when delegates of the various groups making up the Rassemblement Populaire gathered that morning at the Vélodrome Buffalo, buried their differences, took an oath of unity, sang the Marseillaise and the Internationale, and captured or recaptured for the left Joan of Arc, Valmy, Verdun, and the tricolor. Everyone took a solemn oath – 'to defend the democratic liberties conquered by the people of France, to give bread to the workers, work to the young, and peace to all humanity'.[11] Four men and one woman came forward, in a ceremony purposefully recalling the Fête des Fédérations of July 1790, to pledge the allegiance of the regions they represented. Orators struck a note of conciliation, patriotism, unity, and defiance of fascism. Intellectuals like Nobel Prize winner Jean Perrin, Paul Rivet, Henri Barbusse and Paul Langevin took part. Later that day stirring parades took place in the capital and all over France. In Paris, Daladier, Blum and Thorez marched together as political symbols of the unity of the Front Populaire and gave the clenched-fist salute, the differences between them submerged for the moment.

At the end of July Thorez was accorded a place of honour at the Comintern's Seventh World Congress in Moscow, where the Popular Front policy was formally promulgated. A policy that had begun as a tactical operation in response to the threat of fascism in France – corresponding as it did to Soviet foreign policy needs – had become the basis for a new communist worldwide strategy, with implications for developments in Spain, Chile and elsewhere.

The Rassemblement Populaire still had to be formally organized. Fifty organizations had already committed themselves; eventually there were ninety-eight.[12] Representatives of the ten largest organizations that had signed the appeal for the 14 July celebration formed an organizational committee and in the next six months sought to draw up a programme. To allay Socialist and Radical concerns it was agreed that the new coalition would not curtail the political parties' independence of action, nor be a new party or super-party; that in the coming elections no candidate would run as a candidate of the Rassemblement Populaire alone; and that local Popular Front committees would not be permitted to bypass the party organizations in nominating candidates. During the formulation of the programme itself the PCF played the moderate role to the hilt. When the Socialists pressed for broad economic reforms, including the nationalization of key industries and control over the banks, they found themselves confronting an alliance of Radicals and Communists opposing such sweeping reforms.[13] The PCF pressed for a minimum programme that would retain the support of the Radicals and not alienate a broad base of moderate middle-class supporters. Agreement was reached only on the

[11] For the oath and excerpts of speeches see Bodin and Touchard, *Front Populaire 1936*, pp. 23–5.

[12] For the complete list see Lefranc, *Front Populaire*, annexes, pp. 445–7.

[13] Jules Moch, *Le Front Populaire, grande espérance* (Paris, 1971), pp. 87–95, is useful for these and other negotiations.

nationalization of the munitions industries (a political, not an economic reform, designed to curb the power of the munitions makers), greater democratic control over the governance of the Bank of France, and the establishment of a national marketing authority for wheat and other grains. With compromises all along the way, the programme emerged as no more than a catalogue of economic 'demands' (*revendications*) on behalf of various social groups especially hard hit by the depression – the working class, farmers, civil servants, small businesses. The political planks focused on the need to dissolve the fascist leagues and to defend democratic liberties. The text on foreign policy contained ambiguities, calling for a halt to fascist aggression but stopping short of military measures; the formula proposed was collective security through a strengthened League of Nations and continuing efforts at disarmament.[14]

Final agreement on the programme was reached on 10 January 1936, only a few days before a common programme was also signed by the parties of the left in Spain, a month before the Spanish Popular Front won its electoral victory in the Cortes on 16 February. Even if it posed no revolutionary threat – any more than did the Frente Popular as a parliamentary initiative – the Popular Front in France as in Spain deepened the division of the nation into two blocs. The reform planks of the programme were modest even if, as in Spain, the rhetoric was bold enough for the political right to cry 'revolution'.

Despite its limitations and ambiguities, its failure to include structural and other economic reforms, there was cause for enthusiasm and anticipation of a left-wing triumph in the spring elections. For the first time in the Republic's history the political parties of the left had reached an agreement on a common platform. Moreover, the Rassemblement Populaire was more than an electoral coalition, it drew its support from the labour movement and other organizations of the left. The Socialists, excited by the Rassemblement Populaire but still concerned over their own freedom of action, worked out a pragmatic formula for the coming election. Each party would campaign with its own party platform and with its own candidates. In the second round of elections the old rule of republican discipline would prevail – though now broadened to include the PCF. The parties of the Rassemblement Populaire would then support the candidate of the left who led on the first ballot. With a parliamentary victory, the

---

[14] The programme is reproduced in *L'oeuvre de Léon Blum*, vol. 4, part 1, *1934–1937*, pp. 225–9 and in Lefranc, *Front Populaire*, annexes, pp. 441–5.

Rassemblement Populaire's manifesto would serve as the programme of the parliamentary majority and the cabinet.

That same month the Radicals grew closer to the left-wing coalition. Herriot and the Radicals withdrew from the Laval cabinet, provoking its collapse. In the aftermath Daladier replaced Herriot as president of the party. On the other hand, the Radical Albert Sarraut, not known for his friendliness to the Communists, formed the new cabinet. The destiny of the new coalition was still uncertain when a dramatic physical assault on Léon Blum on 13 February 1936 – a near lynching by rightist extremists – instantly recreated the atmosphere of February 1934. Many believed correctly that the extremist press and the agitation of the rightist leagues had contributed to the attack. Even the moderate press recalled the frequent incitement to assassination in previous months. The Popular Front quickly received authorization from the Sarraut government for a protest demonstration for the following Sunday, 16 February – the only stipulation was that the tricolor be displayed equally with the red flag. Although arranged in haste, it was one of the most impressive of all the Popular Front demonstrations. More than half a million men and women marched from the Panthéon to the Place de la Bastille in a solemn and dignified procession. In Blum, a democratic socialist, Jew, humanist, and victim of a fascist attack, the left saw a symbol of all that was democratic, humane, and civilized in the Republic. Still another manifestation of unity, of a different kind, was the reunion, after many months of negotiations, of the CGT and CGTU, divided since 1922. In March 1936 the reunited labour confederation held its first joint congress. Meanwhile Hitler's remilitarization of the Rhineland that month, accomplished with impunity, reminded everyone of the Nazi threat to peace.

As the country prepared for the April elections the conservatives, fearful of a left-wing majority, hammered away at the left's past failures and at the fragility of the Popular Front coalition. The right-wing journalist, Henri de Kérillis, encouraged conservatives to conjure up the unrest in Spain:

Our friends must utilize to the fullest the events that are currently taking place in Spain where the electoral victory of the 'Popular Front' has instantly created a serious revolutionary situation. The parallel between that situation and the political situation in the two countries is striking. Spain is today our guinea pig [*notre cobaye*] and everything that unfolds there constitutes for us a supreme warning.[15]

---

[15] For this and similar citations from the right-wing press see Bodin and Touchard, *Front Populaire* 1936, pp. 40–6.

Similar warnings foretold other parallels of 'anarchy and disorder' should the Popular Front win in France. The Spanish Popular Front played the same role in the spring of 1936 that the Russian Revolution played in the French elections of 1919.

As the election campaign drew to a close in April, the leaders of all parties, for the first time, spoke directly to the people over national radio. In his speech Blum called for the rational management of society and pledged labour reforms like collective bargaining and paid vacations. He reasserted the need for broad structural reforms in the economy, but made clear that his party would scrupulously adhere to the Rassemblement Populaire's manifesto despite its limitations, as the programme of a left-wing majority and a left-wing government. 'The contract', he said, 'exists'.[16] Daladier vigorously defended the Radical programme but also reaffirmed support for the Popular Front as a broad coalition for the defence of the Republic.

It was Thorez who captured the occasion, in a burst of rhetoric about patriotism and unity which went far beyond anything previously heard. He called for the unity of 'workers in the cities and the workers in the fields, workers by hand, and workers by brain'. He took credit for the idea of the 'Popular Front of work, liberty, peace' and of unity of action of 'radicals, republicans, democrats' (apparently still unable to bring himself to include the word socialist), and the 'union of young people'. He now extended his appeal to Catholics and others as well, to create 'the union of the French nation':

We stretch out our hands to you, Catholic worker, employee, artisan, we who are non-religious because you are our brother and because you are like us crushed by the same worries. We stretch out our hand to you, volunteer in the service of the nation, you, war veteran in the Croix de Feu, because you are a son of the people ... We communists who have reconciled the tricolor flag of our fathers and the red flag of our hopes, we call upon you, all workers, farmers, and intellectuals, young and old, men and women, all of you, people of France, to join our struggle and to make your voices heard on 26 April.[17]

Never had the PCF appeared as such ardent champions of national unity and patriotism as in Thorez's appeal to create a 'strong, free, and happy France'.

The elections resulted in a decisive parliamentary victory for the Popular Front coalition, even if not a tidal wave or crushing triumph in the popular

[16] *L'oeuvre de Léon Blum*, vol. 4, part 1, *1934–1937*, pp. 234–44.
[17] Bodin and Touchard, *Front Populaire 1936*, pp. 52–3.

vote.[18] The left-wing vote was 5,420,000 to the opposition total of 4,223,000. The parties of the right, already weaker than the left in 1932, showed only a slight decline (1.5 per cent) in voting strength. On the left the Radicals suffered a sharp setback, paying for their identification with the cabinets of the previous legislature. The Socialists showed a small gain in popular vote. The Communists were the big winners, doubling their vote from 783,098 in 1932 to 1,468,949. In the second-round ballots the Popular Front strategy worked. The Socialists increased their seats from ninety-seven at the end of the last legislature to 146 and for the first time in republican history were the leading party in the new Chamber; the Radicals dropped from 158 to 115; the Communists dramatically increased their representation from ten to seventy-two. With its smaller affiliated parties the Popular Front could count on 376 seats to the opposition's 222. The Popular Front had won a decisive parliamentary majority; what remained in question was the coherence and stability of the coalition in the trials ahead.

In less than two and a half years the country went from the *émeutes fascistes* of 6 February 1934, which had toppled a Radical cabinet, to the investiture on 4 June 1936 of a Socialist prime minister – France's first Socialist premier, heading a Popular Front coalition of Socialist and Radical ministers with a common governing programme to which Socialists, Radicals, and Communists had put their contractual signatures. (The PCF pledged support to the cabinet but declined to join.) The Popular Front enjoyed a clear parliamentary majority and a mandate for change. It had the support outside parliament of the organized labour movement and a broad spectrum of other organizations of the left. The first signals quickly appeared that many supporters saw it as something more than a mere parliamentary victory. The elections triggered a wave of unexpected and unprecedented factory occupations that became the largest strike movement in the history of the Republic. Under pressure of the sit-down strikes, and not on the basis of the Rassemblement Populaire's programme alone, the Chamber, with reluctant Senate support, enacted sweeping labour legislation – collective bargaining rights, paid holidays, a forty-hour week, the latter inspired by but not explicit in the Popular Front programme.

A few weeks later, four days after the Popular Front's supporters celebrated their electoral victory and the new labour reforms on Bastille

---

[18] The most authoritative analysis of the 1936 elections remains Georges Dupeux, *Le Front Populaire et les élections de 1936* (Paris 1959).

Day 1936, news of the military uprising in Spain broke. The Spanish Civil War and the non-intervention agreement that followed were among the events that would shatter the momentum and unity of the Popular Front.

The Popular Front itself, in its original incarnation, scarcely lasted through the resignation of Blum's ministry on 22 June 1937 – about thirteen months – although it lingered on formally until 1938. Yet during its formative period and at its height it remained one of the most exhilarating experiences of the interwar years. Pierre Mendès-France, a young Radical at the time, said, looking back upon it: 'No, it is not by error that the working class and the entire French left have preserved for the years 1936–1938 the memory of an era of uplifting struggle ...'[19] And Georges Lefranc, historian of the French left and himself a participant in the events, recalled: 'The French lived it as a great adventure.'[20]

[19] *Cahiers de la République*, September–October 1960, cited in Bodin and Touchard, *Front Populaire 1936*, pp. 9–10.
[20] *Front Populaire*, p. 9.

The origins and nature of the Spanish Popular Front

SANTOS JULIÁ

Whilst there may not seem to be a great deal of point in attempting to oppose a well-established convention, I should like to propose in this essay that before the Civil War there existed in Spain no political entity which can properly be called a Popular Front. It was only after the war had started that there emerged in many places committees, denominated 'popular front', whose function was to negotiate with the anarchist trade union, the CNT, for control of executive positions on the various defence committees. But as regards a formal agreement between political parties to create a government coalition complete with a programme for the defence of parliamentary democracy, I think that the use of the term Popular Front is entirely misplaced until the emergence of the aforementioned committees constituted by Socialists, Communists and Republicans. The supreme expression of these, of course, would be the May 1937 Negrín government itself, the origins of which one must seek in the process which led Communists and Socialists to agree a unity of action initiative in April 1937. With this in mind, rather than clarifying the origins of the front, or the manner of its constitution, I will be attempting to explain the reasons why a Popular Front did not exist in Spain before the outbreak of the Civil War.[1]

[1] For the former theme, see the author's paper, 'On the making of the Spanish Popular Front', American Historical Association, One Hundredth Annual Meeting, New York, 1985.

The origins of the Spanish Popular Front

The reasons for this failure reside in the fact that within the Spanish left as a whole during the 1930s the most important group was the trade unions. Contrary to what happened in other countries, in Spain the 1930s were not dominated by fascism's ascendency but rather by the trade union invasion of the political sphere. Between 1931 and 1934 the socialist General Workers' Union (UGT) and the anarcho-syndicalist National Confederation of Labour (CNT) witnessed hundreds of thousands of workers – perhaps as many as two million – swelling their ranks, while the gains of the political parties of the left could be counted in mere tens of thousands. It was also true that the outstanding feature of the unions' historical development in Spain had been the demand for complete independence from the political parties and the right to intervene directly in political affairs on an equal footing.

The first consequence of the unions' very singular historical trajectory was that, with the arrival of the Republic in 1931, the UGT became part of the national government while the CNT began an assault against the same state with which its socialist counterpart had become identified. Two years after the Republic's declaration, a UGT which had seen its aspirations to reform frustrated also initiated an insurrectionary offensive against a regime which it had come to view as having betrayed its popular origins to become irremediably bourgeois. The preparation of this offensive was sometimes undertaken in conjunction with the CNT by means of the creation of joint union committees at the local or provincial level: and duly, after the anarchist-inspired workers' risings of 1932 and 1933, there followed that of October 1934, associated with the socialist trade union.

Thus while in France in October 1934 Thorez was proposing a 'vaste rassemblement populaire' to defend democracy against the fascist threat, for the trade unions in Spain defeat had put an end to the first insurrectionary cycle which had sought to go beyond the Republic and the parameters of democracy in order to establish what the CNT called the social revolution and the UGT the possession of total political power. In the period immediately following the first insurrectionary cycle's failure, neither of these two unions was in a position to promote a political initiative the objective of which would have been to resurrect the coalition of the left in order to defend the Republic from the threatening forces of political reaction in Spain.

With the unions suffering enforced closure and workers' leaders both in jail and bereft of a political strategy, at the end of 1934 there emerged from the weakest sectors of the left – that is, from the political parties – two

25

proposals. These, whilst very different in origin, content and scope, were both destined to reduce the left's fragmentation and division, which had greatly facilitated the access of the Catholic right to the government of the Republic in 1934. The first proposal came from the Spanish Communist Party (PCE), which at that stage was extremely small and consequently lacked any real influence among Spanish workers. The second proposal emerged from the Republican Left (Izquierda Republicana) and more particularly from the party's leader, Manuel Azaña, who, after his release from prison, had risen phoenix-like from the ashes of the electoral disaster of 1933 which had also been very much a personal political defeat.

Without abandoning their basic ideological line of the rising of the broad popular masses to seize political power and the subsequent establishment of a workers' and peasants' government, from October 1934 the Spanish Communists set themselves a particular goal. This was to forge an organizational link with anarchist and socialist workers. They attempted to exploit fully the sense of disorientation and disorganization in both trade unions in order to promote *frente único* committees at grass-roots level – that is, committees in factories, workshops and neighbourhoods. The PCE also tried to force the socialist and anarchist leaders to accept the concept of *frente único* or united action at national level. They hoped that if this policy could be developed 'with intelligence and determination', it would estab-lish some kind of political sympathy between itself and a working class which had traditionally been hostile to the communist organizations. Joint committees and workers' alliances, factory and neighbourhood committees were seen as ideal instruments for extending the process of 'systematic recruitment' and for assisting the 'revolutionary working class of other political affiliations' to take the 'decisive step into our party'.[2]

The single mindedness with which this policy was pursued meant that the complementary strategy which the International had mapped out for its Spanish section – namely the constitution with the republican parties of the so called 'popular anti-fascist blocs' – was relegated to a position of secondary importance. The marginalization of Spanish republicanism at the end of 1934, the clear suspicion felt by the working class in its regard, and also the fact that the events of October 1934 could be seen as evidence that the Spanish workers had already taken things beyond a mere defence of the bourgeois Republic, made such a strategy seem scarcely relevant to

---

[2] See letters of 29, 30 October 1934 from the PCE's Central Committee to the organization secretaries of various provincial committees, Communist Party Archive (hereafter CPA): VII–107, VIII–112 and VIII–13.

the circumstances. After some debate, and not a little confusion, the PCE leaders decided not to take any immediate action and to leave it to the workers' alliances to effect the creation of the 'popular blocs'.[3]

The formation of the 'popular bloc' depended, thus, on the response of the Socialists to the workers' alliance and unity-of-action initiatives – since nothing could be expected from the anarchists in this direction. However, after the Communists' hopes had been raised by the creation of a joint socialist–communist committee, albeit one whose function was carefully circumscribed to the distribution of substantial Soviet aid to the prisoners of October 1934, the PCE leaders were obliged to accept the obvious, that the Socialists were not interested in unity-of-action initiatives.[4] To all the PCE's proposals of united action, joint signatures on manifestos, the constitution of committees, the appearance of speakers at joint meetings, the merging of trade unions, the PSOE and UGT leaders, and especially Largo Caballero whose authority on both the party and the union executives was undisputed, responded at first with extreme reticence, later by rejecting the suggestions and finally with a blanket of silence.[5]

Although it would be true to say that the attitude of the two socialist executives did not have a uniform effect in all Spain's provinces and regions, the absence of progress towards unity of action at national level did paralyse both organizational rapprochement and unity of action at the grass roots. By the beginning of November 1935 – a whole year after the policy's initial implementation – no advances had been made. Indeed some regression had occurred, as, by the autumn of that year, the few workers' alliances which had managed to survive into 1935 were, at best, in a fairly unhealthy state and often entirely inoperative.[6]

Without establishing joint committees with the Socialists it was practically impossible for the Communists to make any headway where the republican parties were concerned. It was not that the PCE neglected to make overtures in this quarter: indeed the communist organization proposed unity of action initiatives to the Republicans and it invited them to

[3] José Díaz to the political bureau of the Catalan Communist Party, 17 November 1934 and the circular 'to all party committees', 2 March 1935, CPA VIII–116, X–137.

[4] For the joint committee and its restricted brief, see the minutes of the PSOE and UGT national executives, 4 and 6 December 1934 respectively, in the Fundación Pablo Iglesias, Archivo Histórico (henceforward FPI AH) 20–3 and AARD xx. For the PCE's disappointment, J. Díaz to the political bureau of the Catalan Communist Party, 26 April 1935, CPA X–136.

[5] Minutes of the meetings of the UGT's national executive, 17 January, 25 April 1935, FPI AH.

[6] For the Workers' Alliances at the end of 1935 and the blame attributed to Largo Caballero, see the 'Minutes of the Central Committee of the POUM', 5 January 1936, p. 6, FPI AH.

establish joint anti-fascist committees or to join in what was, by that point, being called a 'popular anti-fascist concentration'.[7] But insofar as all these proposals came up against the same objection from the Socialists, then the PCE was only able to secure some minor successes with the smallest and most peripheral republican parties, such as the Izquierda Radical Socialista or the Partido Republicano Federal. It was entirely unrealistic to have imagined that the major left-wing republican parties, Azaña's Izquierda Republicana and Martinez Barrio's Unión Republicana, would have even considered making a pact with the Communist Party, among other things because as the year went on it was clear that these parties were promoting a strategy to which the PCE was almost entirely superfluous.[8]

The other sector on the political left interested in establishing some kind of coalition consisted of the republican parties. These groups had suffered fairly bad erosion as a result of October 1934, but they were beginning to recoup their forces under Azaña's tutelage. Jailed for his alleged support of both the Catalan and Asturian rebellions and tried twice, Azaña emerged, immediately upon his release, as the only hope for the restoration of the Republic such as it had been originally conceived in 1931, as a motor of reform.

Straightaway Azaña was aware of the powerful rebirth of republican sentiment and decided, after some hesitation, to place himself at its head so as to channel it in the direction of what he termed 'the redemption of the Republic'. Given the impossibility of an understanding with either the Radical Party or the president of the Republic, both of whom he held responsible for the Republic's deliverance to its enemies, Azaña demanded the dissolution of parliament (the Cortes) and new elections. In order to strengthen his demand he effectively transformed the nature of republicanism in Spain. He removed it from what had been its natural habitat – *tertulias* (café society) and coteries – where it was gradually being stifled, and promoted a popular movement, chiefly through a series of massive open-air meetings which culminated in October 1935 in the famous meeting at Comillas on the outskirts of Madrid. There Azaña addressed

---

[7] See references to letters received from the communist organization in the minutes of Izquierda Republicana's national executive, quoted in the 'Querella por rebelión militar contra don Manuel Azaña y don Luis Bello', Archivo Histórico Nacional, Tribunal Supremo, 2–1, pp. 361ff.

[8] For Azaña's explicit rejection of any alliance with the PCE, see his letter to Prieto, 20 April 1935, M. Azaña, *Obras completas* (Mexico, 1968), vol. 4, p. 559.

the largest gathering that any European politician has ever been able to mobilize without recourse to paramilitary methods.[9]

At the same time as he was mobilizing this massive popular movement, Azaña also proposed to all the other left-wing republican parties a pact or 'republican understanding'. Its object was to ensure that any return to power would not mean a minority republican government whose very survival depended on the support of other political forces. Azaña defined clearly his personal position and that of his party and he invited the others to accept the package, and with it his leadership, by means of an agreement to be based on a common programme of government. The essence of this was to be a reaffirmed commitment to the policy of reform initiated by the first governments of the Republic but abandoned subsequently after the coming to power of the Radical Party and the CEDA.

Whilst a rapprochement was occurring between the republican parties, Azaña renewed his contacts with the Socialists in order to put to them the absolute necessity of 'building a strategy which will allow us to look towards the formation of a political bloc sufficiently powerful to win the first battle with which we are confronted'.[10] Azaña well understood the problems which the radical or union wing of the socialist organization would have in accepting his proposal and he thus addressed himself to the leaders of the party's moderate or 'political' sector. In essence, his plan consisted in presenting the republican programme to the Socialists so that their proposals could be incorporated into it. In addition, socialist participation in an 'electoral front' was requested, but on the understanding that the government which resulted from victory at the polls would be an exclusively republican one. From these premises the Republicans concluded two things: the Socialists would have to desist from those points of their programme which could never be accepted by a republican government and, secondly, when the time came to discuss the distribution of places on the candidate lists, it would have to be accepted that the Republicans be apportioned a majority of these.[11] It was only under such conditions that a republican government would be prepared to commit

---

[9] For a report of the event, H. Buckley, *Life and Death of the Spanish Republic* (London 1940), p. 182; for Azaña's role in the formation of the Popular Front electoral pact, see S. Juliá, *Orígenes del Frente Popular en España* (Madrid, 1979), pp. 27–41 and P. Preston, 'The creation of the Popular Front in Spain' in Helen Graham and Paul Preston (eds.), *The Popular Front in Europe* (London, 1987), pp. 84–105.

[10] Letter to Prieto, 16 January 1935, M. Azaña, *Obras completas*, vol. 3, p. 591.

[11] Prieto to the PSOE's National Committee, 16 December 1935; for the minutes of this important meeting, see FPI AH, 24–1, pp. 63ff.

itself to the realization of the coalition's programme, in that it would have, to carry it through, a clear republican majority.

Spanish socialism's moderate wing – which had a majority on both the national committee and the national executive of the party, but not on those of either the UGT or the socialist youth – accepted Azaña's basic plan and sought to turn it into official party policy. The PSOE's communication channels with the Republicans had been cut the previous year and caution was essential if hostility was not to be aroused in its radical wing. At the head of the latter stood the undisputed authority of Largo Caballero. He enjoyed almost unanimous support among the UGT leadership. In addition, Largo Caballero was buoyed up by the near adoration of a significant sector of the socialist youth and he could count on three unconditional supporters on the PSOE executive of which he was president.

The very least which can be said is that the necessary caution was not employed. Indalecio Prieto, actively encouraged from the very beginning by the leadership group which supported him, was soon setting a rapid pace towards a pact with the Republicans. The famous 'Vidarte circular', which opened up the debate over the possibility of an alliance with the Republicans, was interpreted as the beginning of an official rectification of the line that the Socialist Party had followed since the elections of 1933.[12] Despite the fact that this circular was also approved by Largo Caballero, the publicity afforded it, and the very fact that the policy advocated therein was an initiative of the most notorious 'centrists' in the PSOE, provoked an energetic reaction from the party sector which had been closely associated with Caballero since their collective imprisonment in Madrid after October 1934. Backed by members of the executive committees of all three socialist organizations – the UGT, socialist youth and the party – Caballero sent a letter of protest to the PSOE executive which signalled the birth of the *caballerista* faction proper.[13] It hardly constituted standard procedure within the PSOE that the youth and trade union leaderships, supported by a minority on the party executive, should have joined forces to protest about the latter's political behaviour. However, the most important point to note here is that the reaction of the *caballeristas* had the effect of paralysing all official negotiations with the Republicans and of postponing indefinitely the resolution for which Prieto was petitioning.

[12] For a copy of the circular, see the Servicio Histórico Militar, Madrid, cabinet 46, dossier 63.
[13] Minutes of the PSOE's National Executive meeting, 8 May 1935, FPI AH.

Without rejecting the principle of collaboration with the Republicans, Largo Caballero effectively blocked any formal advance in that direction.[14]

Neither was Largo prepared to move in the direction proposed by the Communists. Before the summer of 1935 the PSOE and UGT executive committees, both headed by him, lacked any political line. At the Socialist Party executive's meeting on 8 May, a letter from Prieto was read out 'proposing the re-establishment of contact with the republican parties'. A second letter, from the PCE, proposed 'the creation of an anti-fascist front, the bases for which shall be worked out in advance by the Socialist and Communist parties'. The minutes for this executive meeting are extremely sparse in respect of the ultimate fate of these two proposals: 'all decisions were postponed'.[15]

The postponement was still in force in autumn 1935 when the collapse of the Radical Party increased fears that the CEDA might assume leadership of the government. The Socialists persisted in their rejection of the workers-cum-popular front proposed by the PCE, while the electoral front suggested by the Republicans remained a non-starter. The situation's most serious aspect was that the intensification of the dispute inside the PSOE, which had occurred during the summer, prevented the Socialists from establishing their own alliance strategy with other groups on the left.

The factor which thus precipitated the need for a coalition was entirely unconnected with the internal dynamic of the party and union organizations on the left. The political crisis, becoming more acute as a result of the Strauss and Nombela scandals, made elections an immediate necessity. Without further delay, Azaña formally contacted the Socialist Party executive on 14 November to propose, on the collective behalf of the republican parties, that an electoral coalition be formed. Two days later the executives of the Socialist Party, union and youth organizations, in joint conclave in Madrid's Modelo jail, approved the resolution put to them by Largo Caballero.

The proposal of an electoral coalition was accepted, but in addition to the representation of the Socialist Party on the committee charged with the formulation of the programme and selection of candidates, that of the Communist Party and the UGT was also demanded. It was between 14 and 16 November 1935 that Largo Caballero also took two other decisions which would have important consequences. He proposed to the Communists that their trade union should join the UGT and also decided that the

14 Largo to the PSOE's National Committee, 16 December 1935, FPI AH, 24–1, p. 31.
15 See the minutes of the meeting, FPI AH, p. 73.

programme which the PSOE and the UGT would elaborate for the elections should first be submitted for approval to the PCE and its union. This meant that authority to negotiate with the Republicans was being transferred to a joint committee of Socialists and Communists.[16]

The *caballerista* strategy consisted in accepting simultaneously the proposals which the PCE and the republican parties had been suggesting to the Socialists since the beginning of the year. In paying court to the Communists Largo's intention was to strengthen his own bargaining position *vis-à-vis* the Republicans and also to prevent Prieto from assuming a predominant position within the PSOE. Of course this strategy did alter certain fundamental aspects of the project as originally conceived by Azaña and Prieto. Firstly, the role of the Socialists was reduced by the fact that they were to be only one component on a joint committee and, secondly, the PCE was being conceded a protagonism which no one, except at that moment Caballero, was prepared to accept. At root, the pact was a republican–socialist agreement to which other more peripheral parties and organizations might adhere once its terms had been finalized, but under no circumstances was it envisaged that these groups should be represented on the committees negotiating the agreement itself.

Faced with the substantial changes to the accord which Caballero's demands implied, the Republicans rejected the whole idea of admitting the PCE to the electoral committee whilst the centrist Socialists, at Prieto's behest, brought about the resignation of Largo Caballero from the PSOE's national executive.[17] From that point on – 16 December 1935 – Caballero ceased to consider himself a man of the party and, indeed, ceased to be considered as such. Exclusively identified with the UGT, he would make of the union a stronghold and on its leadership bodies would enjoy a substantial majority, at least until the May 1937 crisis. It was also from the end of 1935 that the UGT began to reassert its political independence, and to behave as a separate political party. Henceforward its political initiatives were to be entirely its own: the union leadership refused to accept any political guidance from the PSOE. Thus, from December 1935, the Socialists had two political leaderships which were not only entirely independent of each other but also diametrically opposed.

[16] For the minutes of the meeting of the UGT's National Executive, FPI AH, p. 215; the minutes of the meeting of the three executives in F. Largo Caballero, *Escritos de la República. Notas históricas de la guerra en España* (Madrid, 1985), p. 255.

[17] For the Republicans' refusal, Largo Caballero, *Escritos*, p. 287. For the latter's resignation, see the minutes of the PSOE's National Committee meeting, 16 December 1935 (cited above, note 13).

With Socialists divided, the UGT refused to have anything to do with the electoral committee. No representative was appointed to discuss either the programme or the allocation of places on the candidate lists. Nevertheless, even though the union was absent from the committee's deliberations, the UGT's political stance was still the crucial determinant of the ultimate form of agreement. Because of its attitude the coalition established was a purely circumstantial one, limited to the electoral period and involving no post-electoral commitment from any of the signatories.[18] The programme would be an entirely republican one, with the socialist inclusion limited to a declaration of political objectives, expressly excluded from any future programme of republican government. Finally, also as a result of UGT pressure, all the parties and labour organizations excluded from the negotiations would be required to manifest a symbolic involvement by signing the final version of the programme.

Everyone came thus to appear as part of a pact which had been negotiated by two groups only – the PSOE and the Republicans. And if just two groups had been involved in establishing both the programme and the lists of candidates, the Republicans alone would be required thereafter to assume government responsibility. The heterogeneity of the signatories – parties, unions, youth organizations – scarcely disguised the very limited commitment which each had acquired in signing, just as the disparity of their ultimate objectives and the fragility of the alliance itself remained equally visible. Everyone agreed that only the prospect of elections had made feasible a coalition and thus that the latter would remain viable only for as long as electoral victory remained a joint goal. After that each group would be free to pursue its own political objectives without any sense of constraint such as a commitment to support a government coalition would have produced.

Once formed the coalition proved to be an excellent instrument for procuring electoral victory but the worst possible tool of government. The fact that any future government was certain to be an entirely republican affair was a source of great comfort and reassurance to liberal opinion and the middle classes. The moderate Socialists were content to see the renewal of the traditional alliance with the Republicans which they perceived as a step along the road to their own future participation in government. Those UGT militants who feared further frustration and disappointment, should Socialists return to govern alongside Republicans, felt confident that Largo Caballero would ensure that such a scenario was never realized. The

---

[18] See extracts from Largo's electoral speeches in Juliá, *Origenes*, pp. 225–7.

PCE's supporters were delighted to see that, at last, the party had been able to escape from an isolation which had reduced it previously to powerlessness. They were particularly pleased to see that this had been largely possible because of the assistance of Largo Caballero, the most prestigious leader of the UGT.[19] The Young Socialists, who had already gravitated into the communist orbit, would mobilize all their forces – substantial indeed in the cities – to assist the left, confident that its triumph in the elections would mean a decisive step towards the future revolution. Even the anarchists recommended that this time their militants should vote. Indeed it was inconceivable for them to oppose a coalition formed with the express intention of passing a general political amnesty for all those either imprisoned or discriminated against after October 1934.

The forces of the Spanish left, so badly fragmented along lines which set union against union, and these against the political parties, were thus united for the elections. That it was a precarious unity was openly displayed during the electoral campaign itself: it proved impossible to organize a single joint meeting. The primary objective of every party and union was to preserve its own identity, and not to become confused with the rest. Above all, future independence of action had to be maintained. It is, then, hardly surprising that the joint republican–socialist committee (the only one in Spain which can genuinely be denominated a Popular Front committee) ceased to function, indeed to exist, as soon as the task for which it had been created had been realized. With the elections won, and at precisely the moment when the threat posed by political reaction was greatest, the forces of the Spanish left found themselves bereft of any common political direction or objective. Without any need to consult his erstwhile allies, the new prime minister, Azaña, proceeded alone to choose his cabinet.

The government of the Republic, which owed its very existence to a coalition of the left, was thus unable to reflect, in its composition, that coalition's real nature. The Popular Front dissolved as a political entity and even the prospect of municipal elections (in the event never held) could not bring about its reconstitution.[20] In such circumstances, with the political parties of the left unable to reconstruct any common front, the political initiative passed back once more to the unions. First an amnesty, then re-employment and indemnifications, and finally new labour con-

---

[19] *Mundo Obrero* (PCE), 2 January 1936.
[20] Although an attempt was made to revive the republican–socialist committee as the 'Central Popular Front Committee'. See relevant correspondence, FPI AH, 24–10.

tracts and the repossession of agricultural land – these were the goals of the growing wave of labour mobilization in both urban and rural Spain which began immediately after the electoral triumph of February 1936, reaching a high point in May and June of that year. It is important to realize that, with few exceptions, the great wave of strikes which broke across the country when the unions regained control of their headquarters and began the process of rebuilding their organizations was devoid of any single political direction or leadership. Neither the PCE nor the PSOE was in a position to channel towards political objectives the most powerful mobilization of organized labour that the Republic had so far witnessed – a mobilization at times the result of joint efforts by the UGT and the CNT. The Communists were quite simply jeered off stage when they attempted to introduce more moderate proposals at workers' mass meetings. The PSOE, which had by this point severed all its organizational links with the UGT, no longer sustained with the latter's leadership anything but a relationship of open hostility. In Spain there was no one who could utter with any authority the equivalent of the famous epithet pronounced by Thorez around this same time to the French strikers.

It was precisely the organizational split in the socialist movement which prevented the republican government from broadening its base when Azaña became president of the Republic in May 1936. Azaña tended towards the view – although perhaps without any great conviction – that the time had come to reintegrate the Socialists into the Republic's government. However, his exploratory investigations came up against the irreducible opposition of Largo Caballero, whilst the UGT executive made it clear that it would consider itself absolved from all its political obligations should a Socialist be called upon to form a government.[21] As a result of the UGT's opposition, there would be no coalition government and the one which was constituted, without Azaña at its head, neither was, nor even seemed to be, coherent or capable. While Madrid was poised on the edge of a general strike, in parliament the monarcho-fascist opposition took heart and the military openly prepared to rebel. With the government in such a state, it could only be a matter of weeks, perhaps even days, before the conspiracy exploded out of the barracks into the streets.

The Spanish Popular Front was different from its French counterpart, both in its origins and nature, because the make up of the political left in the two countries was likewise quite distinct. In Spain, the decisive political influence was to be found in the two powerful trade unions whilst

[21] Minutes of the meeting of the UGT's National Executive, 7 May 1936.

the political parties were, relatively, much weaker. In addition to the unions' enormous strength, one also has to remember that the PCE counted for almost nothing. This meant that there was no possibility of a unity of action agreement between the Socialist and Communist parties such as might then have been extended to include the Republicans in something which could have been termed a Popular Front.

The two great trade unions' rejection of a workers' front with the Communists encouraged the rapprochement of the republican parties and the PSOE. But, again, the refusal of the UGT, which had just emerged from the experience of the Asturian revolution and had no faith in either the Republic or the Republicans, prevented any advance down that particular road. At the same time, the Socialists' internal struggle was rapidly acquiring all the characteristics of an organizational split between the labour union – the UGT – and the political party – the PSOE – which culminated in the resignation in December 1935 of the principal leaders of the UGT from their seats on the PSOE's national executive committee.

It was this *de facto* split which transferred the political initiative of Spanish socialism to the trade union – this because of the greater influence of the labour organization – leaving the political party without any real base from which to build up its strategy of collaboration with the Republicans to its logical conclusion. This same split was also responsible for the PCE's inclusion in the January 1936 agreement. But above all it was this split which precipitated the period of union hegemony over the political spectrum of the left as a whole – a predominance which would end by destroying the so-called Popular Front as a political entity.

The hegemony of the unions was given a crucial boost both by the spring 1936 strike movement and the social revolution which followed the military coup of 18 July. The most complete manifestation of this hegemony was to be found in the second government of Largo Caballero, and its ultimate aspiration in the attempt to form an entirely union government, as was being suggested in March and April 1937. Faced with such an eventuality, and in order to oppose the 'new Saturn', which, according to a circular issued by the socialist executive, 'had determined to devour the political parties', the PSOE proposed to the PCE that a joint committee be constituted to agree a common action pact.[22] Indeed the PSOE went as far as to contemplate seriously the possibility of socialist–communist unification. Looking back, we can see that it was upon the basis of the common

[22] See the PSOE National Executive's circulars to the party base in January and March 1937, examples of both in the Servicio Histórico Militar, cabinet 46, dossier 63, file 3.

36

action pact between the PSOE and the PCE that the parties of the left – Communists, Socialists and Republicans – constructed their May 1937 offensive. This was the culmination of a political pact to which the term Popular Front can appropriately be applied, and which in Spain emerged as a political response to the traditional predominance of the trade unions.

The French Radicals, Spain
and the emergence
of appeasement

H. HAYWOOD HUNT

The French Popular Front could not have existed without the Radical
Party. It was the French Communist Party which saw this most clearly
and which took the initiative in opening the way for the Radicals to join the
communist–socialist alliance, thereby extending what would otherwise
have been a narrowly based working-class alliance into a major political
force. Yet just as the Communists helped to create the alliance with the
Radicals, so they helped to weaken it, and ultimately destroy it, in large
part because of their reactions to events in Spain.

During the interwar period the Radical Party was pivotal: it was always
solicited to form, or help form, the government during the governmental
crises of the era. Even after the Popular Front electoral victory of May
1936, only a minority government could be constituted without the
Radicals.

The Radicals were individualists while most of their partners were, or
said they were, collectivists. The Popular Front itself was simply a vari-
ation on a perpetual theme of French political life: that the country voted
left or right; that there was a party of movement and a party of order.[1] The

This paper is based upon one presented at the Popular Front Conference held in April 1986
at Southampton University. Attendance at the conference was made possible by a grant
from the European Division of the University of Maryland. This paper is written in memory
of my father.

[1] A theme developed in François Goguel, *La politique des partis sous la IIIe République* (Paris,
1946).

Radicals always considered themselves to be on the left of the political spectrum, but they were also a party of order *par excellence*. Radicals wanted social progress but only through order, discipline and legality. The explanation for this apparent paradox lay in the fact that the Radicals were such a mirror image of the contradictions which were France: both a revolutionary and a traditional country.[2]

In 1924, and again in 1932, the Radicals had constructed an effective electoral alliance with the French Socialist Party. One of the major reasons for the success of these past understandings had been the self-defeating electoral strategy of the French Communist party. The logical allies, in ideological terms, for the French Socialists (SFIO), would, of course, have been the Communists (PCF). However, communist policy before 1934–5 was one of rigid exclusivity. Even worse than the bourgeoisie were the socialist 'class traitors'.[3] The result was that the working-class vote was often split between Communists and Socialists in the first round under the two-round electoral system, leaving the Radicals with the plurality of the left-wing votes. In the second round the alliances came into play, with the Socialist, more often than not, withdrawing in the Radical's favour. The Communist candidate was always maintained, but Communist voters, on the whole, followed French political tradition rather than central committee orders and cast their votes for the best-placed candidates of the left. This, in many cases, was the Radical. The result was that in the 1932 legislature the Radicals won 160 seats while the Communists won eleven.[4] Consequently before 1936, the Radicals could contemplate associating with the Communists because they were of relatively minor political importance. Only in certain areas, like the Seine-et-Oise, was the PCF a major political force. In much of France where the Radicals were strong, such as the southwest around Bordeaux, the Communists were insignificant.[5]

[2] This peculiarity of radicalism is illustrated in the conservative Radical paper *L'Ere Nouvelle* (Paris) which had two articles on the same page of its 13 July 1936 issue: one emphasized radicalism's revolutionary roots and the other the Radical concern for order. Cf. editorial, *Journal des Débats* (Paris), 29 March 1936, hereafter *Débats*; Arthur Huc (who wrote for the Radical *Dépêche de Toulouse*), *Hommes et doctrines* (Paris, 1935), p. 172 and Dr Ricolfi (president of the Radical Federation of the Alpes Maritimes) in *Le Petit Niçois*, 16 June 1936.

[3] See, for instance, an article by Maurice Thorez in *La Correspondance Internationale*, nos. 29–30, 15 April 1933, *Oeuvres de Maurice Thorez* (Paris, 1950), book 2, vol. 5, pp. 92–6.

[4] Of the Radical deputies elected in 1932 fully one-third (fifty-three) would *not* have been elected without the left-wing votes which had been cast in the first round for the Socialists or Communists, while thirteen of this number were elected only because of votes cast for them by citizens who had voted Communist on the first ballot.

[5] L'Homme de Pas-Perdus, *France de Bordeaux*, 13 October 1934; see also Peter J. Lamour, *The French Radical Party in the 1930s* (Stanford, 1964), p. 175.

While the Radicals normally presented themselves as a party of movement at the elections, when they sat in the legislature they demanded the maintenance of republican order above all else. Ever since the Stavisky riots of 6 February 1934 and the subsequent paramilitary demonstrations by the rightist leagues, the principal threat to republican order, and to the Republic itself, seemed to come from the new right which looked for inspiration to Italy and Germany.[6] On the other hand, the Communists were beginning to metamorphose into patriotic Frenchmen whose chief desire, at least in the short term, was the defence of the Republic. The increasing moderation of the Communists between 1934 and 1936 surprised everyone, including the Radicals who found that the Communists were prepared to adopt much of the Radical programme as their own. Although the Popular Front parties might have different economic and social doctrines, underneath they were all republicans, concluded some Radicals.[7]

The opening to the Radicals was supplied by Daladier, the leader of the pro-Popular Front sector of the party. In October 1934, with the cantonal elections in view, Daladier wrote an article directed at his old electoral allies, the Socialists. In it he pointed out 'that the famous formula *class against class* does not fit with the present political facts of life'. If the Republic was to be saved from what he, and many others, saw as the danger of fascism, then the working class by itself was not enough: 'when dictatorship had only the working class against it, as in Italy and Germany, it triumphed ... Republican defence requires the cooperation of all democrats ... and vigorous middle-class support.'[8]

Daladier's appeal may have been directed at the Socialists but it was the Communists who responded. Julian Racamond, of the communist trade union confederation (CGTU), wrote to an associate of Daladier's suggesting an approach.[9] On 9 October Thorez, the PCF's leader, called upon the

[6] The Radical Federation of Allier, controlled by Lucien Lamoureux, the conservative Radical and minister of commerce in 1934, demanded that the leagues be dissolved (*France de Bordeaux*, 16 April 1934); cf. Emile Roche, *La République* (Paris), 15 April 1934; Edouard Daladier to the Radical Congress of Clermont-Ferrand, reported in *La République*, 13 May 1934; editorial, *L'Oeuvre* (Paris), 5 November 1934; and Jacques Kayser (a left-wing Radical), *France de Bordeaux*, 10 November 1934.

[7] Léon Archimbaud (Radical deputy), *Montagne de Clermont-Ferrand*, 21 December 1936. Jacques Duclos, the Communist Party secretary, said that the Radicals and the PCF joined the Popular Front for the same reasons, *L'Humanité* (Paris), 28 June 1936; cf. Kayser, *La République de l'Oise*, 11 July 1936.

[8] *Le Petit Provençal* (Marseilles), 4 October 1934.

[9] Racamond to Charansol, the Daladier archives of the Fondation Nationale des Sciences Politiques, Paris, 1DA6, dossier 6, subdossier a, hereafter 1DA6, Dr 6, sdr a.

Communist–Socialist Coordination Committee to extend their cooperation to new political and social forces. A day after that Thorez specifically mentioned Daladier and his article in a speech at the Salle Bullier in Paris and suggested a 'Rassemblement Populaire'.[10]

Although contacts were established with Daladier (and other Radicals), in October 1934, another year elapsed before an agreement could be reached. A major reason for the Radicals' circumspect progress towards the Popular Front was the partisan publicity given by the communist newspaper, *L'Humanité*, to the October 1934 Asturian rising in Spain. Clearly, if the French Communists were sanctioning violence and unrest in Spain they could not be suitable partners for the Radicals, since association with such disorder would risk alienating middle-ground support for the French Popular Front.

In the course of the negotiations for the Popular Front alliance the Radicals found, to their surprise, that the Communists were backing them, in most cases, against the Socialists. In Radical eyes the alliance was directed first at winning the elections, then at protecting the Republic and its institutions and finally at preserving peace. If the Radicals wanted order at home, in international affairs they wanted peace. The 'party of movement', observed the Radical journalist, Pierre Dominique, had always been the party of peace at any price and it had won elections on that platform.[11]

The importance of peace as a basis for the Popular Front needs to be stressed. Yet for the parties of the French left, as for most other parties, agreeing the objective of avoiding war proved far simpler than agreeing a route to its attainment. It was to be events in Spain which polarized political opinion over the relative merits for French security of intervention or non-intervention, of an active or passive defence policy.

During the first half of the 1930s Spain had experienced considerable civil disorder and the evident process of political and social polarization led

[10] *L'Humanité*, 11 October 1934. This was the first use of 'Rassemblement Populaire' (the term preferred by most Radicals at the time) and the official name of the grouping which the Radicals joined. 'Popular Front' was first used a short time later (22 October 1934) by Marcel Cachin, director of *L'Humanité*.

[11] *La République*, 16 February 1936. Others to talk of France's desire for 'peace at any price', included Marcel Déat, *France de Bordeaux*, 23 December 1935; Georges Hoog, *La Jeune République* (Paris), 5 January 1935; Archimbaud in a speech at Laval d'Aix, reported in *Le Petit Parisien*, 7 January 1936; Paul Elbel, a conservative Radical deputy, *La République*, 15 January 1936. On the day the left-wing Radical paper *L'Oeuvre* reported the Rhineland's remilitarization (8 March 1936) on page 1, it reported on page 7 that an 'International Youth Conference for Peace had made great progress with its pacifist ideas.' Félicien Challaye in *Vendredi* (Paris), 31 January 1936, said defeat was preferable to war.

the Radical Dominique to ask whether there would not soon be a Spanish Mussolini or a Spanish Lenin.[12] After the Frente Popular's electoral victory both the Socialists and the Communists in France claimed that the workers' organizations had saved the Spanish Republic. The French left argued that it would emulate its Spanish counterpart whilst the French right warned that the election of the Popular Front in France would only provoke civil strife of the Spanish kind.[13] The Radicals were unsure of what to make of the Frente Popular's victory. André Pierre in *L'Oeuvre* announced that they should rejoice; the Radical deputy François de Tessan concluded that the Frente Popular had won because it was defending democracy. But Dominique was more cautious, urging his readers to watch events in Spain.[14] Trouble in Spain might lose the French left votes in the forthcoming elections. The anti-Popular Front press, accordingly, began to feature reports on the continuing unrest in Spain.[15] On the whole, the Radical papers found it difficult to take any firm position on the situation in Spain. Before the outbreak of the civil war they normally tried to play down the internal disorder, blaming it on the extreme right or ignoring it completely. In the end the Radical press had recourse to the accurate but unsatisfying explanation that 'there is no possible comparison between our political and social situation and that of our neighbour'.[16]

Certainly France and Spain were different. As the Spanish president, Manuel Azaña, admitted, democracy was a recent development in Spain and consequently there was a lack of deeply rooted republican tradition.[17] The Spanish middle class was insubstantial and therefore weak while there was a large, active anarchist element. The French middle class was of significant size and there were few active anarchists. In France there was general consensus that the best form of government was the Republic and

[12] *La République*, 15 January 1936.

[13] André Leroux, *Le Populaire*, 18, 19 February 1936; Duclos, *L'Humanité*, 18 February 1936; Cachin, *L'Humanité*, 19 February 1936. The warnings of trouble may be found in Pertinax, *L'Echo de Paris*, 20 February 1936; Lucien Romier, *Figaro*, 20 February 1936; Pierre Bernus, *Débats*, 21 April 1936; editorial, *L'Ami du Peuple* (Paris), 18 February 1936 and Saint-Brice, *Le Journal*, 18 February 1936. Cf. Lillian Parker Wallace and William C. Askew (eds.), *Power, Public Opinion and Diplomacy* (Durham, North Carolina, 1959), p. 269.

[14] Pierre, *L'Oeuvre* 21 February 1936; de Tessan, *Le Petit Niçois*, 28 February 1936 and Dominique, *La République*, 21 February 1936.

[15] *Débats*, 19 April 1936. *Gringoire* (Paris), 10 April 1936; editorial *Le Temps*, 14, 21, 23 April 1936; the section of Daladier's fragmentary memoirs entitled 'Campagne electorale commune: victoire commun' in 1DA6, Dr 6, sdr b, pp. 33–4 and Albert Vigneau and Vivienne Orland, *F∴ M∴ et Front Populaire: nous conduira-t'on aux horreurs d'Espagne?* (Paris, 1935 sic).

[16] Louis Darrès, editor *Le Petit Niçois*, 23 July 1936.

[17] As reported in *Débats*, 18 April 1936. This was also the opinion of Wladimir d'Ormesson, *Figaro*, 22 July 1936.

that recourse to the ballot box was preferable to resort to the bullet. The Spanish and French socialist parties also projected different images. Whilst Blum's moderation had its counterpart in the political stance of Indalecio Prieto, the leader of the parliamentary wing of the Spanish Socialist Party, the revolutionary rhetoric of veteran left socialist, Largo Caballero, was unwelcome to the mainstream elements in the French Popular Front. The Spanish Radicals, who had joined with the Spanish right by 1933 and were virtually eliminated from Spanish politics in the February 1936 elections, had only superficial popular support, unlike the French Radicals who could count upon strong local support in their respective constituencies. Even if one were to claim that Anzaña's Republican Left (Izquierda Republicana) was similar to the French Radical Party, as did the former deputy from Valencia, Julio Just, the similarity was a superficial one. While Spanish republicans of whatever leaning had little experience of government or the exercise of political power, their French counterparts had, for over thirty years, regularly controlled key ministries.[18]

In the run up to the French election the Radical and pro-Radical press either said little about the turmoil in Spain, or treated it as mere banditry. Only a few papers, like L'Oeuvre, occasionally ran articles, as the election approached, attempting to show that the Frente Popular was engaged in a difficult, but laudable and widely supported process of reform. Conservative journals also discussed Spain, but seemingly to little effect, except on the right's own supporters. A sufficient number of these shifted rightwards to permit the election of a clutch of Doriotist and Croix de Feu deputies who constituted the neo-fascist Parti Populaire Français and Parti Social Français in the chamber after 1936. As these voters went to the polls, Daladier noted wryly that the French right had talked more of Spain than of France.[19]

After the elections, the subject of Spain and its troubles evoked little comment in the Radical papers. Attention was first directed at the formation of the new government and the distribution of offices, until the

[18] Claude Nicolet, La radicalisme (Paris, 1967), pp. 91–92. Just's comments were made in the (published) discussion at the Blum Symposium, 26–7 March 1965. See Pierre Renouvin and René Rémond (eds.), Léon Blum: chef de gouvernement, 1936–1937 (Paris, 1967), pp. 372–3, hereafter Blum Symposium.

[19] Paris-Soir Dimanche, 26 April 1936. The articles in L'Oeuvre in 1936 appeared, for instance, on 24 March and 12 April (Jean Nocher), 19 April (Denise Moran), 20 April (editorial), 21 April (Moran), 19 May (Louis Fischer), 8 June (Pierre), although it is worth noting that Pierre published an article on 13 April headlined 'Spain has nothing to do with our electoral discussions'. Cf. Jacques Delpierré de Bayac, Histoire du Front Populaire (Paris, 1982), p. 195.

wave of strikes and factory occupations began to take up ever more of the Radical-oriented press. In May the Radicals reacted cautiously, but by July they were both concerned and angry. The labour unrest undermined the power of Blum and his party when dealing with the Radicals who had joined the Popular Front in order to maintain republican order and legality.[20] Blum had specifically pledged that he would work within the bourgeois republican context. Without the Radicals he could not make the republican system work, either in the Chamber or the Senate. It was in the Senate, dominated by conservative Radicals, like Joseph Caillaux, that the anger was greatest, especially at the loose talk by Pivert and the Gauche Révolutionnaire who rejected the Senate's authority, suggesting that the masses should take to the streets to help the government overcome the Upper Chamber's obstructionism.[21] Blum, like most Socialists, rejected these suggestions, not only because he advocated the parliamentary road to socialism, but also because he feared that revolution in France would lead to civil war and even foreign invasion.[22] Hitler had already spoken to the French ambassador in Berlin, André François-Poncet, of his 'fear' of communist revolution in France, and hinted that he could not tolerate such an eventuality. François-Poncet assured him that both the Radicals and the Socialists would act against any attempt at revolution.[23]

Hitler's claim that there was a danger of communist revolution breaking out in France was bolstered by Dominique's campaign in *La République*.

[20] Guy Bourdé, *La defaite du Front Populaire* (Paris, 1977), pp. 9–10; Kayser, 'Le parti radical-socialiste et le Rassemblement populaire, 1935–1938', *Bulletin de la Societé d'Histoire de la Troisième République*, 14 (April–July 1955), 280. Appeals for law and order were issued by Radical Committees (see e.g. *La République*, 16 June and 4, 8, 19, 21 July 1936). As regards the Radical press, even the left-wing *L'Oeuvre* began to get nervous in early June. Radical parliamentarians began publicly to demand order: Georges Bonnet (reported in *L'Oeuvre*, 27 June 1936), Camille Chautemps (*L'Oeuvre*, 29 June 1936), Daladier (*Débats*, 3 July 1936).

[21] Marceau Pivert, *Le Populaire*, 15 August 1936. Caillaux talked of the Senate's growing anger in a letter of 30 July 1936 to Roche, in the Roche–Caillaux archives of the Fondation Nationale des Sciences Politiques, Paris, in ERJC9, Dr 1, hereafter ERJC9, Dr 1. In a speech at Toulouse (*Le Populaire*, 25 October 1936), Blum reaffirmed his determination to remain within republican legality. Cf. Georges Lefranc, *Histoire du Front Populaire* (Paris, 1965), p. 225.

[22] Blum to Suzanne Blum, 9 July 1942, in Georges Lefranc, *L'expérience du Front Populaire* (Paris, 1972), pp. 48–9. Daladier believed that Blum feared civil war or a general war over Spain, in 1DA7, Dr, 1 srd a. For fear of German aggression against France see Archimbaud to the Radical Federation of the Gard, reported in *Le Petit Niçois*, 5 October 1936 and Albert Milhaud, *Le Petit Provençal*, 20 December 1936.

[23] Hitler's implied threat may be found in François-Poncet to André Blumel (Blum's *directeur du cabinet*), 10 October 1936 (report of 2 September conversation) in Ministère des Affaires Etrangères, *Documents Diplomatiques Français, 1932–1939*, Second Series, (hereafter DDF 2), vol. III, document 334.

This insisted that the strikes constituted a communist conspiracy to bring about revolution and to draw Hitler's attention away from Russia. The plans, Dominique asserted, had only been cancelled at the last minute (on the night of 11–12 June) thanks to La République's exposé of the plot.[24] While these charges were unsubstantiated, their objective, quite clearly, was to separate the Communists from the majority, and, eventually, to destroy the Popular Front. If there was any plot at all, it was by the spiritual leader of La République, Caillaux and his acolyte, Emile Roche, the paper's director, to break up the Popular Front.[25] It was not long before other Radical leaders and deputies began to climb on the bandwagon. Chief among them were men like Camille Chautemps, a deputy premier, and deputies like Georges Bonnet, Léon Meyer, Georges Potut and Gaston Riou.

It was in the midst of this internal crisis over the strikes and the Communists' role therein that, on 17–18 July 1936, the Spanish generals launched their military coup. It was only at this point that the press friendly to the Radicals rediscovered Spain. At first even Roche voiced his sympathy for the Spanish Republic.[26] Most of the Radical press expressed moral support for a legally elected government, and in some of the provincial papers, like Dépêche de Toulouse, articles in 1936–7 frequently express sympathy as much for a Republic engaged in a battle against militant clericalism as against fascism.[27] Fighting clericalism, after all, had been the Radicals' original raison d'être.

In the end, however, Spain received little more than sympathy from France. Starting from the assumption that it was France's primary objective to remain out of the war, Dominique began, in full accord with the rightist press, a campaign for French neutrality over Spain. The fears of

---

[24] La République, 11 and 18 July 1936.

[25] The Caillaux–Roche archives show that Caillaux himself used La République as his stalking-horse. See, for instance, Caillaux to Roche, 30 July 1936 in ERJC9, Dr 1 and in the epilogue to Caillaux's memoirs where he said he believed he had to stem the disaster spawned by the Popular Front, in ERJC8, Dr 2.

[26] La République, 30 July 1936. In his otherwise useful work on the Radicals, Serge Berstein (Histoire du parti radical, vol. 2: Crise du radicalisme, Paris, 1982, pp. 457–8) says of Dominique's attacks on the Communists, which began on 24 May 1936 (Berstein mistakenly says 31 May), that 'Almost daily from this date he warned the French against following the Spanish example ...' Examination of La République, however, shows that, in all, between 24 May and 24 July 1936 (when he began his campaign against French intervention in the Spanish Civil War) he mentioned Spain on only six occasions (2, 19, 26 June and 20, 21, 23 July 1936).

[27] Pierre Mille, 22 January 1937. On sympathy but no involvement see: editorial, Le Petit Journal (Paris), 21 July 1936; Darrès, Le Petit Niçois, 24 July 1936; Pierre, L'Oeuvre, 28 July 1936; editorial, L'Ere Nouvelle, 14 August 1936 and editorial, L'Oeuvre, 15 August 1936.

La République could only have been aggravated by the strikes and demonstrations in favour of aid to the Spanish Republic which were often instigated by communist and socialist trade union officials.[28] At this point Dominique suggested that the PCF, following Comintern instructions, wanted war, either to deflect Hitler's attention away from Russia or in the hope that the chaos of war would give the PCF a chance to make a revolution in its wake.

The details of the government's adoption of the policy of non-intervention between the end of July and early August have been exhaustively studied. Most prominent Radical leaders supported non-intervention – whether they were inside the government (Chautemps and Foreign Minister Delbos), or outside it (especially Herriot, the Radical president of the Chamber). Only Pierre Cot, in the government, and the old progressive Radical, Archimbaud, outside it, favoured aid for Spain. The Radical Party's leader, Daladier, who was also Blum's war minister, seems to have been prepared to align with the prevailing opinion, despite his doubts about the policy. In the end, in his unpublished memoirs, he noted that once the decision for non-intervention had been made, no French military equipment under his control reached Spain.[29] This, however, was not so much because he felt bound by the government's decision, but because the equipment was so desperately needed by the French military for its rearmament programme. It was of great concern to the Radical leader that French rearmament was continually delayed by both the strikes and the Popular Front's introduction of the forty-hour week.

Certainly many reasons underlay the adoption of the policy of non-intervention, most of them reflecting Radical fears. They feared provoking an attack by Germany. They feared being deprived of British support. They feared a war for which they were not prepared. To Radicals, civil insurrection in France was also a danger which might bring revolution in

---

[28] Léon Jouhaux (head of the largest union confederation in France, the CGT, at this point unified with the communist CGTU), *Vendredi* (Paris), 21 August 1936; Maurice Harmel, in the CGT's official organ *Le Peuple* (Paris), 5, 20 and 23 August 1936; André Marty (later the International Brigade commander), *L'Humanité*, 12 August 1936; Racamond, as reported in *Le Populaire*, 20 August 1936.

[29] IDA7, Dr 4, sdr a. Prior to the government's decision for non-intervention, aid to Republican Spain was sent, from 8 August 1936. Chief but not sole organizer of assistance was Pierre Cot, French air minister. See Cot's testimony, 1 August 1947 in *Commission d'Enquête Parlementaire sur les èvènements survenus en France de 1933 à 1945: Témoignages* (Paris, 1951–2), vol. 1, pp. 273–4; Madeline Astorkia, 'L'aviation et la guerre d'Espagne: la cinquième arme face aux expériences de la guerre moderne', *Colloque Franco-Allemand* (Bonn, 1978), p. 9 and annexe v. See also Pierre le Goyet, *Missions de liaison* (Paris, 1978), pp. 227–8.

its wake. Finally, they feared that whoever won the Spanish Civil War – be it the 'fascist' Franco or the 'Spanish Lenin' Largo Caballero and his communist allies – France would find no comfort in the outcome.[30] For the Radicals the choices seemed so unappealing that they selected non-intervention, as the least unsatisfactory option available.

Non-intervention was widely supported by conservative Radicals. Some in the party, however, like those represented by *La Frontière* of the Territoire de Belfort, clearly found the policy difficult to understand. Others, like Jacques Kayser, on the party's left, slowly and grudgingly came to support it.[31] Others, like those associated with *Le Petit Niçois* and *L'Oeuvre*, developed a schizophrenic approach to the subject: often loudly supporting the Spanish Republicans but, at the same time, accepting that they had to follow their government and its decisions.

Although the Radicals could and did put pressure on Blum, it is clear that the prime minister, after due reflection, accepted the policy of non-intervention which the Quai d'Orsay and Delbos initially put forward.[32] Blum took a calculated if reluctant decision that the price to be paid for a consensus permitting the Popular Front's social and economic reforms was non-intervention. Certainly Blum was a man of exceptional intellect, but he was also a successful politician. When the time came to make a choice, he made the only one possible, the only one which would allow him to keep the crucial parliamentary support of the Radicals. Pragmatism led Blum to ignore the efforts of the PCF and of certain trade union leaders like Jouhaux, to convince him to send aid to Spain. Yet at the same time Blum succeeded in swinging large and initially hostile Parisian working-class crowds behind his policy, as at Luna Park in September and before that at the 'Peace Gathering' at St-Cloud. At Luna Park Blum defended the integrity of the Popular Front against the communist proposal for broadening the alliance into the French Front. This would have brought the defence-minded French right into a national union

---

30 Herbette to Delbos, 2 December 1936, DDF 2, IV, document 80; Dominique, *La République*, 24 and 26 July 1936; editorial *Quotidien* (Paris), 30 July 1936.
31 *La Frontière* was the radical deputy Edmond Miellet's paper. From 21 July 1936 it published messages of support from the left and generally attacked the French right for hypocrisy. After September, however, Spain generally disappeared from the paper. Early in the Civil War Kayser too supported 'aid' (generally unspecified) for the Republicans (see meeting at the Buffalo Velodrome, as reported in *Le Populaire*, 26 August 1936), but later in the year even he was supporting both the Republicans and the policy of Blum and Delbos (*Le Petit Niçois*, 14 October 1936 and *France de Bordeaux*, 9 January 1937).
32 Daladier said, in his unfinished memoirs ('La Guerre d'Espagne'), that the policy was devised by Chautemps, 1DA7, Dr 5, sdr a. Cf. Jean Zay, Blum's minister of education, in *Souvenirs et solitude* (Paris, 1945), pp. 114–15.

government whereby the domestic reform programme would have been jettisoned in favour of an active foreign policy against Hitler, to be pursued in collaboration with the Soviet Union. At Orléans, just prior to the Radical congress at Biarritz, Blum laid the groundwork which enabled the pro-Popular Front Radicals to defuse Roche's attempt at the congress entirely to dismantle the alliance.[33] Blum knew that for the Socialists to emerge with any credit from leading the Popular Front government he had to remain in power to offer his social reforms a chance to take root. Handing over to a Radical, especially under pressure from Caillaux and the Radicals in the Senate, very probably would have led to the dismantling or undermining of some, if not all, of the Popular Front's achievements. Blum's skill and political acumen are evident in the fact that he successfully isolated Caillaux after the latter had finally engineered the downfall of the government in June 1937. Caillaux was surprised to be bypassed by President Albert Lebrun when the Chautemps government was formed. To obtain his year in office, Blum had to accept non-intervention. He did so out of his sense of the political constraints of the moment. While it is fair to say that the Radicals, as the political pivot in parliament, had a key role in pushing through non-intervention, there was clearly very little opposition either from within their own party, from Blum's Socialists or from the parties of the right.

While events in Spain were undoubtedly registered in the Radical Party, from the leadership down, the influence of these events was never direct or simple. Few in France, even among the Radicals, seemed to connect the wave of strikes in Spain, which pre-dated those in France, with the unrest at home from May onwards. Few Radicals saw Spain as either an omen for their future or a model for them to emulate. Except when the question of non-intervention arose, most Radicals had little to say about Spain. Yet, aside from the strikes, it was over Spain, and particularly the communist attitude to Spain, that the Radicals began to distance themselves from the PCF and then from the Popular Front. This put Blum on the defensive and turned him into a typical 1930s premier whose chief concern came to be to keep his government afloat. This, in turn, meant maintaining the *status quo*: internally and internationally. In both cases it meant appeasement. First Blum had to appease the workers, then he had to appease the worried

---

[33] Blum spoke at Luna Park on 6 September 1936, concluding that 'war is only possible when one admits it is possible', pamphlet in 2BL4, Dr 1. At St-Cloud he concluded: 'To want peace means to want it against all obstacles, against all dangers, against all risks', as reported in *Le Petit Niçois*, 10 August 1936. The text of his speech to the Radicals at Orléans may be found in 2BL3, Dr 3. Cf. Lefranc, *Histoire du Front Populaire*, p. 208.

Radical middle class whose loudest spokesmen were to be found in the Senate, and finally he had to appease Hitler, Mussolini and Franco by refusing to supply arms to the Spanish Republicans. Except for the Communists and a few others, this foreign policy also satisfied the widespread desire in France for peace at any price, even if it eventually became the peace of the grave, the concentration camp and the police state.

The Spanish army and the Popular Front

MICHAEL ALPERT

The simplest thing to say might be that Spanish officers disliked the Popular Front and so they rebelled against it. But the lapidary style fails to answer the question that must be posed: what was the *provocation* of the Popular Front government of February 1936, to use Carolyn Boyd's paradigm of *disposition, provocation* and *opportunity*, that incited the Spanish army to rebel?[1] Indeed, is the question posed at all properly? Was it the government, or its deeds, or what it was feared it might do, or perhaps what it would not do, which led to the army's decision to overthrow it? Were these fears and hatreds justified in any sense that we can appreciate, or was the army acting for no other purpose than to pull the chestnuts out of the fire for a selfish oligarchy, which headed an unjust and reactionary economic system, legitimized by a Church unable or unwilling to accept challenge?

Again, was there something in the *disposition* of the Spanish officer corps which inclined it to act as a tool of political and economic interests? Were such interests identical with the army's own? What was the inner structure and self-perception which allowed the army to rise in rebellion against a constitutional regime?

This is a large number of questions to be answered. One path to answering them, which will lead to others, is an examination of the peculiar status of the Spanish army in the late nineteenth and early twentieth-

[1] Carolyn Boyd, *Praetorian Politics in Liberal Spain* (Chapel Hill, 1979), preface, pp. ix–x.

century liberal state, or perhaps the relation of the Spanish state with its army.[2]

The army was a conscript force, with some professional units stationed in Morocco. Military service was relatively short. Officers spent their time training recruits and often in second, non-military jobs which they needed to supplement their poor salaries. There was sparse opportunity for soldiering except with the elite units in North Africa. There was little regimental tradition. To this extent, the army was a model of the forces of the modern liberal, bourgeois state, rather than of the pre-revolutionary armies or the small and highly-trained ones of countries such as Great Britain. But in other respects Spain was not such a state. For one thing, it never had a European role to play, nor had it enemies who would threaten it. It had enough difficulty with the Moroccan protectorate without the need to seek a wider empire. Internally, Spain's indicators of population density and distribution, illiteracy, urbanization, proportion of the working population in the various sectors of the economy, and government by oligarchy and *caciques* – local dominant squirearchies or political bosses – all pointed to a country which by the establishment of the bourgeois-reformist Second Republic in 1931 was still, to a considerable extent, underdeveloped. The changes brought about by the 1931 to 1933 reforms of the Republic are not meant to be undervalued but, if Spain is looked at synchronically rather than diachronically, its comparative backwardness in 1936 is striking.

Because of the gap the Spanish army was not synchronized with its own formal structure or that of the state, but rather more with its own historical tradition and sociological form. Its structure was that of the army of a liberal-bourgeois state, but its attitudes were more those of a pre-revolutionary estate.

These attitudes had evolved through historical developments from the end of the eighteenth century. Within these one constant which would, in my view, be a precipitating factor in 1936, was the tradition by which the Spanish military controlled public order. This was a tradition, deeply rooted in the *ancien régime*, based on the role of the captains-general, senior officers who enjoyed maximum administrative, political and judicial authority in the region over which they were appointed. Moreover, the

[2] See S. Payne, *Politics and the Military in Modern Spain* (Stanford, 1967); Boyd, *Praetorian Politics*; J. Busquets, *El militar de carrera en España* (Barcelona, 1967); F. Fernández Bastarreche, *El ejército español en el siglo XIX* (Madrid, 1978); Michael Alpert, *La reforma militar de Azaña* (Madrid, 1982); G. Cardona, *El poder militar en la España contemporánea hasta la guerra civil* (Madrid, 1983); M. Alonso Báquer, *El ejército en la sociedad española* (Madrid, 1971).

lower judicial and administrative roles were often played by the local military governor.[3]

Perhaps the major feature in the role of the military in public order was that it was able to declare a state of war – that is, to bring an area under military jurisdiction – merely by invoking the *Ordenanzas Militares*, or King's Regulations, of 1768, which gave the army both the right and the duty to police public assembly and to include cases of public order within its own jurisdiction.

Whatever the suitability of such a system might have been for the eighteenth century, the weakness of nineteenth-century liberal reform and Spain's failure to develop a bourgeoisie strong enough to carry out a thorough liberal revolution led to the persistence of a regime of military presence in civilian life which would survive into the constitutional epochs of the last one hundred years. This retarded development of political institutions meant that Spain had unsuccessfully passed through the epoch when liberal armies overthrew oligarchies. When working-class mobilization began to occur at the end of the last century and much more so at the beginning of this one, the officer began to see himself as the guardian of established conservative order.[4]

It would be as well to insist upon this point. The Spanish army's view of its role in the preservation of public order arose from its special position as being entitled to initiate the state of war and to intervene as an army, rather than as citizens at the request of the civilian authorities. Not only this, but the Spanish absolutists of the eighteenth century had used military men to run the country, when their French equivalents employed civilian *intendants*. Perhaps this was why the policing model introduced in revolutionary France was the civilian one with Fouché and the Ministry of Police, while the first Spanish liberal constitution of 1812 retained military jurisdiction. In liberal Spain the rights of assembly, demonstration and expression would always be closely controlled by the military. In addition, military personnel engaged in these repressive functions were subject to their own jurisdiction and not the ordinary courts. Spanish civil governors, unlike their French homologues, the *préfets*, had to fight a losing battle against military predominance. The civil wars and banditry of nineteenth century Spain led to the maintenance of large armies and the custom of military rule. The police force which was formed to put down banditry – the Civil

---

[3] See M. Ballbé, *Orden público y militarismo en la España constitutional* (Madrid, 1983).
[4] See V. R. Berghahn, *Militarism: the history of an international debate* (Cambridge, 1984), p. 69, quoting S. J. Huntingdon, *Political Order in Changing Societies* (New Haven, 1968).

Guard – was and is still to a large extent, militarized. Conflict with the Civil Guard was a court-martial offence, even, for instance, when a poacher resisted arrest.

A militarized police, the absence of a civilian force capable of reacting to public disorder, the use of military jurisdiction, the very limited rights of assembly and strike, made the recourse to the state of war ever more frequent as Spain developed industrially and as its working-class movements and reformist nuclei acquired consciousness.

Since the establishment in 1876 of a constitutional monarchy with a stable regime, the army had not intervened openly in politics. Satisfied as it was with its role in repression and the defeat of attempts to reform its internal structure, it found that the changes occurring in society and the criticisms aroused by the disastrous defeat of Spain in its war with the USA in 1898, together with the army's relatively poor showing in Morocco, required its re-entry into the arena of politics. Press criticism had been silenced by bringing it under military jurisdiction in 1906.[5] Thereafter the army contributed to the repression of disorder caused by the unpopularity of the Moroccan war in 1909 and militarized railway strikers in 1912.[6] In 1917 it moved openly into rebellion, threatening a coup if its demands were not met in the field of its internal conditions, and making and unmaking ministers of war until the Army Act of 1918 ensured that the reform, so necessary in liberal eyes, would not be carried out. The army took a major part in the repression of disorder at the same time as the inquiry into the notorious massacre of Spanish troops in 1921 at Annual in Morocco. Yet, as the cleansing of the Augean Stables of misconduct and political and social error seemed imminent, it was a general, Primo de Rivera, who with the tacit approval of his comrades, solved the political crisis by carrying out an unopposed takeover of power.

The army saw its role as a filler of the political vacuum, as offering a backbone to a Spain riven with particularisms. The army was psychologically prepared to fill this vacuum of authority and social institutions in order to combat what it saw as the demagogy of the progressive alternative.

The seven years of Primo de Rivera's rule only increased the politicization of the army. Large numbers of officers occupied administrative posts at local and national level. Those who took part in the victorious pacification of Morocco in 1925 to 1927 were adulated, perceived as they

[5] See J. Romero-Maura, *The Spanish Army and Catalonia: the 'Cu-Cut' incident and the Law of Jurisdictions 1905–1906* (Beverly Hills, 1977).
[6] See J. Connelly Ullman, *The Tragic Week* (Harvard 1968).

were as fulfilling Spain's christianizing and civilizing mission while conferring on the *patria* the status of a colonial power. That socialists, anarchists and liberal intellectuals criticized this role only indicated, in the eyes of the army and conservative sectors of the population, that they were not patriots. The various poorly-planned attempts at military rebellion by officers who had fallen out with Primo and who were taken up by liberal politicians, by officers displeased with Primo's not unreasonable though arbitrarily implemented reforms, and by groups of younger men who had inchoate revolutionary ideas, only served to increase the politicization of that generation of officers.

This politicization, which probably widened the internal rifts in the officer corps while at the same time sensitizing it even more, increased during the years of the Second Republic. It might be said that the violent personal attacks made on Manuel Azaña, the reformist minister of war in the 1931 to 1933 period, and on his military advisers, helped to create an attitude of almost paranoiac character among the military. Azaña's reforms, it may be contended, aimed at no more than making the army into what it should be in a liberal bourgeois republic on the model of France. The army saw the reforms as an attempt to destroy it, particularly when Azaña abolished the captains-general and began the task of restricting military justice to the ambit of military matters.[7] It could be said that, although repression of disorder during the Republic was still kept in the hands of the army and even though the new corps of Republican Assault Police was commanded by seconded army officers, the army feared that its responsibility and privilege in controlling public order was being eroded.[8]

Perhaps this fear arose, among other sources, from the clearer articulation by working-class organizations of a demand for the dissolution of the paramilitary Civil Guard and the conversion of the army into a civilian militia. Yet the abolition of the army and the arming of a people's militia was merely *proposed* by Madrid Socialists as a change in their party's policy.[9] Nor was there anything in the Popular Front manifesto of 1936 about dissolving the army or the Civil Guard.[10] That Azaña did not take such measures, although the Socialists had hoped that his reforms would turn the army into something like Jean Jaurès's vision of a Swiss-style

---

[7] For the standard criticism of Azaña at the time see Emilio Mola, 'Azaña, el pasado y el porvenir', *Obras Completas* (Valladolid, 1939).

[8] See Manuel Espadas Burgos, 'Orden social en la mentalidad militar española' in M. Tuñón de Lara (ed.), *España 1898–1936* (Madrid, 1984).

[9] R. de la Cierva, *Los documentos de la primavera trágica*, no. 60 (Madrid, 1967).

[10] Ibid., no. 15.

militia, nevertheless did not assuage the army's fears that working-class demands might be met. Perhaps the expression of that unreal fear was a justification for the army's hostility to the Popular Front.[11]

The problem with public order under the Republic was that the famous Law for the Defence of the Republic of 21 October 1931 was directed against the right as much as the left and could be used against the army officers as well. This emerges clearly in the growing criticisms of Azaña's reforms to be found in the military press (incidentally another factor of peculiar significance – why should a few thousand officers have a non-specialized daily newspaper?). Azaña's suppression of the military press because of its subversive and libellous campaigns against him served to increase the polarization between the army on one side and the minister and the republican ideal, which he incarnated, on the other. The military press which re-emerged was much milder and its perusal is not too rewarding. Nevertheless its concentration on crime is interesting, as is its linking of that phenomenon with the maximalist socialist policy increasingly advocated by the leader of the Socialist Party's left wing, Francisco Largo Caballero.[12]

Though on the surface it seemed as if the privileged status of the army in the maintenance of public order was under threat, a closer look at internal war ministry orders shows that military jurisdiction was retained for a wide number of public-order offences, particularly in connection with the policing of strikes and similar manifestations. The senior officers of the police and paramilitary formations remained military, and the government used such forces determinedly against left-wing threats to its stability.

Nevertheless, the trial, sentence to death and serving of a commuted sentence in a convict prison, of the distinguished General Sanjurjo, leader of an ill-planned coup in 1932, acted as a counterweight to any relief the army may have felt. The disgrace of a general serving a term in the company of common convicts rather than in the more suitable and honourable conditions of a military prison was seen as insulting the army.

So far we have not considered the internal attitudes of army officers, their *disposition*, to follow Boyd's paradigm. Did they, for instance, support the ideas of Hitler and Mussolini? Although the military press was concerned at the international aggression that Hitlerism might signify,

[11] See, for example, the autobiography of the air force major I. Hidalgo de Cisneros, *Cambio de rumbo* (Bucharest, 1964), vol. 2, pp. 136–7, who describes the mutual fears of a coup both by officers and men in the air force.

[12] See *Marte*, 1 April 1932 – 30 June 1936 (the Hemeroteca Municipal de Madrid has a fair run of this paper).

army officers admired the abolition of parties and the strict control of expression in Germany and Italy. Likewise the Spanish military admired a tough stance in sentencing policy on crime.[13] Their view of working-class leaders was that they exploited the natural desires of the workers for betterment. Strikes and other such manifestations should be controlled by a more authoritarian constitution, and here the army aligned itself with the views of the major opposition party, the Catholic–conservative CEDA.

In one article attacking the 'hypocrisy' of working-class leaders, the military press introduced free love into the debate. It is perhaps worth speculating that a significant part of the army's dislike of the combination of attitudes that it saw triumphant in the Popular Front victory of February 1936 was sexual in origin. As elements in this tentatively-held view, one might take the frequent appearance of words such as 'virile' and 'effeminate' in the language of conflict used by and in reference to the army. In order to attack Azaña, the libel was circulated that he was a sexual deviant who had been expelled from the military academy for homosexual scandal. At stake in Spain were conservative attitudes towards the status of men and fathers threatened by the independence of women and children, as evidenced in the manifestations of popular militias and youth movements, in which the urban young of both sexes took part. One might go so far as to suggest that the 'free love' which, it was feared, would be the consequence of such behaviour, and which was in effect advocated by some, was really less the true concern than the sexlessness of the feared revolution in society. That young women were not so obsessed with what men felt about them and that young men were beginning to see women as equals was perhaps a genuine if unexpressed fear of the traditional Spaniard. But the army officer had the means of force.[14]

After all, the rightist press told the officer that he possessed a reserve of moral values which were rapidly diminishing in the world. The officer was unlikely to be open to other views given the restricted strata of society from which he was recruited and his style of life. Officers were recruited more and more, through the late nineteenth and early twentieth century, from among the sons of officers and sergeants.[15] They married the daughters of other officers. To auto-recruitment and endogamy must be added their academy training, which was lengthy, beginning as early as the age of

---

[13] See *Marte*, passim.
[14] For the consciousness of a changed attitude towards women during the Civil War, see Ronald Fraser, *Blood of Spain* (London, 1979), pp. 286–9.
[15] See Busquets, *El militar de carrera*, and Fernández Bastarreche, *El ejército español*.

fifteen;[16] and during and after which they had little contact with other young men in the professions and at the universities. The academy acted somewhat like a seminary-style boarding school. It was not only the military arts that were taught but an esprit de corps which instilled in the boy cadet the twin values of loyalty to the abstract concept of a Spain which was politically, socially, and religiously centralized, and loyalty to his brother-officers. Thus he came to hate regional movements, manifestations of ideological nonconformity, dissent and heterodoxy. The army's task was to preserve 'Spanish' values, and therefore the young man hypervalued these. Since by definition all officers shared the same values, loyalty was the absolute virtue. Officers who, for instance, had participated or stood aside in the 1934 Catalan separatist uprising and those generals, often freemasons, whom the Popular Front had placed in positions of command, were 'disloyal'.

The increase in right-wing attitudes had been constant during the late nineteenth century, as the liberal values which the army had defended earlier in the century became merged with conservative ones in the Restoration settlement of the last quarter of the century. The desire to reform the army expressed by dissentients, together with the anti-militarism of working-class movements, especially anarchism which had particular strength in Spain, only increased the polarization of views and attitudes. Nor was the moderating and modernizing effect of a yearly intake of civilian conscripts of any effect, for such was the gap between liberal institutions and actual practice that only the sons of working-class families fulfilled their military service obligations. For varying sums, out of the reach of the poor, middle-class conscripts bought very short service, usually remaining resident at home. Since hardly any officers came from the wealthy Catalan or Basque bourgeoisies the army was insulated from modern currents and the bourgeoisie became largely indifferent to the army except when disaster made them demand reform or a strike caused them to call for military intervention.[17] The absence of pseudo- and proto-military organizations in Spain, on the British model of the Scouts, Boys' Brigade, Church Army, cadet corps, Sea Scouts and so forth, is striking in this connection.

Thus in Spain the army had not been absorbed into the body politic. In spite of the Restoration settlement of 1876 the tradition of the coup was not

[16] Francisco Franco entered the service on 29 August 1907 at the age of fourteen (*Anuario Militar de España*).

[17] Busquets, *El militar de carrera*, and Fernández Bastarreche, *El ejército español*.

dead. It was, however, more difficult to organize than it had been. The coup of Primo de Rivera in 1923 succeeded because none of the forces which might have opposed it was organized. The conspiracies of 1926, 1929 and 1930 and the Sanjurjo attempt of 1932 had collapsed in ridiculous failure. It was generally felt that the age of the military coup had passed. Francisco Franco, chief of the general staff in 1935, had in fact resisted the idea of a coup until the necessary unity of the army was more apparent.[18] He had tried to persuade military ministers and the Civil Guard to take over power when the Popular Front gained its victory in February 1936. But it was a brigadier-general, Emilio Mola, who recognized that a successful coup would need extensive planning and the support of widely different civilian forces to have a chance of success.[19] The officer corps would have to be persuaded to rise by rumours that the government intended, or would be forced, to dissolve the army and the Civil Guard and replace them with a militia. The dismissals, appointments and transfers of commanders by the government which had been brought to power by the Popular Front victory were interpreted as a preparation for a Leninist-style coup by the left-wing socialist leader, Largo Caballero, under the Kerenskyist benevolence of Azaña in the presidency of the Republic and of the prime minister, Santiago Casares Quiroga. Such was the burden of the letter which Franco, writing from his command in the Canaries, sent to the prime minister on 23 June 1936. He referred to the transfer of regiments because of bitter disputes with civilians and to command changes.[20] Possibly this fact – that the government did not insist on the regiments remaining where they were but preferred to calm matters by transferring them – explains the state of unease to which Franco referred.

Whether or not there was any sense of general alarm among the military or whether it had to be aroused, remains an open question. There was never any likelihood of the government dissolving the army or the Civil Guard and in fact Spain was governed by a State of Exception throughout 1936, a state maintained by military and police authority.

On 8 March 1936, at what was apparently the first meeting of the military conspirators, Generals Mola and Franco both insisted that the time of the old-fashioned coup had passed. Civilian support was essential. The decision was taken to rise only if a proletarian revolution took place,

[18] Payne, *Politics and the Military in Modern Spain*, p. 312.
[19] Ibid., chapter 17 for details of the conspiracy.
[20] L. de Galinsoga, *Centinela de Occidente* (Barcelona, 1956), pp. 203–4.

or if Largo Caballero obtained power.[21] On 17 March, Azaña, still prime minister before his elevation in May to the presidency of the Republic, strongly denied rumours of unrest in the army and expressed indignation at crowd attacks on officers.[22] Probably whistling in the dark, Azaña insisted that the army was the Republic's strongest support.

A later meeting of conspirators decided to act if the Civil Guard or the army were dissolved. These fears seem to have been general, though nothing except noisy demands actually seems likely to have happened.

Greater and more justified alarm probably arose through attempts at propaganda among conscripts. Although no troops disobeyed their officers when the latter rebelled against the government on 18 July 1936, there does appear to have been some attempted subversion among the troops on the part of the Spanish Communist Party, organized by the still-surviving leader of one of its factions, Enrique Líster.[23]

The repression of the Spanish fascist group, the Falange, and the arrest of its leader, José Antonio Primo de Rivera, the detention of General López Ochoa, accused of over-harshness in the suppression of the Asturian uprising of October 1934, together with the enforced internal exile of two plotting generals (Orgaz and Varela), were further events which, while not individually causes for excessive concern, went towards creating the climate of desperation which would explain – or justify – the rebellion.

The presence in the Madrid police force of well-known left-wing officers would be seen as intentional, not only for the protection of the regime, but for the deed they committed on the night of 12–13 July when Assault Guard officers murdered the leader of the opposition, José Calvo Sotelo, in revenge for the assassination by rightist gunmen of the second of a number of leftist-inclined officers who had been assisting the socialist militias in their training. Calvo Sotelo had openly stated that the army ought to rise against anarchy in Spain.[24]

In spite of the careful planning of General Mola, his patient negotiations with civilian leaders, and the work of the Unión Militar Española, an officers' organization of conservative tendencies, had it not been for the grotesque murder of Calvo Sotelo it may be doubted whether the loyalty

---

[21] Richard A. H. Robinson, *The Origins of Franco's Spain: the Right, the Republic and Revolution 1931–1936* (Newton Abbot, 1970), pp. 277–8, citing several memoirs of participants.

[22] It was not quite so dramatic. The mob attacked an officer who had arrested a man who had used a knife. They thought that the officer was 'protecting a fascist' (*El Telegrama del Rif*, Melilla, 3 March 1936).

[23] E. Líster, *Nuestra guerra* (Paris 1966), pp. 25–6. I have, however, found no measurable evidence of subversion.

[24] In a Cortes debate on 16 June 1936, quoted in Robinson, *Origins of Franco's Spain*, p. 273.

inculcated at the academy would have inclined so many officers to join the rebels who took over the garrisons on 18, 19 and 20 July 1936. That many officers avoided involvement and quite a number of others refused to rebel and even supported, with greater or lesser enthusiasm, the elected government, is perhaps an indication that things had changed.[25] Praetorianism is perhaps normal in under-developed countries with a low level of industrialization and mobilization. Spain had an army with praetorian style to it but it was, in rebelling against the Popular Front, to come up against a very high level of civilian mobilization. The coup would be unsuccessful and, while few rebels had imagined immediate triumph, fewer still had predicted the major civil war which would ensue.

One conclusion might be, therefore, that the coup of July 1936 was an anachronism, which 'succeeded' only because the plotters realized the need for widespread civilian support and because they included the prestigious Franco and Sanjurjo among their names. As has been seen, golpismo had come into Spain through military plots against absolutism in the early nineteenth century. Liberal governments of the century had preserved the anachronistic features of the army. The vacuum caused by the absence of political elites and institutions required the army to participate. The period during which the army might have been expected to innovate and to overthrow oligarchies lasted longer in Spain than in other countries. By 1876, faced with the mobilization of the working class, by Catalan separatism and by revolutionary ideas which the army thought could not be absorbed, the military became the guardian of the established political order in Spain. This epoch of established and elitist liberalism, beginning in 1875, was unsatisfactory and collapsed, leading to an authoritarian solution, the Primo de Rivera dictatorship of 1923 to 1930. From this angle, the period of constitutional republicanism – 1931 to 1936 – and in particular its 1931 to 1933 years of reformist atmosphere and its six months of revolutionary anticipation or apprehension in 1936, came out of phase. Perhaps they occurred precisely because Spanish society had never before had the chance to become disillusioned with genuine – rather than superficial – liberal institutions.

The army – and this cannot be overstressed – expected to be called upon to maintain public order. From this it grew to see itself as the 'ultimate

[25] For the vicissitudes of officers in the Civil War, see R. Salas Larrazábal, *Historia del Ejército Popular de la República* (Madrid, 1973) and Michael Alpert, *El Ejército Republicano en la Guerra Civil* (Paris–Barcelona, 1977).

recourse to maintain political and institutional normality'.[26] But this was always mingled with a fear of army reform (even though almost all military writers admitted that reform was needed) which in the army mind became associated with chaos, licence, anarchism and bolshevism. It was easy for the army to work up the conspiracy theory which had been prevalent ever since the 1898 disaster, blamed by the left on the army and the navy. Azaña's reforms provoked the construction of a myth according to which he was a pervert who wished to hand Spain over defenceless to the communist–masonic–Jewish conspiracy, well-known to students of right-wing demonology. Azaña, with his ideal of an enlightened, liberal and culture-based society, such as the Republic meant to be, was antipathetic in the army view to its own inflexible and aristocratic code.

In terms of a moderate political position, it might have been reasonable to decide to overthrow the Popular Front government had it given in to socialist demands to abolish the forces of public order, that is the army and the Civil Guard. But only an army which saw its role in such a particular way as the Spanish one did could consider the mere transfer of a garrison or of commanders an attack on the values of society.

[26] R. Salas, in prologue to Payne, Spanish edition, *Ejército y sociedad en la España liberal 1808–1936* (Madrid, 1977).

Soldiers and Socialists: the French officer corps and leftist government 1935–7

MARTIN S. ALEXANDER

On the rue de Varenne, at the entrance of the Hôtel Matignon, office of the prime minister, uniformed Gardes Mobiles snapped into salute at the arrival of Maurice Gamelin, the French army's chief of staff and inspector-general. It was 10 June 1936, four days since the Chamber of Deputies had invested Léon Blum's government by a 174-vote majority, confirming the electoral triumph of the Popular Front. Just two nights earlier, in these Matignon offices, Blum had concluded the tense negotiations for an economic and social settlement which ended the strikes and factory occupations that had crippled French industry since mid-May. This had been a nerve-stretching but exhilaratingly successful first three days for what Blum called his 'exercise of power'. Resistance to the left and its reforming government seemed in disarray. 'A large number of entre-preneurs', Gamelin reflected, 'had lost their heads and panicked . . .'.[1] The conservative parties licked their wounds and opened their post-mortems on defeat. With business bosses as cowed as the political right, the only possibility for repressing the workers' carnival seemed to lie with the army. Perhaps the greatest unspoken question in France that turbulent May was whether the military would cohabit with the Socialists.

The doubts hung heavily as France's most distinguished serving officer strode through the Matignon courtyard to meet Blum. Gamelin noticed the calm prevailing inside the offices, sharply contrasting with the continuing

[1] M. Gamelin, *Servir* (3 vols., Paris, 1946–7), vol. 2, *Le prologue du drame, 1930–1939*, pp. 220–1.

tension outside, product of what the general later decried as 'the criminal demagoguery of the "Popular Front"'.[2] In a spacious ground-floor drawing room, Blum awaited Gamelin. For both this was their first official encounter, encouraging Blum to break the ice by remarking that they were exact contemporaries, born in Paris in 1872. Immediately the well-briefed and elegantly-tailored Jewish lawyer from the Marais charmed the officer whom European leaders knew as France's intellectual soldier.

This meeting, so early after the elections and whilst the Popular Front faced a crowded domestic agenda, acknowledged the menacing European situation after Germany's uncontested remilitarization of the Rhineland in March 1936. Faith in France's military apparatus had been dented by this coup. Moreover scepticism had been stirred over France's ability to help her friends to Germany's east: Poland, Czechoslovakia and Rumania. For Gamelin it seemed imperative rapidly to agree with the Popular Front a high priority for reinvigorating France's defence effort.

Meeting the new prime minister so soon was encouraging for Gamelin; hearing his sentiments proved doubly gratifying. The general departed 'certain that thereafter I could broach anything with him absolutely frankly'. He had candidly told Blum that he felt no affinities at all with marxism. Nonetheless he considered himself a soldier 'with a social conscience'. Chiefly he hoped that the government would insulate the army from political commotion. Blum, according to Gamelin, 'assured me of his favourable feelings towards the military, of his concern for national defence ...: "You must not ... be afraid of the socialists; I guarantee that they now grasp the gravity of the circumstances in which Europe finds itself".' In return Gamelin promised to secure his soldiers' neutrality. The army, he said, was unperturbed by initiatives to extend social justice to the workers. It, he insisted, had to 'lie completely outside the class struggle'.[3]

Behind this affable encounter recalled in Gamelin's smoothly-styled reminiscence, how easily did the French army accommodate the left's installation in 1936? Historians, accustomed to explaining what happened in the past, have in this instance to investigate what did not, since the French experience differs in kind from the rebellion of Spanish officers in

---

[2] Gamelin, written submission to the Vichy Supreme Court of Justice at Riom: 'La politique étrangère de la France 1930–9 au point de vue militaire', p. 21, Blum Archives 3BL3, dossier 1, Fondation Nationale des Sciences Politiques, Paris. I am grateful to Dr N. T. N. Jordan, University of Illinois, Chicago-Circle, for this reference.

[3] Gamelin, Servir, vol. 2, pp. 222–4. The meeting is not recounted in L'oeuvre de Léon Blum: Mémoires. La prison et le procès. A l'echelle humaine, 1940–1945 (Paris, 1955). Cf. J. Colton, Léon Blum: humanist in politics (New York, 1966), pp. 198–203.

1936. In the latter case the causes of insurrection can be researched, likewise the motivations which induced some Spanish officers to side with Franco and the army of Africa yet rallied many others (some 2,000 to 2,500 between 1936 and 1939) to the Second Republic.

For France, though, an attempt must be made to analyse attitudes in an officer corps, perhaps an entire army, sitting on the sidelines, preserving an apolitical tradition. Yet no contemporary survey exists of the moods of the 28,500 officers in metropolitan France and her empire in 1936–7. Sources like memoirs and journals encourage a close focus on the ideological dispositions of the senior ranks, the generals and the two living marshals, Philippe Pétain and Louis Franchet d'Esperey. But in this approach lie further snares. Thoughts about military insubordination – still less plans for insurrection – are understandably sparse in the diaries and correspondence of serving officers. These men, if not quite military vicars of Bray, nonetheless had pay, promotions and pensions to restrain their political prejudices. Most colonels aspired to retire as generals, not as disgraced putschistes. Allowing for such discretion, how far may the army have been silent despite itself? How prevalent were grumbles? Was hostility or simply indifference the predominant sentiment towards the Popular Front?

Gamelin himself was crucial to the general staff's harmonious transition from serving the centre-right governments of Pierre Laval and Albert Sarraut, from June 1935 to May 1936, to working thereafter with the left. Since before the First World War Gamelin had cultivated associations across the classic parliamentary divide. His friends included André Tardieu, the conservative, Maurice Sarraut (a Radical, Toulouse press baron and brother of Blum's prime ministerial predecessor), and the independent socialist Joseph Paul-Boncour. From his military mentor, Marshal Joffre, whom he had served during the 'Marne miracle' of 1914, Gamelin drew the flexibility and personal serenity which characterized his command in the 1930s. Indeed his ascent of the military hierarchy is directly attributable to his nomination by Tardieu (then prime minister) in 1930, as deputy chief of staff. This appointment counterbalanced the abrasive and reactionary General Maxime Weygand, then just promoted chief of staff. Politically distrusted by progressives, Weygand was to be checked by the recognizably republican Gamelin.[4]

In office, especially in the era of the Radical-dominated governments of

[4] Gamelin, *Servir*, vol. 2, pp. i–xxxii. Cf. P. C. F. Bankwitz, *Maxime Weygand and Civil–Military Relations in Modern France* (Cambridge, Mass., 1967), pp. 24–47; J. Nobécourt, *Une histoire politique de l'armée: I: De Pétain à Pétain, 1919–1942* (Paris, 1967), pp. 197–200, 217–26, 236.

1932–4, Gamelin promoted civil–military conciliation. Amid disarmament negotiations, coupled with depression-induced budgetary constraint, he sought undemonstratively to re-establish a political consensus to strengthen the army. In his formula the right to influence policy, even the right to consultation, was earned 'by working completely loyally with ministers and not . . . by sulking . . . lest we risk governments by-passing us altogether'. To cynics, including some critics among the officers, this branded him a 'slave to the politics of the left'. Certainly after Weygand's retirement in 1935 Gamelin became the first officer since Joffre before 1914 to act as both commander-in-chief designate and chief of the general staff. But it was a centre-right government which approved this rare combination of powers. That there was no suggestion by Blum of reducing this position in 1936 reflected Gamelin's comforting approach to exercising command. Germany's military attaché in Paris astutely observed that politicians accepted Gamelin 'because he did not arouse their suspicions or give rise to the belief that he was making himself too powerful'. The general himself wrote later of his conviction that undertaking public service required 'being determined to show absolute loyalty towards the country's legitimate regime' and deference to its underlying institutions.[5]

The politics of Popular Frontism as such undeniably aroused Gamelin's distaste by its polarization of an already divided French society – a tendency from which the Front sprang, but which to Gamelin it seemed 'by introducing its dangerous ideology' also to exacerbate. However, unease at the arrival of SFIO ministers was tempered for Gamelin by the new government's large contingent of experienced Radicals. Yvon Delbos became foreign minister. Radicals also took all three military portfolios, greatest influence as well as responsibility falling to Edouard Daladier, who combined the deputy prime ministership with the ministry of national defence and war. 'Wild men of the left' were thus kept away from sensitive military posts. Moreover the PCF, by refusing office, kept far from the levers of power. This reassured the generals that there would be no security risks inside the political offices of the service ministries. Gamelin viewed the election result with an equanimity born of a practised partnership with Daladier, whose patriotism and political astuteness he respected. Their relationship had begun in 1933 when Gamelin, with only two colleagues, supported Daladier in bitter battles with Weygand over military policy

---

[5] Gamelin, *Servir*, vol. 2, pp. 57, 253, 75; appreciation by Colonel Kuhlenthal in Colonel F. G. Beaumont-Nesbitt, Paris, despatch of 11 March 1937, FO 371, 20693, C2085/122/17, Public Record Office, London (hereafter PRO).

during the depression. In 1936 Daladier had proven credentials as a bulwark between the army and the anti-militarist left on the one hand, the conspiratorial right on the other.[6]

Different soldiers did not all share this unconcern. Yet vituperation was generally expressed openly only by retired officers. One example was Weygand, writing on France's military condition in October 1936. He lashed the left for allegedly infecting the country with anti-patriotism. For him just as for Pétain (who in Gaston Doumergue's 'national union' government after the February 1934 crisis sought the education ministry), the primary school teachers, mostly CGT and SFIO stalwarts, were indictable.

Certainly the majority of the French love their army ... but the cult of the motherland and military duty face dedicated adversaries whose poisonous propaganda is all-pervasive ... Many of these adversaries belong to the state education service ... What sort of soldiers can we expect emerging from *their* schools?

Only restoring 'patriotic education', argued Weygand, would lay the foundation required for reconstructing solid French defences.[7]

Such diatribes from army elders served notice of their prejudice against the left. Did generational change, confining rancorous disputes like Dreyfus to the memories of a mostly retired caste, explain the serving cadre's readier toleration of Blum? Or did the more public and more vigorous criticisms of officers freed from active duty reflect only the imprudence of undisguised opposition to the Popular Front? Two discernible attitudinal patterns help to suggest answers.

On the one hand inside the general staff in Paris, and to a striking degree throughout the home-based officer corps, Gamelin's determination to preserve harmonious civil–military relations profited from his authority and personal prestige. In his seventh year as chief of the general staff by 1936, Gamelin had enjoyed time in which to set the tone that he required among these officers and the field commanders whom he had met and addressed over countless exercises and inspections. Hence in metropolitan France his writ delivered the political neutrality – or at worst political taciturnity – that he admitted was owed to the Popular Front as the legal government. 'With rare exceptions the army staff ... refrained from judging government policy. Under ... Gamelin this respect for absolute

---

[6] Gamelin, Riom submission p. 12, cited above; *Servir*, vol. 2, pp. 88–9, 95–109, 221. Cf. Bankwitz, *Weygand and Civil – Military Relations*, pp. 94–105.

[7] M. Weygand, 'L'état militaire de la France', *Revue des deux Mondes*, Per. 8, cvie année, vol. 35, 15 October 1936, p. 735. Cf. R. Griffiths, *Pétain* (London, 1970), pp. 161–4; Bankwitz, *Weygand and Civil – Military Relations*, p. 273.

discretion on matters of politics – domestic or foreign – became ...
dogma.'[8] In this Gamelin's objective may arguably have been more to
dispel potentially disruptive neuroses among his officers than to convey to
them any enthusiasm for Blum's purposes. The prime minister was 'a great
but misguided mind', Gamelin confided later in his diary. Nonetheless,
notwithstanding motivation, the general attained his goal in urging on his
colleagues the role of *la grande muette*.[9]

Against this, across the continent and in the colonies, distance from
Paris emboldened officers hostile to the left. Advocates of rapprochement
with fascist Italy, like the military attaché in Rome, General Parisot,
watched in alarm at the Popular Front's success. Parisot's like-minded
deputy, Captain Maurice Catoire, vented in his diary his horror at Blum's
election: 'a catastrophic result ... and a triumph for Moscow'.[10] By late
June the agenda of French diplomacy had been politically reordered, to
drop friendship with Mussolini. Delbos and Pierre Cot, Blum's air
minister, were instead concerned to revitalize cooperation with east-
central Europe. Catoire branded this a 'lamentable' foreign policy, 'in tow
to our domestic politics and prey to their vacillations'.[11] Nor was any
warmer affection reserved for the Popular Front among ambitious procon-
sular commanders overseas, to judge by the fealty given the Republic's
Vichyite successors by Generals Noguès and Dentz, in North Africa and
Syria, as well as by Admiral Decoux in Indochina. But perhaps it was
unavoidable that Gamelin could only imperfectly restrain political views
among subordinates enjoying the liberties – and alternative political
environments – offered by service abroad.

In France itself serving officers seldom flaunted prejudiced political
views. The best documented exception to this primary care for their careers
concerned Colonel Charles de Gaulle.

In the office of the national defence secretariat, de Gaulle campaigned
energetically after 1934, in print and through the advocacy of the maverick
right-wing parliamentarian Paul Reynaud, for structural military changes.
Urging the formation of a shock army of six mechanized divisions, de
Gaulle aroused furious controversy by also demanding that this be fully

---

8 R. J. Young, 'French military intelligence and the Franco-Italian alliance, 1933–1939', *The Historical Journal*, 28, 1 (1985), 163.

9 Gamelin, 'Journal de Marche', 6 October 1939, Fonds Gamelin 1K224/9, Service Histori-que de L'Armée de Terre (hereafter SHAT), Vincennes, France.

10 Quoted in R. J. Young, 'Soldiers and diplomats: the French embassy and Franco-Italian relations, 1935–6', *The Journal of Strategic Studies*, 7, 1 (March 1984), 85.

11 Quoted in Young, 'French military intelligence', p. 149.

professionalized. This notion of a long-service career corps was judged unnatural and unnecessary, whilst such a corps was thought unrecruitable by the general staff. Louis Colson, chief of army staff, refused de Gaulle the official *Revue Militaire Française*, asserting that exposition there of the Gaullien concept would risk 'setting a professional army in conflict in officers' minds with the national army'. Conclusively, on grounds of excessive cost, Colson dismissed any likelihood of enlisting and retaining the required additional thousands of career soldiers.[12]

Officers' technical opposition was buttressed by most politicians' hostility to the proposals. For de Gaulle provoked distrust of supposedly 'provocative' armoured forces in general and of socially-isolated, potentially anti-republican, professional soldiers in particular. For republicans the nation-in-arms guaranteed a 'reliable' basis for organizing national defence. Therefore those who spoke against it were mistrusted as possible *officiers de coup d'état* because of the Republic's history of discordant civil–military relations.[13]

Perceptions of large armoured formations as 'offensive' and 'aggressive', inappropriate to democratic France's defensive preoccupations, transcended party boundaries. For instance, pressure was put on Gamelin both in 1935 by the conservative Alliance Démocratique war minister Jean Fabry (a zealously anti-marxist retired colonel and *mutilé de guerre*), and in 1936 by Daladier, with a view to abandoning manufacture of the outstanding Char B battle tank.[14] Yet this was as much a counterattack as a breakthrough weapon.

In this context de Gaulle was inflammatory. He exposed the ambiguous politics of some officers despite Gamelin's pledge of an 'apolitical' army. Unavoidably, in the agitation before the 1936 elections, French military chiefs were exercised by contingency planning in support of the security services, against civil disturbances. General staff officers were first consul-

[12] Colson, letter to de Gaulle, 17 December 1934, Archives Reynaud, 74 AP12, Archives Nationales, Paris (hereafter AN); Etat-Major de L'Armée: Cabinet Colson, 'Note pour le Cabinet militaire du Ministre ...' 11 July 1936, in Gamelin, *Servir*, vol. 3: *La Guerre. Septembre 1939–19 mai 1940*, pp. 516–27. De Gaulle's plans are also in his *Vers L'armée de métier* (Paris, 1934).

[13] See Gamelin's submission in *Commission parlementaire chargée d'enquêter sur les évènements survenus en France de 1933 à 1945: témoignages* (Paris, 1951–2), vol. 2, p. 385. Cf. D. Porch, *The March to the Marne: the French army, 1871–1914* (Cambridge, 1981); D. B. Ralston, *The Army of the Republic: the place of the military in the political evolution of France, 1871–1914* (Cambridge, Mass., 1967); P. C. F. Bankwitz, 'Maxime Weygand and the army–nation concept in the modern French army', *French Historical Studies*, 2 (Fall 1961), 157–88.

[14] 'Journal de Marche: Cabinet Fabry', 11 and 20 September 1935, carton 5N581, dossier 2, SHAT; archives Victor-Henri Schweisguth, 'memento', 4 July 1936, carton 351 AP3, dossier 9, AN.

ted by an 'apprehensive' Paris police prefect, Roger Langeron, during the leftist assembly in the capital on Bastille Day 1935. Fabry, responsible as war minister for the Champs Elysées military pageantry earlier that day, reflected disenchantedly that Parisians, 'patriotic in the morning, were singing the *Internationale* by the afternoon'. Again the evidence suggests that the military identified Daladier as their political safeguard inside the rapidly mobilizing leftist alliance. Minds returned readily to the February 1934 public-order crisis. Consequently it was thought that Daladier (then forced to resign) should prepare against fresh troubles, especially the danger of serious disorder during parliamentary recesses, by personally holding the three hundred senators' and deputies' signatures required for an emergency recall of the legislature. In September 1935 Colson and his deputy, General Victor Schweisguth, considered the 'steps required to strengthen the capital's garrison with a view to preserving order'. Six additional battalions would be needed to keep open 'two corridors, one to Versailles and one to Vincennes, across the "red belt"'. This provision was, characteristically, thought by Gamelin to be overestimated. He, noted Schweisguth, allowed only one extra colonial regiment as reinforcement of the permanent garrison, to secure Paris.[15] Gamelin was, as Britain's ambassador observed, 'a man of quite remarkable ... sang-froid ...'; he was not one to increase the political temperature by provocatively raising the military's profile in the working-class suburbs.[16]

In May 1936 the factory occupations were at their greatest extent. Frightened industrialists, surprised at the suddenness and extent of workers' protests, urged government action to evict the strikers, through the courts, police and troops. Sarraut, a caretaker without a mandate after the election, understandably equivocated, fearing to acquire the stigma of a prime minister 'with blood on his hands' (Daladier's fate after the February 1934 deaths). Nevertheless the situation was by 28 May deemed sufficiently unstable to bring the army again into consultations. Schweisguth recorded that Colson had 'been called to see Sarraut about the factory takeovers. Langeron says that we cannot eject the workers as they are causing no disturbance. That attitude, said Daladier, was how in Italy the fascist seizure of power was prepared.' Despite this warning against

---

[15] J. Fabry, *De la Place de la Concorde au Cours de l'Intendance, Février 1934 – Juin 1940* (Paris, 1942), p. 63; archives Schweisguth, 'mementos', 16 July 1935, 12 and 16 September 1935, carton 351 AP2, dossier 5. Langeron's memoir–diary, *Paris, Juin 40* (Paris, 1946) is unenlightening on the pre-defeat era.

[16] Sir E. Phipps to Foreign Office, London, 5 July 1937, FO 371, 20696, C4888/822/17, PRO.

passivity the meeting broke up unable to concert a response. This was the Popular Front's problem: 'It was agreed to refer it to Blum.'[17]

In contrast to such deference to the new governing majority, de Gaulle articulated an authoritarian personal view of the implications for the army of what he predicted would become a slide into disorder. He had alerted Reynaud that the economic, political and moral crisis was making more likely a breakdown in internal security. He wondered how 'in the mounting tumult (Popular Front or right-wing leagues)' to prevent 'a situation of anarchy, perhaps of civil war ...?' He denigrated the police and Garde Mobile: '15,000 family men scattered the length and breadth of the land'; he doubted their capacities 'if disturbances break out simultaneously in Paris, in Lyons ... in Lille ... and in the countryside'. As for the army, he asserted, it had always had the duty and function in crises of supporting the maintenance of order. 'But how can we expect this when its units are now all formed of voters or natives?' For de Gaulle a professional army was called for as much in view of imminent insecurity at home as because of contemporary tensions in Europe.

Intriguingly, he was invited in September 1936, during a second and calculated CGT strike wave, to a secret meeting with Camille Chautemps, minister of state in Blum's government, a senator and leader of the conservative wing of the Radicals. Chautemps, de Gaulle reported to Reynaud, 'seemed very favourably disposed ... even greatly stressing ... the importance that my specialized corps would assume in current and future public order problems (both at home and in North Africa).' It is hard to dispute Guy Chapman's conclusion that, however exemplary a Frenchman in future, de Gaulle was 'a bad officer, undisciplined and disobedient ...' who risked splitting the army.[18] It is equally difficult to avoid judging the former prime minister Chautemps ruthlessly ambitious, scheming and disloyal, an insincere Popular Frontist and a most dangerous viper for Blum to have lurking in his basket of ministers.[19]

Nevertheless such support for de Gaulle was untypical of most parliamentarians' views. Inside Blum's government, and from the centre across to the democratic right, most shared Gamelin's condemnation of the

[17] Archives Schweisguth, 'memento', 28 May 1936, carton 351 AP3, dossier 9, AN. Cf. Gamelin, *Servir*, vol. 2, pp. 219–20.

[18] C. de Gaulle, *Lettres, notes et carnets, 1919–Juin 1940* (Paris, 1980), pp. 393, 411–14; G. Chapman, 'The French army and politics' in M. E. Howard (ed.), *Soldiers and Governments: nine studies in civil–military relations* (London, 1957), p. 69.

[19] Chautemps twice resigned as prime minister just before crises – February 1934; the March 1938 Anschluss – broke over him. His memoirs, *Cahiers secrets de l'armistice* (Paris, 1963), discuss only 1939–40.

separate professional army. Roger Salengro, socialist deputy mayor for Lille and interior minister from June to November 1936 (politically responsible for police and internal security), emphasized that the Popular Front would enhance French defences against German remilitarization. From the ranks of Blum's senior colleagues only the convinced pacifist Paul Faure, SFIO secretary-general, opposed rearmament outright. The official Radical view was represented by Daladier. In the Chamber in February 1937 he declared himself 'unable to agree with those ... who demanded a career army or ... specialist corps of armoured divisions' because it was 'essential to preserve a proper balance and proportion between the army's various component parts'.[20] Daladier was, in restating this, remaining consistent with his pre-Popular Front position concerning the relationship that he sought between the army and the populace – a relationship of minimal military burdens on taxpayers and conscripts alike. But, even more than this, Daladier was reformulating and modernizing the republican left's conception of how best to reconcile their regime with their army. Instead of de Gaulle's prescription of an ever more technically proficient military caste, but one ever remoter from its government, Daladier conceived of integrating the army back into a society which he thought it should reflect and whose values he wished it to share. To achieve this it would be best, he believed, to reform fundamentally the narrowly professional education received by the rising cadres which contained France's commanders of the future. Young officers, in his eyes, required a more 'civic' training. Approvingly 'he cited Jaurès's submission: "The army should be linked into the elite of the nation." Rather than two years at Saint-Cyr, officer cadets ought to have twelve months at university before their second year at the academy.'[21]

Blum for his part feared not the military institutions which France possessed in 1936–7 (on which he had Gamelin's guarantees) but, apparently with reason, a lurch in a Gaullien direction. Blum had vilified the career army proposed by Reynaud in the March 1935 Chamber debate on extending conscription to two years. Such a corps was to him a 'praetorian' instrument, unacceptable because profoundly antithetical to republi-

---

[20] See Salengro's Denain speech, 7 September 1936, reported by British ambassador Sir G. Clerk to the Foreign Office, in FO 371, 19859, C6327/1/17, PRO. For Daladier's statement see Clark despatch, 24 February 1937, FO 371, 20693, C1597/122/17, PRO. Cf. P. Faure, *De Munich à la 5e République* (Paris, n.d.).

[21] République Française, *Journal Officiel: Chambre: Débats*, 24 May 1927, p. 1597. Daladier's proposed reforms of officer education are found in Gamelin, 'Journal', 11 October 1939. Fonds Gamelin 1K224/9, SHAT.

canism's roots in the *levée en masse* and the citizen soldier. As he quite fairly recollected later, the time was unpropitious for de Gaulle's ideas: violent extra-parliamentary politics was emerging on the streets through the gatherings of the right-wing leagues in 1935. Furthermore Blum thought 'important military leaders – including Marshal Pétain and General Weygand – were more than doubtful; ... [and] a great number of officers were suspect'. Blum's trust lay instead with the ordinary ranks, the 'sons of France's soil and cities' and 'salvation of her free institutions'. He worried what would become of these men if they came under command of some 'blindly obedient praetorian elite'.

For Blum, quite astutely, recognized that the issue of professionalization was a red herring, confusing an important but strictly technical military reform. Blum's view of de Gaulle's scheme was as critical as that of Gamelin and other generals in its observation that

the author and his parliamentary advocate allowed or even aroused a fearful confusion. It seemed, in their minds, that the armoured divisions ... had to *become* the army ... it followed that our effective military power would be placed in the hands of a professional corps and no longer in those of a national army, an army of the people themselves ...[22]

Neither de Gaulle nor Reynaud had taken sufficient precautions to prevent this suspicion. Nor was anything advanced by Blum's interviewing of de Gaulle in late summer or early autumn 1936. The prime minister remained sure that Daladier's and Gamelin's military programmes would meet the technical demands of de Gaulle without carrying the latter's political provocativeness.[23]

If not numerous, then, there were undeniably influential instances of outright military hostility to the Popular Front. Besides Weygand, Pétain and de Gaulle there was the retired General de Castelnau, a bigoted clerical and 1914–18 army commander who was nicknamed 'the booted Capucin' and who, after the Spanish 1936 elections, coined the expression 'Frente Crapular'. But we remain, as Jean Lacouture cautions, 'short of information on the army's state of mind'.[24] Blum grasped that the SFIO's support for internationalism and arms limitation in the 1920s and early

---

[22] Blum, *Oeuvre*, pp. 112–13; *Journal officiel: Chambre: Débats*, 15 March 1935, pp. 1022–53. Cf. Bankwitz, *Maxine Weygand and Civil–Military Relations*, pp. 126–7.

[23] De Gaulle, *Mémoires de Guerre: L'appel, 1940–42* (Paris, 1954), pp. 18–20; Blum, *Oeuvre*, pp. 113–15; Colton, *Léon Blum.*, pp. 225–30; J. Lacouture, *Léon Blum* (Paris, 1977), pp. 335–7 and idem, *De Gaulle: le rebelle, 1890–1944* (Paris, 1984), pp. 252–7; G. Lefranc, *Histoire du Front Populaire* (Paris, 1974 edition), pp. 396–8.

[24] Lacouture, *Léon Blum*, p. 357; Nobécourt, *Histoire politique de l'armée*, pp. 153–67, 203, 221ff.

1930s hardly banked him much credit with which to open his account with the generals. Politicized right-wing officers may have been few, but they made a disproportionate commotion in the press and in salon society. It was hard, then, for a nervous and governmentally inexperienced left to exorcise the spectre of a military menace to their policies, particularly once the Spanish military rebels took on the personification of superficially similar ghouls south of the Pyrenees. Even Gamelin later candidly conceded that 'in their hearts and their heads our soldiers' sympathies favoured Franco'.[25]

Was much menace posed, therefore, by the secret right-wing organizations discovered by the authorities in 1937, the Corvignolles cells and the Cagoule or CSAR (Comité Secret d'Action Révolutionnaire)? The former was an officers' network, clandestinely coordinated by Major Georges Loustaunau-Lacau, one of Pétain's staff. Corvignolles' objective was to prepare in countrywide garrisons for immediate action (even without war ministry directives) in the event of indications of a communist coup. Allegedly the organization could count on ten thousand officers, about one-third of the corps, had it decided to move. Loustaunau claimed success in eradicating pacifist literature from the barracks and in negating what he asserted to be a PCF-inspired subversion campaign directed at conscripts. Yet by February 1938 Loustaunau had been unmasked by an informer, disciplined and removed to the inactive duty list. The CSAR by contrast was civilian-controlled. It enjoyed support with service connections only from a handful of mostly retired officers of extreme-right sympathy like General Duseigneur and Marshal Franchet d'Esperey, who donated to the CSAR one million francs of his personal fortune.

Although Loustanau conferred occasionally with CSAR leaders, the two networks differed crucially in nature and intent. Corvignolles was dedicated to ridding army depots of communist influence and in a last resort to a military defence of the regime against a communist coup. The CSAR on the other hand was *itself* actively subversive, not only working against the Popular Front but against the Republic. Loustaunau indeed was dismayed to learn of CSAR approaches not only to d'Esperey but to senior active generals on the War Council (CSG) which, particularly in the case of General Joseph Dufieux, Inspector of Infantry, obliged Gamelin to demand assurances of non-involvement under oath of honour. But Corvignolles was not tied to the CSAR. Loustaunau distinguished between his defensive counter-coup network and CSAR plotting to install its own

[25] Gamelin, Riom submission (cited above, note 2), p. 13.

rightist regime. The cells and secrecy betray an officer corps ill-at-ease with itself in the socio-political culture of 1930s France, yet a corps of which it has convincingly been demonstrated: 'definite anti-regime plans did not exist in the Command'.[26]

If, then, there should be no exaggeration of the officers' menace to the Popular Front, nor in a wider sense to the Republic, what threat from the left did the officers perceive? The Foreign Office in London in September 1936 judged that 'the spirit and morale of the army is infinitely more healthy than that of the capital or of the civilian population generally'.[27] Did the French high command concur?

Unquestionably it was anxious to reassure foreign observers, especially its sought-after British and Belgian allies. Senior officers spoke confidently, probably in an coordinated campaign to minimize loss of faith abroad in France's capacity to secure herself and help her friends. In this vein Colonel Gauché of French army intelligence affirmed that France was 'not in the state of decay which she is often thought to be by outside observers. Let them only scratch ... and see ...'. French officers still saw military service as an educative and disciplinary agency, that is, as a means of muting extreme political views, as they had since Lyautey published his famous *Du rôle social de l'officier* in 1891. In 1937 the British military attaché talked with a known confidant of Gamelin, André Pironneau, editor of the conservative paper *L'Echo de Paris*. Pironneau felt, and adduced other sources in support, that 'the majority of men joining the army with extreme political views lost the latter rapidly and soon make excellent soldiers ...'.[28]

Evidence does exist of paranoia about pacifist and anti-militarist pamphlets penetrating into the barracks, but more among conservative politicians and 'friends of the army' than in the officer corps. Thus on only his second day in Laval's government, in June 1935, Fabry took pains to tell his staff of his 'decision to fight communism in order to restore confidence to the field commanders'. A sworn enemy of the Popular Front, Fabry lost his Parisian seat to the SFIO in 1936. 'A decent man, but a political operator' in Gamelin's pithy assessment, Fabry was an officer-

---

[26] Bankwitz, *Maxime Weygand and Civil–Military Relations*, pp. 276–7; cf. ibid., pp. 266–75; G. Loustaunau-Lacau, *Mémoires d'un français rebelle* (Paris, 1948), pp. 108–28; J-R. Tournoux, *L'histoire secrète. La Cagoule. Le Front Populaire. Vichy* (Paris, 1962), p. 16 ff.; Gamelin, *Servir*, vol. 2, pp. 253–66, 303–4.

[27] Minute by R. Allen, 25 September 1936, FO 371, 19871, C6616/172/17, PRO.

[28] Colonel F. G. Beaumont-Nesbitt reports in FO 371, 19871, C6616/172/17 and FO 371, 20702, C3753/532/62, PRO.

turned-politician. His prejudices placed him closer to Colonel de la Rocque with his Croix de Feu and PSF veterans and rightists than to the general staff.[29]

Inevitably in the ferment of 1936 left-wing tracts regarded by regimental officers as seditious did reach some of the other ranks. But proven cases of incitement to insubordination were rare. Neither Gamelin nor Daladier was seriously perturbed. Addressing the Radicals' Versailles federation on 28 June the minister took pains to emphasize the close cooperation and common positions unifying the Popular Front government and the armed services. Danger to the latter arose, he insisted, solely from forces outside the political pale, the 'enemies of the Republic' engaged in 'their old game' of social and institutional destabilization. Just three weeks into office Daladier was publicly pledging improvements for the defence services.[30] Likewise concerning the left's bill, enacted on 11 August 1936, for nationalization of selected arms manufacturers, the general staff 'faced the future without misgiving' according to Major Jean Petibon, Gamelin's adjutant. From these beginnings grew the rearmament programme of 7 September 1936.[31]

In a sense bordering on paradox it was fortuitous that the international situation's dangers had become so apparent to the French. These perils significantly helped reconcile army and left by driving them together in common recognition of the urgent need for major military procurements. Indeed the Popular Front's readiness to undertake a defence effort of fourteen billion francs over four years dwarfed anything previously contemplated by conservative governments. It offered a crucial show of intent and realism to French generals. Simultaneously it re-established the credentials of the republican left as heirs to the jacobin tradition of patriotic defence. One ace card of the right – attention to national security – had been spectacularly trumped by the Popular Front. Gamelin confirmed later 'that thanks to M. Daladier's influence we began to secure very important finances ... for our armaments'. Joel Colton likewise credits Daladier with persuading Blum to give the programme official SFIO approval.[32]

From this time, too, Daladier and Gamelin consolidated the army's

---

[29] Archives Schweisguth, 'memento', 8 June 1935, carton 351 AP2, dossier 4, AN; Gamelin, 'Journal', 10 September 1939, Fonds Gamelin, 1K224/9, SHAT.

[30] Reported in Clerk's despatch in FO 371, 19857, C4683/1/17, PRO.

[31] Beaumont-Nesbitt enclosure to Clerk, 11 June 1936, FO 371, 19857, C4248/1/17, PRO.

[32] Gamelin, Riom submission, p. 14, cited above; Colton, *Léon Blum*, pp. 224–5. Cf. R. Frankenstein, *Le prix du réarmement français, 1935–39* (Paris, 1982).

internal stability by implementing measures to enhance unity, high morale and a sense of mission. As Blum had been told at the 10 June meeting with Gamelin, keeping soldiers out of politics required politics in return being kept out of the army. During the factory occupations the general admitted to disquiet about anti-militarist literature directed at the non-commissioned officers, 'seeking to prepare a real revolution, saying to them "Come with us and you'll be the officers tomorrow"'. Consequently Gamelin improved personnel relations, encouraged by the sensitive pragmatism of Daladier. The latter exploited his personal record both as a 1914–18 veteran commissioned in the field from the ranks and as a consistent champion of the lowest military burdens commensurate with an effective national defence.[33]

In November 1936 he successfully met his stiffest test, over revolutionary proposals to democratize the army. This plan, tabled in the Chamber of Deputies' army commission by Robert Lazurick of the SFIO and Marcel Gitton of the PCF, demanded a nation-in-arms modelled on Jean Jaurès's 1913 scheme for a 'patriotic militia'. Lazurick and Gitton proposed allowing trade unionists onto the national defence council (to afford communists access to highly classified strategy papers). They also sought replacement of conscription by paramilitary instruction and the creation in every barracks of *cercles des soldats* affiliated to the CGT – in effect a unionization of the other ranks. Daladier countered that these plans were incompatible with hierarchical military discipline, extending 'illusory promises which neither I nor others could keep without compromising national security'. He had the motion defeated in committee, 'reminding the SFIO and PCF that they were supporters of a government for whose decisions they must take their full share of responsibility'. This was the closest that Gamelin came to awaking to a reality akin to the fantasy-nightmares that occasionally troubled him so long as France had a ministry 'obedient to a socialist imperative'.[34] But in 1936–7 Daladier disposed of a legacy of credibility on the left as well as his rapport with Gamelin and preserved widely acceptable policies by adroitly trading on both.

Relations, then, between the Popular Front and France's officers were stable because of the early promise which Blum gave Gamelin of respon-

---

[33] Gamelin, *Servir*, vol. 2, pp. 220–1. Cf., more generally, D. N. Baker, 'The Surveillance of Subversion in Interwar France: the Carnet B in the Seine, 1922–1940', *French Historical Studies*, 10, 3 (Spring 1978), 486–516.

[34] Army Commission debate, 12–13 November 1936, reported by Clerk in FO 371, 19872, C8231/172/17, PRO; Gamelin, Riom submission, p. 14, cited above.

sible attention to national defence. This was the reassurance required that the left comprehended the preoccupations of the military. Equally Gamelin, a reliable republican with a catholic circle of political allies, had a style that won confidence from his ministerial masters, Blum no less than Tardieu or Daladier.

Nonetheless it bears repetition that evidence on the politics of the French army towards the Popular Front is incomplete. The views of many officers have been documented in substantiating this essay's argument that a civil–military consensus was conserved. Yet this sampling still amounts to only a tiny cross-section of the corps. Our obligation – by the nature of the memoirs and diaries – to concentrate excessively on testimonies of senior soldiers, majors and colonels when not marshals and generals, exacerbates the problem of representativeness. Little is known of the dispositions of the anonymous majority. Yet there was an 'army within the army' of NCOs, subalterns and company commanders, officers in direct daily contact with the 400,000 ordinary soldiers. It can only be surmised whether within them lay different sentiments towards the Blum experiment. Even the professional periodicals only just crack open a view for us of these military minds. When not consumed by minutely technical discussion, as in the *Revue d'Artillerie*, the journals seem larded with unattributable polemic, as in the *Revue des Deux Mondes*, from 'Général Trois Etoiles' or 'Colonel X'.[35]

An image is left, then, of an army insulated from the social and political disorders in 1935–7. The officer corps visible to us was characteristically anti-communist, but open-minded enough and still obedient enough to attempt with the moderate governing left a cohabitation, or anyway a *ménage à trois* of Blum–Gamelin–Daladier. Politically, however, there was an inbuilt fragility in reliance on such a personality-based formula for civil–military harmony. As Lacouture writes: 'Daladier's authority ... was generally admitted. But what would this "authority" have amounted to if the Radical Party's president had been pitched out into opposition?'[36] On the military side a sharper separation of experience was marked out by the Pyrenean frontier. The Spanish army had not undergone a Dreyfus Affair. In France that confrontation cost the army its autonomy so that the 'republic of the Radicals' purged the officer corps in which the young Gamelin rose in the 1900s. Consequently in the 1930s the French army was staffed with republicans; they were anti-communist but they were republi-

---

[35] Cf., however, General M-E. Debeney, 'La mystique de notre corps d'officiers', *Revue Militaire Générale*, 1 (January 1937), 21–3; Chief d'escadron Dassonville, 'L'officier dans la nation', ibid., 3 (January 1938), 89–102.
[36] Lacouture, *Léon Blum*, p. 357.

cans. 1940 showed that the officers' apoliticism could survive the electoral triumph of the left but, with blitzkrieg wrecking the reputations and authority of Daladier and Gamelin, not the military triumph of the Germans. With discipline dissolved the Pétainists were then able to seize what seemed to them a providential opportunity 'to impose a military view of the country's future'.[37] These same men also started that most pernicious of myths that in the Popular Front's spring of 1936 was sown the seed that became the German harvest four years later.

[37] Bankwitz, *Weygand and Civil–Military Relations*, p. 271.

The Spanish Church and the Popular Front: the experience of Salamanca province

MARY VINCENT

Catholic polemicists writing during the Civil War had no difficulty in blaming the Popular Front for the tragic end of the Second Republic. One of the innumerable tracts put out by Catholic apologists in support of the generals' rising baldly stated that the Popular Front was essentially evil, 'a monstrous conglomeration of anti-Catholic political parties' whose tyranny was manifested in its persecution of the 'sacred institutions' of the family, religion and property. Manipulated by international masonry, it intended to deliver Spain to Soviet communism thus betraying both the fatherland and the Catholic religion. Nor did it have a genuine popular mandate as the Popular Front had effectively usurped power after the 1936 elections when, despite the violent and corrupt methods used by the left, the Catholic parties had gained a majority of votes. It was also the representative of a regime which was in itself illegitimate, since the Republic had been voted into power only by the stage-managed April 1931 municipal elections, which had not even consulted most of the conservative rural areas. All this showed that the 'authentic' Spanish nation was represented by the nationalist government: the antithesis of the Popular Front which spoke only for those enslaved by 'exotic and treacherous powers'.[1]

This particular polemic was published early in July 1937. It was,

[1] Ignacio Menéndez-Reigada OP, 'La guerra nacional española ante la moral y el derecho', *La Ciencia Tomista* (*CT*), 163 and 167 (1937), 40–5; 165 and 166 (1937), 177–93.

79

therefore, written with full knowledge of the anti-clerical massacres perpetrated in the republican zone at the war's outset. However, its bitter invective was not simply a horrified reaction to atrocities committed in the government's name. The Church's relations with the Republic had never been happy. In many ways anti-republicanism had crystallized around catholicism. The political right claimed the defence of religion as their foremost aim and the considerable support commanded by Acción Popular, later the CEDA, the most powerful Catholic political grouping, undoubtedly reflected the alienation of many Church members from the republican regime.[2]

The campaign mounted in defence of Catholic interests, however, aspired to something more than merely repealing anti-clerical laws. Despite Vatican policy, which maintained that the Church could not be tied to any one political system but was indifferent to forms of government which were 'accidental' and unimportant, the Spanish Church continued to look for protection from a specific political system. The ideal society was the totally Catholic one; the only government acceptable to the hierarchy was one which would authorize and confirm the Church as holding a monopoly on truth. There was only one God, only one way to achieve salvation, and anything that deviated from this was erroneous, even evil. Any degree of religious or cultural heterodoxy, even private freedom of worship, was unthinkable. The Church could declare its respect for a democratic government but could not accept the social and political pluralism synonymous with democracy.[3]

This unhesitating division between good and evil allowed the presentation of the 1936 elections as a duel to the death between left and right, a battle between communism and catholicism, a confrontation between:

construction and destruction; between the Spain of ancient traditions, religious principles and the conservation of society and the anti-Spain of demolition, church burning and the October revolution [of 1934][4]

---

[2] The initials CEDA stand for Spanish Confederation of Autonomous Right-Wing Groups. For a self-definition, see José Montero, *La CEDA. El catolicismo social y político de la Segunda República* (Madrid, 1977), vol. 2, pp. 593–4. For the founding of AP and the emergence of the CEDA see vol. 1, chapters 2 and 3.

[3] For a detailed analysis of the ideology of the Spanish Church and its development see William J. Callahan, *Church, Politics and Society in Spain, 1750–1874* esp. chapters 6 and 7 and the articles by Frances Lannon, 'The socio-political role of the Spanish Church – a case study', *Journal of Contemporary History*, April 1979, pp. 193–210, and 'Modern Spain: the project of a national catholicism' in S. Mews (ed.), *Religion and National Identity* (Oxford, 1982).

[4] Article by Angel Rosado Acuña, *Gaceta Regional* (GR), 1 January 1936, p. 7.

This language of the two Spains coloured the right's entire electoral campaign. A national organization called the 'Crusade of Prayer and Penance' promoted a campaign of religious cults, 'for God and the Fatherland', to pray for the right's victory. These were designed to attract large congregations. Popular devotions such as the Rosary and the Stations of the Cross were combined with private meditations and sacrifices in one great offering for the successful outcome of elections which were said to be decisive in Spain's destiny:

> Those against Christ have unfurled the banner of destruction and hatred ... the enemies, apostates of their religion and of their birthplace. Those who are with Christ, looking towards Him and Catholic Spain unfurl their banner, white for peace and progress.

Religion and patriotism are here inseparable, and both were endangered by the left's coalition.[5]

The Popular Front's 'banner of destruction and hatred' was, in reality, a consciously low-key and deliberately moderate manifesto put together by a broad electoral alliance which defined itself as an anti-reactionary block.[6] The influence of the Republican parties was paramount in the making of this manifesto which specified that, to the Republicans, the socialist programme of land nationalization was unacceptable. Because of this it was not included in the manifesto and there was no direct attack on property rights. The proposals for agriculture even bore a definite resemblance to those of the Catholic agrarian federations: fostering agricultural credit, eliminating middlemen, revaluing the prices of agricultural produce, and promoting technical education. However, the Popular Front's commitment to re-establishing social legislation and the rule of the Constitution clearly included provision for land reform. While the just redistribution of wealth was fully in accordance with Catholic social thought, the CEDA had repeatedly shown that when this social theorizing was translated into an attack on the estates of the party's supporters it became unacceptable.[7]

The manifesto made no mention of the Church or the religious orders. Education was a major feature and was defined as an 'inalienable function of the state', a tenet contrary to the Catholic one which viewed education as

---

[5] For the 'Cruzada de Oración y Penitencia' see *GR*, 21 January 1936, p. 2, 24 January 1936, p. 3, 8 February 1936, p. 8.
[6] Popular Front manifesto given in Santos Juliá, *Orígenes del Frente Popular en España (1934–1936)* (Madrid, 1979), pp. 216–33.
[7] For a fuller examination of this see Frances Lannon, 'The Church's Crusade against the Republic' in Paul Preston (ed.), *Revolution and War in Spain* (London, 1984), esp. pp. 43–6.

one of the Church's principal rights and duties. The commitment to the Constitution also meant that the religious orders would continue to be barred from teaching. The proposals for schooling were, however, practical rather than ideological, directed towards improving educational standards and facilities. Catholic opposition was, therefore, aroused by what it believed the Popular Front represented rather than by radical proposals for social change. Indeed, the virulence of the Church's campaign in 1936 and its unquestioning support of the right suggests a refusal to countenance government by the left rather than merely an understandable concern with the anti-clerical measures likely to be undertaken by such a government.

From the beginning of the campaign the Spanish hierarchy made it clear that this was no time for neutrality. The cardinal primate, Isidro Gomá y Tomás, issued a pastoral letter in January calling for 'the conquest of political power in the defence of religious interests'. The first duty of Catholics was to 'safeguard the rights of God in society' and vote for God and Spain. Although this pastoral was only directed to the Toledo archdiocese, summaries were published all over Spain. One, which appeared in Salamanca entitled 'The Satanic hatred of religion is the banner of the Left', claimed that the cardinal had instructed the faithful not to vote for the Popular Front since all such votes went to the 'authors and accomplices' of the 1934 Asturias rebellion who were dedicated to the destruction of the Church and the most secure bases of society.[8] Several other bishops also issued pastoral letters, effectively stamping the CEDA campaign with the ecclesiastical licence.[9]

Catholic Action, an umbrella organization set up to coordinate the activities of all lay Catholic groups under the direct control of the hierarchy, followed the bishops in urging its members to fervent prayer. A week before the elections a note was issued from the central committee in Madrid telling members not to forget the fatherland in their prayers and penances. The bulletin put out by the female branch of Catholic Action suggested that the line from the Lord's Prayer 'But deliver us from evil' be used in these devotions. More obviously still, the same bulletin said that Catholic Action was: 'waiting with arms raised to heaven, like Moses on Sinai, sighing for the victory which has to help us restore the things of

[8] Text of Gomá's pastoral given in Anastasio Granados, *El Cardenal Gomá Primado de España* (Madrid, 1969), pp. 306–17. Summary reprinted as an editorial *GR*, 5 February 1936.

[9] Electoral pastorals were issued by the bishops of Tortosa, Barcelona, Oviedo, Málaga, Santander and Tudela. For summaries see *Boletín de la Confederación de Mujeres Católicas de España*, 15 February 1936, p. 2. The bishop of Tudela's is quoted in Ramón Garriga, *El Cardenal Segura y el Nacional-Catolicismo* (Barcelona, 1977), p. 230.

Christ'.[10] Such explicit declarations acted as the Church's rallying call to its powerful network of pious organizations and Catholic defence groups. That a supposedly apolitical organization like Catholic Action could make such an overtly political statement reflects the intimate links which existed between all Catholic groups, both pious and political. There were close similarities of aim and structure between the CEDA and Catholic Action, whilst many of the second group's leaders were also prominent in the first.

Angel Herrera Oria, for example, national leader of Catholic Action from 1933, had been instrumental in the CEDA's foundation and his newspaper, *El Debate*, was its principal press organ. Gil Robles, the CEDA's leader, had spent many years as general secretary of the National Catholic Agrarian Confederation and was also prominent in the Marian Congregations and Catholic Parents' Association. At local levels this overlap between the political and religious spheres was even more striking. In Salamanca, the president of the local branch of Acción Popular, Luis Bermúdez de Castro, was also president of the Catholic Parents' Association and active in the Casa Social Católica, a project begun on the bishop's initiative with the cooperation of Catholic Action. The family of the Traditionalist deputy, José María Lamamié de Clairac, played a leading role in virtually all of the Catholic associations in the diocese. Lamamié himself was involved in the Marian Congregations, the Catholic Parents' Association and the various Catholic Agrarian Federations in Old Castile. He had also helped found in August 1931 the Salamanca branch of the Association of Relatives of Members of Religious Orders, an ad hoc pressure group set up to defend the religious congregations following the expulsion of the Jesuits. This organization was later incorporated into the local branch of the CEDA.

The close links between all these groups show the strength of the forces ready to respond to the cry of 'the Church in danger'. Catholic mobilization had always looked to the unity of all sympathizers in defence of fundamental principles and in 1936 the need for Catholics to stand up and be counted was stressed more strongly than ever. Gomá y Tomás's pastoral called for the unity of Catholics 'before all else', 'above all else' and 'at whatever cost'.

This appeal for united action was given greater weight by the presentation of the Popular Front as the Church's declared enemy, a nihilistic alliance of the forces of evil. The right was firm in its intentions to cauterize

---

[10] *Bol. de la Confed. de las Muj. Cat. de Esp.*, 15 January 1936, p. 1, 15 February 1936, p. 1. Instruction from Madrid reported *GR*, 8 February 1936, p. 8.

all 'unhealthy' elements in the Spanish state. In 1933 Gil Robles had announced the need to purge the fatherland of 'judaising freemasons'. In 1936 he broadened this considerably, saying on the eve of the elections that the party wanted primarily:

to eliminate the sowers of discord who leave the fatherland broken and blood-stained; to eliminate in the realm of ideas that suicidal rationalism which, killing the great universal ideas of Catholicism and the fatherland, had broken with those supreme factors which made up the soul of the nation.[11]

The CEDA called on all its supporters to work against 'anti-Spain', 'against the revolution and its accomplices', obscure figures commonly understood to be marxists, freemasons and Jews. In similar vein, the Dominican Father Carrión published an article in his Order's journal which spoke of those three forces aligning themselves against Spain. Jewish marxists, expelled from ghettos all over the world, came to Spain where 'they settle down and sprawl about as in conquered territory'.[12]

This crude anti-semitic propaganda was accepted and even fostered by the Church. The Jesuit printing house *Ediciones FAX* published the Spanish translation of the *Protocols of the Elders of Zion*. Although widely regarded as a fraud, a review in the Dominicans' journal claimed that its veracity had been shown by recent history. The Jesuit *Razón y Fe* even quoted it as, along with the major papal encyclicals, 'the best summary of modern social science'. It was also serialized in the widely-circulated bulletin of the Jesuit-run Marian Congregations, *La Estrella del Mar*, where its authorship was never questioned. Anti-masonic works also abounded. The most important of these, *Orígenes de la revolución española*, appeared in 1932 and immediately became a best seller. Its author, Juan Tusquets, a professor at the Barcelona seminary and notorious witch hunter, claimed to be able to tell a mason by the position of his handkerchief in his breast pocket.[13]

The prevalence of conspiracy theories for the evils besetting Spain may perhaps be interpreted as revealing the Church's inability to accept either the extent of anti-clericalism in Spain, or that this was due to the Church's failure in its pastoral role.[14] Depicting its opponents as part of the Jewish–

---

[11] First reference quoted Paul Preston, *The Coming of the Spanish Civil War* (London, 1978), p. 48; second reference from Gil Robles's final election address in February 1936. Text given *GR*, 16 February 1936, p. 1.

[12] *GR*, 14 January 1936, p. 4, *CT*, January/February 1936, p. 88, 89.

[13] *CT*, March/April 1934; *Razón y Fe* (*RF*), April 1933; *La Estrella del Mar*, June 1933, December 1934 passim; Garriga, *Cardenal Segura*, p. 200.

[14] Various concerned clerics were beginning to publish studies which showed an unacceptably low level of religious practice in many parts of Spain, above all in the south and in the huge working-class parishes of the industrial suburbs. See, e.g. E. Vargas-Zúñiga, 'El

masonic–communist conspiracy allowed the Church to externalize blame for the strength of the anti-clerical movements. It was neither the Church nor the Catholic elite at fault but rather obscure and satanically-inspired forces, bent on the destruction of all that was true and good; in short, all that was Catholic.

Despite the call for a broad Catholic alliance to combat the Popular Front menace, the electoral battlelines in fact reveal the narrowness of the Catholic label. Athough Gil Robles had tried to bring together groups from the whole spectrum of right-wing opinion, conservative republican to extreme monarchist, what eventually emerged was a series of coalitions constituted according to local circumstances. Most national negotiations, for example those held with Miguel Maura's Conservative Republican Party, ended in failure.[15]

The reasons for the failure of a wider right-wing coalition to emerge are perhaps most clearly shown at local level. In Salamanca the CEDA grouping included the Traditionalist deputy Lamamié de Clairac. This was an established local alliance and was as old as the Second Republic. Maura's Conservative Republicans fielded their own candidate, Tomás Marcos Escribano, once it became generally known that Lamamié would join the monarchists in a rival alliance should Escribano appear on the CEDA list.[16]

Once the decision to stand apart from the CEDA had been taken, the independent candidates met bitter opposition from the right's candidates and the Catholic press. It is difficult to avoid the impression that the centre-right and independent Catholic candidates were excluded from representing the Church essentially because of their republicanism. They accepted plurality within the state and the legal endorsement of views which did not necessarily agree with their own. Their presence on the electoral lists thus meant a blurring of the lines between Republican left and Catholic right, apostate anti-Spain and the true fatherland.

In Salamanca this vitriolic campaign against the centre-right was particularly marked. Yet the two main independent candidates, Marcos Escribano and Filiberto Villalobos, had stood in a semi-alliance with the Bloque Agrario in 1931. Now, however, their old running mate Cándido Casanueva could liken them to cuckoos in the Catholic nest and say that

problema religioso en España', *RF*, July/August 1935, October 1935, January 1936; R. Molina Muñoz, 'La falta del clero y de obras postescolares en Andalucía', *RF*, November and December 1935.

[15] See Preston, *The Coming of the Spanish Civil War*, pp. 169–71.

[16] *El Adelanto* (Salamanca), 9 January 1936, p. 1, 21 January 1936, p. 1.

they were more harmful than the Socialists. Similarly, in the *Gaceta Regional*, the CEDA's provincial press, they went from being 'our dear friends' to 'the hooded enemy'; the revolution under the cloak of order and security.[17] Whereas the right had been prepared to accommodate different shades of opinion in the uncertain circumstances of 1931, such alliances, always uneasy, had become anathema by 1936. A united front meant a monolithic one and those differing from the political norm were identified with the enemy.

Whilst the gulf between the CEDA and the conservative Republicans widened into a chasm, the links between the accidentalists and the catastrophists became overt. One of the two Alphonsine monarchist candidates in Salamanca, the marqués de Albayda, stood down in favour of the CEDA, although he qualified his withdrawal by reiterating his belief that legalist methods had failed and that violence was inevitable. The other refused to withdraw but stressed his admiration for Gil Robles by saying that only a 'tenuous line' separated him from the CEDA leader.[18] Nor did his presence in an accidentalist coalition prevent Lamamié from declaring, in a public speech in the city, that the Republic meant revolution and that universal suffrage was 'absurd'.[19]

Similarly, the CEDA youth organization, Juventud de Acción Popular (JAP), made no bones about its contempt for democracy. 'Our happiest day will be when we stop being deputies', declared one local activist. 'We want to finish for ever with a useless parliament. Spain cannot go on with these debased politics.' The JAP's totalitarianism was well known and widely publicized, occasionally alarming party leaders. However, it was the JAP which had overall responsibility for electoral propaganda during the 1936 campaign and these same leaders appeared at JAP rallies and received the adulation of the *¡Jefe!*–chanting crowds. Nor was this impatience with democracy confined to the CEDA's extremist youth and its monarchist allies. José Cimas Leal, another of the Salamanca deputies and a prominent Cedista, declared at one rally: 'We used the democratic and parliamentary regime, because we had no other, against the manoeuvres of Judaism and masonry.'[20] The CEDA fully intended to be voted into power,

[17] *GR*, 14 January 1936, p. 4, editorial 9 January 1936. On the campaign waged against Villalobos see also Antonio Rodríguez de las Heras, *Filiberto Villalobos, su obra social y política 1900–1936* (Salamanca, 1985), pp. 306–15.
[18] Open letters of the marqués de Albayda, *GR*, 13 February 1936, pp. 1, 8 and Diego Martín Veloz, *El Adelanto*, 28 January 1936, p. 1.
[19] *GR*, 4 February 1936, p. 8.
[20] Martin Artajo, *GR*, 7 January 1936, p. 5; Cimas Leal, ibid., 28 January 1936, p. 8.

but its commitment to democracy went little further. It asked for 'All power for the *Jefe*' and this was just what it intended to obtain: a legally constituted authoritarian government placing an inordinate emphasis on the leader.

The local church's unqualified support for the CEDA coalition reflected its deep-seated preference for authoritarian government. Even the JAP's fascist-style oratory was not enough to induce a greater sense of reserve. When a new branch of the JAP was inaugurated in Alba de Tormes the organization's flag was blessed in a public ceremony in the local Carmelite church just as if it had belonged to one of the Marian Congregations or the Juventudes Católicas. After the ceremony the congregation filed out to join a political rally.[21] Elsewhere, numerous religious cults were offered for the 'salvation of Spain', for 'the Catholic religion and the Spanish fatherland' and even that the 'sons of Salamanca' might return to 'their accustomed faith and compassion'.[22]

At the same time the local branches of Acción Popular were making great play of their piety. The religious aspects of the campaign were particularly emphasized by the female branch of AP, the Feminine Association of Citizenly Education (AFEC), which electioneered in the name of the Spanish woman: she who is, above all else, 'Christian, wife and mother'. On one occasion the election propaganda of these ladies even included a baptism. On discovering the presence of three unbaptised children at one of their rallies the speakers immediately, and successfully, undertook the 'pious task' of persuading the parents to comply with their Christian duties. This accomplished, the children were promptly whisked off to the parish church where they were given the new names of José María, after Gil Robles and Lamamié, Cándido, after Casanueva, and Abilia, after the provincial director of the AFEC. Allegiances to Church and party were thus neatly combined in a ceremony which made quite explicit the associations between the two.[23]

Such blatant links between Church and CEDA lend credence to the claim that God was with Gil Robles and that voting for the *Jefe* would lead to Spain's salvation. This divine endorsement of the CEDA meant that defeat seemed inconceivable. Complete confidence in victory for the righteous at times bordered on the millenarian. As the campaign progressed Gil Robles was increasingly depicted as a gift from God, a man sent

[21] *GR*, 7 January 1936, p. 5.
[22] For a list of these and other cults taking place in the city of Salamanca see the Sección Religiosa, *GR*, 5 February 1936, p. 7, 8 February 1936, p. 7, 12 February 1936, p. 7.
[23] *GR*, 8 February 1936, p. 1, 9 February 1936, p. 8.

by providence to bring Spain back from the brink of the abyss. Polling day, the day of the 'definitive triumph', would initiate a new era of calm and construction, a Spain free of revolutionaries where peace and social justice could reign.[24]

In the face of such assuredness the defeat at the polls in February came as a catastrophe. According to the Catholic view of history ordered by providence the election results had to be accepted as God's will. Although the final triumph was certain, for good must overcome evil, its realization had been delayed. The workings of providence, always mysterious, in this case appeared almost unfathomable. The Popular Front was virtually the sum of all evil yet God had allowed it to win. In asking themselves why God had permitted such a disaster, many Catholics looked inwards to explain their defeat. The crusades of prayer and penance continued in the churches of Salamanca. These soon merged into the customary cults for Lent with their emphasis on suffering and reparation.

The cardinal primate ordered the Stations of the Cross to be held in all dioceses on the first four Sundays in Lent 'for the Church's needs in Spain'. All Catholics were to offer prayers for the divine protection of the Church in 'our' Spain.[25] The Stations of the Cross, the ritual reconstruction of Christ's passion, had assumed a definite political significance under the Republic. Frequently directed by the Jesuits, their character of rogation and reparation ('now I lament my faults and ask Thy pardon') was specifically seen as asking forgiveness for Spain's sins and imploring God's protection for the Church in its hour of need. Those held in Salamanca in March 1936 were particularly well attended.[26]

The way in which the cults for the elections and the destiny of Spain merged into those offered for Lent was fitting. The religious season brought its usual examinations, not only of individual consciences but also of the functions of suffering. In Christian thought suffering is not only inevitable, it is also beneficial. The acceptance and endurance of pain thus cleanses and fortifies the soul. As a particularly homiletic editorial in the *Gaceta Regional* put it: 'pain cures, it does not kill'. The right, therefore, would emerge from their mortification: 'a little better, a little more Christian'.[27]

---

[24] *GR*, 4 February 1936, p. 1, 16 February 1936, p. 1. For more of this kind of millenarian rhetoric in the Salamanca campaign see *GR*, 1 January 1936, p. 7, 14 January 1936, p. 4, 2 February 1936, p. 3.

[25] Decree in *Boletín Eclesiástico del Obispado de Salamanca* (1936), p. 187.

[26] 'Memoria de la Residencia de Salamanca durante estos 25 años, 1918–43', *Bodas de Plata de la Provincia de León S.J. 1918–43*, private publication for the Society of Jesus, p. 18.

[27] *GR* editorial, 5 March 1936.

Many Catholics interpreted the Popular Front's victory in this way; it was seen as retribution, a justified punishment for the shortcomings of the Church and its members. Eduardo Jiménez del Rey, the Propagandist editor of the *Gaceta*, produced a series of articles saying that the right had not deserved victory. Many of its supporters were not sufficiently Christian and had failed to implement the gospel teachings, especially regarding the more equitable distribution of wealth.[28] *La Gaceta del Norte*, Bilbao's Catholic paper, said bluntly that Catholics could not absolve themselves from responsibility for the revolution. The 'humble' had not felt that Jesus was one of them because he had been identified with the rich who had failed to obey the laws of justice and charity.[29]

These arguments held that the true solution to the Church's problems was to implement those social Catholic teachings which had always formed part of the right's political programme but to so little practical effect. This was explicitly stated by the Dominican Father Guillermo Fraile in an article published in July. Fraile argued that masonry and laicism were not causes of the right's defeat but were rather the effects of other, deeper, causes. These he enumerated as the identification of the Church with the social and economic elite and, most importantly, the fact that this elite had virtually abandoned the less fortunate classes. In spite of papal teaching most Catholics were uninterested in the condition of the workers. He concluded that:

It would even be true to say that the Socialists have done more than the Catholics to implement the encyclicals and that there is more Christian content in many of their aspirations and conquests than in the conduct of many who go to Mass but ignore the fundamental precepts of Charity and Justice.[30]

Modern Catholic social thought traditionally sought to steer a middle way between communism and capitalism. It saw the community as the natural unit of society as opposed to the atomized individuals of liberal democracy or the antagonistic classes of socialism and translated this into a vague Christian corporatism which recognized the rights of workers to defend their class interests while still aspiring to the greater goal of social harmony. However, at least in the Salamanca campaign, ideas of corporatism and Catholic syndicalism, those stalwarts of social Catholicism, were conspicuous by their absence.

[28] See, for example, *GR* editorials of 20 February, 26 February, 9 April 1936.
[29] *La Gaceta del Norte*, reprinted *GR*, 3 April 1936, p. 1.
[30] *CT*, July/August 1936. The encyclicals referred to are Leo XIII's *Rerum Novarum* (1891) and Pius XI's *Quadragesimo Anno* (1931).

It was only in the wake of the February defeat that corporatism and syndicalism became prominent issues, again in the context of many Catholics' lack of social commitment. Letters published from the 'anti-marxist workers' of the *sindicatos profesionales* and an anonymous Christian trade unionist stated that the social work carried out by Salamanca's Catholic Employers' Organization had been negligible, and that its members only used labour from the anti-marxist syndicates when the socialist unions were on strike.[31] The supposed unity of aim in combatting the revolution was not sufficient to prevent criticism of the Catholic leaders, both for their policies and for their 'sins of omission'.

The failure to make political capital out of these social Catholic ideas during the elections meant that, when propounded, it was as a means of rectifying the shortcomings of the right rather than as an alternative to the Popular Front's proposals. Indeed the electoral campaign had relied on anti-revolutionary rhetoric to an extent that had left little room for anything else.

This reliance on conspiracy theory and accusations of revolution had left a clear way open for those champions of catholicism who took the Popular Front's victory as signalling the end of the accidentalist tactic. For them the election results meant only that the masses had been deceived into betraying their fatherland. The legalists had failed to win at the polls and now no course remained except armed rebellion. A mass exodus from the JAP to the Falange occurred while the catastrophist groups and the generals began plotting in earnest a rebellion which was, implicitly or explicitly, helped by many Cedistas. The CEDA financiers also now diverted their funds to the Falange.[32] The true Catholic Spain could not submit to the Popular Front, directed as it was by Jews and masons for the nefarious ends of Soviet communism. The insurgents were thus able to turn away from the church's legalist and accidentalist methods yet remain good Catholics because the justifications for their actions stemmed from ideas of revolution and conspiracy which the Church had endorsed and even fostered.

However, most Catholics did not throw themselves into coup preparations. Many began a reappraisal of the right's social and political policies in an effort to find out where these had gone wrong. Yet this does not mean

---

[31] Open letter from the Sindicatos Profesionales de Oficios Varios y ramo de la madera, *GR*, 10 March 1936, p. 7; occasional column by 'a Christian syndicalist', *GR* 17 February 1936, p. 5, 4 April 1936, p. 8.

[32] On preparations for the coup see Preston, *The Coming of the Spanish Civil War* chapter 7; Martin Blinkhorn, *Carlism and Crisis in Spain 1931–36* (Cambridge, 1975), chapter 10.

that they ever came to terms with the new government or that the Church managed, or indeed wanted, to divorce itself from those who led the confessional parties. There was still a determined resistance to cultural and religious change, and fierce opposition to the new government's plans for education. The introduction of a standard certificate of primary education was greeted with horror. The Federation of the Friends of Education (FAE), a leading Catholic pressure group in which Angel Herrera Oria's Jesuit brother Enrique was prominent, published a note objecting vigorously to the new law. Calling on parents to defend their children 'for Christ and for Spain', the note claimed that this kind of public examination could be used by the state to set text books which: 'encourage civil war between rich and poor, laugh at Confession and teach children to rebel against their parents'. In this way the state could ride roughshod over the rights of Catholics and impose laicism in schools regardless of parental wishes.[33] Yet, essentially, the government's aim was merely to improve and standardize Spanish education through a public examination system, something long accepted by the Church in other countries. The Spanish hierarchy, however, refused to accept any modification of its role as prime educator or any encroachment by the state on its control of schooling. Educational liberty meant the freedom of the Church to educate as it saw fit.

Nor was opposition to the Popular Front's legislation confined to the cultural sphere. Despite criticisms within the Catholic right, social legislation was still fiercely resisted. In Salamanca, Jiménez del Rey, notwithstanding his earlier condemnation of the rich who ignored the laws of charity, wrote that the agrarian reform policy was being carried out by anti-patriots on Moscow's orders. They had already paralysed industrial life in France and were now attacking agriculture in Spain. Both policies were intended to destroy the national economies. Popular Front land policy meant nothing less than the destruction of Spain.[34]

Part of the reason for this apparent inconsistency may be that Catholic social thought still relied heavily on the language of charity rather than the language of justice. Charity meant that the rich had a duty towards the poor but justice proclaimed that the poor had a right to what was owned by the rich. For many Catholic contemporaries the first was right, the second was revolutionary. And revolution, as the campaign had shown, was the antithesis of catholicism. The campaign had also shown that the Popular Front was the vanguard of that revolution. Fighting the revolution and

[33] *Nota de la FAE*. Reprinted *GR*, 11 April 1936, p. 2.   [34] *GR* editorial, 3 July.

resisting the new government's innovations, therefore, amounted to much the same thing.

This identification between the Church and the political right was so strong that, when the generals finally rebelled in July, the Church's support was a foregone conclusion. Supporting Franco was said to be the only possible choice for good Catholics both in and outside Spain. Franco was depicted as the repository of the Church's hopes and aspirations, the saviour of Catholic Spain. There was now no possibility of the Church accommodating those of its members who did not follow its line. It could not afford to weaken its position by presenting a divided front. The need for unity had now been defined in explicitly political terms.

This is not to say that the Catholic response to the Popular Front's victory was immediately to prepare for a coup which they knew to be imminent. The vast majority of Catholics only made the decision to bear arms in defence of their faith after 18 July. Yet, in some ways, such preparation was unnecessary. The Church was already armed with a militant rhetoric and a policy of exclusion, both of which were easily channelled into support for Franco. The overwhelming prevalence of such patterns of thinking among Catholics meant that there was no real choice for the Church in July 1936. In the identification with the political right and the exclusion of liberal opinion that choice had already been made.

'La main tendue', the French Communist Party and the Catholic Church, 1935-7

JAMES STEEL

When listeners to Radio Paris heard the concluding remarks of Maurice Thorez's broadcast of 17 April 1936, 'we extend our hand to you, Catholic ...', their reactions ranged from disbelief to satisfaction depending on their political beliefs. Anti-fascists could hardly contain their delight, while militant revolutionaries and anti-clericals scarcely believed their ears. Some Catholics welcomed this gesture of good will in a dangerously divided country, while other Christians denounced it as pure opportunism. Stalin and the Politburo looked on, hoping that the expected result would materialize: a victory for the Popular Front coalition of which the French Communist Party was a member. The Vatican prayed that it would be a mere ripple on the tranquil sea of Catholic France and therefore of little import. In fact the policy turned out not only to be a contributory factor in the Popular Front electoral victory but also qualitatively changed for about a decade the relationship between Communists and Catholics.[1] However, rather than creating unity, as was its avowed intention, 'la main tendue' proved to be divisive. It split the Catholic Church and Catholics as it divided the party and its members. It is the impact of this policy which forms the subject of this essay.

---

[1] For some Catholics 'la main tendue' was 'a farce' (Gaston Bernoville, Le Jour, 20 March 1937, quoted in René Rémond, Les catholiques, le communisme et les crises, 1929–1939, Paris 1960, p. 242), for others 'a gesture of good will' (Gaston Tessier in L'Aube, 26 April 1936, p. 1).

In order to comprehend fully the nature of Thorez's appeal he must be quoted more extensively:

And now we are working ... against the two hundred families and their mercenaries. We are working towards the genuine reconciliation of the people of France. We extend our hand to you, Catholic, worker, employee, artisan, peasant ... because you are our brother and because you, like us, are weighed down by the same cares.

Then, later in the broadcast, Thorez widened his appeal to 'national volunteer, war veteran in the Croix de Feu, because you are a son of our people who like us suffer as a result of disorder and corruption; like us you want to prevent the country from sliding into ruin and catastrophe.'[2]

This later passage in Thorez's broadcast is quoted less frequently than the first. Yet the amplification is equally important since it indicates clearly that the PCF intended to create as broad an anti-fascist front as possible. Also, although 'la main tendue' served a short-term electoral purpose, it became a long-term policy, apparent in both the Resistance era between 1941 and 1944 and in the fact that the strategy has survived as part of French communist policy.[3] It would be wrong to dismiss it as pure electoral opportunism, although such was the response of some opponents of communism, some Socialists and even some Communists themselves.[4] Particular Catholics and Socialists have delighted in signalling the apparent contradictions in the PCF's policies over the years as well as the differences between Communists over 'la main tendue'. Yet, despite a novelty of tone, the policy was as old as the PCF itself and can be traced back to the 1921–2 united front stance. The Catholic press sought to demonstrate that Thorez, like Lenin, was a mere opportunist and that the rapprochement with the Catholics was tactical, whilst the PCF press quoted Lenin to justify a policy which for many Communists and Socialists betrayed socialist principles.[5]

Thorez can hardly be considered a theoretical innovator. There is enough evidence to suggest that as early as 1934 Stalin and the Comintern executive approved of a communist–Catholic rapprochement. Other signs show that Thorez was a rather reluctant executor of this new policy.[6] He

---

[2] *L'Humanité*, 18 April 1936, p. 8. For Blum's attempts at Catholic conciliation see his radio broadcast of 21 April 1936 reproduced in *Le Populaire*, 22 April 1936.

[3] Cf. Georges Marchais, interview for the Catholic paper *La Croix*, as a special edition of *L'Humanité*, brochure (Paris, 1970).

[4] For Trotsky's equation of the Popular Front with the *union sacrée* of 1914 see L. Trotsky, *The Crisis of the French Section, 1935–1936* (New York, 1977).

[5] See *La Semaine Religieuse de Paris*, 15 February 1936; *Sept*, 21 February 1936; *Les Cahiers du Bolchévisme*, 10–11, 15 June 1936, p. 655.

[6] Jane Degras, *The Communist International, 1919–1943: documents* (London, 1971), pp. 334–5.

was perhaps embarrassed by its implicit legitimation of a Popular Frontist approach so soon after Jacques Doriot had suffered expulsion from the PCF for advocating just that strategy. Thorez was, however, won over and implemented 'la main tendue' throughout the Popular Front period.

But if Thorez was no innovator, neither was he an initiator. His speech represented the culmination of an existing campaign. It must be seen as the continuation, on a more formal political level, of movements such as Amsterdam-Pleyel, and associated bodies grouping anti-fascist intellectuals, writers and artists.[7] All of these movements founded by communist and non-communist intellectuals were essentially motivated by anti-fascism and pacifism. The PCF kept a close eye on them and although it did not formally exercise control it had members openly playing leading roles.[8] Organized anti-fascism therefore ante-dated 6 February 1934. Those events acted as a catalyst – but the PCF had been associated with anti-fascism for several years before it sought out anti-fascist allies officially. The nature of communist anti-fascism, prior to February 1934, was sectarian, with anything outside the party being branded 'fascist'. Yet even before 1934 intellectuals, including communist intellectuals, had been to the forefront in the anti-fascist struggle. Thus in this sense an intellectual Popular Front preceded the political Popular Front. Hence it is not surprising that intellectuals played a prominent part in the dialogue between Communists and Catholics over the 'main tendue' initiative – which in turn consolidated their existing anti-fascist endeavours.

To understand the nature of this dialogue the motivation behind the PCF's policy requires examination. There is no doubt that electoral considerations affected the decision to adopt a policy of rapprochement with the Catholics. Thorez was aware of the risk of such a policy being denounced as opportunist. The PCF had come of age with its electoral triumph in 1936, but this very success plunged it into political ambiguity in its position vis-à-vis the Republic. Electoral considerations had taken precedence over ideological ones. If the PCF wanted to be included in a victorious coalition it had to win over part of the peasantry and the lower-middle classes. It could never hope to do this on a revolutionary platform. The PCF had to choose between revolution and reform while being careful not to alienate its rank-and-file support. This explains why

[7] Amsterdam-Pleyel was founded by Henri Barbusse and Romain Rolland in 1932; the Comité de Vigilance des Intellectuels Anti-Fascistes in March 1934 by Langevin, Giono and Alain.
[8] Such as Paul Vaillant-Couturier in the Association des Ecrivains et Artistes Révolutionnaires.

the PCF constantly emphasized that the electoral programme of the Popular Front coalition was not a watered-down communist programme. The alliance's programme had specific short-term aims which, according to the PCF, did not compromise the revolutionary objectives of the party.[9]

The ambiguity of the party's position stemmed from its political discourse, which in turn created difficulties both within party ranks and among those Catholics who might have been attracted to a Popular Front electoral platform. The PCF's main problem was that to win part of an electorate which was predominantly anti-communist it had to project a reassuring image. It had to speak on behalf of a majority of French people, of all men and women of good will, for all those who aspired to a strong, free and contented France. To achieve this in a Catholic country there was no real alternative to 'la main tendue'.

But before the PCF could even think of influencing the electorate, it had to break out of isolation. Immediately there was a conflict of interest between the party and the Church. What the Church wanted to prevent at all costs was precisely what the party needed most: integration in the nation, Frenchness, respectability and legitimacy. This, however, was not in either the Church's interests or the Vatican's in terms of power, influence and prestige. They were determined to do their utmost to deny the PCF its new attributes and consequently tried to keep the party on the fringes of French society as a virtual outlaw. In this respect the February 1934 events crucially assisted the PCF's integration.

It was, however, not only for its own sake that the party had to break out of isolation. Hitler's attainment of power had forced Stalin to rethink his foreign policy. From 1934 onwards, a confrontation with Nazi Germany seemed inevitable and Stalin badly needed allies. Here the PCF could play an important role. If the party was accepted by the French electorate as genuinely anti-fascist, patriotic, democratic and primarily concerned with the well-being of the French working classes and petite bourgeoisie, the way might be open to a rapprochement between the USSR and the western democracies.

One of the problems with 'la main tendue' was that it gave the impression of an overnight change and thus provoked considerable suspicion particularly from the Church hierarchy.[10] Nevertheless the policy

---

[9] See Thorez in *L'Humanité*, 3 January 1935 and Marcel Cachin in *Les Cahiers du Bolchévisme*, 1–2, 15 January 1936, p. 4.

[10] The weekly *Sept*, run by Dominican priests, even accused the Communists of betraying their ideals for electoral gains. See *Sept*, 20 March 1936: 'Moyens impurs – la Trahison des

struck a sympathetic chord with a sizeable proportion of the Catholic rank and file, especially with the young and with some prominent Catholic intellectuals: François Mauriac, Jacques Maritain, Louis Martin-Chauffier, Daniel-Rops, Emmanuel Mounier and even, to a certain extent, leading clergy such as Cardinal Verdier, the archbishop of Paris. Sympathy, however, did not extend to an endorsement of 'la main tendue'. Individualistic above all else, these Catholic intellectuals did not constitute a homogeneous band. They often warned fellow Catholic citizens against the dangers of such an unholy alliance.[11] But their position differed from that of the Church in that they contemplated working with Communists and in some cases did so. In this respect they disobeyed the orders of the French Catholic hierarchy and especially the instructions from the Vatican. Few of them went as far as Martin-Chauffier, a 'left-wing Catholic' who became chief editor of *Vendredi*, a paper supporting the Popular Front. He argued that Soviet social organization came closest to the Christian ideal.[12] However provocative this remark may have been, it nevertheless went straight to the heart of the matter, as did Mauriac when he wrote that the question of unity of action between Communists and Catholics was probably the most serious question that the latter had to face. For him the choice confronting Catholics in 1936 was either to reject the hand extended by Thorez or to accept it unquestioningly.[13] Mauriac was acutely aware of the dilemma facing a Christian at that time since he saw clearly that 'la main tendue' could also be considered an opportunity for Catholics to bring religion to people who otherwise would never come into contact with it. The attraction of 'la main tendue' for Catholics lay in its evangelizing potential among atheistic Communists.[14]

Mauriac's reaction to 'la main tendue' highlights some of the problems which confronted Catholic intellectuals who felt the need for action, whether political or social, and who were painfully conscious of the Church's shortcomings in social matters. They had watched in the 1920s the creation of youth movements specifically for urban and rural Catholics, and had seen Verdier appointed in 1929 to the archdiocese of Paris with the

communistes'; also Georges Izard, *Où va le communisme? L'évolution du parti communiste. Les textes* (Paris, 1936).

[11] *Sept*, for instance, opened its columns to liberal Catholics attracted to practical communism. Nevertheless it was editorially anti-communist. An entire issue (27 November 1936) warned Catholics against 'le mirage du marxisme'.

[12] *Sept*, 27 March 1936. An editorial note dissociated *Sept* from his ideas.

[13] *Le communisme et les chrétiens* (Paris, 1937), preface by François Mauriac, p. 3.

[14] Winning converts was precisely the justification used by Maritain for his fleeting collaboration with *Vendredi*. See *Sept*, 3 January 1936.

aim of heightening the Church's social awareness. But these youth movements were often at loggerheads with the hierarchy, whilst Verdier's voice sounded a lone note against the loud chorus of ecclesiastical conservatism. The French Catholic world was divided over social issues and 'la main tendue' exacerbated these divisions.[15]

The Catholic press was far less homogeneous than its communist counterpart. It shows that the Catholic Church and Catholics had changed considerably in their political attitudes and behaviour since the beginning of the Third Republic. In the late 1920s and 1930s a pluralism existed which eased the PCF's way. The critical independence of some Catholic intellectuals is best illustrated by Emmanuel Mounier's movement *Esprit*, founded in October 1932. This movement and its journal accepted, in the name of Christian values, the possibility of working with Communists and eventually endorsed the Popular Front. But in so doing it antagonized part of the more traditional Catholic electorate, became the victim of a libellous campaign by *L'Action Française* and came close to being condemned by the Vatican shortly after the 1936 elections. Mounier, however, never confused Communists and communism, and was always forthright in his condemnation of the latter.[16]

If individuals like Mounier and Mauriac were prepared to cooperate with Communists, others – such as Maritain, Daniel-Rops and Pierre-Henri Simon – were more cautious and did not advocate acceptance of 'la main tendue'. But neither did they dismiss it outright. Their reaction revealed a degree of unease which, if not directly caused by the PCF's appeal, was certainly brought out into the open by it. Some of these Catholic intellectuals were quick to emphasize, while condemning communism, that communist endeavours in social matters were precisely what Catholics ought long ago to have been practising. It seems that the Communists' position forced some Catholics to question their own outlook on the republican status quo and to search their Christian consciences concerning their own and the Church's role amidst the economic and social stresses of the 1930s. Some lamented the fact that Christianity had abandoned to its arch-enemy, socialism, a monopoly on protesting against social injustice. Even Pierre-Henri Simon, who had no hesitation in

---

[15] *Sept*, for instance, was condemned by extreme right-wing newspapers and by the Jesuits for its 'flirtation' with the Communists. General de Castelnau, an extremely influential figure in Catholic circles, denounced the 'excesses' of left-wing Catholics. See Rémond, *Les catholiques*, pp. 227, 245, 246.

[16] A distinction which was welcomed by the PCF. See Florimond Bonte, 'Communistes, Croix de Feu et catholiques', *Les Cahiers du Bolchévisme*, 10–11, 15 June 1936, p. 660.

condemning Catholic supporters of the Popular Front, was scathing of Catholic conservatives who blindly voted for the right. He was forthrightly critical of what Mounier called 'the established disorder'. This rebellion against instinctive and uncritical political conservatism in the Catholic world was widespread among Catholic intellectuals. Maritain summarized their position when he demanded independence for the 'philosopher', reiterating that 'to the left, to the right, to none do I belong ...'. He concluded that the masses had been alienated from Christianity 'above all as a result of a Christian world unfaithful to its mission'.[17]

Throughout the Popular Front period, numerous Catholic intellectuals and ecclesiastics took up their pens to criticize capitalism in an attempt to put distance between it and catholicism.[18] Their arguments appeared both in reviews like *L'Aube*, *Sept* and *Esprit*, as well as in works by writers such as R. P. Coulet, Maritain, Daniel-Rops, Mounier and Robert Honnert. Obtaining for Catholics a critical perspective on capitalism echoed earlier papal denunciations of the evil of economic liberalism. More importantly still, the intellectuals' stance corresponded to a resurgence after about 1932 of anti-capitalism among individual Catholics, especially Catholic youth. This discontent constituted a potential point of contact for Catholics and Communists. They both agreed that capitalism had failed, that it was unjust, and that the time had come to act against the distress provoked by the economic crisis. In temporal matters, therefore, Communists and Catholics were very close. This was demonstrated by a series of articles in the weekly *Sept* shortly before the 1936 elections.[19] Although the pieces dealt mainly with students in the Latin Quarter of Paris, they nevertheless stressed the prevalence of links between communist and Catholic students. This seems to have come as a surprise and the editorial board of *Sept* reacted swiftly by publishing immediately after the first electoral round a series of articles in which it was stated clearly that not only was Catholic collaboration with the PCF undesirable, but that it was impossible since both doctrines were mutually exclusive. Interestingly a shift of emphasis occurred between the two rounds of the election. After the first the ideological incompatibility of the two doctrines was emphasized, as opposed to possible collaboration on practical matters such as Catholic

---

[17] Jacques Maritain, *Lettre sur l'indépendance* (Paris, 1936), p. 15.
[18] It placed the Catholics in a difficult situation, as Gaston Tessier indicated when he wrote 'go beyond capitalism. But with whom? And how?', *L'Aube*, 24 April 1936.
[19] See *Sept*, January, February and March 1936. Cf. Maritain, *Lettre*, passim; Daniel-Rops, *La Misère et nous* (Paris, 1935), passim; R. P. Coulet, *Communisme et catholicisme: le message chrétien* (Paris, 1939); R. Honnert, *Catholicisme et communisme* (Paris, 1937).

and communist students had stressed in their answers to the *Sept* survey. Had it dawned suddenly on the Dominican priests who ran *Sept* that not only the hearts of young Catholics were at stake but their minds too? Thus what might have become pragmatic cooperation reverted to a straight ideological conflict. Paradoxically, practical initiatives bringing together Catholics and Communists were acceptable to the Church hierarchy only so long as they never went beyond mere statements of good will articulated in *Sept* and its fellow intellectual journals. After the election's first round, with the likelihood of a Popular Front victory, the implications of 'la main tendue' appeared in an unaccustomed starkness to Church leaders. *Sept* adeptly manoeuvred its editorials onto a fresh course, declaring uncompromisingly that 'collaboration with the Communists is neither possible nor desirable for there is not a single issue over which we agree with them'.[20]

It is noteworthy that this intransigence preceded Pius XI's outright condemnation of communism on 12 May 1936. In a speech at the opening of the Catholic world press exhibition at the Vatican the Pope declared communism to be the Church's greatest enemy and the antithesis of Catholic individual, familial and social values.[21] The concern of *Sept* editorialists even before this papal intervention was to prevent any rapprochement between Catholic and communist youth.

This official rejection of 'la main tendue' did not, however, bring all Catholics back to the fold, nor did it end the PCF's effort to win over young Catholics. The PCF considered the Pope's condemnation 'divisive'.[22] Nonetheless it reacted moderately to the increasing papal and Catholic hostility. This restraint paid dividends in that there remained a strong current in Catholic circles favourable to some kind of collaboration. As a result the Church was alive to the risk of antagonizing the younger segment of its rank and file by a systematic rejection of the PCF. Cardinal Verdier stood to the fore in trying to keep ajar a door to cooperation. Yet despite the conciliatory tone, collaboration between Catholics and Communists remained unlikely. Even Verdier's initiatives revealed how far a conciliation had to occur within the structures of the Church. The cardinal reaffirmed the Church's social mission, implying that communism was superfluous but that the Church would work with repentant Communists.[23]

Opposition to 'la main tendue' was strongly entrenched in the Church,

---

[20] *Sept*, 1 May 1936.   [21] See *The Tablet*, 16 May 1936.
[22] Bonte, 'Communistes, Croix de Feu, et catholiques', p. 664.
[23] This was the argument advanced in Coulet, *Communisme et catholicisme*, passim.

but there was also evidence of discontent from the ranks of the Popular Front. Opposition to 'la main tendue' was strongest among the anti-clerical Socialists, but disquiet was also manifest among PCF members. Some criticized Thorez for going too far and this compelled Jacques Duclos to defend the policy in the name of anti-fascism, national unity and solidarity in times of economic crisis.[24] But, aware of the possible charge of electoral opportunism, Duclos indicated that it was preferable for Communists to extend their hands to Catholic workers than to government portfolios.

In its zeal to reconcile the French and to become an integral part of the nation, the PCF (and Thorez in particular), attempted to be all things to all men. Contradictions emerged, enabling the opposition to pit Thorez against some of his faithful lieutenants.[25] PCF militants in many cases feared that marxism would be reduced to a harmless appendage of bourgeois humanism. Paradoxically 'la main tendue' militated against conciliation between Communists and Catholics. It compelled sharp restatements of the two creeds, leaving the exclusivity of each fully exposed.

'La main tendue' as a policy thus caused problems to both the party and the Church. However, whilst the latter referred to dogma and the gospels, to prove the incompatibility of catholicism and communism, the PCF quoted Lenin purposely to legitimize 'la main tendue'. Through its rigidity the Church risked alienating young Catholics who might then be susceptible to PCF overtures. In a way 'la main tendue' was a straightforward application of the traditional communist policy of a united front from below. Such an approach concentrated upon practical issues as a basis for cooperation. Initiatives undertaken in this perspective with Catholic help included support groups for the unemployed, as well as cooperation at local council level in some of the more depressed Parisian suburbs with acute problems in housing, health care and schooling.[26] In this work Communists stressed the affinity between their social commitment and the teachings of the gospels. The fact that some Catholics at the base responded to 'la main tendue' indicates that the PCF's social commitment did strike a chord deep in the Catholic congregations. A politicized social awareness was no longer confined to leading Catholic intellectuals like

[24] *L'Humanité*, 24 April 1936. [25] *L'Aube*, 21 April 1936.
[26] *Sept* mentioned frequent contacts between Catholic and communist students; J. Duclos *L'Humanité*, 24 April 1936 and Bonte, 'Communistes, Croix de Feu, et catholiques', p. 654, mentioned cases of communist militants working with priests to assist the unemployed.

Mauriac, Maritain and Daniel-Rops, men who were already accustomed to diverging from ecclesiastical precepts.

In the final analysis the Church was not prepared to see 'la main tendue' succeed. Thus it always tried to bring the debate back to ideology. Cardinal Verdier remained a notable exception and while he could not condone 'la main tendue' he did attempt to build a bridge between the Church and the Communists. In an environment as politically and socially polarized as France in the 1930s, there was less room for manoeuvre. 'La main tendue' forced the French Catholic Church into a position which it had more or less managed to avoid until then: namely, to have to take sides politically, and to do so openly, between democracy and right-wing totalitarianism. By forcing the Church onto the defensive the policy revealed the reactionary nature of the Catholic hierarchy in France. Its refusal to differentiate between communism and the PCF rendered Verdier's bridge structurally unsound.

Young Catholic intellectuals were disappointed by the attitude of their own Church which made the concrete proposals of the PCF seem all the more attractive.[27] The interest generated in Catholic and communist circles by 'la main tendue' suggests that there was at the time a strong desire for national unity and also widespread concern for the poor and unemployed. This is a useful reminder, fifty years on, that the Popular Front was not only about fighting fascism but was also about countering an economic depression. It would seem that, on the whole, the Church in France underestimated the appeal of what might be called 'practical communism' – not so much because it underestimated the communist propaganda machine but mainly because it underestimated the depth of the malaise within its own rank-and-file congregations.[28]

The obsessive and unwavering resistance of the Church to communist ideology left its hidebound hierarchy increasingly isolated from ordinary church-goers. The latter were commonly ahead of their prelates and priests in their acceptance of joint initiatives with the Communists. This presaged a similar situation between 1941 and 1944 when, once again, Communists and Catholics found grounds for combined action during the Occupation.

[27] Adrien Dansette mentions the suspicion of the Church towards movements such as the Jeunesse Ouvrière Chrétienne (JOC) in his *Destin du Catholicisme français, 1926–1956* (Paris, 1957), p. 105. Conversely one must add the disillusionment that some young Catholics felt towards the French bourgeoisie of which, according to Mounier, 'there was nothing left to be expected', *Oeuvres complètes: recueils posthumes et correspondance* (Paris, 1963), p. 602.

[28] The episode of 'la main tendue' prompted William Teeling to write that 'Perhaps nowhere in Europe is Catholicism fighting a more interesting battle than in France', *The Pope in Politics: the life and work of Pope Pius XI* (London 1937), pp. 215–16.

In these war years, whilst church leaders showed their anti-communist colours by their steadfast support of Vichy, their congregations frequently participated in the Resistance. As a unified movement after 1943 this depended heavily on PCF militants, whilst acknowledging leadership from a liberal Catholic, Georges Bidault.

Trotskyist and left-wing critics of the Popular Front

TOM KEMP

THE LOSERS ARE NOT ALWAYS WRONG

A mass movement which swept millions behind it, the Popular Front burnt itself out in disillusionment and defeat as its left-wing critics had warned from the start. Slandered, ostracized and, in some cases, physically liquidated, these critics, ignored by the masses and isolated in small groups, appeared to be the 'losers'. In the perspective of the fiftieth anniversary they come into their own. Why, then, did they fail to turn the tide of historical events?

ORIGINS OF THE POPULAR FRONT

There would have been no Popular Front but for the tactical turn made by the Comintern as a belated response to the German left's defeat of 1933.[1] It would have been inconceivable without a major turn in the foreign policy of the Soviet Union. The new line was consecrated at the Comintern's Seventh Congress in July–August 1935 – most emphatically in the speeches of Dimitrov and Ercoli (Palmiro Togliatti) – while the French leaders claimed great success had already been achieved.[2]

---

[1] See E. H. Carr, *The Twilight of the Comintern, 1930–1935* (London, 1982).
[2] G. Dimitrov, *The Working Class in the Struggle against Fascism* (London, 1935?); Ercoli (P. Togliatti), *The Fight against War and Fascism* (London, 1935?); and M. Thorez, *The Successes of the Anti-fascist United Front* (London, 1935?).

Trotskyist and left-wing critics of the Popular Front

The Popular Front was designed to confront the twin problems of the growing military threat from Nazi Germany and the spread of fascism. Its novelty lay in the parallel search for international alliances with 'peace-loving' bourgeois states and national coalitions between workers' parties (including communist parties), and capitalist parties opposed to fascism. There was thus a fundamental difference between the Popular Front and the united front advocated by the Comintern in the 1920s.

Opposition to this change of tactic came, unsurprisingly, from anarchists and syndicalists as well as from pacifists who saw in it a preparation for war.[3] Criticism, mingled with signs of approval, came from the parties of the London Bureau.[4] The German Sozialistische Arbeiter Partei evolved towards support while in Spain the POUM joined the Frente Popular pact in January 1936. Some opposition came from within the Comintern and the national communist parties from a minority who saw in the new strategy a turn to the right or were reluctant to break with the class against class policies of the 'third period' (1928–34). In France such an opposition emerged in 1935, publishing a journal called *Que Faire?* and supported clandestinely by some Comintern representatives. Its most prominent supporter, André Ferrat, was expelled from the PCF in 1936 for his opposition to support for the Blum government.[5] His tendency failed to put forward a revolutionary alternative, paradoxically finding a home eventually in the SFIO.

All such critics were liable to be dubbed 'Trotskyist' by Communist Party spokesmen. The genuine Trotskyists, the supporters of the International Left Opposition, were few in number. In France they were organized in La Ligue Communiste and its youth section La Jeunesse Léniniste.[6] From this small group, assisted by Trotsky's analyses, came the most consistent opposition to the Popular Front. Young, inexperienced, lacking roots in the labour movement, but dynamic and irrepressible, they appeared, even to friendly critics, to be dogmatic and sectarian.[7] Such

---

[3] See Jean-Pierre Rioux, *Révolutionnaires du Front Populaire* (Paris, 1973).

[4] See Michel Dreyfus, 'Bureau de Paris et bureau de Londres ...', *Le Mouvement Social*, 112, (July–September 1980).

[5] Dealt with in Pierre Broué and Nicole Dorey, 'Critiques de gauche et opposition révolutionnaire au Front Populaire', *Le Mouvement Social*, 54, (1966). For Ferrat see Philippe Robrieux, *Histoire intérieure du parti communiste*, vol. 4 (Paris, 1984), pp. 211–23.

[6] Yvan Craipeau, *Le mouvement trotskiste en France* (Paris, 1971); an interpretation from his own factional position. A summary of pre-war history in Jacqueline Pluet-Despatin, *Les trotskistes et la Guerre, 1940–1944* (Paris, 1980).

[7] See the comments of Daniel Guérin, a sympathetic critic, in *Front populaire, révolution manquée* (Paris, 1976) and the sharper criticisms of Jean Rabaut, *Tout est possible! Les 'gauchistes' français 1929–1944* (Paris, 1974), member of an anti-trotskyist left-wing faction.

traits were reinforced by the hostility which they provoked from the PCF. Recruiting mainly from the left wing of the SFIO, the Trotskyists showed capacity for growth which exceeded that of other left-wing groups. In the early 1930s, when the official PCF line defined other working-class parties as being some form of fascism, the left-wing opposition had consistently upheld the call for a united front of workers' parties against fascism. Trotsky's writings on Germany provided eloquent support, appealing in vain to the communist parties to take the initiative in mobilizing the working class against the fascist threat.[8] Armed with this policy, the French Trotskyists began to gain some support. Until the right-wing riots of February 1934, which brought fascism onto the Paris streets, the PCF had steadfastly pursued the 'class against class' line, costly as it was in lost membership and influence. Sections of the leadership expressed dissatisfaction with the policy and the February events brought differences into the open. Jacques Doriot called for an agreement with the SFIO while Maurice Thorez continued with the old line.

During the counter-demonstrations in February a powerful current for unity arose spontaneously from working-class ranks. The Trotskyists sought to combine with this current and give it political direction; they were among the pioneers of the call for unity which would, ironically, prepare the way for their own isolation.

THE SITUATION IN FRANCE 1934–5

Although the PCF had more influence among the working class than its membership figures (about 30,000) would suggest, it would be a mistake, both in 1934 and throughout the Popular Front period, to identify its official policy with the moods of the working class or even of its own supporters. At times it was responding to pressure from the base. It found militant workers more favourable to unity in 1934 and less favourable to support for the Radicals in 1935–8. The PCF made its turn towards joint action with the SFIO in the action pact of 27 July 1934. Cooperation with the Radicals and other groups was cemented with the adoption of the programme of the Rassemblement Populaire (the official title of the Popular Front coalition) in January 1936.

The Trotskyists had been pursuing their campaign for the united front from a year or so before the February days. In January 1933 they had

---

[8] Various collections, e.g. *The Struggle Against Fascism in Germany* (New York, 1971). For a comment, see Carr, *Twilight in the Comintern*, pp. 433–6.

called a joint meeting with the Jeunesses Communistes, socialist students and other left-wing groups presided over by the Trotskyist, Yvan Craipeau.[9] Disciplinary measures were taken against the communist youth leaders who took part. Similar efforts were pursued, with some success, in the following year amid growing indications of dissatisfaction with the PCF's 'third period' strategy.

A dramatic change of policy was in gestation following the Comintern's reappraisal of policy, the pressures for a change in Soviet foreign policy and the growing desire in the national communist parties to break out of the straightjacket imposed by the 'third period' if they were to avoid isolation and defeat. Among these prerequisites for the Popular Front (as a political alliance with bourgeois parties, advocated and participated in by the communist parties) the question of Soviet foreign policy was of paramount importance.

The rise of Nazi Germany had thrown it into confusion. Stalin had evidently hoped, at first, to continue the normal (even close) relations which had existed between the two pariah states. The German–Polish treaty of January 1934 indicated that this was increasingly unlikely.[10] A leadership crisis during 1932–5, which finally established the predominance of Stalin, brought a wavering in foreign policy as on other issues. Eventually, in September 1934, the decision was made to enter the League of Nations ('the thieves' kitchen', as Lenin had called it). This implied the acceptance of the existing treaty settlement of Europe, thus smoothing the way for agreement with those countries with the biggest stake in upholding it. Revolution was thereby removed from the agenda. In the Comintern a struggle took place between advocates of the united front headed by Dimitrov and the hardliners, like Bela Kun, who wanted to continue the old policy. Dimitrov's prestige as hero of the Reichstag fire trial was thrown behind the new line and he made the keynote speech consecrating it at the Seventh Congress in August 1935.

How much initiative the national leaderships had is difficult to say; the application of the new line was worked out pragmatically with the old phraseology lingering on. At first Dimitrov had used the term 'united front'

---

[9] Craipeau naturally presents this in a favourable light, *Le mouvement trotskiste*, pp. 75–6, claiming an audience of 1,500, 'absolutely unheard of at this time'.

[10] The Polish treaty must have been a blow to Stalin because on the very day it was signed he informed the Seventeenth congress of the CPSU that relations with Poland were improving. See J. V. Stalin, *Problems of Leninism* (Moscow, 1953). 'Of course, we are far from being enthusiastic about the fascist regime in Germany', he told the Congress. 'But fascism is not the issue here, if only for the reason that fascism in Italy, for example, has not prevented the USSR from establishing the best relations with that country', ibid., p. 592.

but it was soon superseded by the term 'Popular Front', a neologism for an unfamiliar (and for some unnatural) political arrangement. It reflected the Soviet Union's need for allies from the bourgeois states.

The road to the Popular Front in France proved to be a tortuous one, and included some abrupt turns. By the time of the Seventh Congress Thorez was able to report on the new strategy's alleged successes in France: 'The national conference of Ivry which was held more than a year ago', he declared, 'boldly oriented the party along this line in accordance with the thesis so brilliantly developed yesterday by comrade Dimitrov.'[11] The records of this conference suggest that it began with speeches in the old 'class-against-class' vein and that it was the direct intervention of the Comintern which prompted Thorez to turn it round and appeal for 'unity at any price' with the SFIO. This first step on the road to the Popular Front was not an individual, nor even a French initiative.

From then on events moved swiftly. Following the unity of action pact of July 1934 a series of large and enthusiastic meetings and demonstrations took place. The extension of the alliance to include the 'middle classes' became the unaccustomed and reiterated theme of speeches and articles by Thorez and others. In October 1934 Thorez is said to have coined the term Popular Front (though some attribute it to his *éminence grise*, Eugen Fried, or the director of *L'Humanité*, Marcel Cachin). Thorez then became the most enthusiastic proponent of a deal with the Radical Party, which was identified with the 'middle classes'. On 24 October, on the eve of the Radical congress in Nantes, he made a speech calling on it to join 'a Popular Front for liberty, work and bread'. The speed at which the general secretary had moved alarmed some of the Comintern representatives in France, including Togliatti. The vigorous pursuit of close relations with erstwhile 'social fascists' like Edouard Daladier continued with even greater single-mindedness in the following year. The 'success' in France strengthened the hand of Dimitrov in Moscow. Then came the bombshell of the Franco–Soviet pact of May 1935.[12] Its consequences were immediate, straining the loyalty of many PCF members. Symbolically it meant the rehabilitation of the tricolour and *La Marseillaise*. Politically it meant the

[11] Thorez, *Successes*. He recounted how, after the May 1935 Franco-Soviet pact, the PCF had immediately placarded the walls with posters proclaiming 'Stalin is Right!' The agreement with Laval gave Stalin's approval to French rearmament and thus meant that the party had to abandon its anti-militarist stance.

[12] Carr sees the pact as marking 'at last the end of a prolonged period of hesitation and dissension in Comintern. In Moscow Stalin's personal commitment to the new policy was decisive', *Twilight of the Comintern*, p. 152.

abandonment of the Leninist policy of 'revolutionary defeatism' in time of war in favour of national defence and ultra-patriotism.

THE LEFT AFTER THE PACT

Disciplined PCF members may have been temporarily disconcerted by the new line, but apart from a minority they soon accommodated themselves to it. No longer isolated, the PCF took the path which made it a national institution. Other left-wing parties and groups were in disarray; they had to redefine their attitude towards the PCF and the Popular Front. The initiative now lay with the French Communists. They became the main driving force behind the Popular Front. The party possessed a solid apparatus, funds from the Soviet Union and talented propagandists. It enjoyed the prestige of the Soviet Union, now France's ally against the threat from German fascism, and had skilfully adapted to its audience, appealing to peasants, the middle class, Catholics ('the outstretched hand'), and even those misled by the fascists. The party was able to use its influence to determine where the lines should be drawn, seeking links with previously anti-communist politicians while ostracizing those on the left whom it saw as its most dangerous enemies. If necessary, threats and violence were employed to isolate them. 'Trotskyist' became a term of abuse equivalent to 'fascist' or 'scab'. It was no coincidence that the Moscow trials of old bolsheviks unfolded at the same time as the Popular Front; Stalin was emphasizing that he had no revolutionary intentions.

Meanwhile the French section of the International Left Opposition, over which Trotsky had a good deal of influence during his exile in France (July 1933 to July 1935), entered the SFIO as the Bolshevik–Leninist group in July 1934. This move, suggested by Trotsky, followed close on his proposal that the left opposition should no longer consider itself an opposition within the official communist parties but should set its course towards new revolutionary parties and a new (Fourth) International. Discords and splits followed both these decisions. Some refused to enter the SFIO at first, although most later relented.[13]

The Bolshevik–Leninists set themselves the task of mobilizing support among the left of the SFIO for a revolutionary marxist programme. The SFIO constitution allowed them to operate as a group, but they were a small minority in what was evidently a reformist party. The SFIO was

---

[13] The most prominent critic of entryism, and also one of the most talented supporters of the left-wing opposition, was Pierre Naville.

probably four or five times as large as the PCF at this time. Apart from the main current loyal to Blum, the party leader, there were several other groupings. The main left-wing group, the Bataille Socialiste, led by a Parisian lawyer, Jean Zyromski, looked forward to 'organic unity' with the PCF at some future time.[14] It opposed agreement with bourgeois parties, such as the *cartel des gauches* of the 1920s, was favourably disposed towards the Soviet Union but against a policy of bearing arms even defensively in wartime. A younger leader of the wartime generation was also gaining an audience on the left. Marceau Pivert's stance resembled that of the London Bureau; he was an admirer of the Independent Labour Party and Fenner Brockway.

Alarmed by the ease with which the Nazis seized power in Germany, Pivert advocated the formation of workers' defence squads and, with trotskyist support, established the nucleus of such a force.[15] As a pacifist he opposed the policy of national defence of the Blum leadership. Both he and Zyromski might have been expected to oppose the Popular Front. The latter, who adhered closely to the PCF line, came out in favour and, after the Franco-Soviet pact, reversed his former opposition to national defence.[16] By mid-1935 the differences between the two leaders of the SFIO's left had become too wide for them to continue to collaborate and Pivert formed a new group called the Gauche Révolutionnaire. He was influenced by Trotsky's ideas and there was some uneasy cooperation with the Bolshevik–Leninists. Pivert was attracted to the Popular Front by the mass support it obtained and was susceptible to the Blum mystique. In a famous article in *Le Populaire* of 27 May 1936 he declared 'Tout est possible!' and accepted a junior post in the Blum government.[17] He was mercilessly criticized by Trotsky for this slide into 'centrism'.

Once embarked on their entry tactic ('the French turn') the Bolshevik–Leninists tried to win the support of Pivert's followers for a revolutionary policy. At the Mulhouse congress of the SFIO in June 1935 they aimed their criticisms at the Blum leadership. By this time the Franco-Soviet pact

[14] See Donald N. Baker, 'The politics of socialist protest in France: the left wing of the Socialist Party, 1921–39', *Journal of Modern History*, 43, 1 (1971) and also Jean-Paul Joubert, *Révolutionnaires de la SFIO* (Paris, 1977).

[15] With the bizarre name Toujours Prêts Pour Servir. Organized in paramilitary fashion, they acted as stewards at meetings and had a number of clashes with fascist bands. See Rabaut, *Tout est possible!*, pp. 142–3.

[16] Baker is too kind to Zyromski, who drew closer to the PCF (which he eventually joined). In 1938 he congratulated Stalin on the execution of Marshal Tukhachevsky and other members of the Soviet general staff.

[17] He also stage-managed some of the giant demonstrations of 1936 and directed documentary films; the article in question is to be found in Rioux, *Révolutionnaires*, pp. 154–8.

had brought some strange reversals of position. Zyromski was now a supporter of agreement with the Radicals and of national defence. For the Pivertists, however, Popular Frontism allowed militant anti-fascism at home but excluded national defence. Blum, welcoming the change of heart of the PCF, was thinking of 'organic unity', hoping that the issues responsible for the split at Tours in 1920 had been resolved. The debates in which the Bolshevik–Leninists took part proved to be the most acrimonious of the congress. They harassed Blum and were given a hostile reception by the party faithful. While speaking in favour of national defence Blum was needled by youthful interrupters and replied to one: 'Comrade Molinier, I tell you without beating about the bush or oratorical precautions, that if organic unity could be established between the Communists and ourselves, and if, for the reasons which you have given, this unity left outside the party the little group to which you belong, I would be happy to see it happen.' This reply was greeted with applause and some delegates called for the Bolshevik–Leninists to be put out. Later in his speech Blum praised the Communists. 'No one', he declaimed, 'had pushed more ardently, more strongly than they for the constitution of a government in which the Radical Party would take the initiative and the responsibility.' Towards the end he added, 'I am afraid only of one thing ... that the Popular Front should become a means to prevent the organic unity [of the two workers' parties] and I only want the Popular Front with the organic unity of the two workers' parties (loud applause) as a nucleus, as a pillar, as a centre.'[18]

In the two major interventions made by Pierre Naville (one of the Bolshevik–Leninists who had at first been against entry) he addressed himself largely to the Pivertists, calling for a united front as opposed to the Popular Front as a preparation for a revolutionary situation. This was the theme of a series of articles written by Trotsky from November 1934.[19] Needless to say the congress rejected Naville's appeals. Trotsky was accused of applying to France schemes derived from Russian experience. If the Bolshevik–Leninists made less impact than they might have done this was due to their tactlessness and what their critics saw as dogmatism and sectarianism. They took little account of the mood of the congress and even embarrassed some delegates who sympathized with their position. Naville's speeches published forty years later still seem well-argued and retain a serious political content.[20]

[18] Extracts from the proceedings are to be found *inter alia* in *Cahiers Léon Blum*, 17–18 (1985).
[19] *Whither France?* Various editions.   [20] P. Naville, *L'entre deux guerres* (Paris, 1975).

In this period the Trotskyists had their greatest successes in the SFIO's youth movement, the Jeunesses Socialistes. By the end of 1934 they had secured a foothold and were winning new members. The SFIO apparatus tried to get rid of these irritating critics by administrative means. The PCF also had designs on the socialist youth. At the end of April 1935 two leaders of the Soviet communist youth organization (Komsomol), Kosarev and Tchemodanov, arrived in Paris and held a meeting with the leaders of the young Socialists in the presence of Raymond Guyot, secretary of the PCF youth. Thanks to a 'mole' the Trotskyists reported the proceedings in their journal. The Komsomol delegation's mission was to persuade the young Socialists to come out in favour of national defence, to expel the Trotskyists and affiliate to the Communist Youth International. They promised ample funds if this policy was carried out. Fred Zeller and other Socialist youth leaders rejected these advances and the visit became something of a scandal from which the Trotskyists gained.[21] A similar move in Spain was successful and the two youth movements united under the leadership of the Socialist, Santiago Carrillo.[22] In November 1938 Kosarev was arrested by Lavrenti Beria, the Soviet secret police chief, in person, tortured by the notorious Rodos and shot together with the rest of the Komsomol central committee.[23] There is no record of any protest from the parties of the Popular Front.

Having repulsed advances from one quarter the young Socialists had to face pressure from the SFIO's adult leadership. Their leftism and their opposition to national defence, even on the part of those critical of the Trotskyists, was an embarrassment. A delegation was despatched to their headquarters to persuade them to give up their opposition to the party majority, with inducements including selection for local government or parliamentary candidatures.[24] The bait was not taken. A crop of expulsions followed at the movement's Lille congress in July 1935. In January 1936 the majority of the socialist youth in the Seine federation formed an independent movement called the Jeunesse Socialiste Révolutionnaire. Weakened by differences in the leadership and by the split in the Trotskyist movement it was outflanked by the rapidly growing Jeunesses Communistes.

---

[21] Zeller's account (from his autobiography) is in *Cahiers Léon Blum*, 17–18.
[22] Carrillo later became leader of the Spanish Communist Party; see Pierre Broué, *Le mouvement communiste en France* (Paris, 1967), p. 511, n.336.
[23] Robert Conquest, *The Great Terror* (London, 1968), pp. 467–9.
[24] For Zeller's account see *Cahiers Léon Blum*, nos. 17–18.

Trotskyist and left-wing critics of the Popular Front

THE ISOLATION OF THE LEFT-WING CRITICS

As the mass current of the Popular Front swept along, with the PCF very much in control, the left-wing critics of all tendencies became increasingly isolated. Workers and youth entering politics for the first time went instinctively to the traditional parties and unions. They cared little about past differences and accepted the need for unity against fascism and war. Small groups with slender resources, with little experience and lacking roots in the working class, had little attractive power. These groups recruited one by one, not *en masse*, perhaps more from drop-outs from the old parties than from newcomers. On the other hand, the PCF had a well-oiled machine, leaders of established reputation and a layer of active and devoted young full-timers (*les permanents*). It still retained a revolutionary rhetoric, now strongly mixed with nationalism while benefiting from the prestige of the Soviet Union. The Trotskyists, weakened by their own divisions, were absorbed in struggles in the SFIO, which was rapidly overtaken by the PCF as a force in the working class. They were unable to capture even those militants, often spontaneously moving towards revolution, who took the lead in the great strikes of May–June 1936. The PCF set out deliberately to malign and isolate the Trotskyists, including in that term all left-wing critics of the Popular Front, even those in its own ranks.

The anti-trotskyist campaign was stepped up in 1937–8 as the policies of the Popular Front governments produced growing disillusionment. It was synchronized with the Moscow trials which were used to show that Trotskyists were really class enemies and traitors. Meanwhile the SFIO bureaucracy, while establishing close relations with the PCF, took steps to rid itself of its 'own' Trotskyists. Trotskyist forces remained small and, during 1935, had split into two over issues which included whether work should continue inside the SFIO after the expulsion of some of their leading figures and what attitude to adopt towards the Gauche Révolutionnaire. One group launched a 'mass' paper aimed largely at the SFIO's left and was castigated by Trotsky as capitulating to the 'social-patriotic wave' and Pivert's centrism. Trotsky was hardly less critical of the other faction which he accused of conciliationism, failure to put forward an uncompromising programme and a lukewarm attitude towards the Fourth International.[25] Thus during the critical first half of 1936 the most effective critics of the Popular Front were weakened by internal disputes and by lack of decisive leadership.

[25] See *The Crisis in the French Section* (New York, 1977).

Under the pressure of events the two groups (the Parti Communiste Internationaliste led by Molinier and Pierre Frank and the Parti Ouvrier Révolutionnaire of Naville and Jean Rous) merged in June 1936 to form the Parti Ouvrier Internationaliste with *La Lutte Ouvrière* as its paper. The newly-unified organization assumed a notoriety, and even a real import-ance, far in excess of any influence it could have exercised on events. The mass strikes of May 1936 were more a spontaneous working-class response to the Popular Front's electoral victory than the achievement of any group or party. The press, looking for ring-leaders, alighted on the POI. Communist leaders blamed mysterious Trotskyists when they found it difficult to persuade strikers to accept the Matignon agreement. The Blum government also took fright and the first two numbers of *La Lutte Ouvière* were seized on orders from the interior minister, Roger Salengro. Even if all the copies had been circulated the audience would have been small.

The Trotskyists' 'crime' was that they were calling on workers not simply to occupy the factories (which they were doing in any case), but to set up action committees ('soviets') and armed defence squads. Unlike other left-wing critics of the Popular Front, they appeared to be a present danger; there was a suspicious coincidence between what they were saying and what the masses were doing, or might do. It is easy to see that the threat was greatly exaggerated, though 'anti-trotskyism' usefully served a purpose, especially for the PCF.

At the POI's first congress in October 1936 a split again occurred and the movement remained divided down to the latter part of the Second World War. The hope (or the fear) that the Trotskyists would become a pole of attraction for those critical of the Blum government or of the PCF's role in the strikes proved to be illusory. The rapid disenchantment of the millions who had put their hopes in the Popular Front did not benefit the left wing. Indeed, the reflux of 1937–8 hit the left-wing critics as much as it did the traditional parties, and perhaps more.[26]

There is little consolation to be found in the fact that the Popular Front's defeat in France, as in Spain, confirmed the left-wing critics' warning. There remain, it is true, some penetrating analyses which retain their value today. Little of the voluminous writings of the communist parties stands the test of history. As for the vaunted 'conquests' of the Popular Front, they

[26] As Trotsky put it in discussion with C. L. R. James: 'Even so far as we ... had a tide in France it was connected with the Popular Front ... the defeat of the Popular Front was the proof of the correctness of our conceptions ... But the defeat was a defeat and it is directed at revolutionary tendencies until a new tide on a higher level will appear in a new time.' *Writings of Leon Trotsky (1938–39)* (New York, 1969), p. 64.

were made by the strikers, not by the Blum government. The only major planned increase in expenditure was for 'national defence'; there was no welfare state legislation.[27] The 'Blum experiment' failed in its object of overcoming the depression; workers' increased purchasing power was soon eroded by the franc's devaluation, whilst employers were only interested in revenge for the social concessions of 1936. Blum's conception of 'national defence' meant an understanding with Britain; Spain was sacrificed to this object and European war came nevertheless. The final irony was that after the defeat of 1940 (a *divine surprise* for the right), the majority of the deputies elected under the Popular Front banner voted full powers to Marshal Pétain who instituted the kind of regime favoured by the rioters of February 1934. Stalin had, meanwhile, opted for Nazi Germany rather than the 'peace-loving states' of 1935–6, now regarded as war-mongering imperialists. This policy in turn was in 1941 to expose the Soviet Union to grave danger. The left-wing critics may not have been able to foresee such a future in detail but at least they appreciated the contradictions inherent in the Popular Front, unlike those who put their faith in Blum, Thorez and Daladier.

[27] See, for example, Guy Bourdé, *La défaite du front populaire* (Paris, 1977).

The development of marxist theory in Spain and the Frente Popular

PAUL HEYWOOD

After the death of Lenin, the Comintern increasingly saw its activities subordinated to Stalin's changing conceptions of the interests of the Soviet state.[1] Never the source of flexible or progressive developments in terms of marxist theory, the Comintern was, however, forced by the advent of Hitler's regime in 1933 to abandon its sterile ultra-sectarian policy of the previous decade. This had been marked by a damaging excoriation of all social democratic parties as 'social fascist'. The Comintern's new direction culminated in the adoption of Popular Frontism at its Seventh Congress in 1935. The Popular Front strategy, though, was not adopted solely with the short-term aim of defeating fascism. Rather, Popular Frontism was seen also in terms of using bourgeois democracy's institutions to 'prepare the masses for the overthrow of the power of capitalism and to achieve proletarian democracy'.[2]

Such talk of capitalism's overthrow did not seem far-fetched in the context of contemporary developments. In particular, the New York stock exchange crash in 1929 had been taken by European marxists as evidence of the impending collapse of the capitalist mode of production; fascism, in turn, was seen as representing a last-ditch effort to stave off this collapse by

---

[1] On the Comintern, see in particular Fernando Claudín, *The Communist Movement* (New York, 1975); Julius Braunthal, *History of the International* (London, 1967). For documents, see Jane Degras (ed.), *The Communist International (1919–1943)* (London, 1956–65).
[2] Wilhlem Pieck, 'Report on the Activities of the ECCI' in Communist International, *7th Congress Report*, p. 36.

suppressing the working class. Although in this fascism had proved distressingly effective, it did represent, in marxist terms, a response to capitalism *in crisis*. In Spain, as in the rest of Europe, the looming threat of fascism had for some years been exercising the minds of marxists concerned to analyse the phenomenon and formulate a viable response. It was precisely the attempt to confront these problems which characterized a unique period, following the Second Republic's establishment in 1931, in which the Spanish Communist Party (PCE) represented just one of several groupings, and not a particularly important one at that, claiming to derive political action from marxist postulates. Common to them all was the realization, sooner or later, that on their own they were powerless; to defeat fascism and advance towards socialism some form of alliance strategy would be necessary.

The central debate amongst Spanish marxists during the Second Republic became polarized around two issues: the form and shape that such an alliance should take and, more importantly, its purpose. In short, was Spain ready for the transition to socialism? Ultimately the PCE, under Comintern instructions, would gain near absolute political hegemony after the outbreak of the Civil War and scupper all hopes of socialist revolution, a reflection of harsh *Realpolitik*. In terms of theory, however, the striking feature is that the Spanish marxists misread the prevailing socio-political situation, a crucial factor in their failure to evolve an entirely coherent strategy. This much was reflected in the fact that the creation of the Popular Front in Spain owed more to the efforts of the republican leader, Manuel Azaña, than to the pronouncements of any of the Spanish marxist parties.[3] Azaña was convinced by the disaster of the November 1933 general elections, in which a disunited left had been defeated by the right-wing Radical–CEDA coalition, that the Republicans and Socialists must recreate the 1931 alliance to stand a chance in any future election. From 1934 onwards he worked tirelessly towards this goal.

Azaña's main collaborator was Indalecio Prieto, leader of one of the three main factions in the marxist Spanish Socialist Party (PSOE). The PSOE, formed in 1879 and unchallenged until the early 1920s as the sole source of marxist thought in Spain, had split by 1931 between followers of the centrist Prieto, Julián Besteiro, a moderate marxist professor of logic, and Francisco Largo Caballero, leader of the socialist trade union, the

[3] See Paul Preston, 'Azaña, Prieto and the Popular Front in Spain' in Helen Graham and Paul Preston (eds.), *The Popular Front in Europe* (London, 1987); Santos Juliá, *Orígenes del Frente Popular en España (1934–1936)* (Madrid, 1979), pp. 27–41; Santos Juliá, 'Sobre la formación del Frente Popular en España', *Sistema*, 73 (1986), 67–81.

Unión General de Trabajadores (UGT). However, when King Alfonso XIII fled Spain in April 1931, all factions were convinced that the new Republic was bourgeois-democratic. At last conditions were ripe, it was held, for the overdue bourgeois revolution, an essential prelude to the next stage of socialism.[4] The PSOE's role, argued Prieto and Caballero, was to consolidate the Republic in order to help the bourgeoisie make its revolution. Only Besteiro dissented, on the highly deterministic grounds that the Spanish bourgeoisie must be left to carry out its historic mission alone.[5]

What none of the socialist leaders appreciated was that their analysis of the historic moment of the Second Republic was untenable, a fact which subsequently had a profound and damaging effect on both the PSOE and the Republic itself.[6] Central to socialist assumptions was the idea that the new republican leaders represented the bourgeoisie, while the landed oligarchy which had dominated Spanish political life throughout the Restoration Monarchy (1875–1931) was a feudal remnant. This was poor marxism, to say the least. The landed oligarchy had ceased to be feudal in any meaningful sense a century earlier when it started its process of coopting the commercial bourgeosie. This bourgeoisie was small and politically weak, to be sure, but took advantage of the disentailment of church lands in the 1830s and 1850s in order to buy its way into a 'reactionary coalition' with the landed oligarchy, thereby forfeiting its claim to rule in return for the provision of political stability in which to make money. For all its inefficiency, Spain by the 1930s had long been an agrarian capitalist society.[7] The PSOE marxists were guilty of reducing bourgeois revolution to its democratic aspects, thereby ignoring the changes in relations of production which had taken place during the previous century. This fundamental misunderstanding rested on several misconceptions: first, bourgeois revolution was identified exclusively with

[4] See Paul Preston, *The Coming of the Spanish Civil War* (London, 1978), passim.
[5] For Besteiro, see Emilio Lamo de Espinosa, *Filosofía y política en Julián Besterio* (Madrid, 1973), pp. 182–275. On Prieto, see the special edition of the journal *MOPU* 305 (December 1983), 5–51, especially the articles by Santos Juliá and Paul Preston; Alfonso Carlos Saiz Valdivielso, *Indalecio Prieto, crónica de un corazón* (Barcelona, 1984). On Largo Caballero, see the devasting G. Mario de Coca, *Anti-Caballero* (Madrid, 1975; first published 1936), and the introduction by Santos Juliá to Francisco Largo Caballero, *Escritos de la República* (Madrid, 1985), pp. ix-lxvi.
[6] See Preston, *The Coming of the Spanish Civil War*; Santos Juliá, *La izquierda del PSOE (1935–36)* (Madrid, 1977); Manuel Contreras, *El PSOE en la II República: organización e ideología* (Madrid, 1981); Andrés de Blas Guerrero, *El socialismo radical en la II República* (Madrid, 1978).
[7] This analysis draws heavily on Barrington Moore, *Social Origins of Dictatorship and Democracy* (Harmondsworth, 1969), especially pp. 433–52.

industrial capitalism and bourgeois democracy; second, *latifundismo* and *caciquismo* were associated with feudalism; third, Spanish socio-political development was consistently and inappropriately compared with the French model.[8]

The shortcomings of the PSOE analysis of the relation of class forces in Spain were soon revealed. There was no dynamic bourgeoisie in the Second Republic pressing for progressive social change. Instead, the Socialists were confronted by a landed oligarchy which, far from being feudal, organized quickly and effectively as a reactionary conservative bloc to impede as far as possible the Republican–Socialist coalition government's moderate reforms.[9] The resultant confusion within PSOE ranks led directly to the damaging splits which allowed rightist forces to win the elections of November 1933. Largo Caballero, in particular, had soon become thoroughly disillusioned with the new Republic. As minister of labour between April 1931 and September 1933, he was distressed at the failure of his cautious reforms aimed at alleviating the miserable conditions endured by the mass of Spanish landworkers. In response, he was increasingly to express a commitment to revolutionary marxist positions, based on a leninist-style view of the futility of seeking meaningful reform through bourgeois institutions. This process would reach its apogee in early 1936 when he was dubbed the 'Spanish Lenin' by the Communists. In fact their cultivation of Caballero reflected the labour leader's *lack* of marxist credentials: he was accurately identified as the figure most open to manipulation.[10] The key to Caballero's activities had always been his concern to flow with the tide. His revolutionism was never more than rhetorical, informed by a concern to remain popular rather than by any analysis of the socio-political situation in Spain.

Prieto's position, in contrast, manifested a clear consistency, although it was essentially always defensive. Once the Second Republic had been established, Prieto was left without a programme other than to defend the newly-acquired democratic rights so that the bourgeoisie might make its revolution. When he realized that this was not going to occur, his concerns

---

8 For an excellent article on this, see Juan Sisinio Pérez Garzón, 'La revolución burguesa en España: los inicios de un debate científico', in Manuel Tuñón de Lara (ed.), *Historiografía española contemporánea* (Madrid, 1980).

9 See, for example, Paul Preston, 'The agrarian war in the south' in P. Preston (ed.), *Revolution and War in Spain 1931–1939* (London, 1984), pp. 159–81; Edward Malefakis, *Reforma agraria y revolución campesina en la España del siglo XX* (Barcelona, revised edition, 1980), pp. 195–277.

10 See Mikhail Koltsov, 'Ispanskii Denevik', *Novyi Mir*, April 1938, pp. 41–2, quoted in Burnett Bolloten, *The Spanish Revolution* (Chapel Hill, 1979), p. 244.

turned to protecting those gains already made and, in particular, to protecting the PSOE's position. To do this he had no need of marxism. Common sense told him that revolutionary posturing merely played into the hands of the reactionary right. He therefore favoured collaboration with the Republicans.[11] However, in the course of the Republic, the *caballerista* faction would gain control of most of the powerful unions as well as the most important section of the PSOE, the Agrupación Socialista Madrileña (ASM), and the radical youth movement, the Federación de Juventudes Socialistas (FJS). Against Prieto's better judgement, the *caballeristas* were able to ensure that the Socialists contested the 1933 elections alone and opened the door of government to the right. As the rivalry between the two leaders intensified, Besteiro became progressively distanced from the party's decision-making centre. His political marginalization was ensured through a series of devastating articles by Luis Araquistáin, under-secretary to and closest supporter of Caballero at the labour ministry, published in 1935 in the marxist theoretical journal *Leviatán*.[12]

Before then, however, the experience of the CEDA-backed Radical government, elected in 1933 and in power until November 1935, had been leading to the PSOE's 'radicalization'. When three CEDA members were offered ministerial posts in early October 1934, the PSOE took this as a signal for revolutionary action. Concerned that the CEDA represented in certain respects a Spanish counterpart to Hitler's Nazis, the *caballeristas* had for some months been making preparations for a rising, though these were far from thorough. A general strike was called, but it took root only in Asturias, where it turned into a full-scale insurrection. In fact, as Paul Preston has argued, it is possible that Caballero hoped his vociferous calls for revolution would deter the right, thereby obviating the need to call any strike.[13] This primitive essay in the theory of mutually assured destruction back-fired badly. The only destruction which ensued was that of the Asturian revolt and of the Socialist Party, which saw its leaders jailed, its press censored, its Casas del Pueblo closed, and its militants subjected to

[11] See Preston, 'Azaña, Prieto and the Popular Front in Spain', cited above note 3.
[12] Luis Araquistáin, 'El profesor Besteiro o el marxismo en la Academia', 'Un marxismo contra Marx' and 'La esencia del marxismo', *Leviatán*, 13, 14, 15 (May, June, July 1935). Besteiro's response came in the shape of two articles and a book: 'Leviatán, el socialismo mitológico' and 'Mi crítico empieza a razonar', *Democracia*, 15 June, 6 July 1935; *Marxismo y antimarxismo* (Madrid, n.d., but 1935). See Paul Preston (ed.), *Leviatán. (Antología)* (Madrid, 1976); Marta Bizcarrondo, *Araquistáin y la crisis socialista en la II República. Leviatán (1934–1936)* (Madrid, 1975).
[13] Preston, 'Azaña, Prieto and the Popular Front in Spain', cited above note 3.

constant harassment.[14] From this disaster, Caballero and Prieto drew radically opposed conclusions. The former was persuaded that the October 1934 failure was because the PSOE had been insufficiently revolutionary and that it should be 'bolshevized'; the latter, having supported the PSOE's revolutionary line with some misgivings, was now more than ever convinced of the need to regain political power through coalition with the Republicans. Prieto's assessment was to culminate in the Popular Front; Caballero's was to lead to the wholesale loss of the FJS to the Communist Party.

For the PCE, Caballero's new-found enthusiasm for bolshevism was precisely the point of entry they had been seeking. Formed in 1921, the PCE had, until this moment, always been a tiny party, marginal to developments in Spanish political life.[15] With only 800 members when the monarchy fell, the PCE was further hampered by its dependence upon Comintern directives. This was later acknowledged by Fernando Claudín, at the time a leading figure in the communist youth movement, the Unión de Juventudes Comunistas (UJC):

We Spanish communists had the same experience as the 19th century liberals: we had no ideas of our own, developed on the basis of an analysis of Spanish society. Instead of using marxism as an aid to the particularity of the Spanish revolution, we used the Spanish revolution to serve the particular kind of marxism which had been valid for the Russian revolution.[16]

Like the Second International, the Comintern had displayed no particular interest in Spain. Thus, when the Republic was declared, the Communists were unprepared and without specific instructions. They therefore improvised on the basis of the 'ultra-left' line then in force, though in consultation with the Comintern representatives Humbert-Droz and Rabaté, and were roundly condemned for doing so by the Comintern's executive committee (ECCI) when it turned its attention to events in Spain. In an open letter to the PCE central committee on 21 May 1931, the ECCI harshly criticized the leadership for having failed to appreciate the revolution's bourgeois-democratic nature and the role that the Communists

---

[14] On the October rising, see Germán Ojeda (ed.), *Octubre 1934. Cincuenta años para la reflexión* (Madrid, 1985); Marta Bizcarrondo (ed.), *Octubre del 34: Reflexiones sobre una revolución* (Madrid, 1977); Adrian Shubert, 'The epic failure: the Asturian revolution of October 1934' in Paul Preston (ed.), *Revolution and War in Spain 1931–1939* (London, 1984).

[15] On the PCE's formation, see Gerald H. Meaker, *The Revolutionary Left in Spain, 1914–23* (Stanford, 1974), pp. 249–79.

[16] Fernando Claudín, 'Spain – the untimely revolution', *New Left Review*, 74 (July–August 1972), 11.

should have played.[17] As we have already seen, though, the declaration of Spain's Second Republic had nothing to do with a bourgeois democratic revolution.

Like the Socialists, though for different reasons, the Comintern allowed pre-determined theoretical formulations to impede its analysis of the Spanish Republic. For the PSOE, Spain had to follow the French model of development; for the Comintern, it was Lenin's analysis developed at the turn of the century for Russia which was sacrosanct.[18] Again, it was held that Spain was undergoing the bourgeois democratic preliminary stage to the socialist, proletarian revolution. According to Comintern directives.

The Communist Party should under no circumstances make pacts or alliances even of a temporary nature with other political forces ... In no way should it defend or support the republican government ... It should unleash and develop direct action by the masses ... fight as the revolutionary vanguard and guide of the masses, against all attempts to re-establish the monarchy, against all counter-revolutionary plots, taking advantage of such occasions to arm the working masses and conquer new positions for the proletariat and the peasantry.[19]

Thus, when the PCE leadership rallied to the defence of the Republic following General Sanjurjo's abortive *pronunciamiento* of August 1932 in Seville, the Comintern, consistent with its ultra-leftist policy, attacked the Spanish Communists for 'opportunism'. On the very day of Sanjurjo's coup, the headline of *Mundo Obrero*, the PCE newspaper, had read: 'The Azaña government is the centre of fascist counter-revolution'. José Bullejos, the PCE secretary-general, immediately realized the absurdity of such a claim. Taking a lead from the Seville workers who had actively resisted Sanjurjo by launching a general strike, Bullejos issued a slogan demanding the 'revolutionary defence of the Republic'. The ensuing debate between the PCE and the Comintern led to the ousting of Bullejos, as well as Manuel Adame, Etelvino Vega and Gabriel León Trilla from the Spanish party leadership.[20]

In the Comintern-nominated replacement team, the key figures were the new secretary-general, José Díaz, and the propaganda secretary, Jesús

[17] Ibid., p. 2; José Bullejos, *España en la segunda República* (Madrid, 1979), pp. 41–2. The letter is reprinted in Eduardo Comín Colomer, *Historia del Partido Comunista de España* (Madrid, 1967), vol. 1, pp. 287–301.
[18] For the Spanish Socialists' dependency on French marxism, see Paul Heywood, 'De las dificultades para ser marxista: el PSOE 1879–1921', *Sistema*, 74 (1986), pp. 17–49.
[19] Open letter from ECCI to PCE, in Comín Colomer, *Historia*, pp. 295, 296.
[20] See Juan Andrade, *Apuntes para la historia del PCE* (Barcelona, 1979), pp. 45–55; Joan Estruch Tobella, *Historia del PCE (1) (1920–1939)* (Barcelona, 1978), pp. 72–4; and the virulently anti-communist Víctor Alba, *El Partido Comunista en España* (Barcelona, 1979), pp. 130–3.

Hernández. Both were to implement loyally Comintern directives. Humbert-Droz, meanwhile, was replaced by Vitorio Codovilla as Comintern representative. Codovilla, like Palmiro Togliatti during the Civil War, was to play a major role in defining PCE policy. Following the *Sanjurjada*, however, this policy simply amounted to a continuation of the call for a united front from below, a tactic first elaborated in 1921 and reformulated in sectarian guise at the Comintern's Fifth Congress in 1924. For the Comintern, following Lenin's lead, the Spanish Republic was irremediably bourgeois and had therefore to be opposed by the workers, who could expect nothing from it.

The PCE's tiny size meant that its calls for working-class unity had consistently gone unheeded. The rise of fascism, though, and particularly Hitler's accession to power, signalled a widespread recognition within the Spanish marxist left that an effective alliance strategy was vital if Spain was to avoid the fate of Italy and Germany. The most important result of this was the formation of the Alianza Obrera (Workers' Alliance) in 1933 by Joaquín Maurín, leader of the Catalan-based Bloc Obrer i Camperol (BOC). Indeed, Catalonia during the Second Republic was to be the centre of probably the most advanced indigenous marxism ever known in Spain. This was somewhat ironic in that Catalonia was also a stronghold of anarchism, and it was precisely this which had contributed to the PSOE's slow growth there in its first decades.[21] In the 1920s, however, in Catalonia, a group of marxist politicians started to emerge who were to play an increasingly important role until the advent of Negrín's government in May 1937. Principal amongst them was Maurín, a former schoolteacher whose early political inclinations were anarchist, but whose later commitment to marxism–leninism led him to abandon the Confederación Nacional del Trabajo (CNT) and join the Federación Comunista Catalano-Balear (FCCB), the Catalan section of the PCE, in 1924.[22] The FCCB soon fell into dispute with the PCE over what Maurín regarded as the latter's blind obedience to Moscow, whose intransigently sectarian line, he argued, would be costly in Spain. As a result, in 1928 the FCCB was expelled from the PCE, taking with it nearly half that party's total membership. In March 1931 the FCCB merged with the Partit Comunista

---

[21] See Heywood, 'De las dificultades para ser marxista'.

[22] Maurín remains something of a mysterious figure. For highly hagiographic assessments, see Víctor Alba, *Dos revolucionarios: Andreu Nin/Joaquín Maurín* (Madrid, 1975), and Manuel Sánchez, *Maurín, gran enigma de guerra y otros recuerdos* (Madrid, 1976). A recent study of his political thought is Antoni Monreal, *El pensamiento político de Joaquín Maurín* (Barcelona, 1984).

Català (PCC), a dissident marxist party which had refused to join the Comintern, to form the BOC.

The Alianza Obrera's aim, according to Maurín, was to overcome the divisions which had split the workers' movement in Spain and drained its self-confidence. Maurín's central thesis was that a democratic revolution led by the bourgeoisie would be impossible in Spain; to succeed it must be headed by the working class. In a significant advance on the conceptions of both Socialists and orthodox Communists, Maurín recognized that Spain was a capitalist society in which a division existed between bourgeoisie and proletariat. The bourgeoisie had failed to carry out the political tasks of its particular revolution, even though it had become the dominant class. Thus, democratic revolution remained on the agenda; however, since the bourgeoisie had passed the stage at which it could act as a progressive force, the coming revolution would have to be socialist. In short, Spain had to carry through a democratic–socialist revolution or fall prey to counter-revolution and fascism.[23] However, Maurín's insistence that there were *only* two classes in Spain was a gross over-simplification which led him to misjudge the nature of Spanish republicanism. Thus, Azaña was seen as playing a counter-revolutionary role, the perfect representative of the industrial bourgeoisie. Against this, the BOC had to create a workers' front to defeat counter-revolution. The Alianza Obrera was therefore seen as the realization of what Moscow and the PCE had been talking about for some years but had been unable to achieve.[24] Naturally, the PCE was unimpressed, calling it 'the Holy Alliance of the agents of the exploiters against the Frente Unico; ... against communism and against soviets'.[25]

Also unimpressed initially were the Socialists. However, after the November 1933 Radical–CEDA election victory, Largo Caballero led the PSOE into a series of regional agreements with the Alianza Obrera.[26] This alarmed one of the other component groups, the trotskyist Izquierda Comunista, led by Andreu Nin and, like the BOC, mainly based in Catalonia.[27] It was over the relationship between Izquierda Comunista

[23] This is the central theme of Joaquín Maurín, *La revolución española* (Barcelona, 1977; first published 1932). See especially pp. 170–88.

[24] *La Batalla*, 18 May 1933; Joaquín Maurín, 'La Alianza Obrera. Orígenes, características y porvenir', *La Nueva Era*, 1, (January 1936).

[25] Quoted in ibid.

[26] Preston argues in *The Coming of the Spanish Civil War*, pp. 196–7, that Largo's interest in the Alianza Obrera stemmed from his concern to take over the left in areas where the PSOE and the UGT were weak.

[27] On trotskyism in Spain, see Pelai Pagès, *El movimiento trotskista en España (1930–1935)* (Barcelona, 1977), especially pp. 120–8 on the formation of the Izquierda Comunista. See also Francesc Bonamusa, *Andreu Nin y el movimiento comunista en España (1930–1937)*

and the PSOE that Nin would fall out with Trotsky. The exiled Russian leader instructed his former secretary Nin that Izquierda Comunista should infiltrate the PSOE, particularly since Caballero and the increasingly radical FJS held sway in it, to strengthen its revolutionary credentials. In Trotsky's view, the Spanish revolution was under the hegemony of the bourgeoisie and petty bourgeoisie, and the task of Spanish communists was therefore to win over the masses for the coming proletarian revolution.[28] Nin, however, was afraid that the PSOE was too powerful and that his own grouping would simply be absorbed by a party which had always shown itself at moments of truth to be thoroughly reformist. He therefore drew closer politically to Maurín, whose views on the centrality of the struggle between the bourgeoisie and the proletariat he shared and who was also a long-standing friend. By doing so, it is arguable that he opened the way for the PCE to steal a march on the Catalan marxists, for it was the Communists who were to win over the FJS in early 1936. Had the BOC and Izquierda Comunista entered the PSOE and strengthened its left wing, the appeal of the Comintern to the youth movement may well have been reduced.

In the meanwhile, the Alianza Obrera failed in any significant sense to get off the ground. Only in Asturias did it really materialize. Crucially, the key to its success there was the participation of the CNT. Without the CNT, the October 1934 rising in Asturias would have been as easily defeated as those in Madrid and Barcelona. It was this, together with the alarming nature of the policies of the reactionary Radical–CEDA governing coalition, which drove home the point now understood by all Spanish marxists: revolution depended on united action.[29] The problem surrounded both the form of action and the form of union.

The change in the Comintern line when Stalin embarked on his policy of rapprochement with the western democracies in the summer of 1934 allowed the Communists greater flexibility than they had hitherto enjoyed. One of the most immediate results was that the PCE opened relations with the PSOE. It also now solicited entry to the Alianza Obrera, and was thus

---

(Barcelona, 1977). Editorial Fontamara have published a comprehensive anthology: *Revista Comunismo (1931–1934)* (Barcelona, 1978).

[28] Leon Trotsky, 'The Revolution in Spain', 24 January 1931, and 'The Character of the Revolution', 18 June 1931, both reproduced in Leon Trotsky, *The Spanish Revolution (1931–1939)* (New York, 1973). Trotsky's view of developments in Spain was informed by his theory of 'permanent revolution', which rejected the stagist conception of the Comintern and of the Socialists.

[29] See Bernhard Bayerlein, 'El significado de Octubre de 1934 en Asturias. La Comuna Asturiana y el Komintern' in Ojeda (ed.), *Octubre 1934*.

able to claim credit for its last-minute participation in the Asturian rising. This was singularly unjust, given that a central committee plenum agreed on joining the Alianza only on 12 September 1934, and in most areas it took nearly a month to formalize the PCE's entry.[30] Nonetheless, another miscalculation by Largo Caballero allowed the Communists to usurp the glory for Asturias. Caballero, fearful of potential CEDA reaction, denied any participation in the 1934 rising. Such a move was politically extraordinarily naïve, for it allowed the PCE to assume responsibility for the October movement. Caballero's gift to the PCE was not wasted. Taking a lead from the Alianza Obrera, the PCE leader, José Díaz, called for the creation of an anti-fascist popular bloc, in some senses a dry-run of the Popular Front concept. Meanwhile, with the socialist leaders in jail after the Asturian rising, Caballero was persuaded, at a rhetorical level at least, of the need to bolshevize the PSOE. During the same period, negotiations began which were to lead to the Communists' takeover of the socialist youth movement.

The Federación de Juventudes Socialistas (FJS) was headed at the time by the young Santiago Carrillo, who was also editor of its newspaper, *Renovación*. While in prison, Carrillo wrote in collaboration with the FJS president, Carlos Hernández Zancajo, and Amaro del Rosal a highly polemical pamphlet, *Octubre: segunda etapa*. Published at the start of 1935, it poured scorn on what was seen as the traitorous reformism of the moderate and centrist sectors of the PSOE. The only positive aspect to the Asturian fracas, argued Carrillo, was that it demonstrated the need for the PSOE's bolshevization.[31] Ironically, in view of his later career, Carrillo's analysis was in some ways closer to Trotsky than was that of Nin's Izquierda Comunista, and indeed, between the publication of *Octubre: segunda etapa* and the VII Congress of the Comintern, the FJS communicated with the Catalan-based Marxists in a bid to make them join forces with the PSOE. The FJS leaders were particularly impressed by the quality of the articles written by Nin, Andrade and Maurín. Carrillo, in turn, was allowed to use the pages of the BOC's *La Batalla* for articles against Indalecio Prieto, who had been involved throughout 1935 in negotiations with Azaña and Diego Martínez Barrio to resurrect the 1931 republican–socialist coalition.

La Batalla was also, with Largo Caballero's *Claridad*, the arena for Carrillo's polemic with Maurín in August and September 1935 over the

---

[30] See Alba, *El Partido Comunista*, p. 148.
[31] Fernando Claudín, *Santiago Carrillo. Crónica de un secretario general* (Barcelona, 1983), pp. 27–30. Much of the text of *Octubre: segunda etapa* can be found in Bizcarrondo (ed.), *Octubre del 34*, pp. 83–137.

issue of the proletariat's political unification. The FJS leader exhorted the 'trotskyists' to join the PSOE in order to ensure its bolshevization. Maurín, in contrast, held that the PSOE was irredeemably reformist and that a new political grouping should be formed comprising genuinely revolutionary elements of the PSOE along with the PCE, the BOC and Izquierda Comunista.[32] Maurín was already moving towards this goal, and on 25 September the BOC merged with Nin's Izquierda Comunista to form the Partido Obrera de Unificación Marxista (POUM). The POUM has often mistakenly been designated trotskyist; in fact, the POUM quickly joined the London Bureau of Revolutionary Socialist Parties, to Trotsky's disgust.

It could perhaps be argued that the formation of the POUM, which was bound to be mainly Catalan-based, facilitated the PCE's task. Certainly when the Popular Front strategy was announced in August 1935, by Dimitrov, it was taken as a signal by many in the FJS that the time was ripe to join the Comintern. Carrillo, in particular, was increasingly falling under the sway of leninist conceptions of party organization, an influence which was to mark the rest of his political career. The PCE thus concentrated its efforts on winning over the left of the PSOE while simultaneously firing predictable broadsides at the newly-formed POUM. In turn, Maurín rejected the Popular Front, claiming that it signified both the permanent fusion of the workers' movement with bourgeois parties on the basis of Stalin's international policy, and the renunciation of demo-cratic–socialist revolution.[33] Instead, the POUM called for a circumstan-tial electoral pact between a united front of the PCE, PSOE and POUM and the left-wing Republicans. This pact should have a triple aim: to defeat counter-revolution in an election; to achieve amnesty for those imprisoned after Asturias; and to re-establish Catalan autonomy, rescinded by the Radical–CEDA government. Once these aims had been achieved, argued Maurín, each party should follow its own path.[34] Jordi Arquer, writing in the POUM's theoretical organ, La Nueva Era, attacked the Popular Front for being defensively reformist, and for 'castrating' the workers' movement, the only force which could successfully offer resistance to fascism. Arquer expounded the POUM line that the Popular Front mistakenly posed the dilemma facing Spain as one between fascism and bourgeois democracy, whereas the real issue lay between fascism and socialism.[35]

---

[32] For the debate see Ramón Molina, Polémica Maurín-Carrillo (Barcelona, 1978), a reprint with a prologue by Jordi Arquer of the 1937 publication of the articles in pamphlet form.
[33] La Batalla, 23 August 1935.   [34] ibid., 27 December 1935.
[35] Jordi Arquer, '¿Frente Popular Antifascista o Frente Unico Obrero?', La Nueva Era, I, 1, (January 1936).

The PCE's vision of the Popular Front elaborated after the Comintern Congress had the virtues of theoretical clarity and practical coherence; it had the defect that its theoretical clarity was inappropriate to the Spanish situation, while its practical coherence amounted to capitulating before all Azaña's proposals. The republican leader had, since November 1933, been working to recreate the 1931 electoral alliance with the Socialists. Convinced of the non-viability of any revolutionary attempt, Azaña urged the Socialists to exercise restraint in response to government policies. Instead of revolution, which would provoke a terrible backlash, he called for unity. The basis for that unity was contained in a republican declaration of April 1935 which listed the minimum conditions for political cooperation in Spain. Essentially moderate, the seven-point declaration constituted the outlines of the eventual Popular Front programme: it called, amongst other things, for the re-establishment of constitutional guarantees; the release of those imprisoned after Asturias; and the legal existence of trade unions.[36] These would be central planks of the Popular Front programme. In order to make its theory match such a programme, the PCE was obliged to adapt its stagist conception of the revolution: it now spoke of the first stage, the bourgeois-democratic, being divided into two sub-stages. The first of these would be restricted to the enactment of the Popular Front programme, while the second would see the completion of the bourgeois-democratic stage, prior to the socialist stage. This Procrustean approach was probably largely inevitable. The PCE remained at the start of 1936 a very small party with little political weight. To stand any chance of gaining an influence it had little choice but to accept the terms proposed by Azaña and Prieto, particularly as these two were reluctant to include the PCE in their attempted reformulation of the 1931 republican–socialist coalition. Nonetheless, the PCE did play a vital role in that it persuaded the *caballeristas* to join the Azaña–Prieto initiative. This was crucial to the political feasibility of the Popular Front and political health of the PCE.

Largo Caballero was initially very hostile to the Popular Front idea. While all other Spanish marxist groups had been moving towards the realisation that some electoral coalition with bourgeois forces was necessary to ward off the fascist menace, Caballero was reverting to a sectarian stance reminiscent of the Comintern's erstwhile 'class against class' policy. Indeed, the political trajectories of the Communists and the *caballeristas* during the Second Republic mirrored one another almost exactly. The

---

[36] For the other points see Preston, 'Azaña, Prieto and the Popular Front in Spain', p. 98, cited above note 3.

UGT leader's position received intellectual justification through the articles published by Luis Araquistáin in his journal *Leviatán*. Araquistáin opposed an alliance with the bourgeois left, arguing that it would lead to a repetition of the failures of 1931–3.[37] The *caballeristas* argued that the PCE's analysis was incorrect; that there was no need for any anti-fascist bourgeois democratic stage in the revolution. Instead, it was necessary to establish the dictatorship of the proletariat, under PSOE hegemony. Such ideas could only alarm the Communists who suddenly found themselves in the unlikely situation of having more in common with Prieto's centrist grouping in the PSOE than with either the socialist left or the POUM.

The Comintern therefore despatched Jacques Duclos to Spain in December 1935 to try to persuade Caballero of the need to join the Popular Front. Duclos faced a hard task breaking down the resistance of someone who held to his position with all the fervour of the recently converted, but a combination of the Comintern delegate's arguments and the manifest popular success Azaña and Prieto were enjoying with their calls for unity led Caballero eventually to concede.[38] This, together with Azaña's famous speech at Comillas on 20 October 1935, ensured that the Popular Front became a reality. The pressure on other marxist groupings to join became irresistible if they were to avoid political marginalization. Thus both the POUM and the FJS, for all their criticisms of the Popular Front, solicited entry in early 1936. The FJS under Carrillo was in any case moving towards an accommodation with the PCE. In March 1936, Carrillo would be invited to Moscow, where it is probable that he joined the PCE, although formally he remained a member of the PSOE. On his return he worked with Codovilla, the Comintern representative, to unify the FJS with the Unión de Juventudes Comunistas (UJC). In November 1936 he formally announced his incorporation into the PCE, taking with him a large proportion of FJS members.[39]

The POUM explained its decision to join the Popular Front by referring to the need to defeat counter-revolution, but did not give any theoretical back-up to this sudden switch. Trotsky was outraged. In an article published in *New Militant*, entitled 'The Treachery of the POUM', he was scathing of the Catalan group's decision:

[37] Luis Araquistáin, 'La nueva táctica comunista', *Leviatán*, 16 (August 1935).
[38] See Preston, *The Coming of the Spanish Civil War*, p. 144; E. H. Carr, *The Comintern and the Spanish Civil War* (London, 1984), p. 2.
[39] On the unification of the FJS and UJC see Ricard Viñas, *La formación de las Juventudes Socialistas Unificadas (1934–36)* (Madrid, 1978).

The former Spanish 'left Communists' have turned into a mere tail of the 'left' bourgeoisie. It is hard to conceive of a more ignominious downfall ... To enter temporarily into a mass political organisation in order to carry on an uncompromising struggle in its ranks against the reformist leaders ... – that is opportunism; but to conclude a political alliance with the leaders of a reformist party ... on the basis of a deliberately dishonest programme serving to dupe the masses and cover up for the bourgeoisie – that is valor! Can there be any greater debasement and prostitution of marxism?[40]

Grandizo Munis, a trotskyite opponent of Nin and Andrade within Izquierda Comunista and founder of the Spanish section of the Fourth International, was similarly damning. He argued that the POUM should have called on its members to vote for the Popular Front as the only available option against the right, but then immediately after the elections it should have turned against the 'reactionary' new government and appealed for a proletarian revolution. With no small degree of idealism, Munis claimed that the POUM was not prevented from carrying out such a course by its size, but by its opportunism.[41]

Yet in an important sense, once the Popular Front strategy was declared, the theoretical debate was transformed into a straightforward political struggle for hegemony over the unification process. Andreu Nin, the real target of Trotsky's thunder, accepted as much at a POUM Central Committee meeting in early January 1936. Having presented an intransigent report stating that the PCE and social-democrats could never play a revolutionary role in the Cortes, he then noted the important difference between theory and practice.[42] This was a crucial point. Marxists, with their claim to epistemological privilege, always face acute problems when stubborn reality refuses to conform to theoretical schemas. Since the theories are sacrosanct, reality has to be reinterpreted. To a greater or lesser extent all Spanish Marxists during the Second Republic were guilty of a 'creative' reading of reality. In particular, the lack of a clear understanding of the Second Republic's precise nature and the role of its institutions led to costly tactical confusion at key moments. Nonetheless, the period leading up to the Popular Front did see the most lively marxist debate ever known in Spain. Tragically a deadly combination of stalinist manoeuvres and fascist reaction ended not only the development of this marxist debate but in many cases the lives of the Marxists themselves.

[40] Leon Trotsky, 'The Treachery of the POUM', *Spanish Revolution*, pp. 208, 209.
[41] Grandizo Munis, *Jalones de derrota, promesa de victoria* (Madrid, 1977; first published 1948), pp. 247, 248.
[42] See Bonamusa, *Andreu Nin*, p. 262.

The other Popular Front: French anarchism and the Front Révolutionnaire

DAVID BERRY

In considering the Anarchists' attitude to the Popular Fronts, we have to bear in mind Daniel Guérin's distinction between what he calls the Popular Front No. 1 – an electoral alliance between social democracy, stalinism and bourgeois liberalism – and the Popular Front No. 2 – a powerful, extra-parliamentary movement, the initiative for which came from the working class:[1] 'the true popular front, the popular front of the streets and not of the politicians'.[2]

Thus, *Le Libertaire*, most important of the anarchist newspapers and organ of the Union Anarchiste (UA), was careful to distinguish between the Popular Front's leaders – the politicians – and its working-class supporters.[3] The Anarchists enthused over 'the fraternity, the solidarity and the strength of the working class' manifested in the extra-parliamentary movement of 1934 and 1935, and they also took an active part in that movement: the old nineteenth-century anarchist disdain for mass organizations – even for 'the masses' – was now no longer dominant.[4]

The UA was one of the eight organizations represented at the meeting held in the offices of the CGT on 7 February 1934. According to Lefranc, Jouhaux particularly wanted the anarchists to be associated with the call for a general strike: 'fidelity to the ideals of his youth and the desire to cover

---

[1] *Front populaire, révolution manquée. Témoignage d'un militant* (Paris, 1970), pp. 102–3.
[2] *Le Libertaire*, 31 July 1936.
[3] See M., 'La trahison du "Front Populaire"', *Le Libertaire*, 7 August 1936.
[4] Epsilon, 'Bonne Année', *Le Libertaire*, 3 January 1936.

himself against accusations of having sold out to the government'.[5] Its members took part in the strike of 12 February, and during the summer of 1934 they were involved in the Centre de Liaison et de Coordination des Forces Antifascistes de la Région Parisienne – a non-communist rival, more or less, to the communist-dominated Comité Amsterdam-Pleyel.[6] They had a 'profound distaste at having to associate with certain elements'.[7] Nonetheless they decided that 'for the time being, the most important thing is to halt the progress of fascism' and agreed to take part in the demonstration of 14 July 1935.[8] However, the prefect of police refused to allow the anarchist black flag on the demonstration, so the Anarchists took part not as a separate group but with their respective trade unions.[9]

At its Easter congress, held 12–13 April 1936, this tactic was confirmed as policy: the UA could not remain on the touch-line. Anarchists must ally themselves with the non-anarchist left and take part in the mass anti-fascist movement – albeit whilst trying to influence it in a revolutionary direction.[10] It is no coincidence that it was at this conference that the more 'workerist' FCL (Fédération Communiste Libertaire) rejoined the UA.[11] Nor was it unconnected that the next August the opposite faction left to found the FAF (Fédération Anarchiste de Langue Française), condemning the UA for being centralist, authoritarian and too conciliatory towards the non-anarchist left.[12]

Anarchists were active in the strike-wave of May–June 1936, though to what extent is something which has yet to be researched thoroughly. We know that the Paris federation of the UA called an extraordinary congress for 4 June, to discuss tactics, and that hardly anyone had time to attend because they were already too involved in the strikes they were supposed to be discussing. We also know that, from around the spring of 1936, the workerist tendency fought hard to establish factory committees as a base of support for revolutionary policies – though estimates of how successful these were vary, and the policy was abandoned at the UA congress of October–November 1937.[13] First-hand accounts of the spring and summer

[5] See Georges Lefranc, *Histoire du Front Populaire (1934–1938)* (Paris, 1974), pp. 23–4, 441 and Jean Maitron, *Le mouvement anarchiste en France*, vol. 2, *De 1914 à nos jours* (Paris, 1975), p. 27, for a list of other organizations involved.

[6] See Lefranc, *Histoire du Front Populaire*, pp. 56–7.   [7] *Le Libertaire*, 5 July 1935.

[8] Sébastien Faure, 'Liquidons d'abord le fascisme', *Le Libertaire*, 12 July 1935.

[9] See Maitron, *Le mouvement anarchiste*, vol. 2, p. 27.   [10] See *Le Libertaire*, 8 May 1936.

[11] *Le Libertaire*, 15 May 1936. Cf. ibid., 3 January 1936.

[12] See Maitron, *Le mouvement anarchiste*, vol. 2, pp. 87–8. *Terre Libre*, which had existed since 1934, became the organ of the FAF in February 1937.

[13] According to Jean-Pierre Rioux, *Révolutionnaires du Front Populaire, choix de documents 1935–38* (Paris, 1973), p. 350, these committees were successful; according to Jean Rabaut, *Tout est*

of 1936 by anarchist militants also vary in the impressions they give. Joyeux writes that his UA group in the seventeenth *arrondissement* failed to exploit the opportunities afforded to Anarchists by the Popular Front, being subsumed instead into the general enthusiasm for political reform.[14] Faucier, however, claims a more committed involvement:

The anarchists were at the heart of the struggle. At the offices of the Union Anarchiste, there was a continuous coming and going of militants and sympathizers wanting propaganda material for solidarity work with the strikers.[15]

A rather more negative view is provided by Léo Eichenbaum-Voline who asked what the Anarchists were doing and answered his own question critically suggesting, 'Apart from a few isolated individuals lost in the crowd, nothing ... they argued about their differences.'[16]

It is to be remembered, however, that Eichenbaum belonged to the FAF, of which his father Voline was a leading member, and which adopted a much more critical view of the broader labour movement than did the UA or the FCL. Indeed, André Senez specifies that the Anarchists who were most involved in the strike movement were those who were members of both the UA and the CGT, and especially ex-FCL militants.[17] Henri Bouyé admits that 'our movement was not equal to the situation', but also distinguishes between the different tendencies: the greatest offenders in his eyes were the individualists – who were interested neither in the labour movement nor in social revolution – and the CGTSR (CGT-Syndicaliste Révolutionnaire) – who were too isolated.[18] In fact, although our information is still very sparse, some Anarchists did play an important role in 1936: Pierre-Valentin Berthier and Bernard Bouquereau fomented and organized strikes in the tanneries of Issoudun.[19] Bouyé organized a strike of florists in the shop where he worked, drew up their list of demands, and created the Syndicat des Employés et Travailleurs Fleuristes de la Région Parisienne (CGT).[20] Patat created the Syndicat de l'Alimentation; Guyard was a prominent militant at the Sautter-Harlé works; and Roger Caron (of

possible! Les 'gauchistes' francais 1929–1944 (Paris, 1974), p.252, they were not. Cf. *Le Libertaire*, 4 and 11 November 1937, for the debate on this policy.
14 Maurice Joyeux, *Souvenirs d'un anarchiste* (Paris, 1986), p.284.
15 Bulletin no. 26–7 of the Centre International de Recherches sur l'Anarchisme (Marseille annexe): *1886 ... 1936 et quelques autres anniversaires* (Marseille: CIRA, ler semestre 1986), p.47.
16 'Témoignage de Léo Eichenbaum-Voline', in ibid., p.71.
17 'Témoignage d'André Senez', in ibid., p.36.
18 'Témoignage de Henri Bouyé', in ibid., p.59. Cf. Joyeux, *Souvenirs*, p.285.
19 'Témoignage de Pierre-Valentin Berthier', ibid., pp.39–40; and interview with the author, 21 April 1984.
20 Bouyé, 'Témoignage ', pp.56–8.

the JAC [Jeunesses Anarchistes Communistes]) managed to get himself elected to the bureau of the metal-workers' union.[21] By all accounts, one of the greatest obstacles in the way of anarchist involvement in syndicalist activities at that time was the determination of the PCF to maintain its authority within the trade union hierarchies.

The Anarchists were also an integral part of that sector of the labour movement which, throughout this period, adopted a resolutely anti-militarist – and consequently anti-stalinist – stance. They took part in the Centre de Liaison contre la Guerre et l'Union Sacrée, established in opposition to the Stalin–Laval pact of May 1935. Organized by the Révolution Prolétarienne group and the Ligue Syndicaliste, the Centre de Liaison's manifesto and two conferences were supported by the UA, the FCL and even the CGTSR, as well as by other groups and individuals closely associated with the anarchist movement: the pacifists around *La Patrie Humaine* and *Le Barrage*, the Ligue Internationale des Combattants de la Paix (whose president was Sébastien Faure), Henri Poulaille, Ernestan and Simone Weil. In January 1937 Anarchists also joined with the Gauche Révolutionnaire, the Monatte-Louzon group and others to create the Cercle Syndicaliste Lutte de Classes – an attempt to regroup the revolutionary opposition to the policies of Jouhaux and Frachon.[22] Many of those involved with La Révolution Prolétarienne and the Ligue Syndicaliste were themselves, of course, very close to anarchism. So it is clear that only in the sense of a united working-class front was Popular Frontism welcomed by Anarchists.

In July 1935, an editorial in *Le Libertaire* insisted that they welcomed the new unity of action in the labour movement, having been among the first to call for it, but added the caveat that 'we believe it is now necessary to oppose the so-called "Front Populaire", which is a distortion [*déformation*] of that unity'.[23] This was partly to do with the Stalin–Laval pact. For the Anarchists, this pact was a new Union Sacrée intended to maintain 'the status quo established at Versailles, through an alliance of French and Russian imperialism'.[24] In March 1936, *Le Libertaire* declared in banner headlines that 'Popular Front means Holy Alliance, and Holy Alliance means war'.[25] The pact cemented their hostility to the Communists – or

---

[21] Senez, 'Témoignage ', p. 36.
[22] See Nicolas Faucier, *Pacifisme et Antimilitarisme dans l'entre-deux-guerres (1919–1939)* (Paris, 1983), pp. 112–14, 149–51; Rioux, *Révolutionnaires*, pp. 26, 235, 247; Guérin, *Front populaire*, pp. 84, 216, 242–3; Pierre Broué and Nicole Dorey, 'Critiques de gauche et opposition révolutionnaire au front populaire (1936–1938)', *Mouvement Social*, 54 (January–March 1966), 131–3.
[23] *Le Libertaire*, 5 July 1935.   [24] *Le Libertaire*, 10 May 1935.
[25] *Le Libertaire*, 20 March 1936.

nacos (nationaux-communistes), as they became known – and, of course, encouraged them in their belief that the Communists' primary motive in promoting the Popular Front was Stalin's bellicose foreign policy. Attruia summed up the Anarchists' attitude to communist strategy:

It is not the task of true revolutionaries to defend this State against another State – even a fascist one – but to destroy the State through revolution. Their duty is not, as Vaillant-Couturier has written in *L'Humanité*, to oppose 'the permanent threat of a fascist putsch with the barrier of republican feeling in the country and among the forces of law and order' (sic), but actively to prepare a revolutionary response.[26]

But the Anarchists also attacked what they saw as the fundamental deceptiveness of the Popular Front policy, the naivety of believing that anything significant could be achieved by electing a Popular Front government: 'make the rich pay' was a seductive but misleading slogan.[27] This was, of course, a matter of very basic anarchist principles, as the UA's manifesto made clear.[28] Parliamentarianism was the gravest danger to the working class, being no more than an anaesthetic. An electoral alliance with the bourgeoisie was a trick, because it had the working class believe that their interests were the same as their rulers', and a century's experience showed that it was 'always the working class that pays the cost of such alliances'.[29] It was therefore foolish to believe that a Popular Front government would or could achieve what the working class needed. 'Will it ... expropriate the industrialists and the financiers? No. That is not its aim – our good republican Radicals could never subscribe to such a thing.'[30]

Popular Front governments in France or Spain would not be able to achieve what the working class wanted without going beyond the legal framework of a bourgeois parliament, and they would not be able to do that without destroying themselves as coalition governments. Anarchists wondered what would happen then.

Parliamentary resistance? Capitalism has shown in several countries that it is quite capable of overcoming such opposition without lifting a finger. The Popular Front, if it wishes to hold on to power, will have to protect itself by adopting a 'neutrality' which will be greatly appreciated by capitalism. Otherwise, it will be forced to step down. There is no other possible solution.[31]

---

26 D. Attruia, 'Le prolétariat et la lutte contre la guerre et le fascisme', *Le Libertaire*, 7 April 1936.
27 *Le Libertaire*, 3 January 1936.
28 The manifesto was adopted at the UA's Paris congress on 12–13 April. See *Le Libertaire*, 22 May 1936.
29 Ibid.   30 *Le Libertaire*, 5 July 1935.
31 'Les élections espagnoles', *Le Libertaire*, 21 February 1936.

In the spring of 1936, the UA was already promising total disillusion on the part of the working class. 'This experiment will be the greatest confirmation of our ideas on the incapacity of political parties to lead the proletariat to its complete emancipation.'[32] And they were also suggesting that this disappointment might well result in 'a new revolutionary upsurge'.[33]

For the UA, those things that were achieved – from the amnesty in Spain to paid holidays in France – were won not by the Popular Front governments, but through the direct action of the working class itself.[34] For the Anarchists, the direct intervention of the labour movement, unmediated and unrestricted by electoralism, had more progressive potential than the electoral coalition between the Socialist, Communist and Radical Party hierarchies – a coalition which *Le Libertaire*'s 21 August 1936 editorial insisted was a product and not a cause of the spontaneous popular movement.

In Spain as in France, all the parliamentary hubbub surrounding the Popular Front, the shifts in parliamentary majorities and so on – which are persistently taken for causes by commentators who either are blinkered or who have an interest in such misunderstanding – are nothing but the effect of the tremendous dissatisfaction of the masses who have a direct interest in real change.[35]

But it was the Spanish revolution which, more than anything, aroused the imagination and enthusiasm of the French Anarchists. Again, when it came to the question of non-intervention, they were quite clear on the role of the Popular Front government. The working class could and should rely only on itself. 'The defence of Spain in revolutionary struggle must be assured by the French working class, and not by the French nation. The neutrality of the latter must not lead to the passivity of the former.'[36] It must act to destroy pro-fascist forces in France, and constitute 'the Revolutionary front of solidarity with Spain'.[37] Thus the campaign of solidarity for Spain was not a humanitarian effort, sealed off from revolutionary politics in France – the two were closely linked.

So, in analysing the tasks facing the revolutionary left, concerning both domestic politics and the Spanish problem, the UA rejected reliance on a Popular Front government in favour of direct and autonomous action by

[32] *Le Libertaire*, 10 April 1936.
[33] 'Les élections espagnoles', *Le Libertaire*, 21 February 1936.
[34] Editorial, *Le Libertaire*, 21 August 1936.
[35] Louis Ander, 'La lutte de nos camarades d'Espagne' *Le Libertaire*, 10 July 1936.
[36] 'Neutralité de trahison', *Le Libertaire*, 7 August 1936.
[37] Luc Daurat, 'Utilisons le masque gouvernemental', *Le Libertaire*, 25 September 1936.

the labour movement. This was the basis of the revolutionary front policy.[38]

These two underlying principles – working-class autonomy and revolutionary class struggle – implied opposition to the 'neo-reformism', which, according to the anarchist analysis, was basically a more insidious form of fascism, trying to integrate the trade union movement into an increasingly corporatist state.[39] As Séchaud put it: 'We are faced more and more with the dilemma: fascism or revolution.'[40] Therefore as far as international politics were concerned, the UA's call for a revolutionary front clearly espoused traditional 'proletarian internationalism', denouncing the 'myth' of the struggle between 'fascism' and 'democracy', and rejecting national defence, whether in a capitalist or 'state capitalist' country. The implications for the campaign around Spain were clear. One of the UA's main aims in that respect was to unmask the role of foreign imperialisms – British, French and Russian – in the Civil War, and in particular to expose the role of the SFIO and CGT – 'agents of French imperialism' – and of the PCF – 'agents of Russian imperialism'.[41]

The revolutionary front as opposition to the reformist Front Populaire and as 'revolutionary front of solidarity with Spain' were, then, linked in that they were based, initially at least, on the same political analysis.[42] And the campaign of support for Spain was not intended to work only one way, simply as a means of providing material assistance. One of the Anarchists' main aims was to provide a counter-information service to compensate for the failings of the French Popular Front press, which was far from even-handed in its coverage of the various sectors of Spanish anti-fascism. The French working class, 'duped' by its own politicians, would have before them the example of a large and successful revolutionary labour movement, independent of all politicians, and might be inspired by the example.[43] Second, the campaign for international solidarity included repeated exhortations to the workers in transport and armaments manufacturing to take the law into their own hands and supply the Spanish anti-fascists with all they needed – going as far as a general strike, even insurrection, if need be. As Sébastien Faure put it, speaking of the

---

[38] See 'Pour un Front Révolutionnaire', *Le Libertaire*, 20 May 1937.   [39] Ibid.
[40] Séchaud, 'France et Espagne', *Le Libertaire*, 7 August 1936.
[41] 'Pour un Front Révolutionnaire', art. cit.
[42] Daurat, 'Utilisons le masque gouvernemental'.
[43] See Louis Ander, 'La lutte de nos camarades d'Espagne', *Le Libertaire*, 10 July 1936. There were six French-language anarchist newspapers given over entirely to events in Spain.

CNT–FAI, 'Admiring their example is fine. Preparing to follow it is better.'[44]

So what were the results of this policy in terms of practical cooperation? We have already noted the Anarchists' involvement in the mass anti-fascist movement of 1934–5; and the UA's decision at its Easter 1936 congress to give priority in the short term to the need to combat fascism, thus implicitly accepting alliances with other groups on the left. And although between July and October 1936 the UA was involved in a Comité Anarcho-Syndicaliste pour la Libération et la Défense du Prolétariat Espagnol (CASLDPE), along with the CGTSR and FAF – a kind of anarchist front – the UA was also cooperating during the same period with the SFIO, the Gauche Révolutionnaire, the Jeunesses Socialistes Révolutionnaires, the Comité de Vigilance des Intellectuels Antifascistes, Trotskyists, and even, in a few rare cases, Communists.[45] According to Joyeux, his local UA group already had more or less regular contacts with 'related revolutionary groups' even before the revolutionary front policy was adopted: pacifists, the CGTSR, freethinkers, Trotskyists, and the local SFIO section once it joined the Gauche Révolutionnaire. In Wattrelos, there was even a Comité Antifasciste which united Socialists, Anarchists and Communists in one group.[46] Cooperation with Communists was, however, unusual. The Trotskyists were not the only ones to be slandered by the Stalinists in this period. The anarchist press regularly printed reports of physical intimidation and even violence being practised against its members. On several occasions – according to Le Libertaire – the PCF employed the tactic of organizing a local meeting, at very short notice, and sometimes making attendance at it 'compulsory', in order to prevent their supporters and sympathizers from attending another anarchist-organized meeting in the same locality.[47]

In October the policy of cooperation between Socialists and the UA was formalized at a joint public meeting, proposed by the Socialists, on the theme 'For the creation of the Revolutionary Front'. The event was held at the Mutualité on 3 October: Le Libertaire for the 9th claimed an audience of 4,000. It was chaired by Audubert of the SFIO's fifth section and, significantly, Paul Rivet had originally been intended as the main socialist

[44] Le Libertaire, 7 August 1936.
[45] See various reports in Le Libertaire throughout August, September and October 1936.
[46] Joyeux, Souvenirs, p. 275; See also Le Libertaire, 4 September 1936.
[47] See Hobsbawm's comments on the increase of anti-anarchist propaganda by the Communists in the mid-1930s: 'Bolshevism and the Anarchists', Revolutionaries (London, 1977), p. 68.

speaker: in the event, Weiss (probably a misprint for Weitz) of the Jeunesses Socialistes, and Pivert of the Gauche Révolutionnaire spoke for the Socialists, with Ringeas and Faure from the UA.[48] The meeting passed a resolution calling for the creation of an armed Garde Populaire, and defined its position on the Blum government thus: '... a Popular Front which did not attune itself to the revolutionary events which are now taking place in Spain and which will soon spread to France, would be betraying the proletariat of both countries'.[49]

As for the campaign of solidarity with the Spanish revolutionaries, the UA had decided that cooperating only with small anarchist organizations was not achieving good enough results, whereas working together with 'related revolutionary tendencies' had already enabled them to reach much larger sectors of the working class.[50] Their policy was that: 'Outside of its own specifically anarchist activities, the UA is ready, as in the past, to co-operate with all other revolutionary organizations on clearly defined tasks, and particularly for the effective support of Spain'.[51] This was to lead to the creation of the Comité pour l'Espagne Libre. And in fact, despite the pretensions of the CGTSR and FAF at being a French version of the CNT–FAI, the CNT fully supported the UA's policy.[52] On 16 October 1936, Le Libertaire printed a telegram from Horacio Prieto, secretary of the CNT national committee, urging the UA to work together with anyone sympathetic to the cause of Spanish anti-fascism. Durruti's appeal to all French revolutionaries to unite in 'a true anti-fascist front of the people' was also advanced in justification.[53]

This was to widen the existing split in the anarchist movement between the UA on the one hand, and the FAF and CGTSR on the other, the latter rejecting any kind of formal or long-term cooperation with non-anarchists. When the CASLDPE held its congress in Paris, 24–5 October 1936, the UA's proposal for a 'broadened front' was rejected overwhelmingly, since the CGTSR and the FAF had a majority on the central Paris Comité Anarcho-Syndicaliste.[54] The Comité Confédéral of the CGTSR declared at its meeting on 23 October that the UA's new committee 'can in no way

---

[48] See Le Libertaire, 25 September and 2 October 1936.   [49] Le Libertaire, 9 October 1936.
[50] Le Libertaire, 23 October and 6 November 1936.   [51] Le Libertaire, 6 November 1936.
[52] See also Le Libertaire, 7 August 1936 and Archives Nationales/Section Contemporaine F7/14721. Most of the Spanish Anarchists were far more 'popular frontist' than their French comrades.
[53] Le Libertaire, 30 October 1936.
[54] L'Espagne Antifasciste (CNT–AIT–FAI) – organ of the CASLDPE – 28 October 1936 and 7 November 1936.

claim to represent either the CNT or the FAI in France'.[55] A later statement of the residual Comité Anarcho-Syndicaliste went even further and insisted 'As far as we are concerned, those who practise such a liaison cease, *ipso facto*, to be Anarchists.'[56]

The main grounds for dissent from the Front Révolutionnaire on the part of the CGTSR and the FAF were not so much the practice of alliances with non-anarchists as such, but rather the fact that such an alliance was perceived by the dissenters as an organic alliance, a long-term and even organizational link-up which would inevitably entail jettisoning anarchist principles. However, this was not how the UA saw the Front Révolutionnaire. It was made clear that such alliances were temporary: circumstantial cooperation over specific tasks.[57] Thus, contrary to what the CGTSR and the FAF affirmed, the UA's understanding of the kind of revolutionary alliance into which it was entering was that (1) it would last only as long as proved necessary for the achievement of its specific aims; (2) such an alliance entailed no abandonment by any constituent grouping of its own principles or methods of working, beyond those adjustments implied by the will to cooperate; and (3) none of the groupings involved would exploit the alliance for partisan propaganda purposes.

However, this split became more complete as the UA went on to cooperate with an even wider range of political organizations. The most spectacular example was a meeting at the Vel d'Hiv' organized by the UA in December 1936, at which the platform included Léon Jouhaux and Marcel Cachin, the two *bêtes noires* of the anarchist movement, as well as speakers from the FAI (Magrina), the Catalan CNT (Trabal), the Aragon Council (Mavilla), the UA (Huart), the POUM (Gorkin), the Esquerra and the Generalitat (Miravitlles), the SFIO (Zyromski), the JEUNES (Jeunes Equipes Unies pour une Nouvelle Economie Sociale – Joss), and the Gauche Révolutionnaire (Pivert). It is noticeable that Pivert was allowed to speak last and that it was his speech which received most coverage in *Le Libertaire*'s report.[58] But from the autumn of 1936 the UA cooperated regularly with various groups and individuals on the left in organizing public meetings, demonstrations, fund-raising: Jean Rous (Parti Ouvrier Internationaliste), Marcel Fourrier (Comité pour la Révolution Espagnole), André Ferrat (*Que Faire?*, Association Communiste Révolutionnaire), the Parti d'Unité Prolétarienne, the Parti Frontiste,

[55] *Le Combat Syndicaliste*, 30 October 1936.
[56] *L'Espagne Antifasciste* (CNT–AIT–FAI), 7 November 1936.
[57] *Le Libertaire*, 20 November 1936.   [58] See *Le Libertaire*, 30 October 1936.

Robert Louzon and la Révolution Prolétarienne, *la Vague* and – not insignificantly – the 'reformist' Anarchists around the monthly *Plus Loin*, who had been ostracized up until this point because of their support for the war effort in 1914.[59] Although research on this has also been sparse, there is some evidence of local manifestations of the Front Révolutionnaire: in Aulnay-sous-Bois, the Trotskyists and the UA worked together, forming a group about 100 strong and seriously worrying the local PCF.[60] In the ninth *arrondissement* the Jeunesses Anarchistes Communistes and the youth section of the Gauche Révolutionnaire formally merged.[61] Joyeux gives a description of his delegation to joint talks with the local SFIO section, in the seventeenth *arrondissement*.[62]

It is difficult to separate the two aspects of the revolutionary front policy. On the one hand, it was intended as a reprise of the extra-parliamentary movement of 1934–5, able to unite the anti-stalinist left in a revolutionary opposition to the Blum government. On the other, it was a means of drumming up as much support as possible for the Spanish Republicans in general, and for the CNT–FAI and the POUM in particular.

In fact, as things developed, a clear contradiction emerged between the UA's position on the Popular Front and its solidarity work for Spain. At home, resolute opposition to the party hierarchies, to parliamentarianism, and to the myth of the anti-fascist crusade; in Spain, tacit acceptance of CNT ministers and of what was, in effect, a Popular Front government engaged in an anti-fascist war.

In certain ways, the Anarchists were better placed than some to help make the revolutionary opposition to Blum and Jouhaux succeed: they were more resolute in their critique of Blum than the Gauche Révolution-naire; they were better established in the labour movement and less ideologically demanding of potential allies than the Trotskyists. Yet, on the evidence, the policy does not seem to have been a great success. Speaking at the UA's congress of October–November 1937, Charles Ridel (alias Louis Mercier-Vega) – a member of the administrative commission – deplored the political incoherence and inconsistency of the UA, 'which launched the campaign for the Revolutionary Front, only to abandon it later'.[63] According to Joyeux, the UA's adoption of the revolutionary front policy had left each group quite free to contract alliances as and if it wished: both the local membership and the national leadership were hesitant about alliances – a

[59] See *Le Libertaire*, 26 January, 25 February, 1 July 1937.
[60] See *Le Libertaire*, 1 January 1937.
[61] See *Le Libertaire*, 6 November 1936.   [62] See Joyeux, *Souvenirs*, pp. 275–93.
[63] *Le Libertaire*, 11 November 1937.

hesitancy which Joyeux puts down to 'fifteen years of struggle against marxist political parties and reformist syndicalists', and alienation caused by anarchism's failure to prevent many of its supporters defecting to the various marxist groups since the war, an alienation which led many to shrink from further contact with such groups.[64] As for the seventeenth *arrondissement*, although Joyeux claims that the revolutionary front policy initially boosted his group, he and his fellow delegate Edrac felt alienated by the Gauche Révolutionnaire's middle-class intellectuals, and soon stopped attending what they felt was an ineffectual talking shop. For Joyeux the discourses of the various sectors of the revolutionary front were just too distinct.

Perhaps the principal function of the revolutionary front policy was to make possible the creation of the Comité pour l'Espagne Libre in October 1936 and of Solidarité Internationale Antifasciste (SIA) in November 1937. Both were quite successful as solidarity campaigns, but again showed up the inconsistency of the UA's policy. Both involved cooperation with supporters of the Popular Front government. The same policies which were accepted in Spain were opposed in France. There were various reasons for this: the acceptance of a *fait accompli* (the CNT's participation in government), the need to defeat Franco, an unwillingness to criticize a CNT to which the UA was grateful for having put anarchism back on the agenda ... and the existence within the UA of two major tendencies. Louis Anderson, editor of *Le Libertaire* from 1936 to 1939, has described this split within the UA as one between those who were above all pacifists (typified by Lecoin) and those who were above all revolutionary anti-fascists (such as Frémont).[65] It was the latter tendency which produced the revolutionary front as opposition to the reformist Popular Front. It represented a move towards a more workerist and syndicalist view of the Anarchists' role, and towards a less purist attitude to the thorny question of anarchist organization. The stereotypical 'all or nothing' image was rejected in favour of a more constructive, pragmatic and realistic anarchism with heroes like Durruti and Makhno. Revolutionary frontists wanted the movement to leave the anarchist ghetto and become an integral part of the wider revolutionary labour movement.[66]

The UA's other dominant tendency was that typified by Lecoin, a tendency more individualist than collectivist, more pacifist and 'moralist'

[64] Joyeux, *Souvenirs*, pp. 285, 287–8, 289–90.
[65] In conversation with the author, 6 April 1985.
[66] See Groupe d'anarchistes russes à l'étranger, *Plateforme d'organisation de l'Union Générale des Anarchistes (Projet)* (Paris, 1926).

than revolutionary.[67] Lecoin's method – tried in campaigns of a humanitarian nature in the 1920s – was to establish an unelected organizing
committee, and to solicit the help of almost anyone whose name would be
likely to draw attention and support.[68] This method of working mostly
complemented the Spanish tendency to reduce the political conflict to two
camps: fascism and anti-fascism. Lecoin himself tended to see the work of
the Comité pour l'Espagne Libre and of SIA as a humanitarian campaign.

If we accept Joyeux's assertion that 'for decades anarchism has swung
between two extreme tendencies – isolation in its certainties, and the drift
towards reformist or humanitarian organizations – without managing to
find a point of equilibrium between doctrinal intransigence and compromise', then I would suggest that these two extremes were represented in the
late 1930s by the FAF on the one hand, and by Lecoin and his supporters
on the other.[69] In the middle were those who tried to put into practice their
anarchist politics while at the same time, in the interests of effectiveness,
cooperating with other groups whose position on specific points was close
to theirs.

In view of the nature of the Front Révolutionnaire, as understood and
practised by the UA, it would seem reasonable to reappraise Broué and
Dorey's assertion that the Anarchists were always 'a minority swimming
against the stream'.[70] Not only were the Anarchists not as isolated as some
suggest, they also seem to have grown significantly in number in the
Popular Front period, and this was partly a consequence of the UA's
revised ideological position. The JAC, reporting in January 1937 on the
increase in sales of *Le Libertaire*, claimed that since the previous July the
anarchist movement had come to be seen once more as belonging firmly
in the labour movement, and that the revolutionary front policy was
responsible for this. Rabaut claims that, for the first time in forty years, the
Anarchists were again 'l'avant-garde de l'avant-garde'.[71]

Membership of the UA and the readership of *Le Libertaire* had both
expanded during 1935, and after July 1936 the increase accelerated.[72] *Le
Libertaire* believed that the reasons for their new popularity were threefold:
the correctness of their stance on the Popular Front government; their

---

[67] See Louis Lecoin, *Le cours d'une vie* (published by the author, 1965), and Maurice Joyeux,
'Louis Lecoin', *La Rue (revue culturelle et littéraire d'expression anarchiste)*, 11 (1971).
[68] See Lecoin, *Le cours d'une vie*.
[69] Maurice Joyeux, *Ce que je crois: réflexions sur l'anarchie* (Paris, 1984), p. 43.
[70] Broué and Dorey, 'Critiques de gauche', p. 92, fn. 3.
[71] *Le Libertaire*, 8 January 1937; Rabaut, *Tout est possible!*, p. 213.
[72] 'Témoignage de Nicolas Faucier', *Bulletin* no. 26–7 of the Centre International de
Recherches sur l'Anarchisme (Marseille annexe): *1886 ... 1936 ...*, p. 48.

consistent anti-militarism; events in Spain. Between spring 1936 and spring 1937 UA membership more then quadrupled. There were some fourteen other anarchist papers besides *Le Libertaire*, which itself on May Day 1937 – a few weeks after Clichy – printed an exceptional run of 100,000 copies.[73] At the end of 1936 an *école propagandiste* was opened.[74] Throughout the period 1936–8 new anarchist groups and regional federations were formed and links between existing groups strengthened. Disabused ex-Anarchists became active again, previously unaffiliated syndicalists discovered anarchism for the first time, and Socialists and Communists – including several in positions of responsibility – deserted their parties for the UA.[75] The non-anarchist press also began to talk about the Anarchists much more. Even *Le Temps* printed a feature based on police sources, about 'a dangerous resurgence of the anarchist movement': 'It appears that the extremists, who thought that with the rise of the Communists they would see the triumph in France of revolution, insurrection and anti-militarism, are abandoning the Communist Party to go and swell the ranks of the Anarchists.'[76]

Clearly a full assessment of the strength and role of anarchism in this period is something which has still to be carried out; but by the end of October 1937 the leadership of the UA confidently announced that it was 'the only force having the authority and influence necessary to lead the revolutionary movement'.[77]

[73] See *Le Libertaire*, 2 October 1936, 22 April and 13 May 1937 respectively. We are dependent on *Le Libertaire* itself for these statistics.
[74] *Le Libertaire*, 22 January 1937.
[75] See, for example, *Le Libertaire*, 4 December 1936, 8 January, 3 June and 8 July 1937. Anderson, interview with the author, 6 April 1985; Faucier, letter to the author, 27 May 1985.
[76] *Le Temps*, 9 October 1936. The article was quoted in its entirety in *Plus Loin*, November 1936. Cf. 'Ceux qui parlent de nous', *Le Libertaire*, 29 April 1937.
[77] *Le Libertaire*, 11 November 1937.

The French Popular Front and the politics of Jacques Doriot

ALAN FORREST

For Jacques Doriot, as for many of his generation who made the political leap from left to right, the formation of the Popular Front government in 1936 was an event of crucial importance. Following his meteoric rise through the ranks of the French Communist Party during the 1920s, Doriot had broken with the party cadres in the spring of 1934 over Moscow's insistence on a 'class against class' policy, arguing, along with many of the French left, that the first priority was a common front against fascism in Western Europe. Some months later, the PCF would follow him down the same road, but by then Doriot had been denounced for his defiance of party discipline and had finally been expelled from the party in the summer of 1934. Historians differ in the explanations they offer for this act of deliberate defiance. Was Doriot turning his back on his communist roots through a conviction that the party was dangerously wrong, through a genuine commitment to the cause of a 'front commun'?[1] Or was his action motivated rather by his vaulting ambition and irritation with the stubborn refusal of the party leadership to deviate from Moscow's view of the world?[2] Whatever the reason, the outcome is not in question. By 1936 he had established his own political party, the Parti Populaire Français, and had started his drift into an extreme and often brutally anti-democratic

[1] D. Wolf, *Doriot – du communisme à la collaboration* (Paris, 1969).
[2] J.-P. Brunet, *Jacques Doriot – du communisme au fascisme* (Paris, 1986). For his period as mayor of Saint-Denis, see Brunet's earlier work, *Saint-Denis, ville rouge, 1890–1939* (Paris, 1980), esp. chapters 16 and 17.

political discourse – the drift which would lead him to extremes of collaboration and to enthusiasm for the Légion des Volontaires Français in the Vichy period. By 1936, too, he was faced with the reality of the Popular Front government, the very kind of alliance which he had long been advocating from within the communist ranks. As R. W. Johnson has perceptively phrased it, the formation of the Front Populaire had the effect of 'freezing out' Doriot while the Communists enjoyed unprecedented national influence. Doriot could not but oppose and frustrate the new government, since the solution 'for which he had so courageously campaigned was now a threat to his political survival'.[3]

Yet Doriot remained, at least initially, loyal to the industrial workers who had formed his political audience as a young man. He prided himself on his working-class roots and on his practical experience of working life. He held in deep contempt those middle-class dreamers on the right whose politics was derived from Barrèsian nationalism, and continually talked of the workers of the Paris *banlieue* as the idealized stereotype of the sturdy, patriotic Frenchman.[4] In his introduction to Simon Sabiani's book, *Colère du peuple*, he went out of his way to praise his Marseille ally for his proletarian qualities of dynamism and 'coeur', for that love of the active life which he saw as essential to cherishing freedom itself.[5] PPF membership, too, was heavily biased in favour of workers, peasants and small businessmen, which goes far to explain Doriot's social priorities and his sometimes muted criticism of Blum's reform programmes.[6] In this regard, of course, he would claim that it was not he who had abandoned his principles in founding the PPF, but the Communists who had lost their way, becoming complacent and 'embourgeoisés'.[7] His attacks on the Popular Front concentrated on what he saw as their cowardice in giving way to the economic demands of big business, which in turn created deep alienation in the working-class suburbs of French cities. *L'Attaque*, the PPF newspaper in Lyon, summed up this attitude succinctly in its special issue for the cantonal elections of 1938, when it argued that the socially conservative elements of French society had overlooked their national duty, with the result that hundreds of thousands of workers 'pensent russe avant de penser français'.[8]

---

[3] R. W. Johnson, 'Le grand Jacques', review of Brunet's biography in *London Review of Books*, 9 October 1986, p. 9.

[4] *L'Emancipation Nationale* (hereafter *EN*), 4 July 1936.

[5] J. Doriot, introduction to S. Sabiani, *Colère du peuple* (Paris, 1936), p. vii.

[6] Wolf, *Doriot*, p. 192.   [7] J. Doriot, introduction to Sabiani, *Colère du peuple*, p. vii.

[8] *L'Attaque*, 10 October 1937.

The French Popular Front and the politics of Jacques Doriot

Underlying Doriot's pervasive distrust of the Popular Front was his new-found hatred of the Communist Party. Even though there might at times have been some common ground between him and the Radical and Socialist leadership, the role played by Thorez was sufficient to ensure that the defeat of Blum's government became a single-minded crusade whose fire was increasingly concentrated on the communist menace. Communists were accused untiringly of corruption in their municipal fiefs, of dismissing good officials to promote reliable party hacks, of organizing witch-hunts against those courageous enough to oppose them. And, above all, he continually alleged that the party which claimed to stand for the working class was doing incalculable harm to the interests of these very workers, creating social disharmony and leading their members into strikes which they could not possibly win.[9] At every available opportunity he launched himself against the party in what looked like a bid to exact every possible ounce of vengeance for the wrongs which he himself had suffered at their hands. Behind the rhetoric, of course, lay a considerable element of fear: his portrayal of the Popular Front presented a frightening image of dependence on the good will of Thorez, of endless compliance and resignation on the part of Blum. The communist commitment to the Popular Front, he warned, was one dictated by opportunism, not by principle. Communists were a fifth column in France, bent on mischief-making and the spread of revolution. Doriot's collaborator, Paul Guitard, put this rather well when he wrote that politics had always been seen as something of a game in France, a game which the PCF was ideally placed to exploit. The great error of Frenchmen, he argued, was to believe that the Communist Party was simply another political formation, 'un parti comme les autres'.[10]

What made it different in kind from other parties was, of course, its special relationship with Moscow and the Comintern. Soviet behaviour inside the Soviet Union was intolerable enough, but for Doriot the principal danger lay in its international influence, communicated through books, pamphlets and the 'cultural poison' of the Soviet cinema.[11] In his eyes members of western communist parties were often incapable of distinguishing between their own interests and those of their respective countries and the national interest of the vast and aggressive imperial power that was the Soviet motherland. This ambivalence lay at the heart of his own disenchantment with the PCF, and he could not rid himself of the

[9] *EN*, 4 July and 22 August 1936; *L'Attaque*, 20 November 1937.
[10] P. Guitard, *La France retrouvée* (Paris, 1937), p. 15.
[11] *EN*, 24 October 1936.

view that the Popular Front was 'the means of inducing the masses to support the foreign policy of the Soviet Union'.[12] It was a charge he would come back to again and again, lambasting those intellectuals who were too prone to believe Soviet optimism, praising those – like Gide – who finally saw the light and denounced Stalin, or quoting approvingly the fears of individual French communists when, like Renaud Jean, they suggested that the PCF was losing its freedom of thought and action.[13] Convinced that there could be no compromise between French socialism and stalinism, Doriot made it one of his principal goals to win over his compatriots to the necessity of conflict with Soviet Russia. Blum's apparent failure to grasp this salient truth only served to entrench Doriot's view that the prime minister was in his turn a dupe of the Soviet propaganda machine whose opinions had to be denounced and publicly exposed.[14]

In pursuing this campaign Doriot repeatedly returned to the question of the financial links between Paris and Moscow. The proof that the PCF was eternally in Russia's debt and was unable to take independent decisions without first considering Soviet interests lay in the financial obligation of the French party to its paymasters in the East. It was a difficult case to prove, and often his allegations were based on nothing more substantial than insinuation or innuendo. Jacques Duclos, who had been so indiscreet as to challenge Doriot's own financial probity and to suggest that he was dependent on German backers, became an obvious target for PPF venom; and 'l'espion Duclos' was persistently portrayed as Russia's most trusted agent inside the French communist movement. In a powerful propagandist tract published in 1937 under the title *C'est Moscou qui paie*, Doriot outlined the case he had assembled against the Communists. They ran a bureaucratic machine of some 250 officials in France, a richly-financed propaganda office, and a loss-making party press that comprised around forty titles locally and nationally. *L'Humanité* alone, he claimed, was losing several million francs each year. The membership of the PCF was not capable of shouldering a loss on such a scale; hence the logic was compelling, that Moscow was directly subsidizing the running costs of the party and was doing so with one single aim, 'to make propaganda for the Soviets in all cases and in all circumstances'.[15] For the Communist Party, he warned, the threat was grave, since this reliance ensnared them in an unequal and unpatriotic relationship with the Soviet leadership. But for

[12] J. Doriot, *La France ne sera pas un pays d'esclaves* (Paris, 1936), p. 24.
[13] *EN*, 21 November 1936; Doriot, *La France ne sera pas un pays d'esclaves*, p. 31.
[14] *EN*, 4 July 1936.
[15] J. Doriot, *C'est Moscou qui paie: toutes les preuves* (Paris, 1937), p. 39.

France the menace was just as serious. By its gold, alleged Doriot, Moscow had succeeded in detaching a sizeable part of the French population from their national loyalties. In consequence, 'Moscow can direct a large number of French citizens without reference to our national institutions.'[16]

The PPF's own platform was highly nationalistic, and it found this international influence deeply disturbing. The Popular Front was portrayed as the hapless dupe of Stalin's political guile, a coalition government that was generically weak and lacking the resolve needed to guide France through such troubled times. This weakness was of several distinct kinds – it was weak because it was a coalition of several rather ill-integrated parties, weak because it was open to the pacifism and internationalism of socialist ideology, weak above all because it was subject to persistent communist influence and pressure. The PPF attacked the government for adopting what the former saw as socially divisive policies at a time when renewal and national rebuilding were required. It questioned the government's will over the implementation of law and order: was Blum prepared to keep the peace in city streets where left-wing gangs were currently allowed to threaten Doriot's supporters and break up his party rallies? 'Are the prefects of the Republic', he asked angrily, 'under orders from Moscow?'.[17] This was in many ways the most damaging attack of all, that Blum and his ministers were little more than marionettes dancing to the tune of the Kremlin puppeteers. Stalin, he wrote in December 1936 in a tauntingly bitter phrase, 'mène toujours le bal français'.[18] It was a gibe which was difficult for the left to refute.

Stalin's role was seen as most immediately dangerous in the field of foreign affairs. In Doriot's view there was little doubt that Russia was intent on starting another world war, since he believed that the Soviet system needed another war if it were to survive. Anti-fascist speeches from the Kremlin, condemnations of Hitler by members of the Comintern, and warning notes sounded by the PCF all provided Doriot with proof that Russia was on the point of engulfing the continent in a war in which western nations were condemned to destroy themselves for a cause that was not theirs. Stalin he saw as an obsessive warmonger, 'Thorez-la-Guerre' as his most loyal disciple.[19] The outbreak of hostilities in Spain served only to confirm Doriot's worst suspicions, as volunteers – the majority of them organized through Europe's national communist parties – were kitted out and marched across the Pyrenees to defend the Spanish

---

[16] Ibid., p. vi.   [17] *EN*, 24 October 1936.   [18] *EN*, 12 December 1936.
[19] *EN*, 17 October 1936.

Republic. With men went arms and munitions, despatched secretly across the frontier by political interests that were often embarrassingly close to the French government. Doriot's campaigning on Spain was tireless. He argued endlessly the cause of neutrality and non-intervention, and any hint of partisanship by the Popular Front was treated as yet another instance of its weakness and adventurism. In this as in other matters, Doriot's populist instincts were acute. It was Frenchmen who were pulling the chestnuts of 'le petit Père Staline' out of a particularly torrid fire.[20] It was French boys who were being killed and maimed so that Russia could colonize Catalonia.[21] In working-class districts, claimed the PPF, local communist cells were being turned into emergency recruiting stations for Spain, and PCF leaders were deliberately directing their campaign at those without jobs and without hope, perpetrating a blinding fraud on the young workers of the industrial towns. L'Attaque, in its very first issue, drew a clear distinction between the young idealists whose lives were being sacrificed and the calculating and unscrupulous individuals who stood behind them – the political agents and capitalist arms-dealers who callously, almost nonchalantly, sent them to their deaths, the sort of people 'who are to be seen every Tuesday in the dock at the local magistrates' court'.[22] In Paris, Yves-Marie Sicard poked bitter fun at the morality underlying this recruitment exercise: the PCF's commissar, Marty, he explained to the unemployed, would buy them for ten francs apiece, and if they dared to desert, he would have them shot without the least compunction.[23] Blum's government, Sicard scathingly concluded, did nothing to impede such a noble enterprise.

If the PPF pilloried the communist cadres, they stressed the youthful gullibility of those men and boys who allowed themselves to be talked into service. They were the real heroes, the sons of ordinary French families where the father had served bravely in the First World War, families who had worked hard throughout their lives and who woke up in 1936 to letters of farewell from their sons and brothers or to heart-breaking telegrams from Barcelona or Gerona. Under headlines of despair the PPF lingered emotively on the agonies suffered by such families, the shock, the worry and the fear. Personal details were carefully compiled, the reader left to savour the void left by each departure. In Lyon, for instance, they listed the rollcall of boys from ordinary Lyonnais suburbs who had abandoned their

[20] EN, 21 November 1936.
[21] A. D. Rhône, 4M 236, police report for 31 December 1936.
[22] L'Attaque, 20 November 1937.   [23] EN, 30 January 1937.

families, often without a word of warning, fitted out with false passports and papers by the communist cells in Villeurbanne or Vaise. The message was clearly spelt out week after week. The youngsters who were being sacrificed, sent 'au massacre' or 'dans la boucherie', were not rabid political militants but ordinary lads from the four corners of France, lads such as one might encounter in the local bar or on the street corner.[24] They were the victims of Spain; and such was the depth of feeling which the campaign tapped that within a few months Doriot was demanding, to widespread approval, that the government repatriate the thousands who had already crossed the Pyrenees. Blum's silence was taken as further incriminating evidence of his domination by the Communists.[25]

At home Doriot painted a bleak picture of the social disorder which resulted from the Popular Front's passivity in the face of a concerted campaign of dislocation. Spain, after all, was only one of several ways in which Stalin might hope to provoke civil war in France. He also depended on the promotion of political strikes and of street violence in the major cities. The strike movement of 1936, volubly supported by the PCF, appeared to provide all the ammunition he could desire – a clear instance of politically-motivated industrial sabotage to put pressure on a government elected to represent the interests of the workers in the first place. Doriot saw such strikes as being totally unconnected with the workers' real interests, as an unwelcome political intrusion for which responsibility lay squarely with the Communists. As with Spain his campaign enjoyed a strong measure of public support, even in areas where there was little overt criticism of the Popular Front. For throughout France the damage done to the country's industrial infrastructure by the strike movement had begun to arouse a tangible public reaction. With the passage of time that reaction frequently became tinged with irritation and incomprehension, which Doriot was not slow to exploit.[26] His conviction that the Popular Front was being deliberately undermined by communist influence went far to dictate his subsequent political tactics. The Popular Front, he argued, was doomed to failure since it was a bizarre partnership of irreconcilable opposites, an alliance of necessarily contradictory aims. Its decomposition was inevitable, because of the incompatibility between 'a reformism without real reforms' and 'a communism that was not truly revolutionary'.[27] His goal therefore became to help smash such brittle unity as the

---

[24] *L'Attaque*, 20 November 1937; *L'Attaque Paysanne*, 18 December 1937.
[25] *EN*, 13 February 1937.
[26] A. D. Rhône, 4M 236, prefect's report of 22 May 1936. [27] *EN*, 5 December 1936.

Front might possess. The Socialists he depicted as honest men who allowed themselves to be shamefully deceived by their communist allies – in Doriot's colourful imagery the SFIO was allowing itself to be 'plucked' like a chicken by Thorez and his comrades.[28]

But it was on the Radical Party that he lavished his propagandist cares, since they hated any idea of violent revolution and showed themselves to be strongly neutralist over Spain. The Radicals, in Doriot's eyes, were ripe for subversion, especially in those areas, like Lyon, where radical politics was firmly dominated by a local party baron like Edouard Herriot. Here the PPF paper trod with care, attempting to woo the younger radical voters with a strongly anti-elitist approach and addressing open letters to the *mairie* and to 'Herriot-la-Guerre'.[29] In particular, it directed its appeal at those whom it called 'les évolués', men who had once supported the concept of a Popular Front but who had since seen the error of their ways.[30]

With this clientele in his sights, Doriot widened his attack to embrace social and economic issues. His assault on the handling of the economy had to be fairly cautious, in that he had no wish to side with the conservatives and put his working-class support at risk. Hence he tended to concentrate on what he represented as Blum's weakness and mismanagement, seizing on spiralling prices to attack the government for its inadequate control of the economy. Again the public was sensitive to this issue, since rising prices were eroding many of the social gains of the Popular Front. In Lyon, for instance, the prefect reported that local opinion was turned less against the government than against speculators and hoarders: there were fears that big business was using dishonest means to pursue its campaign against the Popular Front, including 'the systematic withdrawal from the market of essential foodstuffs'.[31] This was an upsurge of opinion that did not easily fit in with traditional conservatism, one on which Doriot felt that he might capitalize. But his most comprehensive attacks on Blum focused on the prime minister's inability to support the currency. The SFIO, like other parties of the Popular Front, had promised that it would resist all calls to devalue; in November 1935 Blum had indicated to the pro-devaluation Paul Reynaud that socialist policy would accept neither deflation nor devaluation, a popular if utterly unreal stance that would backfire as soon as his party was in government.[32] Hence both the devaluations over which

---

[28] J. Doriot, *La France avec nous!* (Paris, 1937), p. 17.
[29] *L'Attaque*, 13 and 20 November 1937.
[30] A. D. Rhône, 4M 236, prefect's report of 23 January 1937.
[31] A. D. Rhône, 4M 236, report of *commissaire spécial* to prefect of Rhône, 24 November 1936.
[32] J. Jackson, *The Politics of Depression in France, 1932–1936* (Cambridge, 1985), pp. 192ff.

he presided seemed like humiliating disavowals of his former policy, and the PPF rushed to capitalize. They pointed to the many victims of devaluation, from the peasantry to the middle classes and those with small savings, victims who included, in Doriot's analysis, the Popular Front itself. Devaluation represented for him the most outward symptom of Blum's economic failures. It provided the evidence which he had been seeking that – as he triumphantly proclaimed in July 1937 – 'the Popular Front has been reduced to bankruptcy'.[33]

Much of his economic criticism of Blum was in fact thinly-veiled social criticism, criticism of the effects which his economic measures were having on ordinary Frenchmen. As the months passed, he came increasingly to identify with the losers, to champion the small businessman and the peasant farmer who were, in his view, the real victims of Blum's social legislation. In this respect his approach came to resemble that of the more conventional right, supporting the little man against the big battalions of the state and the trade unions. Peasants, he suggested, were particularly at risk at a time when small farms were being merged and marginal land was being abandoned. They had nothing to gain from the Popular Front, from the banks which wanted to mortgage peasant lands for their own profits, from the Socialists who wished to impose the wishes of the cities and of urban officialdom, from the Communists who wanted to suppress property-ownership and the freedom to work without government regulation.[34] But Doriot's attempts to woo peasants and independent artisans to the cause of the PPF cannot obscure his continued commitment to the interests of the working class. The ideology of the new party, though nationalist, retained a commitment to 'le social', to social reform and social legislation. It would, said Raymond Millet, 'take from capitalism whatever seems useful, but would prevent it from turning the country into a source of profit'.[35] In consequence Doriot was discriminating in his attacks on Blum's social achievement: he censured the CGT's role in measures like the forty-hour law, but was careful to express himself favourable to the aims underlying the reform. Indeed, where he did distance himself from the government's social programme, it was often to chide them for lack of courage or of credibility. Blum, he implied, had done too little for the unemployed, had not pursued a sufficiently vigorous plan to guarantee apprenticeships for young workers, or had allowed the poor to live in

[33] *EN*, 3 July 1937.   [34] *L'Attaque*, 27 November 1937.
[35] R. Millet, *Doriot et ses compagnons* (Paris, 1937), p. 67.

degrading slum conditions.[36] He had betrayed the legitimate aspirations of the working class, while doing nothing to disturb the complacency of big business. It was here that the old communist in Doriot showed through most clearly, since for him it seemed inadmissable that the capitalist structure of France should be allowed to remain intact, with investment decisions reliant on individual whim and the dictates of the market, while unemployment was ravaging the lives of millions. In the words of his Lyon newspaper, Doriot remained an impassioned social campaigner, 'Doriot the worker from Saint-Denis, Doriot who has voted for the social laws proposed by the Popular Front and who, defending the workers against individual greed, battles energetically against social conservatism'.[37]

He most clearly resembled the militant he had been when he was denouncing the freedom of manoeuvre that was allowed to private business interests. The Popular Front, he implied, might talk the language of the working class, yet it did nothing to control the abuses of capital, abuses which were as damaging to workers as they were threatening to the fortunes of small businessmen. Its anti-trust legislation was feeble to the point of being laughable, an act of 'abdication' in the face of business pressure, while the social reforms that reached the statute book risked remaining inoperative because of the determined opposition of 'les gros'. Doriot, it should be stressed, was not interested in extending political power to the workers, believing that the sort of class conflict preached by the left only undermined their real interests. 'We belong', he wrote, 'to that persuasion which demands true harmony between capital and labour', and that harmony could be achieved only by burying the class-against-class dogmas of the PCF.[38] But he remained deeply hostile to big business and to any government which seemed too pliant to their demands. It was the nation, not the individual, that had to be served, and in this regard his judgment of Blum's government became increasingly harsh with the passage of time. Economically he saw France condemned to a long period of decline and mediocrity, largely because the social benefits conferred by the government ate deep into the economic capacity of the country. Socially there were too many losers and too few who reaped any tangible benefit. Inflation, devaluation and high levels of unemployment all contributed to the destruction of the social paradise which the left was intent on creating. Politically the country was exposed and undefended. The

[36] *EN*, 8 August 1936 and 6 February 1937; *L'Attaque*, 11 December 1937.
[37] *L'Attaque*, 4 December 1937.
[38] J. Doriot, *Refaire la France* (Paris, 1938), p. 42.

Popular Front was leaving France in a weaker condition than when it had assumed power, and this came increasingly to outrage his nationalist sensibilities. Zeev Sternhell is, of course, right to see marked similarities between this kind of nationalism and the 'vieille idéologie jaune' of the protofascist right.[39] The PPF was increasingly drawn into a familiar discourse of decline and decadence, of lament for a national interest which had been abandoned to ideologues and internationalists. The enemy within, the invader encamped on French soil, the seed of French social destruction – the images used might vary, but the message was the same. The Popular Front was presiding over the decline of French values and the collapse of French confidence. Its most abiding fault for Doriot and his followers was less wickedness than ingenuousness, the naive assumption that the Communist Party could be trusted or regarded as 'un parti comme les autres'.

39 Z. Sternhell, *Ni droite ni gauche: l'idéologie fasciste en France* (Paris, 1983), p. 183.

The Blum government, the Conseil National Economique and economic policy

ADRIAN ROSSITER

Blum came into office with a nearly impossible economic mission – to increase the purchasing power of the working class in a manner that was permanent, generally felt and yet still under some central control. Retaliatory price increases, patchy distribution of the benefits and macroeconomic rigidity soon undid most of what had been achieved in that respect. The social achievement, on the other hand, was more considerable. The laws restricting the working week to a maximum of forty hours and providing paid holidays are the elements which are most frequently recalled, for they became a kind of political shibboleth by which loyalty to the Popular Front was judged – and which Blum himself invoked as his greatest contribution to the well-being of working people.[1] However, a distant observer comparing the France of 1935 with that of 1937 (or indeed any later date) would immediately realize that an even more profound change had been wrought – by the introduction of compulsory collective bargaining into industrial relations.

That development can be regarded from several points of view. Political intervention fell under three heads. The Popular Front's electoral victory on 3 May 1936 made reform possible, if not inevitable. Then came the great wave of strikes and the Matignon conference which sought to resolve

---

[1] Léon Blum, 'La prison, le procès, la déportation', *L'Oeuvre de Léon Blum*, vol. v, *1940–45* (Paris, 1955), pp. 288–9; see, too, Julian Jackson's essay in this collection.

them.[2] Thirdly, the law of 24 June 1936 made it obligatory to negotiate wages and working conditions by collective contract. But there was also an internal evolution, which operated on quite another plane from parliamentary politics – for collective bargaining evidently depended on direct dialogue between unions and bosses. Indeed, close examination of the procedure involved reveals a surprising degree of cooperation, if not outright complicity, between the opposing forces. The forum for this activity was the Conseil National Economique, a technical council which has been overlooked by most historians. Bosses and workers there were regularly consulted about the precise way that collective contracts, and several other key measures, were put into effect.

This is all the more surprising in that the Popular Front has often been portrayed as a period of unremitting confrontation in domestic politics. One need only consider the successive waves of factory occupations, not just in June 1936, but also later that year, at the end of 1937, and in spring 1938, to be tempted to jump to one of two conclusions. Either collective bargaining was a superficial formality, changing nothing in the fundamental class struggle; or the bosses were still planning to end all statutory relations with the trade union movement, and would ultimately have achieved this as part of their counter-attack from 1938 onwards. Neither judgement seems true to reality. Enforcing collective contracts made a real impact, both in specific, concrete instances and above all on the general attitudes of all three sets of 'social partners'. The Conseil National Economique played an essential part in the process. When one comes to look at the dynamics of this interaction, it appears that the council was not just a battleground for opposing interests, but actually helped their respective positions evolve. Moreover, the law remained in place even after the employers had succeeded in undoing much of the Matignon settlement. In fact, it helped defend them against the only weapon of the workers which they really feared – spontaneous occupation of the workplace. As ever, institutionalization of social relations led to increased opportunities for the protagonists.

The three following sections will show why collective bargaining was still a sensitive question after 1936; how the Conseil National Economique was specially equipped to answer the difficulties arising; and what form its

---

[2] This element was probably even more important than the first one. As with paid holidays, devaluation, and (above all) the forty-hour week, collective contracts *were not actually mentioned* in the Popular Front election manifesto, but were decided at a later stage, in a quite different way from that which is usually recounted: Adrian Rossiter, 'Popular Front economic policy and the Matignon negotiations', *Historical Journal* (July–September 1987).

intervention took. The conclusions will suggest some ways in which consultation of the council helped shape the course of industrial relations during and after the Popular Front.

I

There were both technical and ideological problems to implementing collective contracts. The technical complications stemmed from the traditionally low density of unionization in France. Trade unions were extremely weak until the Popular Front came to power: net membership stood at little over 10 per cent of the work-force, for even the peaks (in coal-mining, merchant marine and the docks) did not much exceed 25 per cent, while certain key sectors, notably chemicals, eastern metallurgy and the food industries, were hardly covered at all.[3] Matters were made worse by sectarianism. Before reuniting during the winter of 1935–6, the communist CGTU and the reformist CGT fought a bitter civil war; after Matignon, a new sort of 'yellow trade unionism' appeared, the Syndicats professionnels français, closely linked to De La Rocque's PSF; and the Christian CFTC was a constant third element. The huge jump in numbers after June 1936 was not an unqualified advantage, for it meant that experienced activists were spread very thinly on the ground, tending to lose touch with their militant new recruits, which exacerbated fears of communist 'infiltration', particularly in private heavy industry. On the other side, individualism again took its toll – there were often rival producers' associations; the French entrepreneur disliked revealing secrets even to his chosen confederates; and he would not willingly authorize others to negotiate on his behalf. Finally, there was the inherently complex nature of the French economy, with businesses ranging from large, modern factories to artisan workshops, a widespread preference for the specialized luxury market, and regional variations in the cost of living and in availability of transport, raw materials or alternative employment. When all these factors came into play in a single trade, it would be extremely difficult to create a comprehensive collective contract.

The ideological difficulties came only from the employers, though that simplification of matters was quite recent. Even in 1934, the Communists had denounced all collective bargaining as class collaboration.[4] This position was clearly symptomatic of their isolation in a separate, weaker

---

[3] Pierre Laroque, *Las rapports entre patrons et ouvriers* (Paris, 1938), pp. 310–11.
[4] Conseil national économique, *Les conventions collectives de travail* (Paris, 1934), p. 97.

158

confederation, but it underlies how important reunification of the CGT was to the Popular Front. The bosses' objections were equally tactical, for they correctly assumed that they had more to lose by recognizing trade unions' right to represent the work-force *en bloc*, than they could hope to gain by organizing a common front themselves. But their self-interest conveniently sheltered behind two questions of principle: first, that individualism was in fact the best guarantee of the laissez-faire, free-market liberalism on which the French economy had been based, at least in appearances, since the Revolution.[5] If workers and employers relied on summit organizations to contest their differences on the national stage, the state would inevitably be expected to conciliate and arbitrate – which could only increase its burden at a time when it was already under tremendous strain. Secondly, union pluralism turned the choice of negotiating-partner into a political statement, rather than an objective commercial decision.[6] Why should entrepreneurs be expected to assume such responsibilities, when the French state itself had refused, for largely diplomatic reasons, to recognize the CGTU throughout the 1920s and 1930s?

At one level, the May strikes and the Matignon conference changed everything. There was a massive increase in union membership, so the CGT became more representative of the workforce in general; the bosses were forced to rally behind the leadership of the Confédération Générale de la Production Française (CGPF); Blum and his ministers presided over an empirical, one-off arbitration, and the collective-bargaining law was passed by parliament almost unanimously. But the fundamental problems remained and, without adequate provision, they would certainly arise again, for the special conditions of May–June 1936 could not be expected to last indefinitely.

The new law had two key features. The first was that the contracts must be negotiated by fully competent bodies, so as to ensure that they answered the real needs of the trade in question, and to maximize their chances of lasting. The second point was to create a mechanism whereby such agreements could be extended over as large a field as possible, and might take in employers and workers who had not participated in drafting them, even indirectly. Otherwise, a substantial element in each profession would either cling to a separate arrangement (possibly negotiated many years

5 Richard F. Kuisel, *Capitalism and the State in Modern France* (Cambridge, 1981), pp. 1–30.
6 Adrian Rossiter, 'Experiments with corporatist politics in Republican France, 1916–1939' (D. Phil. thesis, Oxford, 1986), pp. 162–3.

before), or even carry on without one at all. Thus both features of the law (competence, and 'extension') turned on the key question of *representativeness*. Unlike previous legislation, which merely recognized collective bargaining as a legally acceptable activity, the 1936 law was restrictive: only 'the most representative organizations' in a particular trade and region were allowed to negotiate such a contract. Similarly, in order for the minister of labour to make it compulsory – without which the anomalies and free-riders would continue unabated – he had to establish that this was in the general interest, that all the original clauses remained valid and appropriate, and that the earlier signatories were still genuinely 'representative' in the new context.

This work was evidently far too technical and urgent for parliament to debate each instance where extension might be required; yet, since the principle involved was one of submitting individual liberties to the general will, it clearly belonged to the political domain. The response, as is well known, was to pass just a *loi cadre* on 24 June 1936, that is to say, a piece of enabling legislation whereby parliament approved the principle and then empowered government to implement it in each specific sector, according to a general procedure.[7] What is not usually appreciated is that although this manoeuvre answered the legal difficulty, it did not in itself provide a political solution. These questions were rather too sensitive – certainly too time-consuming – to be entrusted purely to the traditional mechanisms of the ministry of labour; indeed, under such circumstances they might well not win the lasting support of the trade unionists and businessmen who would have to put them into effect. On the other hand, neither the Socialists in government nor their interlocutors in the CGT would willingly have turned to the third power in the state, the judiciary, for they felt that judges were too conservative to defend the workers' interests adequately.[8]

As the introduction has already suggested, the Popular Front's strategy was to entrust the essential part of the task to the Conseil National Economique. This was itself a significant departure, for after a promising start that body had come to be regarded with indifference by most Radicals, mistrust by doctrinaire Socialists, and outright hostility by the Communists. Still more surprising is the realization that the council's action helped to maintain the momentum of the new economic policy after

---

[7] *Journal officiel de la République Française, lois et décrets* (henceforth: J.O.), 26 June 1936, pp. 6,698–9. For parallels with the forty-hours law, and the general importance of *lois cadres*, see André Philip's comments in R. Rémond and P. Renouvin, *Léon Blum, chef de gouvernement 1936–37*, 2nd edition (Paris, 1981), p. 102.

[8] Joel Colton, *Compulsory Labor Arbitration in France 1936–1939* (New York, 1951), pp. 46–7, 51.

Blum's fall in June 1937, and even later, when Daladier reverted to a centre/right majority.

II

The Conseil National Economique (CNE) was set up by the Radicals in 1924–5, responding to demands by the CGT that worker representatives should help plan official economic strategy. Various other interests (such as industrialists, farmers, cooperatives, academics) were also brought in, so as to produce a general economic advisory council, of the sort then much in fashion throughout the capitalist world. In the French case, however, its task was essentially one of 'information', in that it produced only studies and recommendations, which government and parliament might *optionally* take into account.[9] It intervened in politics even less than, for instance, Weimar's *Reichswirtschaftsrat*. In its first ten years, 1925–35, the CNE suffered from the repeated failure of both left-wing and right-wing governments either to guarantee its status with a definitive law, or even to use its existing facilities to the greatest possible extent. Yet there are certain aspects which merit comment.

First, there is the way that its membership was defined: a special decree determined which specific bodies (unions, business federations, etc.) were the most typical ('les plus représentatives') of the socio-economic activities to be consulted.[10] But the choice of delegate was left entirely to those pressure groups, and no outside interference was permitted. The principle of granting authority to 'most representative organizations' came directly from the constitution of the International Labour Organization; in 1936, it would answer some of the trickiest aspects of legislating for collective contracts. Secondly, the CNE structure rejected the simple worker–boss parity characteristic of many other advisory bodies in France: it contained several 'experts' and interests straddling the left/right divide, for example the association for large families, regional transport offices and local government agencies. Thirdly, even in its earlier, provisional period, the council produced a wide range of reports on important technical questions – economic infrastructure, international action against the depression, and, at the end of 1934, a detailed study of collective bargaining, which openly regretted its comparative rarity in France, and suggested how matters might be improved. The bosses who had let that report through

[9] *JO*, 17 January 1925, pp. 698–700.
[10] *JO*, 11 April 1925, p. 3703 (an *arrêté* dated 9 April).

were virtually disowned by their organizations, and, as happened all too often in the period, no legislative action resulted. But the machinery was kept moving, and the 'social partners' stayed in contact, however wary; under the totally different conditions after May 1936, this tradition was to count for a great deal, and the council acquired a new importance.

Indeed, the next vital step came even before that juncture. In early 1936, each house of parliament held a debate on the CNE, and passed a bill granting it full legal status and administrative autonomy. Thus – my fourth point – the provisional period was definitely over, and historians who fail to take account of this are again in danger of underestimating the institution. However, this was scarcely a Popular Front measure: it came in the 'stalemated' fifteenth legislature, for its passage into law represents the sole success of the special parliamentary commissions formed after the 6 February 1934 riots. Moreover, the PCF rejected its implicit class collaboration; the Radicals showed little interest, despite their links with the council's origins; and, as we shall see, most Socialists were muted in their support. The bill's sponsors were all left-wing dissidents: Joseph Paul-Boncour, Paul Ramadier, Louis Sellier, Georges Potut.

The conflict of ideas behind any project to incorporate economic interests into the democratic system represents at once the most difficult aspect of the CNE, and also one which, for lack of space, this essay will treat only briefly.[11]

There is an inherent ambiguity in such a council. Is its primary function representative? Or is it a nakedly privileged forum for special interests, a sort of mandate accorded to economic competence and expertise? Neither notion can readily be reconciled with classic republicanism: the former because an 'economic chamber' would undermine the political assemblies; and the latter because any attribution of power to expertise would be inherently undemocratic. A recent study shows how these dangers and contradictions were never fully overcome: limiting the council's role to one of respectful advice helped defuse the tension, but did not resolve it.[12] During the late 1920s and 1930s, some socialist theoreticians were tempted by rationalization and planning, and the internal logic of their argument would have required building the economy around a series of joint councils, more or less modelled on the CNE; but, by the end of 1935, the campaign for a plan had been defeated. Thus the official socialist reaction

[11] For more details, see Rossiter, D. Phil., pp. 108–42.

[12] Giuliana Gemelli, 'Une institution ambivalente: le Conseil national économique', *Urbi*, 10 (1987), 92–9 – an abridged translation of an article in *Rivista di Storia Contemporanea*, 4 (1984).

to the new council in February 1936 was scarcely enthusiastic: 'those vital nationalizations, which are the only thing to bring the crisis to an end, cannot conceivably come from the CNE, *an essentially conservative body*'.[13]

However, these equivocations did not strike at the heart of the council, and the historian cited above is rather misleading when she portrays its role after 1936 as the 'fluttering vector' of a 'fragile social consensus'.[14] A firm counter-indication comes from Emile Roche, a contemporary politician who went on to preside over the equivalent council during the Fourth Republic:

> A good historian of the CNE would have to distinguish between two periods, the first being when the 1925 legislation was in force, and the second after the reform of 1936. He would then show how the Council found its role significantly increased in that second period. But if he based his argument only on government acts and parliamentary bills, he would scarcely reveal the full extent of the progress achieved.[15]

For once, these hints of an 'untold story' are more than wild innuendo or an impossible challenge – the archives of the CNE survived both the Occupation and subsequent upheavals, and, recently discovered in the Palais d'Iéna, where they had been hidden even from the Archives Nationales, they give a unique insight into economic affairs in interwar France.[16]

The reform of March 1936 actually changed the basis of the council quite profoundly. Under the 1925 arrangement, representation came under three heads – consumers, labour, capital – which were only roughly subdivided between agriculture, industry and commerce. There were several reasons for this vagueness, not least that the alternative, a really hierarchical structure, would have seemed all too close to the reactionary, anti-capitalist model advocated by Action Française supporters, and

---

[13] *Le Populaire*, 13 February 1936 (emphasis added).

[14] There are also a couple of slips which, though minor errors of scholarship, have wider implications for her analysis: the reform of the CNE is wrongly attributed to the Popular Front government; and the council's general secretary, Georges Cahen-Salvador, is confused with his son Jean (who was the actual author of the work on interest-group representation which she cites).

[15] Emile Roche, 'Georges Cahen-Salvador: le secrétaire-général du CNE' in Anon, *Georges Cahen-Salvador 1875–1963*, no date/place (subsequent to funeral service at Conseil d'Etat, 23 February 1962), p. 20.

[16] For a few more details, see Rossiter, D.Phil, p. 344. My thesis (esp. pp. 305–26) made use of this source to investigate another aspect of 'corporatist politics' in the Third Republic – compulsory cartellization. The present essay is based on further spot checks into the collection, which has now been transferred to the Archives Nationales, but is still being classed and catalogued: where possible, I shall cite alternative archival or semi-public sources (e.g. the CNE *Bulletin*, of which there is an incomplete run in FNSP library), but on occasions I shall have simply to indicate: CNE, plus a description of the document in question.

actually being initiated in neighbouring Latin countries. In 1934–6, however, under the impetus of the eminently anti-fascist Paul-Boncour, the council was reinforced by twenty *sections professionnels*, which did bear some superficial resemblance to Italian *corporazione*. They were strictly *paritaire*, that is to say under the equal and joint management of employees and bosses, without any third-party intervention; and they had the same objective of embracing all the interests and expertise within a particular trade. But these *sections* had no innate right to regulate their profession, and they were created in the most even-handed, flexible manner imaginable. In April and May 1936, a massive census was undertaken of trade associations, unions and organized interests in France; on the strength of the replies received, a draft decree defined the different categories and the relative allocation of delegates. The CNE itself debated and approved these measures, and only then did they become law.[17]

The process had a triple significance. For the first time, there was a systematic classing of the economy oriented around unions and their own methods of demarcation.[18] Secondly, the CNE had in effect been asked to give an opinion on a draft decree, *before* it was published or became fixed in law – this was a notable widening of its customary authority, and the happy results seem to have favourably impressed those responsible for preparing the Popular Front's economic legislation, for the precedent was soon copied. Thirdly, the reform of March 1936 had actually created a new strength out of the council's ambiguities. It was still only consultative, and yet the question of representativeness had been addressed by creating the *sections*. These were the basic units, the essential agents, of the new CNE, but they were prevented from usurping all its functions by the continuing pre-eminence of the *commission permanente*, to which all resolutions had to be submitted. Power operated there on a tripartite basis: just over a third of the seats went to workers' representatives and their allies; slightly fewer were held by the CGPF and Chambers of Commerce; and the remainder were attributed to agriculture, with a sprinkling of 'experts' and special interests. Thus each part of the council answered a different need – the *sections* provided specific professional expertise, but being *paritaire*, could not break a deadlock between workers and bosses; the *commission permanente* considered matters from the strategic point of view, because the summit organizations predominated there; the Assembly was the sovereign body,

[17] *JO*, 16 April 1936, p. 4084; 23 July 1936, pp. 7749–51.
[18] Their census replies are already available to the public, and represent a precious source of data for the social historian: Archives Nationales (AN), CE 10 to 33.

'a living representation ... the most exact and the most direct possible, of all economic interests in the country'.[19]

III

This mixture was precisely what the Blum government needed to enact its social legislation as effectively as possible. The *lois cadres* on collective contracts and the forty hours leaned heavily on the CNE's recommendations for their implementation. An elaborate process involving at least four stages was devised. A union or professional body requested that the measure in question be extended to its particular sector; the ministry invited replies from all other parties concerned, and drafted a text; this went to the relevant *section* of the CNE for its comment, which was then reviewed by the *commission permanente* (this extra stage was successfully imposed by the council – the government had envisaged direct consultation of the *sections*, which would have been against CNE rules); finally, these two formal opinions were submitted to the ministry for consideration. Each subsequent decree and *arrêté* contained in its preamble the phrase 'having consulted the Conseil National Economique'. Some examples from the collective-bargaining act will show how and why this procedure mattered.

On 12 June 1936, a collective contract, covering most aspects of metallurgy and mechanical engineering in and around Paris, was signed between the CGT and the local bosses' union, GIM, plus the Citroën company, which was not a member.[20] In December, the *arrêté d'extension* drafted by the ministry came before the twelfth *section* of the CNE. The workers and employers there not only approved it, but stiffened its provisions by rejecting a protest from a coach builders' federation, for they were able to prove that this body had paid a contribution to GIM funds, and thus GIM had a valid claim to speak on its behalf.[21] That decision was perhaps not surprising, for almost half the bosses on the twelfth *section* were signatories to the contract, and needed to cover against unfair competition from companies paying lower wage rates; the unions' interest was self-evident. However, this 'shared responsibility' – not to use a stronger expression – amongst the CNE members went rather further, and governed the great majority of their interventions in the collective bargaining act.

[19] Joseph Paul-Boncour, *Journal officiel, Débats parlementaires, Chambre des députés*, 11 February 1936, p. 334.
[20] The full title of GIM was 'le Groupement des Industries Métallurgiques Mécaniques et Connexes dans la Région Parisienne.
[21] AN, F²² 1633, *avis* of twelfth *section*, 11 December 1936.

165

When the same contract came up for renegotiation in 1938, the *section* rejected two (conflicting) requests for special treatment – one from workers in the suburbs, demanding the full Parisian cost-of-living allowance; the other from bosses in the same area, the Seine-et-Oise, asking to be exempted from the contract altogether, on the grounds that conditions there were entirely different from in the capital.[22] On another occasion, the twelfth *section* allowed a 'national' agreement (one negotiated without any geographical limit, and signed by the most representative organizations at summit level) to subsume various regional ones, for it was held that 'special conditions' obtained: public authorities being a major client here, the same terms should be presented all over the country. This decision had the effect of depriving locally representative bodies – on both sides of industry – of the right to veto any contract in their particular area, and was, strictly speaking, illegal; certainly, the ministry could not have carried it off if the CNE had refused its assent.[23] To take a third example, an overwhelming majority of workers and bosses on the *commission permanente* decided that even in a sector like house-building in the Savoie, where 85 per cent of companies were run by self-employed craftsmen, the federation of artisans should not be recognized as 'most representative', but instead an escape clause 'reserving all rights and opportunities for the artisan class' should be appended to a patently inappropriate agreement.[24]

Perhaps the most thought-provoking evidence is numerical/chronological: under the high noon of the Popular Front (in precise terms, from June 1936 to 15 March 1937, by which time the 'pause' was in full operation), only thirteen draft *arrêtés* were received by the CNE; by the end of 1937, however, a further 125 had passed through the system, requiring the *sections* to meet more than sixty times; between January and May 1938, there were ninety-five more under consideration; in the next six months (a period of mounting disagreement, prior to virtual abandoning of the forty-hours law in November 1938), the council reported on no fewer than 163 *projets d'extension*; and at the height of the employers' counter-offensive from December 1938 to February 1939, ninety more compulsory contracts (including amendments resulting from arbitration decisions) were approved.[25] These figures suggest two points. The frequency with which

---

[22] AN, F²² 1633, *avis* of twelfth *section*, 18 August 1938.
[23] *Bulletin périodique du Conseil National Economique* (henceforth, *Bulletin*), I (October 1936 – January 1938), 81.
[24] CNE: *commission permanente* minutes, 8 February 1937.
[25] See respectively, *Bulletin* I, 2 and 77; II (February–May 1938), 46; III (June–November 1938), 30; IV (December–January 1939), 38.

collective bargaining was made compulsory increased steadily from 1936 to 1939; over the five periods defined above, the rate progressed from 2, to 13, to 19, to 27, to 30 contracts per month. Secondly, it proceeded by a different rhythm from the ebb and flow of the Popular Front: indeed, it actually accelerated at moments of greatest tension, whatever the outcome. Note that these were all real, individual negotiations; the figures do not include temporary renewal of existing contracts by order of parliament, as happened in July 1937 and January 1938; thus each one implies the imposition of collective bargaining in an area where it had previously been optional. It cannot be claimed that these contracts were uniformly 'good' for the workers, nor that the CNE's advice was always followed by the labour ministry, but the general sense of its intervention was well defined by its general secretary, Cahen-Salvador:

Our task has been not so much to reconcile disputes between bosses' and workers' delegations, as to settle conflicts of interest separating signatories to the contract (employees and employers together) from those who until then shirked from applying it. Our *sections* have had to undertake real arbitration.[26]

Given that establishing collective bargaining had been for years one of the CGT's most persistent demands, the continuation of the practice under the 'neo-liberal reaction' of 1938–9 must, on balance, be regarded as a significant development.

Moreover, the mechanism of consulting the CNE gave vested interests an opportunity to air grievances before the authorities could present them with a *fait accompli*; and, on chosen ground, the council's resistance could be surprisingly effective. At the end of July 1938, during negotiations for modification and renewal of the metallurgy contract, the CGT insisted on making it apply to certain toy manufacturers, on the grounds that the material used (metal) counted more – for it was easier to define – than did the purpose to which it was put (making toys). Ramadier, a genuinely sympathetic minister, only temporized, promising a 'special decision' on some other occasion. However, two weeks later, Pomaret, the new minister appointed precisely to unblock restrictive practices, decided to caution prefects against unnecessary confrontation on this issue:

For sure, CNE recommendations cannot bind the courts, whose supreme right it will be, if required, to give judgement on any claims or disputes arising ... However, you are doubtless well aware that the council possesses *such moral*

---

[26] CNE: general secretary's report, 15 March 1937, p. 11.

authority, thanks to the rules governing its membership, that the opinion which it has expressed on this question *has a force which one could scarcely overestimate.*[27]

It is striking how wide-ranging were the terms in which the minister couched his warning, and that they referred to the CNE, not to the CGT: under the prevailing circumstances, the unions could not have achieved such a victory on their own.

Three further instances of important CNE action should be cited. In the first few months of their work, the *sections* often sent contracts back for redrafting, demanding more provision against 'abnormally low wages' or in favour of skilled workers, before they would approve them – according to Cahen-Salvador, the bosses and workers there generally agreed on this point.[28] Secondly, CNE intervention could sometimes restrict the scope of the law, rather than widen it: whenever a contract was extended, the *commission permanente* insisted on eliminating anything extraneous to the conduct of industrial relations *per se*, even important concessions which had been agreed in the original, on-the-spot negotiations. Thus it ruled out any clause which sought to affect relations with third parties (whether through controlling prices or by restricting cartels), or which limited the hiring of new personnel (the 'closed shop' was specifically forbidden), or which obliged businesses to open and shut at particular times.[29] Indeed, contracts tended to be silent even about the forty-hour week and arbitration, leaving these issues to be regulated by the specific national legislation. This development, which stemmed directly from the council's decision not to let contracts exceed their strictest possible limits, was of vital importance, for it focused bosses' hostility on other items of policy, leaving collective bargaining intact. Moreover, it meant that the contracts themselves were potentially 'neutral' and might eventually be deployed in the employers' interest.

Thirdly, the council revealed at a very early stage a crucial ambiguity concerning the 'extended' contracts. Since they originated from private bargains negotiated between free agents, they were subject to civil law only; on the other hand, surely the act of extension granted them the same force as a 'statutory edict or regulation'? But the law made no special provision for enforcement, and implied that an extended contract would correspond in all respects with the spirit of its original. In theory, then, no one outside the firm could prevent the owner from making a private deal

---

[27] AN, F²² 1633, ministry of labour circular to prefects, 5 September 1938 (emphasis added).
[28] *Bulletin* I, 80 and 88–9.   [29] *Bulletin* I, 87–91.

with his workforce to ignore a contract, *although it had been made 'obligatory'* – for third parties cannot initiate a civil lawsuit.[30] If businessmen had secretly prayed for a loop-hole to save them from compulsory collective bargaining, this was surely it. Yet all their representatives on the CNE *commission permanente* immediately consented to give labour inspectors the task of *enforcing* extended contracts, and then during debate in General Assembly on 15 March 1937, they tacitly admitted that this meant equipping them with powers under the criminal law. Even more surprising, they accepted that the practical effects (wage rises) of a compulsory contract should be backdated at least as far as the beginning of the extension procedure, and possibly right back to the date of the original free contract, for otherwise some bosses might be tempted to procrastinate, and confront the others with unfair competition.[31] The Conseil d'Etat denounced this as retrospective legislation and, naturally, the Popular Front dared not insist. Nonetheless, a year later, the council renewed its report in the same terms.[32] This time the demands about using labour inspectors were enacted – by one of Daladier's decree laws, which are usually presented in a purely conservative light.[33]

IV

How then, can the CNE's activity best be summarized? One cannot claim that it consistently enabled business and labour to impose their will on political circles – though they came close to such a result on those (relatively rare) occasions where they had interests in common. Rather, the council played a crucial part both in implementing the Popular Front's social policies, and then in revealing some new possibilities inherent in them. Without that intervention, the programme would have been heavily subject to the whims and prejudices of senior civil servants and judges: indeed, the logic of the *lois cadres* had led at least one historian to state dogmatically that such was the case.[34] Still more important, a full

---

30 CNE, dossier on 1936 collective-bargaining law: Ivan Martin initial report, 30 January 1937; *commission permanente* minutes, 1 February 1937; General Assembly, 15 March 1937.
31 Conseil National Economique (rapporteur Ivan Martin), *Les problèmes posés par les conventions collectives du travail* (Paris, 1937), pp. 9–11.
32 CNE, dossier on 1936 collective bargaining law: *commission permanente* minutes, 21 June 1937; General Assembly, 28–9 March 1938, 'Avis concernant les modifications à apporter à la loi du 24 juin 1936'.
33 *JO*, 3 May 1938, p. 4956 (articles 17 and 18).
34 Theodore Zeldin, *France 1848–1945*, paperback edition (Oxford 1979, 1981), vol. 1, pp. 276–7; vol. 5, pp. 311–12.

appreciation of the Council's role offers a new insight into how some employers reacted to the changes in society which the Popular Front was both mirroring and provoking.[35]

Collective contracts, together with arbitration, ended up covering the bosses' Achilles heel – their relations with a militant workforce which, for much of the period, threatened them with occupations of their property. The Blum government and its immediate successors were aware of this, and toyed with the idea of 'neutralization' – enforced closure of the workplace pending any arbitration judgement; but, once the Senate had vetoed that option, the system no longer held any terrors for the *patronat*. Collective bargaining was no hindrance to the employers' counter-attack, which was concerned far more with cutting labour costs than with fostering true competition. As was shown above, the CNE ensured that when contracts became obligatory, they had to drop all clauses relating to prices and cartels. On the vexed subject of work time, they tended to defer to the forty-hours law. That, in turn, was slowly undermined – in order to step up production despite shortages of skilled labour (an idea itself first mooted on the CNE and its off-shoot, Chautemps' Comité d'Enquête sur la Production). By these roundabout means, businessmen at last got what they really wanted – not so much an increase in hours worked, as a reduction in over-time payments.[36] Only then was the essence of the Popular Front social legislation perverted, for the total wage bill had been reduced and profits restored, while prices continued to gallop. But collective bargaining still remained in place. Indeed, the bosses had achieved their objectives precisely by living with it, and adapting it to their needs.

Yet the ultimate victory perhaps lay with the other side. Even under Vichy, contracts were negotiated between separate employers' and workers' federations, and the dossiers referred to the ministry of labour. Collective bargaining became an intrinsic part of French industrial relations. In this rather ironic respect, the CNE proved to have been a most effective agent for the reforms of summer 1936.

[35] For more details on the evolution in *patronal* thinking after May 1936, see Rossiter D.Phil. pp. 282–326; and compare with Ingo Kolboom, *La revanche des patrons* (Paris, 1986), which arrives at similar conclusions by a quite different route.

[36] Robert Frankenstein, *Le prix du réarmement français* (Paris, 1982), pp. 277–81; and Elisabeth du Réau, 'L'aménagement de la loi instituant la semaine de quarante heures' in R. Rémond and J. Bourdin (eds.), *Edouard Daladier, chef de gouvernement* (Paris, 1977), pp. 132–42.

Social and economic policies of the Spanish left in theory and in practice

J. M. MACARRO VERA

The Popular Front electoral pact in Spain was negotiated between the representatives of the republican groups and those of the Socialist Party (PSOE). The latter were also acting on behalf of the other working-class organizations which would eventually subscribe to the pact. During the negotiations specific political and social measures were discussed. Leaving aside those which were rejected outright – such as the nationalization of land and banks – this essay will concentrate on the measures over which agreement was reached. For these would form the basis of the future government's programme.[1]

The political amnesty was just such a measure, discussed in connection with the reinstatement of workers dismissed because of the events of October 1934. The republicans claimed to be sympathetic towards them, but with one proviso: neither the workers who had taken the jobs of those dismissed nor those employers who had acted without political malice should be victimized. The socialist representatives, on the other hand, stood firm on this point, possibly because reinstatement was the only union (UGT) proposal in a programme which had been drafted by the PSOE executive.[2] In the public sector, it was left up to those formulating the

---

[1] The PSOE and PCE programmes and the minutes of the meetings between Socialists and Republicans to negotiate the Popular Front pact in the Archivo Histórico (henceforward AH) –25– 29, Fundación Pablo Iglesias (FPI) *Documentación CN del Frente Popular.*

[2] Ibid. letter dated 24 November 1935 accepts the PSOE programme, adding only that 'all those singled out because of October 1934 should be reinstated'.

legislation to finalize the policy on reinstatement. In the private sector, cases would be submitted to the *jurados mixtos*, the arbitration committees on which workers, management and government were all represented.

Over land reform, the PSOE proposed nationalization, with the exception of those smallholdings farmed directly by their owners. Nationalized land would be granted in perpetuity to the agrarian unions. Tools and machinery would also be expropriated. One standard tax would replace the existing plethora. The Communist Party (PCE), for its part, drew a distinction, demanding land expropriation – for either individual or collective exploitation – only in certain cases: the nobility, large land-owners, the Church and lands which had previously been subject to a seigneurial regime. However, as the PCE also demanded both that communal land should be returned to the municipalities and that state-owned land should be settled on the peasantry, it is not clear how many of those possessing medium-sized holdings would remain exempt from the proposal. On all other points the PCE coincided with the PSOE. As is well known, the republican groups were absolutely opposed to the nationali-zation of the land. Equally well known are the terms of the electoral agreement: the protection of small and medium farmers – particularly by means of fiscal measures, loans, the revaluation of agricultural prices – and a general reactivation of land reform with the emphasis on revising the structure of land ownership.

As far as industry was concerned, the keynote remained protection within an orthodox framework geared mainly to supporting the private sector. Thus while the social legislation of 1934–5 was repealed *en bloc*, the Republicans refused to consider resurrecting that which dated from the reformist biennium of 1931–3. Republican opposition meant that the municipal boundaries law would remain inoperative, whilst they also refused to approve the law governing workers' control proposed by the Socialists. Nor could the Republicans accept the suggestion, made by the PSOE and the PCE, that sanctions against those employers who flouted the labour law should extend to imprisonment. Moreover, when it was agreed to establish a legal minimum wage, the Republicans declared that this would have to be set at an extremely low level because of the economic crisis. Thus, under the terms of the Popular Front programme, the possibilities for social legislation came to be seen as contingent upon the state of the economy as a whole – 'the general interests of production' was the expression coined. Although the principle of social legislation was reaffirmed, the precise formulation of 1931–3 was not.

But all of these extremely detailed agreements were immediately swept aside by virtue of the way in which the political amnesty was implemented. Popular political protagonism predominated over the niceties of republican intent as massive numbers of detainees left the gaols.[3] Even more crucial was the law providing for the obligatory reinstatement of those workers dismissed from January 1934 onwards, either for their political views or because of strike action. This differed substantially from the legislation projected in the electoral programme since it included private employers. They were required to re-employ their entire 1934 workforce and also to pay compensation in respect of all such staff. This naturally posed serious problems of increased costs which could not necessarily be absorbed by increased production. The threat of unemployment also hung over such replacement workers as might prove surplus to the new situation's requirements.[4] The way in which the electoral agreement had been exceeded threatened the Popular Front's very existence as a cross-class initiative in that the new measures inevitably affected in adverse fashion many of the small and medium employers whose support was essential to its survival. It must also be noted that although the economy had recovered from the crisis levels of 1933, signs of improvement were as yet slight.[5] Indeed it is fair to suggest that whatever the political or moral justification for the 3 March decree implementing a blanket reinstatement policy, it ran counter to the declared intent of protecting and promoting industry. An additional violation of the electoral agreement occurred in May when the *jurados mixtos* were re-established in their 1931 form, thus further undermining the spirit of moderation which had been the pact's keynote.[6]

Unsurprisingly, the way in which the electoral agreement had been exceeded had political as well as economic consequences. The net result was the alienation of many employers. Claims that the reality of the reinstatement policy was ruining many businesses may have been exaggerated. Nevertheless problems did arise for some companies and it remained

[3] For the PCE's support of popular protagonism and criticism of the republicans' over-legalistic approach, *Mundo Obrero*, 24 February 1936. See also *Documentación CN del Frente Popular* for the debate between republicans and socialists over the extent of the amnesty measure.
[4] Government decree in *Boletín del Ministerio de Trabajo*, February 1936.
[5] For a bibliography on the economy during these years, see the author's article, 'Una fuente para el conocimiento de la depresión de 1929: los "Indice Registro de Sociedades" de Hacienda', *Revista de Historia Contemporánea*, 3 (1984).
[6] For a highly critical analysis of these measures, J. Montero, *Los Tribunales de Trabajo (1908–1938). Jurisdicciones especiales y movimiento obrero* (Valencia, 1976), pp. 193–8.

the case that many employers believed the spirit of the Popular Front agreement had been violated, which in turn jeopardized the rationale of the strategy. The progressive Republicans tended to stress the self-interest which fuelled the employers' complaints, pointing out that in 1934 they had been more than happy to accept conservative legislation sanctioning the dismissals.[7] This was correct, but the economic problems resulting from the reversal of this situation remained, as did the employers' sense of uncertainty. This anxiety resulted from the fact that they saw themselves as being victimized for availing themselves of what, two years previously, had been the law of the land – albeit an extremely partisan one. The employers' unease was compounded by the realization that the republicans had turned out to be less than staunch defenders of the moderation enshrined in the Popular Front's electoral pact.

The Popular Front victory saw a veritable avalanche of labour demands. These descended on an economy that was scarcely able to absorb the labour costs which had resulted between 1931–4. Yet while the improvements obtained by Spanish workers during this period were more than a depressed economy could sustain, they were still insufficient to relieve the poverty of the majority.[8] Indeed living standards dropped after October 1934. Thus in 1936 there was a concerted attempt on the part of the working class to recoup previous gains and even to extend these.

In spite of the unreliability of the statistical records, unemployment continued to provide the backdrop to worker demands.[9] But an analysis of the origins of strike action reveals that it was not the fundamental cause. The strike wave seems to have begun in April 1936, reaching its peak in June, by which time the whole country was affected.[10] The strikes were aimed not only at increasing wages but also at reducing the length of the

---

[7] Diario de las Sesiones de Cortes (DSC), 16 April 1936, p. 341.

[8] The problem over absorbing the wage rise stemmed from the fact that company profits habitually depended on increasing the product price rather than on reducing production costs, S. Florensa, 'Economia y politica económica de la Segunda República', Arbor, 426–7 (June–July 1981); also J. Palafox, 'La crisis enconómica', Revista de Occidente, 7–8 (November 1981), 65–6.

[9] Boletin del Ministerio de Trabajo, January 1936, pp. 74–5 casts some doubt on the exactness of the statistics, suggesting a lower figure in reality. On unemployment see also F. Bermejo, La II República en Logroño: elecciones y contexto politico (Logroño, 1984), pp. 413–16; J. Casanova, Anarquismo y revolución en la sociedad rural aragonesa, 1936–1938 (Madrid, 1985), pp. 67–8; and the author's La utopia revolucionaria. Sevilla en la II República (Seville, 1985), pp. 67ff. and pp. 85–6 for an analysis of who bore the financial brunt of the crisis.

[10] Statistics on strike incidence from the Boletines del Ministerio de Trabajo – although the reports published could be as much as two months out of date.

working day.[11] In that their occurrence coincided with the revival of the *jurados mixtos* in their 1931 form, it is not surprising that the protests from employers' associations began to mount. Many expressed the fear that their end as a class was in sight.[12] This was an extremely emotional response. Yet there can be little doubt that, in spite of the employers' offensive against both the unions and government legislation, some firms did go bankrupt because they could not meet the increased labour costs.[13] Clearly this meant the erosion of the basis of the Popular Front. It was union policy to oppose closure and to petition to be allowed to take over the firms in question. Whilst this had far-reaching political implications, which naturally went beyond the parameters of the Popular Front, there could be no guarantee that such appropriations would ensure future profitability. Neither could a 36-hour week or retirement at sixty guarantee work for all.[14] Nevertheless, the joint union offensive (UGT/CNT) would continue until the summer.

In addition, the Popular Front saw the revitalization of agrarian reform. February 1936 brought an end to eviction proceedings unless the cause was non-payment of rent. There were decrees to remedy the situation of dispossessed tenants, to provide for new land settlements and there were even plans to have the Institute of Agrarian Reform (IRA) declare land in those municipalities with high unemployment levels to be of 'social interest' and therefore expropriable. On 25 March 1936 the famous occupation of estates by landless peasants in Extremadura occurred. Such direct action became widespread, leaving the IRA with no option but to legalize such seizures *a posteriori*. Although agrarian reform was one of the most radical demands of the Popular Front programme, the reality of change had overflowed its parameters. The IRA's declaration in February is striking in this regard: 'The concept of private property, with all its

[11] A 44-hour week was re-established in metallurgy and construction. See for the strike wave and working conditions: J. M. Macarro Vera, *La utopia revolucionaria*, pp. 38, 79–80, 459ff.; M. Cabrera, *La patronal ante la II Républica. Organizaciones y estrategia (1931–1936)* (Madrid, 1983), pp. 299–300; L. German, *Aragón en la II República. Estructura económica y comportamiento politico* (Zaragoza, 1984), pp. 101–2; see R. Vinyes, *La Catalunya Internacional. El frontpopulisme en l'exemple catalá* (Barcelona, 1983), pp. 304ff.; and A. Balcells, *Historia contemporánea de Cataluña* (Barcelona, 1983) for conflicting views over the relative tranquillity of Catalonia; for strikes in Granada, C. Viñes, *Médio siglo de vida granadina. En el cincuentenario de Ideal (1932–1982)* (Granada, 1985), pp. 346–50; see also F. Bermejo, *La II República en Logroño*, pp. 408–11; J. Casanova, *Anarquismo y revolución*, p. 99.
[12] M. Cabrera, *Las organizaciones patronales ante la República'*, Arbor, 426–7 (1981), 165; see also her previously cited work, *La patronal*, pp. 301–6.
[13] For examples in Seville, see the author's work, *La utopia revolucionaria*, p. 462.
[14] As proposed at the CNT's congress. See *El Congreso Confederal de Zaragoza*, CNT (1955), pp. 180–1.

privileges and prerogatives, is, as far as the land is concerned, now obsolete in fact as well as thoery.'[15]

Thus it is clear that the reality of direct action was daily outstripping the objectives of the Popular Front programme as agreed by the coalition's members. In that this radicalization was effectively being sanctioned or legitimized *post hoc* by the government, the latter clearly needed to redefine its political objectives in order to maintain the Popular Front's coherence and credibility. This was especially so in that the ascendancy of organized labour was adversely affecting the economic interests of other classes and was thus straining the relationship between the components of the Popular Front. If the initiative was to survive as a cross-class coalition then a clear statement of intent was needed from the government. The questions which must be addressed are whether such a redefinition ever occurred, whether the policies discussed above were consistent with the electoral pact's objectives and with the Republic as a regime of 'democratic liberty', above specific 'economic and social class demands', and, finally, whether an economic policy ever emerged which was capable of synthesizing the competing claims of labour and capital.

In his ministerial statement of 15 April 1936, Manuel Azaña, as prime minister, declared that the most pressing issue of the moment was the economy. The main objective was to ensure its stabilization, the pursuit of which would inevitably involve conflict with the interests of the working class as epitomized by the spate of direct action. The stabilization of the foreign debt was crucial if Spain's key exports were not to be hit. This was a real threat if, by defaulting on payment, vital imports of raw materials were jeopardized. With economic stabilization in mind Azaña announced a package of fiscal measures and also a public works initiative – although this had to be self-sustaining and could not just be seen as a palliative for local ills or as means of relieving 'the burden of hunger'. The public works policy had to be a cautious one to avoid the risk of inflation – Azaña's greatest fear. Consequently, while wage levels had to be protected they had equally to be controlled so that the chances of achieving a balanced economic policy would not be reduced.[16]

The evidence furnished by the right regarding the dire state of the national economy – the rise in inflation, the depreciation of the peseta, the fall in share prices – all confirmed the reasonableness of Azaña's proposals. While the right accepted the prime minister's economic objectives, the parliamentary interventions of the labour movement's political representa-

[15] Cabrera, *La patronal*, p. 293.   [16] DSC, 14 April 1936, pp. 283–7.

tives demonstrated their lack of any economic analysis – something they shared with the CEDA's Gil Robles. While in October 1934 the PSOE left had abandoned socialization as an objective, because of its likely failure given the inherent weakness of Spanish industry, it was, by 1936, calling for the complete socialization of industry. This about-turn was not satisfactorily explained. The PCE's economic objectives remained limited. It called for a 44-hour week, first for workers in the iron and steel industry, but subsequently to be extended to the rest of the labour force. The object was to reduce unemployment; something which could also be achieved, in the party's view, by expropriating the Church and redirecting its wealth.[17]

Azaña had certainly defined in the Cortes his economic objectives, but not the specific policies to secure them. Thus the spokesman of the Lliga, the party of the Catalan *patronal*, wondered if it was really possible to speak of an established economic policy at all? Some days after Azaña's speech of 15 April this query received a reply of sorts when the industry minister blamed the right for the lack of an economic strategy. It had left chaos behind it in government and while a proper plan was being elaborated the Popular Front was proceeding in accordance with certain basic principles of justice and integrity.[18]

But justice and integrity alone could not guarantee the success of Azaña's proposals. And neither were these compatible with the unions' demands – nor even with the original proposals contained in the Popular Front programme. The reduction of the national debt was hardly compatible with the public works programme. Hence the rapid resignation of the treasury minister, Gabriel Franco, who could not both implement spending cuts and increase budgetary resources in order to finance public works.[19] The blanket reinstatement of workers also caused problems, especially for smaller businesses. The Popular Front parties were unable to respond to the right's complaints or its calls for the setting up of a tribunal to examine reinstatement cases – except by generally denouncing its role in 1934–5. Whilst this certainly diminished the right's moral authority, it was hardly an adequate response either to the substance of its questions, or to the economic problems facing the country in 1936.[20]

The internal contradiction of the Popular Front in economic matters was manifest. The left's programme had been swamped by the demands of the working-class parties and organizations for immediate social reforms at the

[17] Ibid., pp. 292–319.   [18] DSC, 30 April 1936, p. 547.
[19] J. Avilés, *La izquierda burguesa en la II República* (Madrid, 1985), pp. 296–8.
[20] DSC, 16 April 1936, p. 341; 30 April 1936, p. 542; 5 May 1936, pp. 575–88.

same time as the Republicans, as the governing minority, had to apply the brakes, if Azaña's objectives were to stand a chance of success. The disagreement between the Republicans and the political representatives of the labour movement reflected a basic truth; the Popular Front had no coherent economic policy. All that existed was a series of often contradictory measures deriving from the electoral pact. There was no clearly established order of priorities. The restrictions on expenditure, the balancing of the foreign debt and the control of inflation necessitated, at the very least, a reformulation of the electoral programme.

This lack of an economic policy was manifest in Casares Quiroga's inaugural speech as prime minister in May 1936. He could make no more specific a statement than to announce the implementation of agrarian reform, reactivation of the 1931 social legislation, and the provision of a further 100 million pesetas to be added to the 90 million already approved by the previous government for public works to combat unemployment.[21] And in May, when the Cortes discussed a bill authorizing a subsidy of 25 million gold pesetas to the government from the Bank of Spain, in order to remedy the lack of foreign exchange consequent upon the deficit in the foreign trade balance, the finance minister, Enrique Ramos, was unable to respond adequately to the case brought by the right. He fell back on the inherited financial crisis and the flight of capital as his only justification for the measure. These were certainly real considerations, but the fact remains that the minister used them to deflect the right's questions about rising company costs at a time of decreasing productivity.[22]

The same lack of an economic strategy emerged in the crucial matter of a tax on the profits from the sale of personal assets. Such a measure formed an integral part of the Popular Front programme's fiscal objectives. But as the government had not yet elaborated any concrete proposals for implementing tax reform, it had to suffer the brunt of the right's attack in silence. The Popular Front government had no means of replying when the charge was levelled that the Spanish left was the only one in Europe, indeed the world, without a fiscal strategy. Whereas, elsewhere the key to the policies of the left was exactly this. The Spanish right went further, adding that a clear choice had to be made between a deflationary and a reflationary policy. The left, however, was silent. As was to become the norm in

---

[21] DSC, 19 May 1936, p. 693. Out of 8.5 columns only 0.3 column of Casares's speech concerns the economy.

[22] DSC, 29 May 1936, pp. 983–1007.

economic debates in the Cortes, the PSOE and PCE very rarely intervened.[23]

The difficulties arising from the absence of an economic strategy – if we take this to mean a coherent set of measures with a clearly established order of priorities – were compounded by the labour movement's activities. The unions demanded a higher standard of living for workers. This was accompanied by a noticeable increase in production costs, coupled with reduced investment and the prospect of a further loss of competitiveness. Such a combination destroyed the feasibility of the Popular Front programme as an inter-class initiative.

This disparity between the front's political programme and the political practice of its signatories, in economic matters, gave the right the opportunity to praise Léon Blum's strategy, designed to reconcile the interests of labour and capital in a plan of national reconstruction. The French prime minister's respect for trade union independence, the system of collective work contracts and the national uniformity of wage rises – all contrasted favourably with the chaotic state of affairs in Spain where inter-union rivalry was rife and where no national standard of wages or work conditions existed for any single industry. Even the monarchist leader, José Calvo Sotelo, defended Roosevelt's plan for increasing wages in line with productivity levels, since this would stimulate domestic consumption without narrowing profit margins.[24] Casares Quiroga made no reply. The only Popular Frontist to take up the economic theme was the communist, Vicente Uribe. He declared simply that the economic crisis could not be blamed on the coalition's policies, but was rather the result of the actions of the landowners and finance capital.[25]

The situation was a delicate one. With one eye on the June 1936 Matignon agreements in France, the Spanish republican parties were demanding stern measures to bring both workers and employers into line. They feared that, otherwise, the petit bourgeoisie, faced with a wave of industrial conflict, would end by embracing fascism.[26] Even the PCE was calling for moderation in the strikes, while the UGT struggled desperately

---

[23] DSC, 11 June 1936, pp. 1,306–13, which included some incisive criticism by the CEDA deputy, Bermúdez Cañete, on the left's total lack of a fiscal policy.

[24] Blum's policy defended by Calvo Sotelo and Ventosa in DSC, 19 May 1936, pp. 699–708 and 16 June 1936, pp. 1,383–4. Calvo Sotelo's speeches were habitually bi-partite – a technical economic section and then a separate political intervention, anti-democratic and fascist in tone. It is noteworthy that the economic interventions were never challenged by his opponents.

[25] DSC, 19 May 1936, p. 718.   [26] Avilés, *La izquierda burguesa*, pp. 301–4.

to channel the wave of worker demands, its problems compounded by the internal division of the socialist movement.[27]

The situation over agrarian reform was scarcely less confused. The first full-scale debate on this in the Cortes revealed the severe limitations on the scope of reform. There was controversy over the resettlement policy being pursued by the new administration, but equally over the fact that a number of land settlements granted after 1 January 1935 had been rescinded. These actions can be explained as part of the Popular Front's attempt to counter the CEDA's 'agrarian counter-reform'. However, the fact that rural dwellers were being dispossessed of land on which they had previously been settled, simply because such settlements had been organized by the CEDA, meant eroding the peasantry's support for the Popular Front. Equally erosive were the settlements on the land of medium-sized tenant farmers.[28] Similarly the policy of distributing landless labourers among landowners, a common practice with local mayors, could often have unfortunate results – although the intention was simply to alleviate the dire level of poverty and thus stop farmworkers from starving. The Unión Republicana deputy, Fernando Valera, encapsulated the problem. 'The settlement policy is really intended to meet a social need which is particularly acute at present.' But the driving sense of urgency brought with it considerable problems, especially when the allocation of the landless damaged the interests of small peasant proprietors. The tension was only increased by the giving of preferential treatment over the allocation of work to socialist and communist workers. Although, as the agriculture minister indicated, a partisan approach was to be discouraged, it only redressed the balance, given that the landowners themselves favoured rightist workers. The negative impact of such a situation was doubled by the fact that those alienated by the proceedings were the social sectors on which the Popular Front's viability ultimately depended.[29]

The economic objective of the Popular Front's agrarian reform was to improve the lot of the majority of the peasantry. But the government's fundamental error lay in presenting its social legislation in isolation,

---

[27] For the contradictions of PCE policy in 1936, see the author's *La utopia revolucionaria*, pp. 433ff. Socialist debility was often the result of the internal struggle being waged between the party (PSOE) and union (UGT) leadership; for evidence of this, see the minutes of the PSOE parliamentary minority, 16 June 1936 AH–18–7, FPI. For the UGT leadership and the strikes see the union executive minutes for May–July, FPI.

[28] DSC, 29 April 1936, pp. 492–518.

[29] DSC, 30 April, 5 May, 6 June 1936. In Córdoba small landowners and tenants had to make a financial payment in lieu of having workers settled on their land, M. Pérez Yruela, *La conflictividad campesina en la provincia de Córdoba 1931–1936* (Madrid, 1979), p. 204.

leaving the economic measures for later. This had the effect of emasculating the entire initiative for, without a coherent economic strategy, the social policy could amount to little more than a short-lived display of moral commitment.[30] It is hard to see how even the policy of settlement itself could be of much benefit to those at whom it was aimed, given that there was only an average allocation per recipient of 5.5 hectares.[31] The clearest indication of its fundamental non-viability came from the minister responsible for the settlement process who considered a 40 per cent success rate as the most that could reasonably be expected.[32] He was thus unable to respond to the charge that the policy created 'either privileged parasites or miserable wretches'. The reality of the situation made a nonsense of the claim that settlement would establish a new class of smallholders which, in turn, would stimulate small-scale domestic industry.[33]

In practice the agrarian question could not be solved in isolation. With thirty-six inhabitants per square kilometre, no country could be entirely agriculturally based. As the CEDA deputy, Antonio Bermúdez, pointed out, such a situation made industrialization essential. But this would have to be undertaken in the context of a national economic strategy such as the Popular Front had never elaborated. Bermúdez also pointed out that the policy of settlement had enormously increased production costs. He demanded: 'where in the world would one expect those sectors most affected by the crisis to be required to succour the unemployed?' The replies of both Ricardo Zabalza for the PSOE and Antonio Mije for the PCE failed to address the issue. Both confined themselves to the usual attacks on the right for its policies during the conservative biennium of 1933–5. By contrast the Unión Republicana deputy, Valera went straight to the heart of the matter. While accepting that the settlement programme was a socially useful policy, he wondered what could be done to solve the problem of rural unemployment where there was a balance of payments deficit, a budgetary deficit and when the industrial sector was unable to absorb even those workers entitled to reinstatement after October 1934. It

[30] DSC, 1 July 1936 for agriculture minister Ruiz Funes's references to the government's social legislation. He declared that the measures which constituted its economic strategy proper were still pending. But these alone could have made the social package a viable proposition.

[31] The figure derives from the division of hectares occupied from March to July 1936 (572,005) by the number of peasants settled (110,921), in E. Malefakis, *Reforma agraria y revolución campesina en la España del siglo XX* (Madrid, 1971), p. 432.

[32] Ruiz Funes in the debate on the repeal of the 1935 agrarian reform law, DSC, 27 May 1936, p. 925.

[33] DSC, 1 July 1936, pp. 1759, 1774, 1792.

was a reasonable query, but one to which the Popular Front coalition had no answer.[34]

The absolute impossibility of tackling the land question, except as part of a national economic plan, emerged clearly from the Cortes debate on the harvest on 1 July 1936. The right raised the question of wages, the reduction of the working week, the unions' refusal to set production targets and the use of machinery. The labour minister, Juan Lluhí, after countering the right's arguments, went on to establish the government's criteria regarding the harvest: production costs had to reckon with a living wage because it was unacceptable that profit should be based on the payment of starvation wages. The minister favoured a production target but declared that machinery should only be brought in if the full use of human labour could be guaranteed. The very reasonable demand that a living wage be paid would necessarily involve increased production costs, especially if it was accompanied by a reduction in the working week. This, in turn, would mean a rise in the price of agricultural products to the consumer. This would have been one means of alleviating the situation considerably, although it would have involved abandoning the price control on bread in the cities, which was considered sacrosanct. Production targets were rejected outright by both the PSOE and the PCE, while an embargo on the use of machinery as long as there was still unemployment made the cost of the harvest prohibitive.[35] Designed to address the immediate problems, the measures in question were thus all stop gaps and remained entirely uncoordinated.[36]

From this issue of the harvest the right sought to make political capital. In return both socialist and communist deputies lost no time in pointing out that the right had become as quick to criticize the government for its inaction as it had been slow to act on its own account previously. Such point scoring characterized the polarization of the age. Nevertheless, in economic terms, it appears that the cost of collecting the harvest did exceed its market value.[37] This charge, based on the ministry's own statistics, was levelled at the agriculture minister, Mariano Ruiz Funes, during the

---

[34] DSC, 30 April 1936, p. 541, 5 May 1936, p. 577–83, 6 June 1936, p. 596 for interventions by the left and right which reveal both an avoidance of the issue and a lack of understanding where economics were concerned.

[35] Zabalza put the case against production targets – seen as an employers' ruse to cut wages, DSC, 1 July 1936, p. 1783.

[36] DSC, 1 July 1936, pp. 1,743–815.

[37] E. Malefakis, *Reforma agraria*, pp. 426–8, 437–8 and M. Toñón de Lara, 'Rasgos de la crisis estructural a partir de 1917', *La crisis del Estado Español* (Madrid, 1978), pp. 36–9.

debate and his performance in replying was visibly less self-assured as a result.[38]

Socialist and communist deputies insisted on the right's moral bankruptcy because of its own past actions in the countryside. They demanded that, in view of the right's boycott, the harvest should be appropriated and the task of collection be entrusted to the municipal authorities or directly to the peasantry. Once again, the left was more concerned with hitting political targets than with solving the practical economic problems of agriculture.[39] The harvest might indeed be saved as a result, but the cost of its collection would remain equally ruinous, the price having to be met either from union or municipal funds instead of by the landowners.

The inadequacies of the left's policies were fully exposed. If the system of agricultural exploitation in the Spanish countryside was to remain unaltered it would require some backtracking on the government's part and a serious attempt to find another route to reform. But, whatever the case, a national economic strategy reaching beyond the declarations of the electoral programme would be essential. Vital too was the political will to remain faithful to the idea of class compromise and to the political objectives which had informed the Popular Front's creation.

An appraisal of this kind could equally well be applied to industry and commerce. Although these sectors did not experience the crisis levels apparent in the Spanish countryside, there was a similar clash of class interests. Workers' demands came up against the interests of many small employers who were seen as constituting the foundation of the Popular Front. Both the Madrid construction strike, referred to above, and the non-payment of urban rents in Seville had a considerable effect on this class of small proprietors and landlords.[40] In the countryside as in the cities, they were affected by union action, while in the Cortes they were the victims of both the utopian projects and the doctrinal rigidity of the governing majority. For example, the latter was not deflected for one moment from its course when, during the debate on the proposed return of the common lands to the municipalities, it was pointed out that much of this land had already been handed over to small peasant proprietors.[41] In

---

[38] DSC, 1 July 1936, p. 1765.   [39] Ibid. pp. 1,781–5, 1,796–9.

[40] For the construction strike, Santos Juliá, *La izquierda del PSOE (1935–1936)*, (Madrid, 1977) and 'Luchas obreras y políticas de Frente Popular en Madrid, 1931–1936', *Estudios de Historia Social*, 16–17 (1981), 140–1. For the rents in Seville, see the author's *La utopía revolucionaria*, pp. 41–2, 457ff.

[41] It was approved that both municipal and common land sold since 2 May 1808 should be returned to the municipalities. This would have involved possibly the largest shift in land ownership in Spanish history, see the debate in DSC, 26 June, 1, 7, 9, 10 July 1936,

the same debate, the socialist, Zabalza, said emphatically of this social group, 'today we are witnessing the triumph of the large landowners, just as the factory is defeating the craftsman.... Faced with this reality, the marxist groups have a more rational perspective of human progress, support the concept of worker collectives.... we want mechanized collectives, not individual ownership which is disastrous for most smallholders.'[42]

Notwithstanding Zabalza's explicit declaration of the historic failure of the Spanish petite bourgeoisie, the crucial point remains that both worker demands and the mediocrity of the republicans' economic policies were alienating this group from the Popular Front. Faced by this alienation there were only two possible solutions. The first was to accept the consequences of the split and to reinforce the proletarian bloc – which implied addressing the whole question of the seizure of political power, even though this would effectively mean the end of the Popular Front. The other option was to carry on attempting to make the Popular Front viable – which would mean limiting worker gains since these inevitably clashed with the interests of the small proprietors and businessmen.

However, while no sector proposed the strengthening of the proletarian bloc, all access to a reconstituted Popular Front, via the reform of government policies, was blocked. Indeed, this latter course would have required a redefinition of economic priorities and of their social repercussions in 1930s Spain. What is indisputable is that none of the economic recipes contained in the Popular Front programme had any value or relevance and that those charged with their implementation were in utter disagreement.[43] Azaña had bypassed the Popular Front programme in proposing a middle-of-the-road economic policy which sought to balance sectional interests. But in July 1936 it would seem that none of the Popular Front parties was even concerned to face up to the economic conundrum.

[42] DSC, 10 July 1936, pp. 2,049–50.
[43] There is no evidence that any such redefinition of economic policy was ever considered. For a serious analysis of the alternatives, S. Juliá, 'Luchas obreras', pp. 140–1 and 'Corporativistas obreros y reformadores politicos: crisis y escisión del PSOE en la II República', *Studia Storica*, 1, 4 (1983). See also the author's *La utopia revolucionaria*, pp. 456ff.

Women, men and the 1936 strikes in France

SIÂN REYNOLDS

When Suzanne Lacore, a retired schoolteacher in a Dordogne village, heard that Léon Blum was about to offer her a junior ministry in his government in 1936, she hastened to decline it in advance. Blum responded:

Ma chère amie,
I will not bow to your refusal . . . You will not have to run anything [*diriger*], simply to encourage [*animer*]. Above all, your role is to be there, for *your mere presence* will signify a great deal. (my italics)[1]

This essay will not be concerned with the women ministers of 1936, but they make a suitable starting point for asking how we can begin to assess the 'presence' of two sexes in France in the Popular Front period. Surprisingly often, even today, in many general histories of the French Popular Front, or indeed the Third Republic, the classic reference to Léon Blum's famous three ministers accompanies a notable absence of women from the rest of the text. Women's symbolic presence in the government, made clear in Blum's letter, remains symbolic in historical writing. The by now rather large body of writing, published or unpublished, on 'women in the Third Republic' still seems, however good its reputation, to be confined

[1] Léon Blum to Suzanne Lacore, late May 1936, reproduced by Lacore in *Vétéran Socialiste*, 18 (March 1960)

to a sort of 'territory of the women's historian', rather than integrated into 'total history'.[2]

The terms 'women's history' and 'feminist history' are sometimes used interchangeably, sometimes opposed to each other. Here, women's history will be taken to mean a history with women as its subject matter, feminist history one that tries to look at all history using the concepts of gender and gender relations. Although this essay *will* chiefly be concerned with women, my purpose is to try to suggest a feminist reading of a particular event, the strike wave of 1936 which was such a prominent feature of the Popular Front in France, asking the question 'in what ways were the strikes experienced differently by men and women?' – while bearing in mind that neither men nor women had any single unitary experience.

As much as anything else, feminist history is a way of writing and a use of language. The past being another country, it is not surprising that they speak differently there. Contemporary sources cannot always answer our questions using our terms. So to take one instance, quite an important one for what follows, descriptions of the strikes in May–June 1936 often do not distinguish between men and women workers. The French word *ouvrier*, meaning a male worker, is used in many of the sources, including archives, statistics and the contemporary press, even when referring to industries where we know that the bulk of the workforce were women, *ouvrières*. Simone Weil, the author of one of the most striking first-person accounts of factory life in the 1930s, who was working with other women in segregated shops most of the time, herself talks of *ouvriers* when making any general points about the working class. Secondary sources are often unhelpful too, because their authors have not been concerned to ask questions about gender. So despite the considerable literature on the Renault automobile firm, for instance, it is not easy to find out from it how many women were working there in 1936.[3]

If primary sources pose some problems, and if the approach of much of

---

[2] The gap between the two bodies of literature is wider in France than in English-language publications. H. Dubief, *Le déclin de la IIIe République* (Paris, 1976) and J. Mayeur, *La vie politique sous la IIIe République* (Paris, 1984) are fairly typical in citing the ministries without further reference to women, whereas J. F. McMillan (who has of course also written about women in the Third Republic) incorporates women's history into his *Dreyfus to De Gaulle* (London, 1985) to a degree rare in general works.

[3] Neither P. Fridenson, *Histoire des usines Renault* (Paris, 1972) nor B. Badie, 'Les grèves du Front populaire aux usines Renault', *Mouvement Social*, 81 (October–December 1972) has much to say about women. From A. Touraine's *L'évolution du travail ouvrier aux usines Renault* (Paris 1955) it *is* possible to discover that there were 3,110 women working at Renault in the late 1930s (p. 87), but we have to deconstruct Touraine's own calculations to work out that this meant about 12 per cent of the workforce, and they are not mentioned again.

the secondary writing is unsatisfactory, there is at least now a substantial body of descriptive 'women's history' which makes it more possible to attempt some sort of synthesis. Much of this material is in the form of unpublished but easily accessible French theses. These represent what Michelle Perrot has called 'the primitive accumulation' phase in women's history and, despite the rather uneven quality of the research, are today the starting point of any serious study. What follows is indebted to some of this research.

WOMEN WORKERS IN THE 1930S

To have some kind of perspective on the strikes, a few preliminary remarks on women's employment in the 1930s are called for. Practically all the statistics derive from the censuses taken between 1906 and 1936. There are a number of analytical studies based on the census data, which agree about the overall trends.[4] Briefly, the number of women 'active' in the economy peaked just after World War I (when many still had their wartime jobs) at 39·6 per cent of the workforce; began to decline during the 1920s; and dropped somewhat between 1931 and 1936. Secondly, setting aside the large number of women still working in agriculture, there was a shift out of the industrial sector into the services sector. By 1936, women only represented 27·6 per cent of the industrial workforce (34 per cent in 1906). It is now thought, however, that official figures inadequately reflect a more complex reality since so many women moved into and out of work on a short-term basis, particularly during the depression. One has only to read Simone Weil's *Journal d'usine* of 1934–5 to appreciate the irregularity of many workers' lives – the lay-offs, the waiting outside factory gates, the trek from one place to another in search of temporary work. And Catherine Rhein's thesis on a Paris oral history project confirms the discontinuous nature of many women's work.[5]

Women had rarely been employed alongside men doing identical work: in the earlier part of the century, they had been concentrated in domestic service and industrially in the textile and garment sectors, all of which were

---

[4] See J. Daric, *L'activité professionnelle des femmes en France; étude statistique* (Paris, 1947); M. Guilbert, 'L'évolution des effectifs du travail féminin en France depuis 1866', *Revue Française du Travail* (September 1947), pp. 754–77. The figures are presented in accessible form in Evelyne Sullerot's chapter 'Condition de la femme' in A. Sauvy (ed.), *Histoire économique de la France entre les deux guerres* (Paris, 1984) vol. 3; and by H. Bouchardeau, *Pas d'histoire les femmes* (Paris, 1977), p. 144.

[5] C. Rhein, 'Jeunes femmes au travail dans le Paris de l'entre-deux-guerres' (Doctorat de 3e cycle, University of Paris–VII, 1977), pp. 249ff.

in decline in our period. Their wages were uniformly low, sometimes barely more than half a man's, and they were even less likely than men to join a union, in a period of low union membership overall: 8 per cent of the CGT, though 25 per cent of the Catholic CFTC. New jobs in the tertiary sector (in catering or in chain and department stores) were low-paid too.

What is particularly interesting in view of the strikes is the finding suggested by Sylvie Zerner in a recent thesis, based on a very close reading of the census figures,[6] that the overall decline of the numbers of women in industry masks what was actually a shift into the more advanced sectors of French industry – light engineering, food production, chemicals, electrical goods, automobiles and so on, where American-inspired modern work processes were in use. In this area women were overwhelmingly OS (*ouvrières spécialisées*), that is semi-skilled workers using machines in one stage of the production process. Once more, they were rarely in direct competition with male workers. Although now increasingly in the same industries as men, women were still segregated, this time by their status. They were not so much moving into a man's world as into a women's world where the only men they saw were skilled mechanics coming to fix their machines when they went wrong – a situation which some had temporarily experienced during World War I.

Zerner has interesting things to say about the *mentalités* of women who made this transition, and her analysis digs under the familiar arguments about why women workers accepted low wages. Most girls were still being given a wildly inappropriate 'vocational' training in sewing; many took a first job in dressmaking. In the sewing trades, speed *was* skill: outworking in particular was a form of sweated piecework where the woman was constantly working against the clock. Thus such women moved from an archaic isolated piecework ethic into a modern workplace piecework ethic. They were not employed on assembly lines but in industries where individuals supervised their own machines. An obsessive attitude to turning out the required number of pieces could become a reflex. Simone Weil's experience, as described in *La condition ouvrière*, vividly conveys the despair that (as a raw and clumsy beginner) she felt about trying to turn out the hundreds of bolts asked of her, in the jobs in engineering she took in 1934–5, as well as the pride taken in their rapidity by the women around her. Bertie Albrecht, another intellectual who took a low-paid job, this time in the Galéries Lafayette workshops in 1937, reported that when women

[6] S. Zerner, 'Ouvrières et employées entre la première guerre mondiale et la grande crise' (Doctorat de 3e cycle, University of Paris–x, 1985).

went home after a day on piecework tying and labelling goods, their families had to appeal to them to slow down ('Calme-toi, tu n'est pas aux Galéries!').[7]

Low-paid, non-unionized, concentrated in certain areas of the labour market, and with a particular history of work-patterns, the women workers in French industry in 1936 cannot, one is forced to conclude, be regarded as sharing identical circumstances with their male equivalents. At the same time, there was no such thing as a unitary 'women workers' experience': a woman's age, marital status, number of children or elderly dependants accounted for considerable differences in day-to-day experience. To take just one example, married women were not entitled to unemployment benefit.

THE ELECTIONS AND STRIKES OF 1936

Where, if anywhere, do these women fit into the formation of the Popular Front and the excitement of the approaching elections of April–May 1936? Women were not of course allowed to vote under the Third Republic, though they were by no means absent from political life, as the iconography of the period amply reveals. Perhaps most significant in the context of this essay, which is concerned with the industrial strikes, is the fact that women's wages were a major issue in the election campaign by left-wing parties. Not that this was made explicit: the condemnation of 'starvation wages' by communist and socialist politicians was voiced in more general terms, attacking previous governments for allowing the working class to bear the brunt of depression. But every time a *salaire de misère* is actually quoted, it turns out to be a woman's full-time wage (indeed it could hardly be otherwise, given women's rates of pay). We do not, at this stage, hear the sound of women's voices. In an all-male election, male orators were talking about women without saying so, and perhaps without clearly realizing it themselves. It is not until after the strikes that the occasional voice of a woman gets through complaining of low wages. Thus Jules Moch recalled the shock of seeing a woman delegate turn to her boss during the collective bargaining in June for the grocery foodchains like Félix Potin, and saying:

Look Monsieur, this is what I earn. You seem to trust me because I am a saleswoman at peak hours and a cashier the rest of the time. With what I earn, I

[7] Reproduced in A. Fourcaut, *Femmes à l'usine en France dans l'entre-deux-guerres* (Paris, 1982), p. 235.

can't even buy a pair of stockings a month, after paying for my keep. When I need a winter coat, will I have to prostitute myself?[8]

The gates of women's speech were only to be unlocked by the strike movement.

The strikes broke out in the interval between the election results and the formation of Blum's government. They began in the second week of May, reached a peak in early June, just after the Matignon accords, and gradually declined thereafter, although their 'rolling' nature meant that some went on into July. Certain aspects of the strikes are well known, though their relevance to the men/women divide is not usually explored. They were overwhelmingly in the manufacturing sector and in large-scale commerce. Civil servants, transport workers, teachers, postal workers did not strike: by and large it was the least unionized sectors which struck, the most unionized which did not.[9] Factories near Paris, particularly in light engineering, food production and so on were prominent in the movement, as, eventually, were the big department stores. Thus most of the women workers about whom we have been talking found themselves caught up in the strikes – for many of them the first time they had participated in a strike at all. Later comment and contemporary press reporting frequently make some reference to the 'naivety' of many of the strikers, though without relating it to sex, arguing either that it proves the spontaneity of the movement, or that it rendered it vulnerable to manipulation. But there are no systematic figures of any kind about the sex distribution of the strikers, evidence of which remains fragmentary and dispersed.

Many images of the strikes and factory occupations have been captured on film, and eye-witness accounts survive. The images often suggest a mainly supporting role for women: doing 'womanly' things, like bringing a basket of food to the factory gate to husband or son, or knitting to while away the time while someone plays an accordion. Alternatively, some accounts refer to the 'greater combativity of women' or see them as Pasionarias: 'The women spoke too, they were pretty wild, worse than the men, real furies.'[10] Is it possible to see beyond the ministering angel and

---

[8] *Léon Blum, chef de gouvernement 1936–7, actes du colloque* (Paris, 1967) p. 98.

[9] Antoine Prost, 'Les grèves de juin 1936, essai d'interprétation', ibid., p. 73. Prost points out that union membership was very low in metals, food and textiles, but does not relate this to the sexual division of labour.

[10] First quotation from P. Birgi, 'Femmes salariées, syndicalisme et grèves de mai-juin 1936' (Mémoire, ISST, 1969), p. 64, which contains much useful descriptive material; second quotation from M. Couteaux, 'Les femmes et les grèves de 1936, l'exemple des grands magasins' (Maîtrise, University of Paris–VII, 1975), which is more analytical in approach. Both are essential reading.

the harpy, and learn anything new about the participation of women in the movement, in particular how it differed from that of men?

Perhaps it is not such a bad idea to start with the knitting – it is certainly a pervasive feature of pictures and recollections. 'I have never knitted so much in my life' – Mme B. in Galéries Lafayette.[11] The reporter from *Le Populaire*, also commenting on a department store, where women employees were in the majority, wrote: 'We can go round the shop . . . It is a real beehive of embroidery and knitting. They will have woollies for the whole of next winter.'[12] A law student, whose account is often described as a classic, reported of one factory:

In the courtyard, the women are sitting in the shade, sewing, reading or darning socks. This evening at 8 o'clock, they will be allowed to go home. On the steps, the men are playing cards, drinking beer – wine and spirits are not permitted by the strike committee.[13]

This picture is repeated a hundred times in various forms. What seems to emerge is that these hours of enforced leisure were lived by most men as precisely that – leisure, to be spent doing things like drinking, smoking, playing cards. For women, leisure seems not to be totally possible – it is as if they feel idle hands are guilty hands. In an age when many clothes were still made at home, every spare moment – in the métro, in lunch breaks – went on knitting. This should not really surprise us of course – but the 'explosion of joy' of 1936 is often described as the discovery of leisure. For women, this was only half true.

Next, one might turn to what could be termed matters of maintenance. This would include not only the basket at the factory gates, but working in the canteen to make meals for strikers. Undoubtedly, for many women, the occupations did mean having to provide food. But there was also a form of maintenance related to materials. Quantitative estimates are impossible and men were also involved, but it does seem that women were particularly concerned to prevent waste of perishable goods endangered by the strike. Thus in a fur workshop, 'the women workers are treating the skins to prevent them being spoilt'.[14] In food manufacture, in particular, there were risks of damage. The leader of the food federation in the CGT later recalled that 'women did extra work to put the foodstuffs being processed at the time in a safe place. The women were more concerned about this

---

[11] Couteaux, 'Les femmes', p. 100.
[12] *Le Populaire*, 18 June 1936 (also quoted Couteaux, 'Les femmes', p. 66).
[13] H. Prouteau, *Les occupations d'usines en Italie et en France 1920–36* (Paris, 1937), p. 143.
[14] *L'Humanité*, 5 June 1936.

than the men; it was because they really [*concrètement*] know the value of food.'[15] Sometimes – significantly – maintenance was a new experience for women: when in a Gennevilliers cotton mill, 'the women workers cleaned the machines', it was the first time they had been allowed to touch them.[16]

A third area to explore is something which seems to emerge fairly clearly from all archives, newspapers or memories. That is, that there was a difference between the action of women in all-women factories and those in mixed enterprises. Where women made up the entire workforce, they organized their occupations, composed their lists of grievances, formed delegations to deal with the management and so on. Where the workforce was mixed, even if women were in the majority, the organization was invariably handled by the men (with or without some women representatives), and many of the women were sent home (or allowed home, as some put it). Thus in two TSF (radio component) factories, the all-women labour force occupied the first, while in the second one, which was mixed, women were sent home.[17] In a Corbeil shoe factory employing many women workers, 'only the men, about 120, remained on site'.[18] In Fives-Lille, in the huge textile factories, 'all women' – the vast majority – 'young people of both sexes and men over 50 were allowed home', leaving the youngish adult males in charge.[19] Marcelle Vallon, who worked at the Magasins Réunis, commented that 'the movement was organized by the men, and in the delegations you met men only'. They thought women 'couldn't put two ideas together' she comments, and they only asked her because 'she's middle-class, she will be able to cope'.[20] In the photo in *L'Humanité* of the Galéries Lafayette delegation to the employers, there are five women and twenty men – an approximate inversion of the sex balance of the workforce.[21] Here, as in so many other areas of life, it seems that women were perfectly capable of handling their own affairs when they had to, but in mixed situations, even where women were the majority, men took control and women accepted it. I do not mean to imply any lack of solidarity here – the men would often stand out for women's wage demands when they could have settled earlier – simply that both sexes appear to have accepted that if men were present, they took charge. Much as we

15 Quoted by Birgi, 'Femmes salariées', p. 64.   16 *L'Humanité*, 6 June 1936.
17 *L'Humanité*, 26 May 1936.
18 Archives Nationales (AN), BB 18 3011, correspondance des procureurs généraux relative aux grèves de 1936. (Series BB 18 3007–3012).
19 AN, BB 18 3009, Douai region, 4 June 1936.
20 Quoted in Birgi, 'Femmes salariées', p. 63. Cf. M. Colliette's account of the chain store Aux Magasins Réunis, in G. Lefranc, *Histoire du Front Populaire* (Paris, 1965), annexe.
21 *L'Humanité*, 21 June 1936.

might like to think otherwise, women's collusion, or to use a more neutral word acquiescence, in the men's taking charge has to be reckoned with. Thus some women's experience of the strikes was as full participants; others were deprived of any initiative.

It has to be remarked here, making a fourth area of debate, that one of the main reasons why women were sent home was to avoid accusations of immorality. *Gringoire*, the right-wing paper, talked about 'orgies' behind the factory gates. *Figaro* quoted a striker's wife who had seen 'photos of the men leaning on window-sills with women workers'. *Le Petit Bleu* quoted another wife as saying 'those women are going to use the strike to take away our husbands. Oh, there'll be some ructions on the home front when all this is over.'[22] The left-wing press retorted that everything was highly respectable: *L'Humanité* said that 'strike pickets' in a department store, 'stay all night, and the other employees, and *all the women*, go home, to return next morning at 9 a.m.'.[23] Renault did the same thing. Monique Couteaux, who has looked at the strikes in the *grands magasins*, perceptively remarks that the right-wing press tends to stress sexual difference in its reports – presenting women as either unwilling victims or as sexual objects – while the left-wing press seeks to smoothe over sexual difference, praising women for being just like men: 'as firm in their resolve as the workmen', 'worthy of their companions' and so on.[24] But both sides identified women as a potential source of immorality. It would probably be unwise to shrug this off: crises and emergencies *are* erotic, and the atmosphere of collective euphoria no doubt heightened sexual feelings. But not for the first time, women are perceived (by male journalists and strikers' wives alike) as the source of disturbance – and working-class women were divided.

The words of one striker's husband on the other hand remind us (fifthly) that something else was going on besides such excitements. He and his wife were both on strike, 'but not to the same degree. "She, well she's gone mad. She stayed eight days and nights at the factory, without setting foot in the house. I had to wash the kids, comb their hair and wipe their bottoms for a week."' His wife reportedly said: 'I'm staying, out of solidarity.' The end of the story was that he went to the factory with a gun to fetch her home, eight days' child-care being more than flesh and blood could stand (and clearly a new experience). The Catholic fortnightly which reported this incident commented, if not exactly approvingly at least understandingly, that he was ready to kill in the interests 'of a higher ideal than corporate solidarity

---

[22] *Le Petit Bleu*, 11 June 1936, quoted with other examples, Couteaux, 'Les femmes', p. 73.
[23] *L'Humanité*, 17 June 1936, my italics.   [24] Couteaux, 'Les femmes', pp. 77–8.

– the family'.[25] The family was something most women knew all about. Corporate solidarity was something else again. It is not exaggerating to say that for many women (for many men too, but arguably with more preparation) the strike movement was their first experience of any truly collective action. Their industrial experience had been in the main very different from men's, although there had of course been strikes by women workers before.

One group of women workers particularly fascinated the press: the salesgirls in the department stores. The poignant contrast between the compulsory elegant dress and make-up of these mainly young women, and their long hours and starvation wages, apparently shocked the stores' customers. L'Humanité described, as if it would come as a surprise to its readers, an overheard conversation between 'two young and pretty salesgirls from the Galéries Lafayette', who spoke of 'the bosses being choked' at 'seeing that the workers could hold out'.[26] It was of such women (often the daughters of manual workers), and the new experience of collective activity they had undergone, that Henriette Nizan was thinking when she wrote, after the strikes:

Their knitting or a novel used to isolate them in the métro or the train, the only public place where they would have been allowed to talk and exchange ideas. Then they would go home and try to keep up a life style that was out of step with the life they were really leading ... Will they now return so easily to their narrow selfish way of life? Will they abandon their communal warmth? I don't think so ... They have experienced the joy to be had by living in an atmosphere of mutual trust.[27]

From this kind of comment, of which there is no shortage, especially in the left-wing press, it is tempting to conclude that precisely because they were less used to thinking in collective terms, women's experience of the strikes overall was more intense than that of men: the dramatic events of June 1936 were a greater irruption into their lives. It has been argued that this was a turning point for the integration of women into the working class, and for some of the writers on women in this period this has become something of an article of faith, one moreover which redounds to women's credit.[28] The working class must after all be a good thing for women workers to integrate with, and if we are concerned to distinguish between men's and women's experience of the strikes, this surely is one answer.

[25] Dossiers de l'action populaire, 25 June 1936, pp. 1,542–3, survey of strikers' homes.
[26] L'Humanité, 9 June 1936.
[27] H. Nizan in Vendredi, 25 June 1936.
[28] Birgi argues this, and M. Colin in Ce n'est pas d'aujourd'hui (Paris, 1975), in a section drawing on Birgi's mémoire, states it more forcefully.

But it is not an answer I find wholly satisfactory, or rather it begs a number of questions. If women were joining the organized working class – by taking out a CGT card for instance as millions of workers of both sexes did in June 1936 – they were being recruited into a male world, with its own rules and customs, one that had long ignored women or wished them out of it. If they joined this world it was on men's terms, not theirs. Integration implies that the new arrivals change the composition of the original mass in some way, and that from then on the interests of all will be represented. It is not at all clear that this was what happened in 1936. It is not even easy to discover how many women did join the CGT and for how long. Antoine Prost, who has written the most thorough statistical study of the CGT's massive recruitment in the period, hardly refers to women at all. It is certainly true that by the classic norms of visibility in the labour movement, such as being named delegate to union conferences, more women are suddenly visible in 1936–7, as an analysis of the relevant volumes of the great Maitron biographical dictionary shows (an exercise incidentally of great interest to women's history). It remains unclear how many women remained in trade unions during the years 1937–9 when union or rather CGT membership, of both sexes presumably, fell away almost as quickly as it had risen in 1936. We simply have to say that we do not know the extent to which women identified themselves with the class struggle as defined by the men who, beyond any doubt, were organizationally dominant during the strike movement. What is more, class solidarity is widely assumed to be the dominant emotion, and it tends to mask any examples of specific women's solidarity.

This gives special interest to one piece of evidence coming from Madeleine Tribolati, at the time a young clerk and one of the few women to take part in the collective bargaining talks in her sector, doing so as a representative of the CFTC, the Catholic trade union confederation. She told Michel Launay that when she happened to meet women delegates from the CGT, 'they would find themselves on common ground defending aspects to do with "the female condition". Their male colleagues, whatever their union allegiance, were greatly struck by this'.[29] To appreciate the unusual nature of such an alliance it should be remembered that relations between the CGT and CFTC were so hostile that the CGT would not agree to the CFTC being represented in the union delegation to the Matignon

---

[29] M. Launay, 'Le syndicalisme chrétien en France 1885–1940, origines et développement' (Doctorat d'état, University of Paris–Sorbonne, 1981), p. 2,304, and note 725 (a thesis full of interest on women's unions in the CFTC).

conference. And the CFTC was in a difficult position during June 1936: officially opposed to strikes and class confrontation, it was nevertheless drawn into the movement. It recruited members in the aftermath, generally, it is thought, from people who wanted to counter CGT influence.

This brings us from the question of women's solidarity with the movement to the question of their opposition to it, which must be part of the equation too. It is not easy to distinguish women's opposition, as such, to the strike movement, given the nature of the sources. But if women were by and large strangers to the world of unions, by the same token one would expect there to be a certain amount of resistance from women workers, at least as much and possibly more than from men. The evidence is extremely patchy but certainly during the autumn – when the euphoria of June was a faded memory, and when the strikes were renewed in an atmosphere of bitterness and recrimination – a few rather dramatic instances of aggression between women office workers and manual workers based in the same firm are on record, the former being opposed to further strikes. Sometimes hostile women workers or forewomen were singled out by workmates for a 'conduite de Grenoble' – a 'rough ride' home.[30] Qualitative evidence comes from Catherine Rhein's oral history witnesses: she found enthusiasm for the Popular Front and the strikes only from those women in her sample who had worked at Renault and Citroën, in big factories where everyone came out. Some of the other respondents had antagonistic memories, or felt that they had been obliged to go along with something they did not really believe in: 'on a été syndiquées', one of them said – 'we were unionized', rather than 'we joined the union'.[31] Neither women's support nor their solidarity can be taken for granted.

Just as women's experience during the strike, with all its variations, differed from that of men, so their experience of the consequences is equally hard to assimilate to that of men. No one has really examined the grievance registers for sexually specific demands and that is well beyond the scope of this essay. Here and there – and the department stores again come to the fore – the *cahiers* contain a women's demand: notably the right for shop assistants to sit down for five minutes in every hour; the provision of a crèche (some stores already had one) and coded demands about arbitrary sackings (a covert reference to sexual harassment).[32] Evidently there were such demands to be voiced, though how loudly it is hard to say. What is

[30] E.g. AN, BB 18 3009, Bordeaux region, 11 December 1936; BB 18 3011 (the famous 'Cusinberghe affair'); BB 18 3007, Aix; BB 18 3012, Grenoble, July 1936 – all cases where women workers were at odds with strikers.
[31] Rhein, 'Jeunes femmes', p. 280.   [32] Couteaux, 'Les femmes', p. 66.

more significant, though not perhaps really surprising, is the absence of a call for equal pay for equal work. The *cahiers* invariably call for pay rises, and usually for a higher percentage rise for low-paid workers (as the Matignon accords specified), which meant in practice that women's wages received a substantial boost. But they were still left as the lowest-paid workers, and nowhere apparently were voices raised (by either sex) for any equalization of men's and women's earnings.

This did not pass completely unnoticed at the time, but feminists outside the labour movement seem to have reacted most. Thus Maria Vérone, of the Ligue Française du Droit des Femmes, wrote to Jouhaux, secretary of the CGT, and Salengro, the interior minister, about the absence of equal pay from collective bargaining. Huguette Godin wrote an article in *Le Quotidien* asking whether the omission was because the employers had opposed it or because workers of both sexes had failed to raise the issue. At a meeting held by the communist Jacques Duclos in July, two women teachers said that they had gone to address strike meetings at a department store in June and had been warned by CGT officials not to 'raise the question of equal wages in front of all these raw recruits to trade unionism, who had only joined the CGT the day before'. They had complied out of union discipline, but now they asked why the question was out of order. (They received no satisfaction from Duclos, whose reply was evasive.)[33] The politician G. Lhermitte, who supported feminist demands in parliament, wrote in 1938 to Daladier pointing out that the *conventions collectives* had not only enshrined the principle of unequal pay, but that if percentage wage rises were thereafter granted, the gap between men's and women's wages would grow even bigger.[34]

It seems likely that equal pay was omitted from the strike demands not by any oversight but because those in charge of negotiations – generally the CGT – thought it too radical a demand, while women were either too timid to suggest it or themselves regarded it as impossible. They cannot have been unaware either of the danger to women's employment that equal pay might bring, in the industrial sector (it had been achieved for schoolteachers and some post office workers as early as the 1920s). The reality of the danger is demonstrated by what happened to women metal-workers after 1936. The wage rises, while not giving equality, had closed the gap

---

[33] *Droit des femmes*, July 1936; cf. also Couteaux, 'Les femmes', p. 79.
[34] AN, F 60 246, letter from G. Lhermitte to Daladier, then prime minister, about women's suffrage and equal pay, 15 November 1938.

quite considerably between men's and women's wages. Catherine Rhein quotes a report of 1938 which says that:

The difference between the male and female wage is no longer large enough for industrialists to give preference to female labour, which is less regular and less skilful [*habile*] ... [they blame] the large wage rises for women laid down in the collective agreements, as well as the difficulty experienced by women workers over a certain age in adapting to the techniques which change frequently with changes in production.[35]

Whatever the truth about adaptability, women's pay rises may have helped to tip the balance against them. Certainly while men's unemployment peaked in 1935 (and can thus be linked with the male election) women's unemployment did not peak until much later – 1938–9 – and was submerged in the slight but overall general recovery. The recovery, such as it was, partly provoked by the increased armaments expenditure initiated by the Blum government, was felt most in heavy industry which chiefly employed men. At the very least, this points to a differential pattern of employment and unemployment as between men and women.[36]

There are other differences too: while women were probably affected about equally with men by the problems of the post-Matignon situation – firms closing because they could not afford the social legislation, lay-offs, further strikes and so on – they did not always enjoy the benefits. To have your two weeks' paid holiday, you had to have worked for the same firm for a year – something many women had not. The first year, the special *billets* Lagrange – railway vouchers for travel to the sea – were not made available to women heads of family or women workers with an unemployed husband (though this was changed for 1937). Bertie Albrecht reported that many of the women in the Galéries Lafayette chose to devote their new day off (the result of the forty-hour week) to 'thoroughly doing out the house'.[37]

CONCLUSIONS

The picture is full of complications and no more than a fraction of the potential questions have been touched on here. But one can say with some firmness that women's experience of the industrial turmoil of 1936 cannot simply be assimilated to men's, nor is it possible to point to a single unitary women's experience. The women of the industrial working class with whom this paper has been concerned might have experienced the strikes

[35] Rhein, 'Jeunes femmes', p. 281.   [36] Ibid., p. 285; cf. Sullerot, 'Condition', p. 429.
[37] Fourcaut, *Femmes à l'usine*, p. 237.

in any number of ways: as active participant; enthusiastic but excluded newcomer; reluctant recruit to a union; active resister; young girl sleeping away from home for the first time; unemployed wife of a striker, bringing food and worrying about money – and so on. All these roles were possible within an overall experience in which *both* class and gender played a crucial part, interacting with each other. At the time, and later, such interaction was hardly perceived, the perception of gender taking a particularly rigid form. The words of the men of the Popular Front unequivocally indicate that they assumed an essentially domestic identity for working-class women, whether they were employed or not. We find Duclos calling on 'the women of France to unite for the protection of their homes' and 'the future of the race', and the secretary of the garment-workers' federation of the CGT claiming that women's participation in the strikes 'meant it really was a matter of defending [our] bread, the home, the survival of our children' and that it confirmed 'the eminently natural character of our demands'.[38] This effortlessly equates women with 'natural' demands rather than industrial ones, and assumes that the 'natural' role of women is to care for children – the single woman worker for instance (which is what the majority of his new union members were) does not have a place in the scheme of things. Such statements indicate the difficulty of thinking of women as proletarians in their own right. The sexual division in the working class was simultaneously visible and invisible – making it possible for a historian like G. Dupeux to write in a widely-read textbook a sentence like the following: 'The CFTC before 1936 had drawn most of its support from office workers and women; now it had more support from the working class.'[39]

It would be wrong to suggest that such habits of mind were peculiar to men. Catherine Rhein commenting on the memories of the women in her study says: 'I have to say so because they say so, and they insist on the point: the crisis, the recession, unemployment, newspapers, trade unions and politics were all domains or concepts reserved for men.' Yet all these women had been employed, were affected in their daily lives by the slump, read newspapers, in some cases joined unions, later got the vote. The readiness of women to say one thing while living another may bring to mind notions of false consciousness or alienation. Suzanne Lacore, with whom this essay began, and who is often quoted as a symbol of women's

---

[38] Birgi, 'Femmes salariées', p. 51.
[39] G. Dupeux, *French Society 1789–1970*, trans. P. Wait (London, 1976), p. 212. (Many women in the CFTC were textile workers, both before and after 1936.)

progress towards equality under the Popular Front, showed in a pamphlet of 1932 that even she, an unmarried schoolteacher, regarded the working-class woman as the provider of comfort to 'the valiant fighter', that is, the man of the house.[40]

Even such a tentative and fragmentary feminist reading of the strikes of 1936 as this can perhaps raise some awkward questions about the unity of the working-class experience of the Popular Front in France and challenge the (sometimes unwitting) unisexual bias of so many general historical accounts.

[40] *Femmes socialistes*, brochure (1932), quoted in Couteaux, 'Les femmes', pp. 61–2; cf. Rhein, 'Jeunes femmes', p. 242.

From clientelism to communism: the Marseille working class and the Popular Front

DAVID A. L. LEVY

This chapter originates in an attempt to understand the nature of the Popular Front as a mass movement and as a provincial as well as Parisian phenomenon. Marseille is a particularly interesting example to study from this perspective because while its working class participated fully in the Popular Front their movement represented a profound change in the city's political traditions. The aim here is to demonstrate how the Popular Front movement combined together with other economic changes to produce this transformation in the local political system and to lay the basis for widespread working-class organization and action. This account is based on a more detailed study of the 1934–8 strikes in Marseille, but the focus here is on the political and social context rather than the factory floor.[1] The chapter looks first at the special nature of Marseille's political and economic system prior to the Popular Front. Secondly, consideration is given to those economic factors which undermined Marseille's claims to specificity. The third and final part examines the way in which the Popular Front movement built on these changes both to speed up and secure the transformation from clientelism to class politics. The chapter's argument is not that this process was completed during the 1930s but rather that the success of the Popular Front movement in Marseille was both a con-

[1] This chapter summarizes some of the findings of my unpublished doctoral thesis, 'The Marseille working-class movement, 1936–1938' (D.Phil, Modern History, Oxford, 1983). I am grateful to the Leverhulme Trust for the financial support they provided for this research.

sequence of, and itself accelerated, the change in the local political system. The account therefore seeks to advance the process of rediscovering the local origins of a Popular Front movement which has too often been described purely in national or at best Parisian terms.[2]

THE SPECIFICITY OF MARSEILLE

Marseille's sense of uniqueness within France was founded upon three factors: its geographical location, its economic activity, and most importantly, its unusual population structure. Perched on the southern edge of the country Marseille was clearly part of France but an extremely unusual one. The city had traditionally been dominated by its port, whose activities encouraged this sense of separation from the mainland. The port served less as a gateway to France than as a port of transformation for the Mediterranean. Raw materials were imported, processed in the city, and then re-exported across the Mediterranean. This pattern of trade was centuries-old and increased Marseille's identity as a Mediterranean rather than a French community.

The city's Mediterranean identity was reinforced by its population structure. In 1936 the 200,000 foreigners accounted for almost one-third of its population.[3] Over half of these foreigners (125,000) came from Italy and the rest from Spain and other Mediterranean countries. But these figures do not give a true impression of the local population. They exclude people naturalized after coming to Marseille. Also since large-scale immigration to the town had been underway for eighty years a far larger number of people were themselves children of immigrants.[4] In addition the largest single category of Mediterranean migrants and the one with perhaps the strongest sense of identity – the Corsicans – were never included in these figures on *foreign* immigrants.

This unusual population structure combined with port employment's seasonal and informal nature to create a set of social relations which posed

---

[2] There are still no full-length published studies of the Popular Front at local level. Jacques Kergoat, *La France du Front Populaire* (Paris, 1986), has used many of the unpublished theses and mémoires dealing with provincial experiences of the period, but he only gives vague source references and uses local evidence in an often haphazard way.

[3] The official census figure for the Marseille population in 1936 was 914,232. But this figure was grossly inflated, and most local historians suspect that the genuine figure was nearer to 620,000. See Levy 'Marseille working-class movement', chapter 1 for more details on the population structure and the reasons for census fraud.

[4] William Sewell, *Structure and Mobility: the men and women of Marseille, 1820–1870* (Cambridge, 1985), gives an admirable description of the city's immigration and population structure in the nineteenth century.

problems for those keen to organize workers along class lines. For many of the foreign workers in Marseille their primary sentiment was one of insecurity, both towards the state which treated them as aliens, and towards employers, who in a time of high unemployment, and with casual labour markets, could pick and choose workers at will. The competition for jobs within the working class and the migrant's fear of the official bureaucracy meant that many were more inclined to seek security through the loyalty of the clan rather than through that of their class.

The Marseille political system reflected local economic and social realities in that it too seemed more Mediterranean than French. Patronage and clientelism reached their peak in the town during the 1920s and early 1930s. Immigration's rapid pace in these years combined with the decomposition of the Radical Party's political hegemony nationally. The rapid succession of elections (which took place annually in Marseille between 1928 and 1932) supplied an environment in which ideologically-based political commitment was low, and where there was a sizeable group of people to be mobilized on a clientelist basis in elections, on the understanding that their political patrons would facilitate integration into society.[5]

Immigration provided the basis for Marseille's unusual political practices, and it was above all the Corsicans and Italians who helped the local political machines function. These immigrants did not arrive at random, but rather came from villages with a tradition of migration to Marseille. As they arrived they brought with them their villages' clan structures, which were then reinforced in the face of the new, alien environment. The novelty surrounding the re-establishment of traditional clan structures lay in the way they were adapted to a society with a stronger state, and where access to the political machine unlocked certain rewards. Democracy rapidly transformed the traditional clan system into a spoils system.[6]

The operation of a spoils system facilitated the political mobilization of migrants in a city with a traditionally low level of political and electoral participation. The constant expansion of municipal employment between the mid 1920s and 1938 was the most public evidence of this system at work, but it was well known that poor relief through the local *Bureau de bienfaisance* fulfilled a similar function. These practices were perfected by Simon Sabiani between 1929 and 1935 when he effectively controlled the

[5] See Levy, 'Marseille working-class movements', chapter 4.
[6] See F. Pomponi, 'a la recherche d'un "invariant" historique: la structure clanique dans la société corse', *Pieve e paesi* (Paris, 1978). I owe this reference and some of the interpretations here to A. Chenu, 'Industrialisation, urbanisation et pratiques de classe: le cas des ouvriers de la région marseillaise' (Thèse, sociologie, University of Toulouse–Le Mirail, 1981).

local council. Politicians like Sabiani not only offered employment to their supporters, they also offered the *titularisation* which was the key to permanent employment. The promise of *titularisation* was most commonly made between the two electoral rounds to those municipal employees who could be persuaded to vote for the ruling party in marginal areas. These practices were only the natural corollary of a system where security, and above all job security was seen as being in the hands of local politicians. Even a middle-ranking local politician could favour members of his clan on an extraordinarily large scale. The example of the migrants who came to Marseille from the Corsican settlement of Calenzana provides just one illustration of the system at work. That almost half of these migrants succeeded in obtaining prized public sector employment had a great deal to do with the presence in the town of some powerful Calenzanais political patrons – Jean-François Leca, an SFIO local councillor, and the brothers Guerini, who were close friends of the SFIO leader, Henri Tasso, and controlled one of the city's most powerful criminal operations.[7]

The role of the clan in obtaining employment was reflected in the activity of several local trade unions, particularly those in the docks and public sector. Access to many jobs was effectively controlled by the few powerful trade unions in the city, whose bosses were either political leaders in their own right or had close contact with influential local politicians. From the very beginning of the 1920s, for example, it was the municipal workers' trade union which presented the relevant local council committee chairman with the names of those workers who should be employed. Practices such as these, where one joined a trade union *before* beginning work, and precisely for the purpose of obtaining it, contributed to a clientelist system's operation and the accompanying downgrading of ideological motivations.[8]

Clientelism was accompanied by political corruption and violence. These aspects of local life were most obvious in and around the port where they complemented the traditional illegal activities ranging from prosti-

---

[7] Calenzanais showed a great reluctance for manual occupations. Their contacts were sufficiently good to ensure that few of them were relegated to that sector. 42 per cent of their number went into the *fonction publique* while 43 per cent obtained other white-collar jobs. M-F. Maraninchi, 'Un exemple de migration dans l'entre-deux-guerres. L'exode Calenzanais' (Mémoire de maîtrise, University of Provence, 1971), p. 101. On crime and corruption in the SFIO see Levy, 'Marseille working-class movement', pp. 169–72.

[8] Clientelistic considerations prevailed over those of efficiency in the case of municipal employment. The number of workers employed by the city administration increased by 2,000 from 1930 to 1938, but only 123 of these posts were advertised for open competition. See Levy, 'Marseille working-class movement', p. 178.

tution to smuggling and theft. But in the 1920s and 1930s the violence and corruption spilled over into political life. Local gangsters found that political parties were only too ready to accept their services, as bodyguards and election agents. The scale and range of electoral fraud was extensive and criminals could be useful in supplying 'flying' voters who could move from one polling station to the next, vote in the name of dead people or sailors known to be at sea, or simply intimidate political opponents.[9]

The SFIO in Marseille was closely implicated in these clientelistic and corrupt practices. They were used to consolidate the position of a party whose ideology, locally, provided little to distinguish it from its Radical Party rival. Indeed, in many respects the success of the Marseille SFIO lay in its ability to assume local Radicalism's mantle and then to complement it with the support of large parts of the local Corsican and Italian communities. The SFIO deliberately tried to appeal to the electorate on a very broad basis, cutting across classes, stressing local and traditional Radical Party issues such as anti-clericalism. In normal times this approach often produced electoral success but it limited the number of workers who were sufficiently enthusiastic about the party to become active members. Only one-third of party activists were working class.[10] The inability of the SFIO to implement radical change in Marseille despite its sizeable representation in the Chamber of Deputies and its frequent control of the local council probably caused a certain disillusionment with political remedies amongst the local working class. Most affected were those native-born groups least likely to be utilizing the local clientelist system.

The Marseille SFIO tended to describe itself primarily as a defender of local interests rather than in class or ideological terms. Ideologically orthodox, but apparently only passionately so when attacked from the left, the SFIO tried to present itself to the populace as the most efficient political negotiator to whom Marseille's interests might be entrusted. By concentrating in parliamentary election campaigns on its ability to obtain favours for Marseille in Paris, it encouraged the very localism to which it was appealing. Electors were even more inclined to see the political issues discussed in Paris as being remote, and to view the SFIO as their political

---

9 These measures were perfected by Simon Sabiani, who was the effective, although not the official mayor of Marseille from 1929 to 1935. For more details on Sabiani see J-A. Vaucoret, 'Un homme politique contesté: Simon Sabiani (biographie)' (Thèse de 3ème cycle, University of Provence, 1978).
10 M. D'Agostino, 'L'implantation socialiste à Marseille sous le Front Populaire' (Mémoire de maîtrise, Aix, 1972), p. 68.

patron in negotiations with the state in an enlarged version of the patron–client relationship on which the party functioned locally. This perspective allowed little room for the consideration of potential conflicts of interest within the city. Instead, men such as Henri Tasso, a shipper, SFIO deputy and mayor of Marseille from 1935 to 1939, were sent to Paris to defend the port and its associated industries with little consideration of whether everything that helped the port might be of equal help to those who worked in it. This approach to politics was ill-suited to meet the coming challenge of a more class-based, national, and ideologically-charged political movement as represented by the Popular Front.

The strong point of the SFIO's localism was that it rested on a dense network of community structures in the city. Groups such as the Amis d'Instruction Laique (AIL), the local anti-clerical association, provided the working-class base for the SFIO, and with it a tissue of collectively organized activity at the level of the *quartier* which could form the basis for later political initiatives. The SFIO won control of the AIL movement just after the First World War largely because there was no other contender. The PCF viewed anti-clericalism as a bourgeois deviation from the class struggle, while the other candidate, the Radical Party, had lost credibility among the local working class. The AILs were a valuable asset. Their membership of 13,000 was more than twice that of the SFIO. The forty-two AIL groups in Marseille were present in almost every part of the city. Their number, though, was greatest in the working-class areas, even if their day-to-day running was usually assured by members of the middle class, most commonly teachers. With an SFIO local councillor or party activist on the management committee of almost every AIL group, the organization provided the party with a useful platform. When one of the AIL's numerous football or basketball teams played a match, it was usually an SFIO dignitary who presented the prizes. There was a constant interaction of this kind between the party and the AILs. The difficulty for the SFIO was that it won control of this movement precisely at the time when the issue on which it was founded, anti-clericalism, was declining.[11]

THE IMPACT OF ECONOMIC CHANGE

In the 1930s there were various challenges which called into question both Marseille's sense of separation and specificity in France, and the highly

---

[11] See B. Bouisson, 'L'anticléricalisme à Marseille entre 1919 et 1939' (Thèse de 3eme cycle, Aix, 1971), p. 112, and Levy 'Marseille working-class movement', p. 150.

original pattern of community and politics in the city. Some of these challenges were internally generated but others derived from changes brought about by the Popular Front.

Much of the Marseille's originality depended on its prime economic function, that of the port. But in the interwar period this traditional domination began to be called into question. The new generation of chemical and petrochemical industries tended not to be located in and around the historic centre of Marseille but rather inland towards the Etang de Berre. This industrial dispersal took place in response both to the overcrowding of the old industrial areas and because of the undesirability of locating potentially dangerous industries too close to the city centre. A new network of canals made the move possible and created inland ports which soon challenged the supremacy of Marseille itself. The effects were dramatic. Increasingly, Marseille's main economic activities came to be based away from its historic centre and were directed more to the domestic than the foreign market. The new factories were financed by national and even international, rather than by local capital. Their managers were more likely to be professionals appointed by a remote company in Paris or London than the sons of well-known local captains of industry. These changes in economic structure called into question Marseille's previous sense of separation from the mainland. They also undermined the previously established community structures based on the old working-class *quartiers* in and around the port. Fewer workers could now live and find employment in the city's traditional working-class areas. They had to choose between moving to new, often incomplete, industrial suburbs, and spending up to an hour commuting. The new factories were far larger than those of traditional local industries. In place of the port's informality the new industries substituted routine, discipline and control as employers and managers tried to impose local adaptations of American-inspired, modern line management methods and to create more rational production systems. Traditional industries had been protected from these developments, partly through local insularity and pride, but also because Marseille's favourable location meant that they were able to monopolize the captive Mediterranean and colonial market where there were fewer pressures to keep costs down. The newer chemical and engineering factories, by contrast, worked in a far more competitive environment and were under more pressure to control labour costs since their clients were far freer to choose suppliers elsewhere in France or Europe.[12]

[12] Ibid., chapter 2, passim.

New production techniques produced a depersonalization of workplace relations which compounded the effects of the accompanying dislocation of old community ties. Together the change made life rather easier for those communist activists who argued that the old SFIO cross-class appeal based on local solidarity and appeals to vague ideas such as anti-clericalism no longer made sense. In the 1920s and early 1930s Communists had proposed instead a politics which made the workplace the centre of its attention, arguing that the conflicts and issues raised at the factory were of prime importance. By the mid 1930s these arguments carried more weight than before but Marseille was not yet a purely industrial and proletarian city even if it was moving in that direction. The traditional bases of local politics had been weakened but Communists needed a new alliance strategy and a less sectarian approach if they were to progress.[13]

THE POPULAR FRONT AND THE TRANSFORMATION OF THE POLITICAL SYSTEM

Fascism and its antithesis, anti-fascism, provided the opportunity for change in the local political system. Its rise first in Italy, then in Germany and Spain, had a particular resonance in Marseille. The large number of immigrants from Spain and Italy who had often remained unmoved by domestic French left-wing politics, suddenly discovered in anti-fascism an issue and campaign which had a particular meaning for them. Italians in Marseille had long been interested and active in anti-fascist activities, since many of them were refugees from Mussolini, but Hitler's seizure of power and the 6 February 1934 riots combined with Franco's uprising in Spain to create a sense of immediacy about the anti-fascist cause which previously had been lacking. Paradoxically, in Marseille it was this *international* aspect of the Popular Front movement which succeeded in mobilizing for a national campaign those parts of the population which had previously remained unmoved by domestic left-wing politics.

If fascism seemed a real threat to Marseille's immigrant population, the city's position, halfway between the Spanish and Italian borders, and the strength of local right-wing groups must have made it seem equally genuine to many French-born inhabitants too. The 20,000 or so people in the Bouches-du-Rhône who were prepared to join extreme right-wing groups such as the Parti Populaire Français and the Parti Social Français in the mid 1930s outnumbered the local PCF and SFIO memberships

[13] Ibid., chapter 5.

combined. The numerical strength of these extreme right-wing and often avowedly fascist groups lent urgency to the anti-fascist campaign and led many local people to be swept into the Popular Front movement.

The Comintern's change of line in 1934 meant that the PCF was to play a key role in mobilizing anti-fascist feeling and in transforming it into a campaign for the Popular Front of all republican forces. Previously, Communists had only been interested in narrowly class-based campaigns and had embraced local workers' traditional disdain for Parisian parliamentary politics. Now they argued in favour of a broad coalition, partly to mobilize a grass-roots campaign, but also to deny political power to anti-republican forces. This change in line had a particularly striking impact in Marseille. Communist support for the Popular Front breathed new life into a republican reflex which had seemed worn out after so many years of being used to give a radical appearance to the essentially moderate and pragmatic local Socialist and Radical parties. Anti-fascism assumed anti-clericalism's old role first by creating a popular political and social movement, and then, strikingly, by marrying this at the base with a particular political programme. This force was channelled through the political parties and then implemented via the Third Republic's traditional parliamentary machinery.

The new movement built on some of the strengths of the old associational tradition. Popular Front political, social and recreational committees could build on the framework of groups like the Amis d'Instruction Laique. But if some of the Popular Front's structures were marked by continuity with local political traditions, the mood surrounding the new movement showed a marked break with the past. The cosiness of the corrupt local political system was disrupted. National, and even internationally-based ideological politics were introduced into a city where most politicians had argued that politics was strictly about practical, local issues and could be solved by action at local level, or if necessary by an additional subsidy from Paris. The local Communists succeeded in persuading many Marseille electors, even those who did not vote for them, that the government in Paris did matter, that national politics were relevant to Marseille, and in more than a purely instrumental way. Partly this represented the triumph of a more ideological view of politics, but it marked the triumph of a participatory view as well. The Popular Front movement was perceived as a crusade. As such participation in demonstrations, at meetings and in discussions over the parties' programmes was encouraged. This was markedly different from the old view of Marseille politics where a vote was purely a commodity to be sold to whichever politician could promise a job or obtain the fullest order book for the local shipyard. Workers were encouraged to discuss their demands and to help formulate a political programme in ways not before experienced. There was also a new readiness to talk about how a Popular Front government could help a working class which had previously viewed the central state's activities with wariness or at best indifference. The Matignon agreement and the new industrial relations system which followed Blum's election showed just how important governmental action could be for the organized working class. The new system of collective contracts, compulsory concili- ation and arbitration tended to force local conflicts into a fresh mould, imposing a new rhythm on the successive rounds of strikes and generaliz- ing the resolution of conflicts. The result was that after June 1936 more demands were channelled through the trade union hierarchy and towards the state's representatives: either the mayor, prefect, or minister of labour.

The Marseille SFIO failed to reap the benefits of the new political situation. Local SFIO leaders saw the communist share of the Marseille left-wing vote increase dramatically.[14] Similarly, increases in party and union membership profited the PCF far more than the Socialists. The clientelism of the Marseille SFIO was ill-equipped to deal with the challenge presented by the Popular Front's passionately ideological mood, with its crusades against fascism and the two hundred families, and with the vast increase in working-class expectations which it stimulated. With the Popular Front, voters expected more than simply jobs, housing or the other favours that socialist patrons had previously provided in exchange for votes. Besides, the municipality was facing bankruptcy and funds which had traditionally oiled the wheels of the local political machine were exhausted.[15] The attempt to set up socialist workplace groups known as Amicales Socialistes (AS) represented a belated attempt at national level to fight off the increasing communist domination of the factories and trade unions. But in Marseille the AS movement made little headway in the large

---

[14] First-round parliamentary election results in Marseille for Communists and Socialists expressed as a percentage of votes cast are as follows:

Date	PCF	SFIO
1924	6	47
1928	10	48
1932	10	44
1936	29	31

(Source: Levy, 'Marseille working-class movement', p. 109)

[15] After 1937 the level of municipal indebtedness meant that no new workers could be recruited.

private-sector factories where the Communists had been so active. Instead, the AS seemed more like an adaptation of past clientelist practices as municipal and other public-sector employees joined in the hope that with a socialist prime minister, AS membership would secure them wage rises and greater job security. Having failed to profit from working-class mobilization generated by the Popular Front campaign, the Marseille SFIO was to suffer later by identification with a government whose performance fell far short of workers' admittedly inflated expectations.

The SFIO's loss was the Communists' gain. Before 1934 the PCF did appallingly badly in Marseille, in both membership and votes. At the end of 1933 the party had only two hundred members in the city. But after February 1934 Communists were active in a whole range of factory and community-based activities which produced an influx of recruits and extended the party's influence.[16] Communists were among the most energetic organizers in the docks and among public-service workers, stealing the ground from underneath the cautious *confédéré* leaders in each sector. The PCF also devoted considerable efforts to organizing workers in the local engineering factories and in the newer chemical and petrochemical plants. As the idea of the *Rassemblement Populaire* was extended to include almost anyone who was not accused of being a member of the 'two hundred families' there was a similar extension of communist efforts at organization. PCF militants became active in the old socialist-influenced community groups, and also set up new associations which recruited sympathizers not yet ready to join the PCF itself. The whole mood of the Popular Front, with its sense of unity, and the priority which it placed on political activism and ideological rather than clientelistic appeals, tended to aid a party like the local PCF which could present itself as the most active proponent of anti-fascism, the prime mover behind the Popular Front, and the defender of the working class against the 'two hundred families'. The party was also successful in its campaigns to 'clean up Marseille', as people tired of the constant scandals, corruption and criminality associated with local political life. The PCF persuaded many local people that politicians did not have to be corrupt and motivated only by self-interest. It held up its local leaders, the deputies François Billoux and Jean Cristofol, and the CGT leader, Charles Nédelec, as examples of men with personal and political morality above reproach. The claim was somewhat overdone. What was

---

16 Whereas in 1934 PCF membership in the *département* was only a tiny proportion of that of the SFIO, by 1937 the PCF with 10,000 members was way ahead of the SFIO's 8151. Levy 'Marseille working-class movement', p. 114 and appendix 8.

true was that these leading Communists were uncompromised by any public association with the local criminal fraternity. And since they were relatively recent arrivals in Marseille, without experience of elected office, they had had little opportunity to engage in political corruption.

Communist successes among the working class meant that the party rapidly won control of the newly reunited Union Départmentale and Union Locale of the CGT. The complaints of socialist trade unionists about communist entryism were, on occasions, justified. But arguments about the need for the political independence of trade unions had no effect in a city where everyone knew that control of key trade unions such as the dockers, sailors, and council workers, had always been regarded precisely as the prerequisite of political power. After June 1936, however, the expansion in union membership and changes in the industrial relations system meant that control of the local union movement conferred even more power than before. In 1937 and 1938 the PCF repeatedly used its control of the CGT for strictly political ends. On occasions their purpose was to bolster Popular Front governments, but after summer 1938 the aim was far more to incite industrial unrest designed to challenge the Daladier government and, with it, the Munich agreement.

Communist opposition to the Daladier government made little headway in Marseille. For the Marseillais the natural accompaniment to anti-fascism was pacifism and Daladier's attempts to avoid war were welcomed. Nevertheless, the debate over Munich within the local labour movement reflected the way in which the Popular Front experience had changed the climate of Marseille working-class politics. Before the Popular Front, quiescence, parochialism and clientelism were the norm in Marseille. After the Popular Front national and international concerns impinged much more on the life of the local working class. Ideologies and mass mobilization increasingly replaced the naked search for spoils and patronage which had previously provided the stuff of Marseille politics. The politics of class came to haunt the practitioners of clientelism. Corruption, clientelism and patronage all continued, but after 1936 politicians in Marseille were forced to recognize that their clients were aware of the wider world and were, on occasions, ready to mobilize to make demands upon it.

A reinterpretation of the Spanish Popular Front: the case of Asturias[*]

ADRIAN SHUBERT

On 4 October 1934 the workers of the Spanish coalmining region of Asturias rose in armed revolt against the government of the Second Republic. This was intended as part of a nationwide rising planned by the Socialist Party (PSOE) to overthrow the right-wing republican government. The aim was to prevent what it saw as the menace of a fascist takeover and then to install a government committed to sweeping social reform. However the socialist rising was incompetently planned and only in Asturias did it materialize. But there the PSOE's limited objectives were immediately exceeded by a radicalized working class which initiated a full-scale social revolution under the banner of the Alianza Obrera, (Workers' Alliance). The Asturian 'Commune' lasted two weeks before it was defeated by 26,000 troops from the Spanish army and Foreign Legion. Widespread and vicious repression ensued.[1]

The memory of the Asturian revolution persisted in Spanish politics from October 1934 until the Civil War's outbreak in July 1936. The Popular Front, the vehicle by which the left returned to power in February 1936, was one of its by-products. Yet if the history of the Spanish Popular Front is well known, ironically the Popular Front in Asturias itself has

---

[*] The author wishes to thank Lola de la Calle of the University of Salamanca for her help in gathering research material for this article.

[1] On the causes and course of the Asturian insurrection see my book *The Road to Revolution in Spain* (Champaign-Urbana, 1987).

suffered neglect.[2] Such meagre scholarship as has been devoted to it deals exclusively with its political aspects.

My purpose in this essay is to redress the balance and to suggest – the scarcity of sources prevents anything more definite – that the Popular Front in Asturias was more than just a regional expression of a national political alliance. Rather, it had its own life, addressed local as well as national concerns, and went beyond the narrow sphere of electoral politics.

THE POPULAR FRONT IN SPANISH POLITICS

The Popular Front was formally created on 15 January 1936. It was a broad electoral coalition of six political parties: Unión Republicana (UR), Izquierda Republicana (IR), Partido Socialistra Obrero Español (PSOE), Partido Comunista de España (PCE), Partido Sindicalista and the Partido Obrero de Unificación Marxista (POUM), together with the socialist union confederation, UGT, and the Young Socialists. The alliance presented a single list of candidates in the elections held on 16 February. It pledged parliamentary support for a government to be composed solely of Republicans and for the implementing of the programme outlined in the manifesto. Its major points were amnesty for 'all political and social crimes' committed before 15 November 1935, defence of the constitution, agricultural reform, parliamentary reform, protectionist measures for industry, intensification of public works, tax reform, educational reform and new social legislation. The measures proposed in the crucial area of agricultural reform were extremely modest; more credit and lower taxes, a new tenancy law and a land policy for 'settling peasant families'.[3]

This electoral alliance was a form of leftist unity to prevent the right remaining in power after the elections. For the Republicans, who both inspired and dominated it, the Popular Front was equally a means of avoiding social revolution by reassimilating the working class's principal political organization – the PSOE – into a progressive, reforming Republic. It represented a return to the formative political alignment of the Second Republic; the 1931 coalition between Republicans and Socialists. The project was initiated by Manuel Azaña and strongly supported

---

[2] The best study of the Spanish Popular Front is S. Juliá, *Orígenes del Frente Popular en España, 1934–1936* (Madrid, 1979).
[3] *El Sol*, 16 January 1936.

by Indalecio Prieto of the PSOE in the face of violent opposition within his own party.[4]

Although the first steps towards what was to become the Popular Front were taken in the spring of 1934, by consolidating three republican groups into Izquierda Republicana, the coalition's real beginnings lay in the Asturian insurrection's failure in October 1934. The government's clumsy attempt to implicate Azaña prompted the final coalescing of centre and left-wing Republicans in April 1935. More importantly it allowed Prieto – unconvinced of the wisdom of either the September 1933 break with the Republicans or the October 1934 insurrection – publicly to advocate an agreement with the Republicans.[5] From April to December 1935 he struggled against those within the socialist movement – especially the young socialist leadership – who rejected this approach. For Prieto's opponents, the lesson of October 1934 was that the PSOE had to be converted into a disciplined revolutionary party on the bolshevik model.[6]

The Asturian insurrection and its implications were at the heart of the creation of the electoral alliance known as the Popular Front. But that alliance was only one of a number of competing formulae for leftist unity in Spain after October 1934. Another was the Popular Front as elaborated by the Comintern at its Seventh Congress in July–August 1935. In Spain, this strategy was championed by the PCE. But the party's relative marginalization – even after October 1934 – meant that the Popular Front in the Spanish context continued to turn on a republican–socialist axis. A second, more important, alternative was the Alianza Obrera, a revolutionary, anti-fascist workers' front proposed by Joaquin Maurín, the POUM leader and a dissident Communist.

Maurín had formulated the strategy of a workers' front in 1933 in response to Hitler and had hoped to establish workers' alliances throughout Spain. But anarchist hostility and socialist suspicion prevented this except in Asturias, where an increasingly radicalized working class forced local Socialists and Anarchists to combine in March 1934. Both official and dissident Communists joined later. The October events only confirmed Maurín's belief that the Alianza Obrera was the best organization for the working class. Throughout 1935 he unavailingly attempted to interest the PSOE, and especially the increasingly radicalized Largo Caballero. Faced with socialist apathy and the increasing support at the

---

[4] P. Preston, 'Manuel Azaña y la creación del Frente Popular, 1933–1936' in V. Serrano (ed.), *Azaña* (Madrid, 1981).
[5] I. Prieto, *Posiciones Socialistas* (Madrid, 1935).   [6] *Octubre, segunda etapa* (Madrid, 1935).

base for some sort of electoral alliance, Maurín and his party were eventually obliged to adhere to the Popular Front pact, even though they took no part in its creation.[7]

THE MAKING OF THE ASTURIAN POPULAR FRONT

Nationally the Asturian October was both central to the Popular Front's genesis and, as a political model, the principal alternative to it. In the region itself, the October events were the crucial determinant of the political debate. Of course, Asturians never lost sight of the wider political context of which they were a part and this context conditioned, or at least informed, regional developments. However, the making of the Asturian Popular Front did more than merely produce a local copy of a national realignment.

As at national level, the Asturian Popular Front began with a rapprochement for electoral purposes among the republican left's parties. As early as May 1934 the Asturian branch of Izquierda Republicana was in contact with the Radical Socialists, the supporters of Miguel Maura and the tiny Partido Republicano Democrático Federal of Gijón with 'the principal object of a firm leftist unity leading to the creation of a single party'.[8] The latter responded that they would support a federation of parties in which each retained its personality. However, no further references occur to this subject until May 1935, when the party received another letter from IR 'expressing satisfaction at our party's desire ... to arrive at an understanding for the next electoral struggle'.[9]

By this time, the question of an electoral alliance had outgrown the rather narrow confines of the republican left to include the PSOE. The region's most prominent socialist leaders, such as Ramón González Peña and Amador Fernández, fully supported Indalecio Prieto's efforts to create an electoral combination with the Republicans. González Peña had played a prominent part in the October 1934 insurrection, being known as the rising's 'generalísimo'. Nonetheless his experience of revolution had not shaken his life-long belief in electoralism and reformism. In the internal party polemics which erupted after October 1934 he publicly expressed himself firmly on the side of Prieto against those who wanted to 'bolshevize' the party and to purge the non-revolutionaries.

[7] J. Maurín, *Revolución y contrarrevolución en España* (Paris, 1966).
[8] Libro de Actas, Partido Republicano Democrático Federal, 9 May 1934, Gijón, Legajo K5, Archivo Histórico Nacional, Sección de la Guerra Civil (AHN-GC), Salamanca.
[9] Ibid., 20 May 1935.

By late March 1935 the left's attacks had prompted him to write to Prieto that both he and Fernández, leader of the powerful Asturian miners' union (SMA), fully supported his idea of an electoral alliance: 'If it should come to a split in the party, rest assured that I identify with your ideas, as does Amador ... It is my view that there should be an anti-fascist front for the election to end the repression and bring those responsible to trial. Then we require a congress to determine the party's strategy.'[10] Addressing the Madrid section of the socialist youth, González Peña gave a more detailed description of the alliance he envisaged. This proved, in the event, a fairly accurate depiction of the future Popular Front.

Just now I see no alternative to fighting the elections on the basis of an understanding with the parties of the left – from the Republicans to the Syndicalists – provided they accept. Our weapon should be a programme of measures to be taken immediately. Among these the most interesting would be the transfer of deeds of ownership to the present tenants on the land. This would exempt only the small farmer who works the land with his family.[11]

González Peña's position was echoed in the newspaper *La Tarde*, which first appeared late in May 1935. (Although there was no indication of who was behind the new weekly it was essentially the principal socialist daily of the region, *Avance*, closed down in October 1934, under another name.) *La Tarde* called the occasion of Azaña's speech at Valencia, the first of his three open-air speeches, 'a magnificent day for the reconquest of the Republic. More than anyone else Azaña embodies the true spirit of the Republic.' The paper demanded a 'close alliance of liberals, republicans and men of good faith'. However the editors betrayed what would always be the abiding Asturian interest in the pact when they announced that 'the alliance will have only one programme: amnesty, amnesty, amnesty'.[12] The following week the paper was even more optimistic. 'If any doubt remained about the unity of the Republicans it has disappeared ... What most frightens the Republic's enemies about the Valencia demonstration is the form in which don Manuel expressed himself, his clarity ... Everything is within reach; electoral coalition with a programme for governing, based on the support of the forces to their left.'[13]

The national debate received the most attention but an equally impassioned one was taking place among the Asturian Socialists. However, the issues were not entirely the same, nor could they have been given the

---

[10] *Documentos socialistas* (Madrid, 1935), pp. 145–6.   [11] Ibid., pp. 150–1.
[12] *La Tarde*, 27 May 1935.
[13] Ibid., 3 June 1935.

existence of such a radicalized working class and the recent revolutionary experience. The Asturian debate's centre of gravity lay leftward of that in the party as a whole.[14] Julián Besteiro's followers, the principal targets of the socialist left nationally, were all but ignored in the north. The struggle there was primarily between the supporters of Prieto and the republican alliance and the advocates of bolshevization. But instead of finding expression in such terms, the key issue was the form that working-class unity should take: the Alianza Obrera or a single marxist party.

The first major contribution to the debate came from young socialist leader, Santiago Carrillo, the foremost proponent of purging the PSOE. Advocating the creation of one united marxist party, Carrillo rejected as 'unacceptable' the turning of the Alianza Obrera into a nationwide organization, 'which implies that the parties will have to give up their leading role'. For Carrillo the Alianza Obrera constituted a federalist approach to meet the needs of the moment. But it could be no substitute for a single party and youth organization embracing the entire marxist proletariat.[15] Carrillo was immediately attacked by miners' leader Amador Fernández. Although at the national level Fernández supported Prieto, in the regional debate he presented himself as a defender of the Alianza Obrera against the concept of organizational unity. The former was superior because it allowed a number and variety of organizations to work together while each retained its identity and independence. It was also much more feasible: 'To fuse various parties into one successfully is much more difficult to do than to propose.'[16]

On 23 November Silverio Castañón, a young socialist leader, in prison under sentence of death, defended the Alianza Obrera as a revolutionary weapon but also urged the PSOE not to 'look down on any legal means – especially elections – that may be useful in mobilizing the masses'. Although not believing that socialism could be achieved by electoral means, he saw the need to oust the right from power. 'I support a temporary alliance – although with a specific programme – with all the least unworthy elements of the left to end this chaotic situation of unbridled rightism. But there can be no question of our party being represented in the cabinet.'[17] Jesús Ibáñez, who supported both marxist unity and the Alianza Obrera, opposed a purge of the party, but from a clearly revolutionary standpoint: 'We must eliminate from our midst any democratic illusions in the knowledge that any new collaboration, however

[14] P. I. Taibo, *Asturias, 1934* (Gijon, 1984), vol. 2, p. 207.   [15] *Asturias*, 26 Oct. 1935.
[16] Ibid., 2 November 1935.   [17] Ibid., 23 November 1935.

revolutionary its claims, cannot provide the working class with fully socialist solutions.'[18]

Imprisoned members of the region's youth socialists also contributed to the debate. They issued two letters, displaying 'a vehement opposition to the position of the young socialist executive and the authors of the pamphlet *Octubre*'. The executive and the pamphleteers demanded the bolshevization of the party through a purge of Besteiro's wing. The Asturian youth required 'to know why [the socialist youth executive] had not participated in the revolutionary movement. [They also] rejected the theses of bolshevization and marxist unity within a single party and called for an alliance with the republican left in the next elections'.[19]

The Asturian Socialists were not alone in debating how to confront the political situation at the end of 1935. The CNT's regional federation did likewise, although its debates were 'more subterranean'.[20] While most Asturian Anarcho-syndicalists had supported the Alianza Obrera in 1934, against the rest of the CNT and the AIT, the question of what position to take over the forthcoming elections and the Popular Front proved much more divisive. The division had a precedent in the controversy caused by the decision of the Asturian *cenetistas* exiled in France to join early in 1935 the Comité de Unidad de los Refugiados Políticos Españoles which included the PSOE, PCE, UGT, BOC, Sindicatos de Oposición, Republicans and the French and Spanish Red Cross. This decision was criticized at the time by French Anarchists as well as later at the May 1936 CNT national congress.[21]

For Asturian Anarcho-syndicalists there was no question of revising their fundamental 'apoliticism'; the issue was how to secure the freedom of those gaoled in October 1934. As Niceto de la Iglesia wrote to Avelino González Entrialgo, exiled in Belgium: 'presently those who say we should participate in the election constitute a majority. We believe, not in parliaments, but that the prisoners must be freed and our meeting places opened'.[22] Another friend, Horacio Argüelles, wrote that 'if the CNT committees promote an abstentionist campaign, as now looks likely ... it will lead the organization to disaster'.[23]

In February 1936, shortly before the election, the Asturian CNT held a poll of its members which even reached those in the Cárcel Modelo in

[18] Ibid., 14 December 1935.   [19] Taibo, *Asturias*, vol. 2, p. 205.
[20] Ibid., vol. 2, p. 197.
[21] Ibid., vol. 2, pp. 194–5.
[22] de la Iglesia to González Entrialgo, Gijón, Leg. J12, AHN-GC.
[23] Argüelles to González Entrialgo, Gijón, Leg. J12, AHN-GC.

Oviedo, although the prisoners refused to express an opinion lest they unduly influence the others. The debates in the regional plenum held to resolve the issues were, according to Fernando Solano Palacio, 'violent'. But in the end the plenum voted 'to participate in the elections and to recommend that members vote for the candidacy of the left', although no public declaration was made.[24]

The debates in the CNT were undoubtedly heated because they involved fundamental questions of political and moral principle. Something of the anguish is caught in the letters sent to González Entrialgo by his companion, Olivia Díaz, between November 1935 and February 1936. On 13 November she was optimistic about the elections; 'at least the atmosphere is clearly favourable. The prisoners count for a lot. You hear many people who say that before anything else all those men must be freed. Yesterday Niceto said that if the left wins you will all be home by 14 April.'[25] At the end of January 1936 she described the rally which she had attended in the Salón Popular in Gijón. PSOE, PCE and IR representatives addressed the large and enthusiastic audience, 'with many people left outside for lack of space'. Olivia was impressed by the Republican, Carlos Martínez, because 'he gave the most details and ... seemed very reasonable', although he was strongly critical of the CNT's abstention campaign in the 1933 elections. She herself opposed abstentionism and accused one anarchist said to be advocating it of having used influential connections to stay out of gaol.[26] In her last letter before the election she captured the dilemma facing the anarchists. Participation in electoral politics was unavoidable 'for the sake of those in prison ... we must vote and do everything possible to free them from the clutches of the enemy'.[27]

The decision taken by the CNT regional plenum to recommend that its members vote for the left was crucial to the Popular Front's success in Asturias. In November 1933, when the CNT had pursued its ¡No Votad! campaign, the right won Asturias with 127,000 votes compared to a combined total of 113,000 for the parties of the left. The PSOE, PCE and IR had received combined totals of 8,909 and 836 votes respectively in the two CNT strongholds of Gijón and la Felguera. By comparison, in 1936 the Popular Front received 21,955 and 3,217. This was an increase of 15,000 votes, more than the difference between right and left in 1933 and enough to account for virtually all the difference in 1936, when the gap between the

[24] Taibo, *Asturias*, vol. 2, pp. 213–14.
[25] Díaz to González Entrialgo, 13 November 1935, Gijón, Leg. J12, AHN-GC.
[26] Ibid., 31 January 1936.   [27] Ibid., 7 February 1936. Author's italics.

ten leading candidates of the Popular Front and those of the right was slightly over 16,000 votes.[28]

THE ELECTION CAMPAIGN

Following the signing of the left's electoral pact on 15 January 1936, the most pressing task was the allocation of candidacies and the selection of candidates. During his campaign to establish the alliance Prieto had assured PSOE members that their party would receive the number of candidacies proportional to its electoral strength.[29] In practice this was not the case. Candidacies were divided between the PSOE and the Republicans so as to allow the latter to govern alone. The other working-class parties would receive their candidacies from the PSOE's share. At national level this meant that, based on the 1933 results, each candidature given the Republicans represented 8,552 votes, while each socialist place represented 12,775.[30] This inequality also existed in Asturias. On the strength of the 1933 results the Socialists should have secured ten places on the list, the Communists two and the Republicans one. In fact the Socialists sacrificed their party interests, taking only six places compared to two for the Communists and five for the Republicans.

Since PSOE rules required that candidates be chosen by local organizations, the Popular Front committee's role became that of approving local decisions. The socialist candidates were chosen in a poll (*antevotación*) held on 30 January. The top six were Matilde de la Torre with 1,413 votes, Inocencio Burgos 1,340, Ramón González Peña, 1,304, Amador Fernández 988, Belarmino Tomás 904 and Francisco Largo Caballero 989.[31] González Peña chose to stand in Huelva and Largo Caballero Madrid; consequently they were replaced by Marciano Moreno Mateo and Graciano Antuña. Three of the six, Fernández, Tomás and Antuña were in exile and facing charges for their part in the October rising. The PCE's candidates were Dolores Ibárruri (La Pasionaria), and the imprisoned Juan José Mansó.

The Popular Front's electoral campaign was an active and diverse one which the provincial committee attempted to coordinate. On 24 January it urged all the member parties' local sections to create local committees and even parish sub-committees to forward all campaign plans to Oviedo:

---

[28] Taibo, *Asturias*, vol. 2, pp. 216–17.   [29] Prieto, *Posiciones socialistas*, pp. 123–4.
[30] Julía, *Orígenes*, p. 146. These figures do not include Catalonia.
[31] *La Tarde*, 5 February 1936.

'Once each committee is established it should send to this provincial committee a list of the events to be held in the locality, indicating the time, date and place and if possible mentioning any themes of special local interest which could be raised in order to boost our propaganda.'[32] It is unclear whether such a high degree of coordination was achieved but certainly there were numerous electoral events over a large part of the province. Between 15 January and 15 February *La Tarde* mentions 139; one analysis estimates there were in excess of 300 in seventeen days.[33]

The Popular Front campaign generated enormous enthusiasm, especially among the working class. Olivia Díaz describes the fervour in Gijón. At a talk given by Matilde de la Torre on 'The Woman in the Twentieth Century' she found 'the hall was already full to overflowing and there were lots of people in the street outside'.[34] When Alvaro de Albornoz of IR, the senior candidate on the Popular Front list, arrived in Oviedo from Madrid on 21 January the station was crowded with well-wishers.[35] Attendance at many rallies reflected the enthusiasm: at Mieres, a socialist stronghold, 6,000 attended a meeting called by IR, and another in Olloniego drew 5,000.[36] The editors of *La Tarde*, on 13 January, declared, 'Without setting great store by democracy, on with the elections then. But none of us should expect anything different from what we already have. We are the men of October and towards October we continue.' Within a week, though, they had changed their tune, noting 'the delirious enthusiasm spreading throughout Asturias as Popular Front rallies are held'.[37]

But why did the Popular Front campaign generate such enthusiasm? The principal attraction was undoubtedly the prospect of an amnesty for the prisoners of October. That was what motivated Olivia Díaz and other anarchists who chose to support the Popular Front. On the basis of a set of interviews, the historian Taibo concluded that so crucial was the amnesty that 'the other elements of the Popular Front's programme disappeared from view'.[38] Its overwhelming importance emerged through events which followed the announcement of the Popular Front's victory. The day Azaña replaced Portela Valladares a riot broke out in Gijón's Coto prison. This provoked a widespread work stoppage and a march on the gaol. In Oviedo's Cárcel Modelo a prisoners' committee took control as a large crowd gathered outside. A group of newly elected deputies,

---

[32] *La Tarde*.   [33] Taibo, *Asturias*, vol. 2, p. 214.
[34] Díaz to González Entrialgo, 7 February 1936, Gijón, Leg. J12, AHN-GC.
[35] *La Tarde*, 22 January 1936.   [36] Ibid., 15, 22, 29 January 1936.
[37] Ibid., 13, 20 January 1936.
[38] Taibo, *Asturias*, vol. 2, p. 214.

including La Pasionaria, visited the authorities to secure the prisoners' release. This provoked a celebration in all the mining towns and in Sama the town band met the returning prisoners at the railway station.[39]

While amnesty was central to the Popular Front's appeal, and was perhaps the only part of its official programme to which people in Asturias paid much attention, it was not the sole point of attraction. During the campaign speakers at Popular Front rallies associated the coalition with local issues of interest to the working class. At one rally in Lieres the former socialist mayor justified socialist participation in the Popular Front by referring to immediate pragmatic needs. Although he then went on to link the need for the nationalization of the mines to the election.[40] Similarly, in Mieres, disgruntled bakery workers suffering unpaid overtime working were enjoined not merely to vote for the left but to campaign energetically on its behalf.[41]

THE POPULAR FRONT AFTER THE ELECTIONS

Nationally the Popular Front's structure never extended beyond the election committee which had guided candidate selection. Only Republicans and Socialists had sat on this committee and once the election was over neither side showed much interest in. Prieto had little use for it; for him it was 'the political parties and parliamentary caucuses which count'.[42] Azaña too wanted to return to normal political instruments, in his case cabinet and parliament.

In Asturias, however, the Popular Front continued to function after 16 February 1936. In late March the Popular Front's provincial committee organized a major demonstration to protest against 'the constant fascist provocations against proletarian and republican elements'.[43] The meeting, addressed by PSOE, PCE, IR and young socialist speakers, was attended by about 20,000 people. The list of demands presented to the civil governor included the immediate implementation of the Popular Front programme, the reinstatement of all workers dismissed for political reasons, immediate indemnity for the repression's victims, urgent measures against unemployment, the disarming of all fascists and replacement of the labour ministry's provincial delegate.[44] The provincial committee also arbitrated when local

---

[39] Ibid., pp. 219–23; D. Ibarruri, *El unico camino* (Barcelona, 1979), pp. 224–32.
[40] *La Tarde*, 22 January 1936.
[41] Ibid., 27 January 1936.   [42] J. S. Vidarte, *Todos fuimos culpables* (Mexico, 1978), p. 99.
[43] *La Tarde*, 27 March 1936.   [44] Ibid., 30 March 1936.

committees proved unable to agree over candidate selection for municipal elections.

It was at the local level that the Popular Front showed greatest vitality and where the impulse emerged to turn it into a vehicle for working-class demands and action. In Trubia the committee snubbed a number of local businesses under the banner 'Comrades: boycott those who live off the *proletariat* and betray it.'[45] In Figaredo the local committee ostracized until May three employers and one doctor 'as a sanction of their conduct as enemies of the cause of the workers and the Republic'.[46]

With time workers became increasingly disenchanted with the Popular Front government and its slowness at meeting their demands. Some began seizing the initiative themselves. Nowhere was this clearer than in Gijón, where the alliance between Republicans and working-class parties broke down in early spring. In May, 'when the local Popular Front committee was little more than a memory', the residents of the working-class district of El Llano created a new committee which sought to engage the concern of the Republican-controlled city government on the district's needs. This was seen by *Avance* as the way to 'carry out the true work of the Popular Front'.[47]

These types of activity were both localized and sporadic. In June *Avance* published an editorial on 'the tasks of the Popular Front' in which it complained of the local committees' weaknesses and the general lack of popular mobilization, calling on them to compensate for the national government's failings.

There is a Popular Front committee in every village in Asturias. They were not created solely to carry out electoral propaganda. What the national government is failing to do can well be carried out at the local level, specifically municipal problems whose solution would fulfill some of the electoral promises.... We must always keep in mind the type of enemy we are facing. If there are weaknesses at the top in confronting him this is to a great extent due to the passivity from below. Security can only come from the enthusiasm of all.... The Asturian Popular Front has lain dormant as an organ of regional politics.[48]

CONCLUSION

The incipient transformation of local Popular Front committees into independent political protagonists pressing working-class demands ran counter to the determination of Azaña and Prieto to resume traditional

[45] Ibid., 2 March 1936.   [46] Ibid., 11 May 1936   [47] *Avance*, 2 July 1936.
[48] Ibid., 28 June 1936.

parliamentary politics and to assert the power of central government. The existence of such conflict between state power and local institutions foreshadowed developments in Asturias during the Civil War.

Following the military rising of 17–18 July 1936 municipal governments were immediately replaced by numerous local war committees, whilst the unions assumed control of the most important sectors of the local economy. The most crucial of these committees was the provincial Popular Front committee in Sama de Langreo, headed by the socialist leader Belarmino Tomás. In September this committee moved to Gijón and Tomás was appointed governor of Asturias and Leon by the Republican government.

As the representative of the state, Tomás and his committee (in December 1936 renamed the Consejo Interprovincial de Asturias y León) sought to counter the fragmentation of political power which had occurred in July. They also sought to reverse some of the revolution which had accompanied it. The local committees were dissolved and replaced by traditional town councils, small businesses seized by the workers were returned to their owners, private banks were allowed to reopen, the appropriation of land was halted and the worker militias converted into a regular army.

The object in view was to increase the effective prosecution of the war against Franco. However, the Republicans were unable to stem the nationalists' northern offensive in the summer of 1937. As the Basque country and then Santander fell, Asturias remained isolated, facing attack from the east and west. At this point the conflict between national and local interests reached crisis point. On 24 August, in a desperate attempt to stave off defeat, the Interprovincial Council assumed sovereign political and military authority.[49] This autonomy was shortlived. On 1 September the Nationalists attacked Asturias. Seven weeks later Republican resistance collapsed and on 21 October the war in the north came to an end.

[49] There is no complete history of the Civil War in Asturias. These are two popular histories: O. Muniz, *Asturias en la Guerra Civil* (Salinas, 1976), and *Historia de Asturias* (Salinas, 1981), vol. 8. J. Ambou, *Los comunistas en la resistencia nacional republicana* (Madrid, 1978) is an account by a communist participant, while F. Solano Palacios, *La tragedia del norte* (Barcelona, 1938) is an account by an anarchist participant.

'Le temps des loisirs': popular tourism and mass leisure in the vision of the Front Populaire

JULIAN JACKSON

'Le temps des loisirs': thus ran an article in the communist magazine *Regards* in 1938. The theme was not novel: with the introduction of paid holidays (*congés payés*) and the forty-hour week in June 1936, 'leisure' (*loisirs*) had become the catchword of the age. One of Blum's most remarked-upon appointments was that of Léo Lagrange to the new post of under secretary of state for the organization of sport and leisure. Defending his government in 1942, Blum referred to his pride that 'through the organization of work and leisure', he had brought 'a ray of light into difficult lives'. As the Popular Front becomes increasingly sanitized by history, the *congés payés* loom ever larger as its supreme achievement. The photographs of crowds waving from departing trains have become as much a symbol of 1936 as the barricades have of 1968.

With its first legislative act, therefore, Blum's government left the domain of politics and entered that of legend. In doing so it achieved a fundamental aspiration. Unlike 'planism', the other strategy which claimed to offer resistance to fascism in the 1930s, the Popular Front centred its defence of democracy around the parliamentary Republic. Not the least of its aims, therefore, was to provide a mystique for democracy in an era susceptible to other myths, to reinvigorate the republican idea in France. That this should be attempted in the field of leisure was particularly significant since most contemporaries recognized that the 'organization of leisure' was something in which the fascist states had been

226

pre-eminently successful. Even the Communists could refer admiringly to the achievements of Nazi Germany.[1] In offering itself as the salvation of democracy, the Popular Front government proposed a more interventionist conception of government. Its solution to the Republic's institutional crisis was the opposite of that provided by the preceding governments of Laval and Doumergue. They had flirted with constitutional reform or governed by decree, in order more effectively to confine the liberal state within its minimalist role. The Popular Front, in contrast, while posing as the defender of constitutional traditionalism, presented its activist view of the state's role as the only means of salvaging parliamentary democracy.

Throughout its existence the Popular Front was thus poised uneasily between the exigencies of politics in the age of the masses and its mission to preserve parliamentary democracy – to save liberalism by fusing it with mass politics. This tension was acutely expressed in the person of Blum himself, the fastidious rationalist who addressed huge crowds while surrounded by all the paraphernalia of politics as theatre. Indeed in the age of mass politics it is difficult to distinguish where politics end and leisure begins: the 14 July Popular Front demonstrations consisted of both celebration and political protest. The Popular Front turned politics into carnival and *fête* into politics. It liberated politics into the widest possible arena. *L'Humanité* reporting on a meeting in February 1937 gave as much space to the entertainments as to the political content.[2] It was significant that many meetings took place in sports stadia – the Vel d'Hiver or Buffalo stadium – and that in his model for a *centre de loisirs*, presented at the 1937 Paris Exposition, Le Corbusier included an arena for political parades. But while this fusion of public and private, politics and recreation, was integral to totalitarian strategy, it fitted less obviously into the Popular Front's vision which aimed to show, in Lagrange's words, that democracy also was capable of 'creating a vast organization of sport and leisure'.

Before considering the Popular Front's response to this challenge, we should note that the demand for greater leisure had played little part in the movement's origins. Although *congés payés* had been on the CGT's agenda since 1925, union organizers did not find them a mobilizing issue in the early 1930s, and they were not even included in the Popular Front programme. The shorter working week had been on the left's agenda since

---

[1] J-V. Parant, *Le problème du tourisme populaire* (Paris, 1939); J-P. Depretto and S. Schweitzer, *Le communisme à l'usine* (Paris, 1984), p. 223.
[2] *L'Humanité*, 6 February 1937.

the beginning of the depression, but as part of an anti-unemployment strategy not as a *politique des loisirs*. Partly this was a consequence of the fact that leisure, during the crisis, was only too familiar as the enforced idleness of short-time work. Partly too it occurred because socialists traditionally preferred to stress the redemptive possibilities of work – not escape from work. The introduction of the eight-hour day and the postwar debate on rationalization had slightly modified this situation. Thus in 1919 the CGT had established a commission on leisure, but in the 1920s the unions' main activity was directed towards defending the eight-hour day. Their thoughts on how to use the new leisure derived from their conception of recreation as self-improvement.[3]

The failure of working-class organizations to establish a policy on leisure before 1936 also reflected the fact that the concept of leisure had been used by American business managers. It risked being seen, therefore, less as an authentic vision of working-class redemption than as part of a strategy of scientific management. It was not, however, a strategy which had been much taken up by French employers who tried to circumvent the eight-hour legislation rather than viewing it as a means of raising productivity. Since the First World War a number of employers had begun to take in hand the leisure activities of their workforce, but this policy, conceived in a spirit of nineteenth-century company paternalism, was usually intended to inculcate a corporate spirit.[4] The Citroën workers, forbidden to circulate in the factory, were shown films on the factory as a whole. Their perception of the factory as space was ordered for them by the management.[5] The workers' organizations attempted to resist such strategies of social control – this was one aim of the communist and socialist sports federations – but their efforts were hindered by mutual recriminations, at least until the two federations united to form the FSGT in December 1934.

The government's early uncertainties regarding a leisure policy were reflected in Lagrange's initial attachment to the health ministry; not until the fall of Blum's government was Lagrange's post transferred to the education ministry. The shift signified the emergence of a clearer view. But action was urgently needed. Even if the demand for greater leisure had figured little in union propaganda during the early 1930s, this was largely because the idea seemed politically inconceivable. Once during the strikes of 1936, the impossible became conceivable, *congés payés* emerged as a major

[3] G. Cross, 'The quest for leisure: reassessing the eight-hour day in France', *Journal of Social History*, 18, 2 (1984), 195–208.
[4] G. Etienne, *L'utilisation des loisirs des travailleurs* (Paris, 1935).
[5] S. Schweitzer, *Des engrenages à la chaine: les usines Citroën* (Lyon, 1982), p. 102.

aspiration, revealing a significant feature of the strike movement. Throughout France the strikes represented a protest against the previous years of 'rationalization' at least as practised during the depression: the speeding up of production targets and tightening of factory discipline. One classic depiction of the results of this process is Simone Weil's *La condition ouvrière*, her account of life in an engineering factory in 1934. Weil's narrative is a litany of fear, boredom and exhaustion. Renoir's film for the PCF's 1936 election campaign, *La vie est à nous*, has a scene attacking the factory timekeepers. The historiographical tradition portraying the factory occupations of 1936 simply as an explosion of joyous liberation at release from this factory discipline can be overplayed. Nonetheless it reflects a truth about them as a collective interruption of the daily round, an escape within the factory – from factory time – just as later the first *congés payés* represented an escape from the factory as space. But, although the famous factory celebrations of 1936, the dancing in factory yards, were real enough, as time passed they became less a spontaneous outburst than a strategy to preserve morale. In the words of one Renault unionist: 'we needed to keep the men in the factory ... and this climate of festival was an excellent way of doing so'. His factory was visited by variety artists and sporting heroes.[6]

In short, the strikes of 1936 posed in embryo the 'problem of leisure' about to be confronted by the government. Just as the strike committees rapidly organized leisure, to prevent the inactivity of the occupation from degenerating into a disorder susceptible to exploitation by their adversaries, so too the government needed to counteract the right's attacks on Lagrange's 'ministry of idleness'. One author in 1939 expressed fears that without guidance the workers would be exposed to 'the dangers of alcoholism, debt and moral depravity'. The left shared such fears even if it expressed them less luridly.[7]

In defining an attitude towards leisure a vital role was played by Lagrange who quickly integrated his policy into the Popular Front's political vision.[8] Four themes stand out. First, 'to allow the youth of France to discover joy and health through the practice of sport'. 'Joy', 'youth', 'health', 'happiness' are recurrent ideas in Lagrange's speeches. The emphasis on the young was to demonstrate that democracy also was capable of harnessing the revolt of youth. Secondly, Lagrange argued that

[6] B. Badie, 'Les grèves du Front populaire aux usines Renault', *Mouvement Social*, 81 (1972), 88.
[7] Y. Becquet, *L'organisation des loisirs des travailleurs* (Paris, 1939).
[8] G. Proteau, *Le message de Léo Lagrange* (Paris, 1950).

a generalization of leisure would create 'moral unity' and 'bring together the different elements of French youth'. He advocated the setting up of local *clubs des loisirs* by means of which 'the miner, the artisan, the peasant, the mason, the clerk, the teacher will gradually understand the unity of human labour'. This was leisure as a version of the *main tendue*, an expression of the Popular Front's ambitions towards *rassemblement*. Thirdly, the aim was to generalize participation in sport and democratize both tourism and élitist sports such as skiing or aviation. Finally, Lagrange stressed that his aim was not to 'regiment' leisure but to reconcile liberal individualism and totalitarian effectiveness. Encouraging different sectors of the population to meet through recreation would develop the 'sympathy and respect' necessary in a democracy.

Joy and youth, *rassemblement* and unity, participation and democratization, liberty and democracy: these are classic Popular Front themes. In attempting to realize them we find Lagrange intervening in a wide area of activities: organizing cheap rail transport (the Lagrange tickets) and providing subsidies for sports facilities. But the limited resources at his disposal severely restricted his capacity for direct action. The burden of implementing his policy fell on the Popular Front's many constituent organizations. This was, however, a deliberate preference as much as a consequence of financial necessity. Lagrange saw the state as 'a guide'; Georges Lefranc of the CGT's Workers' Education Institute (CCOE) argued for 'pluralism ... federalism in the field of leisure'.[9]

The reliance on extra-governmental initiatives also underlined the triple character of the Popular Front as government, electoral coalition and mass movement. One manifestation of this was an extraordinary efflorescence of committees and associations in a political culture generally characterized by a low level of associative life. The forming of committees was a vital part of the Popular Front experience, from the vigilance committees of 1934 to the strike committees of 1936. This development was simultaneously a sign of the politicization of French life in the mid 1930s, an expression of the Popular Front as a movement spilling beyond the boundaries of the left's traditional organizations and, finally, an implicit refutation of Nazi *Gleichschaltung*. Popular Front meetings brought together an eye-catching variety of associations. In contrast to the regimented conformity of German and Italian parades, demonstrations in France proclaimed the vitality of her democracy by means of the colourful patchwork of independent organizations on view. This was certainly true in the area of leisure where

[9] G. and E. Lefranc, *Le syndicalisme devant le problème des loisirs* (Paris, 1937?), p. 45.

many groups prepared to meet the situation created by the recent social legislation.

Among these were the CGT, the youth hostel movement, the FSGT (whose membership grew from 42,000 in 1935 to over 100,000 in 1938), the communist Popular Tourist Association (ATP), the 'Holidays for All' organization founded by a group of primary school teachers, the local Popular Front committees themselves, as well as many recently established local leisure committees.[10] These organizations all saw their task as furnishing tourist information and providing the kind of assistance the traditional tourist organizations seemed unwilling to give. Thus in the absence of the *syndicat d'initiative* the Menton leisure committee met the first train loads of holidaying workers in the summer of 1936.[11] But, in the words of Holidays for All, the Popular Front aspired to be more than 'a cut-price copy of bourgeois tourism'. Leisure had to become a 'daily lesson in solidarity', the prelude to a 'more perfect social harmony'. But here also a balancing act was required between the collective and the individual. Unlike the Nazi 'Strength through Joy' programme, the Popular Front organizations inclined against collectively organized tours. Special cheap trains were provided for particular groups of workers but the CGT's tourist bureau opposed the 'group mentality' of such collective excursions.[12]

Among the organizations encouraged by Lagrange was the youth hostel movement, especially the Centre Laique des Auberges de Jeunesse (CLAJ). The expansion in the number of youth hostels under the Popular Front, from 250 in June 1936 to 400 by December, owed something to the new demand for cheap holiday accommodation but also to the fact that they propagated an ideology in tune with Popular Front values. Lagrange saw them as the prefiguration of a fraternal society. For the CLAJ's magazine *Le Cri des Auberges*, each hostel was a 'miniature republic of the young ...uniting young intellectuals, workers and peasants'.[13] Hitherto the movement had been largely middle class; in the future an appeal had to be made to the workers. The CGT hoped that the CLAJ would recruit among workers to free them from bourgeois conformism and teach them to use their leisure constructively. Although the youth hostel movement was racked by arguments over issues such as hitch-hiking and vegetarianism, formal politics were discouraged: 'No politics ... Leave your passionate

---

10 On these organizations see, F. Bloch-Lainé, *L'emploi des loisirs ouvriers et l'éducation populaire* (Paris, 1936).
11 *Le Front Populaire de Menton*, 1 September 1936.
12 *Vendredi*, 16 July 1937; 7 May 1937 ('La CGT et les loisirs'); *Regards*, 13 May 1937.
13 *Le Cri des Auberges de Jeunesse*, March 1936.

discussions to the city and give yourself up to the joy of breathing fresh air.'[14]

The CGT's tourist bureau also aimed to bring together town and country. Established in spring 1937 it laid on excursions, organized a holiday saving scheme and arranged accommodation for holidaying workers in peasant households, to encourage 'greater cooperation between rural and urban workers'. For those coming from the provinces to Paris, courses were arranged by the CCEO for *guides-compagnons* whose task would be to show visiting peasants that Paris was not a 'modern Babylon'.[15] A variant on this theme of tourism as an instrument of *rassemblement* was added by the PCF deputy Victor Barel, an ATP organizer. By reviving the depressed tourist industry the Popular Front would retain the allegiance of 'this middle class that our enemies want to separate from the bloc of workers'.[16]

Not only would the paid holidays bring the French people together, they would also allow the workers to know their country. This reconciliation between the masses and 'their' nation, was an essential element of Frontist strategy, especially as conceived by the Communists who celebrated the genius of France in her artists, language, climate and geography.[17] As Barel remarked, paid holidays would allow every Frenchman to 'take physical possession of the geography of our country'.[18] 'The metal workers have returned from their holidays: France is there to be discovered thanks to the paid holidays' proclaimed *Regards*. This theme was not only exploited by the PCF. *Syndicats*, journal of the anti-communist wing of the CGT, printed a letter from a postman describing how his only previous visits to parts of France outside his home province had come during military service: now the workers could know France 'other than simply through geography classes and the cinema'.[19] Just as the June factory occupations had represented the reappropriation of factory space, so in August the workers could take possession of their country – like the Marseillais patriots in the quintessentially frontist film, Renoir's *La Marseillaise*.

But geography was not to be separated from history: to know France was to know her past. To coincide with the 1939 Tour de France the communist historian Jean Bruhat wrote a series of articles in *L'Humanité* about the

[14] Ibid., December 1936.
[15] On the Bureau, *Syndicats*, 15 April 1937; *Le Peuple*, 10 April 1937, 8 May 1937.
[16] *Journal Officiel, Débats* (Chamber), 28 July 1936, p. 2,175.
[17] For example, P. Vaillant-Couturier, *Vers les lendemains qui chantent* (Paris, 1962).
[18] *Journal Officiel, Débats* (Chamber), 28 July 1936, p. 2,175.   [19] *Syndicats*, 15 April 1937.

impact of the revolution in each of the regions visited by the race. This neatly fused travel, sport and history.[20] The CGT's *guides-compagnons* attended courses on the history of the Paris region. And this was not just any version of history. Although the Popular Front's consensual aspirations led it to embrace the widest possible historical heritage, history did not thereby become neutral. Just as Renoir's *La Marseillaise* shows us not revolutionary heroes but common people, so the *guides-compagnons* were to emphasize the role of the 'anonymous masses' previously hidden in 'the shadows of royal majesty and imperial pomp'.[21]

Thus the Popular Front never forgot that it had enemies. If the notion of *rassemblement* represented one face of frontist discourse, the idea of conquest was the other. The two ideas converged in the theme of the 200 families, an instrumental myth which identified the enemy *and* delimited it, showing the people of France united against a band of irreducible enemies. The workers had therefore to *conquer* their leisure. Hitherto, in CGT eyes, sport had been a 'formidable enterprise of social corruption'. By taking control of their own leisure the workers would free themselves from the grip of 'industrial seigneurs'.[22] The communist union leader Benoît Frachon put the case for union control most forthrightly: 'If the worker wants entertainment, his union is there to provide it. If he is in difficulty, his union can supply the solidarity he needs. If he wants to make a trip into the country, his union will help him.'[23] Thus throughout the factories of the Paris region the unions set up sports clubs and leisure committees. The CGT launched the slogan 'a club in every factory'. By April 1937 the Renault factory had twenty-one football teams and clubs for every other sport.[24]

It is in this context that we must view the Popular Front's response to the right's attacks on the *congés payés*. Although gibes about proletarianized beaches were real enough, there was little serious opposition to the paid holidays. The Popular Front press, on the other hand, delighted in retailing right-wing sneers. The wife of a metal worker described how the hotels of the Côte d'Azur had feared that the workers would eat with their hands: 'they were certainly amazed to see that we knew how to use a fork'.[25] Such enemies were necessary; without them there could be no victories. Whether exaggerated or not, right-wing attacks nonetheless hit

20 J. Bruhat, *Il n'est jamais trop tard* (Paris, 1983), p. 102.
21 G. Lefranc, *Les luttes du peuple parisien* (Paris, 1937?) (Lefranc's course for the *guides-compagnons*).
22 *Le Peuple*, 30 March 1937 ('Les loisirs des travailleurs').
23 B. Frachon, *Le rôle social des syndicats* (Paris, 1937?), p. 21.
24 Depretto and Schweitzer, *Le communisme à l'usine*, p. 224.   25 *Regards*, September 1937.

at one fundamental feature of the Popular Front: the assertion of a working-class *presence* in a highly compartmentalized society – a presence on the cinema screen, in the street and, now, on the beaches.

To confine a discussion of the Popular Front's conception of leisure to sport and tourism would be to accept a compartmentalization of human activity totally antithetical to its vision of the world: 'it is against compartmentalization and for the creation of a complete man that we are struggling' declared *L'Humanité* journalist Paul Vaillant-Couturier. Lagrange's *chef de cabinet*, Edouard Dolléans, talked of the need to develop 'the total individual'.[26] 'Break down the barriers' was one of the slogans of 1936. *Loisirs intellectuels* were as important as *loisirs physiques*. The communist Maisons de Culture organized 'camping and culture' sections; the CGT's tourist bureau aimed to 'link art and culture to tourism'. Although the Popular Front had devoted little attention to *loisirs* before 1936, it had developed a cultural line which meshed with the unexpected expansion of leisure.

The major role in defining the Popular Front's cultural policy was taken by the PCF.[27] Its main features were cultural defence and cultural democratization. The triple struggle of the Popular Front for liberty, bread and peace was also a triple defence of culture against bookburners, speculators and cultural barbarians. Culture had to be rescued from the hands of a privileged elite. Or, to quote the communist J. Berlioz, 'culture must become republican in the etymological sense of the word'.[28] The Popular Front saw the creation of numerous cultural organizations dedicated to realizing this reconciliation between the people and art: the *maisons de culture*, the People's Music Federation (FMP), the People's Association for the Friends of Museums (APAM), the Association for the Development of Public Reading (ADLP).

The new situation created by the 'conquest of leisure' gave these bodies their opportunity. They in turn helped the labour movement to organize leisure. A visit to the Exposition arranged by the printers' union was reported as follows: 'this organization of leisure by the union ... offers a concrete justification for the increased leisure granted us by the forty-hour week'. The visitors were guided by Julien Cain, the Bibliothèque National-ale's director and a sponsor of the ADLP. This was said to show 'the harmony reigning between intellectuals and workers in the field of

[26] *Peuple et Culture*, 20 October 1936; *Le Musée Vivant*, June 1936.
[27] On the Popular Front and culture, see P. Ory, 'La politique culturelle du premier gouvernement Blum', *Nouvelle Revue Socialiste*, 10–11 (1975), 75–93.
[28] *Journal Officiel, Documents parlementaires* (Chamber) (1936), no. 1,285, p. 405.

leisure'.[29] The organization of cultural activities was also taken in hand by local leisure committees which were often affiliated to the Comité National des Loisirs, founded by Albert Thomas in 1929. Up to 1936 its action had been extremely restricted but between 1936 and 1938 the number of affiliated committees rose from 119 to 400.

The Popular Front's aspiration towards cultural democratization was intended to be more than a simple repetition of that movement of intellectuals towards the masses witnessed after the Dreyfus Affair. Culture was not to be offered to the workers; they had to take it for themselves. For the FMP the slogan 'Aller au peuple' was insufficient: 'it is not enough for intellectuals to go to the people; the people must come to the intellectuals'.[30] This implied that the workers should take over the organization of their cultural leisure activities. Thus the CGT founded its People's Theatre and one *maison de culture* exhorted the unions to call upon it rather than 'capitalist impresarios' when providing entertainments.[31] Workers were also urged to participate in artistic creation themselves: those at the Bloch factory mounted an exhibition of their painting, while the Renault workers exhibited their sculpture.

Taking control of one's culture did not necessarily mean transforming it. The call for a 'people's culture' was not to be fulfilled by repudiating the existing cultural heritage: 'there is no such thing as an art for the people ... there is simply art'.[32] The first objective was, therefore, to open to the people those areas of culture from which they had been hitherto excluded. The possibility of a clash between the demands of the avant garde and the objective of cultural popularization was sidestepped: the composer Koechlin (a member of the FMP) saw the masses' musical ignorance as a guarantee of their comprehension. Among painters Leger argued that education had imposed false artistic values inherited from the Renaissance: children's natural creativity should be allowed to express itself. It was indeed in the visual arts that the most vigorous arguments occurred over the relationship between cultural modernism and mass culture, but all participants agreed at least with the painter Ozenfant that art could only rejuvenate itself by 'drawing its sap from the popular masses'.[33]

The ecumenicalism of the Popular Front's defensive cultural stance – cultural 'apoliticism' was the motto of the *maisons de culture* – did not

---

[29] *Syndicats*, 7 October 1937.   [30] *L'Art Musical Populaire*, 1 May 1937.
[31] *Peuple et Culture*, 20 January 1937.
[32] Ibid., 20 March 1937.
[33] C. Koechlin, *La musique et le peuple* (Paris, 1936); P. Gaudibert, 'Le Front populaire et les arts plastiques', *Politique Aujourd'hui*, October 1974, pp. 105–21; *Commune*, May 1935.

preclude the drawing of *some* boundaries. Just as in their physical leisure the workers had to be saved from the temptations of the café or passive spectator sports, so too they had to be rescued from degraded forms of 'popular' culture – Tino Rossi, American gangster films – imposed by the bourgeoisie on the worker 'to humiliate him, abase him, drug him'.[34] This is not to say that existing cultural forms would not be affected by their confrontation with a mass audience. Artistic life would be stimulated by an audience for which art was not merely a distraction. Koechlin tried to distinguish between 'light popular music and genuine people's music, expressive of the people'. And Vaillant-Couturier suggested one route towards this quest for a modern folklore:

> During the June strikes there emerged a whole musical folklore, a folklore of songs. There was not a factory which did not have its songs ... did not put on some play; all this represents the surge of interest by the French people in music and theatre.[35]

This returns us once again to the enforced leisure of the 1936 strikes.

Defining the Popular Front's objectives regarding leisure is easier than assessing its achievements in the field. First, we must not exaggerate the extent to which the population made use of the new access to leisure. For most workers holidays remained an impossible luxury in spite of the Lagrange tickets. Almost 550,000 of these were purchased in 1936, 907,000 in 1937, 1.5 million in 1938. Although not insignificant, these figures only represent a small proportion of the eligible population. Holidays did not become a feature of French working-class life overnight.[36] For those unable to afford a two-week holiday there was the possibility of weekend excursions: the number of weekend train tickets doubled in the summer of 1936 while traffic on *grandes lignes* increased by only 10 per cent. Where did the first holiday-makers go? Beaches were a popular destination, usually those nearest to the point of departure. But for many of their beneficiaries the first paid holidays represented less a 'discovery of France' than a 'retour au pays': in the Côte d'Azur many new 'tourists' seem to have stayed with their families.[37] What the experience of *congés payés* meant to the first holiday-makers is impossible to say. Various Renault workers described their holidays in the union newspaper. Some used the language of schoolbook platitudes, some the idiom of the Popular Front (it was necessary to 'strengthen the fraternal links' with 'our peasant brothers').

---

[34] *Peuple et Culture*, 20 January 1937.
[35] *L'Art Musical Populaire*, August/September 1937.
[36] F. Cribier, *La grande migration de l'été* (1969), pp. 44–6, 248–52.
[37] Parant, *Le problème du tourisme*, pp. 122–4.

Others were suddenly confronted with a France whose existence they had not suspected: Brittany was in 'the Middle Ages'.[38]

The hope of using leisure as an instrument of *rassemblement* proved a chimera. The youth hostel movement remained a middle-class preserve: in 1939 the CLAJ of the Paris region was still urging its members to increase propaganda in factories, which had remained 'almost virgin territory for us'. As for using youth hostels to unite townspeople and peasants, there were numerous reports of incidents between youth-hostellers and peasants offended by the more libertarian aspects of the movement. For its part, the *Cri des Auberges* was shocked that peasants sought out the bistro and cinema could they not be taught to love nature?[39] The Popular Front, in short, remained an essentially urban phenomenon. Frequently the Popular Front tourist organizations had to remind workers that summer holidays coincided with harvest time for the peasantry; tact was necessary.

Even in the factory, however, it is not clear that the Popular Front succeeded in imposing its vision of leisure. After the June 1936 strikes the level of industrial unrest remained high in spite of the efforts of the CGT leaders. One historian has suggested that the CGT attempted unsuccessfully to stem this 'revolt against work' by linking the organization of leisure to a productivist rhetoric: increased productivity in the workplace would be compensated for by greater leisure outside it. But the workers, it is argued, opposed this strategy, rejecting any return to anything approaching previous production targets.[40] They had struck to escape the tyranny of the time keeper. But perhaps this was less a 'revolt against work' than a revolt against the modern concept of a strict distinction between work and recreation, against the whole idea of 'leisure' which, far from being a revolt against factory time, is dependent on it, as its antithesis. For not only did the Popular Front organizations find difficulty in persuading the workers to return to work, on occasions there were reports of workers taking clandestine jobs in their leisure time. They had, that is, to be persuaded not to work during their 'leisure'.[41] The Popular Front's productivist vision of leisure clashed with the pre-modern attitudes of many workers.

But in its notion of leisure as cultural self-improvement, the Popular

---

[38] Depretto and Schweitzer, *Le communisme à l'usine*, p. 225.
[39] *Ceux des Auberges*, June 1939; *Le Cri des Auberges*, February 1938.
[40] M. Seidman, 'Work and Revolution: Bourgeoisies and Working Classes in Paris and Barcelona in the 1930s' (Amsterdam thesis, 1982).
[41] F. Cahier, 'La classe ouvrière havraise et le Front populaire 1934–8' (Memoir, Paris, 1972); *Le Populaire*, 29 July 1936; *Le Front Comtois*, 3 October 1936; G. and E. Lefranc, *Le syndicalisme*, p 14

Front looked back towards the early years of the century rather than to the mass cultural consumerism of the postwar years. And yet in practice it was to prefigure the latter more than it continued the former. Certainly the Popular Front's cultural experiments were not entirely without impact. The cultural visits organized by the APAM reached some 25,000 people; unions hired the Opéra to lay on performances of well-known operas for their members; *Le Peuple* commented that in entertainments organized by unions popular comedians had often been replaced by serious artistic performances. But more common was the complaint that not enough was being achieved in the cultural field. The experiment of a weekly cheap night opening of the Louvre for trade unionists was abandoned for lack of demand, and Léger relates that when he offered his services as a popular lecturer on art at Lille, he encountered an audience of 100 professionals and no workers.

Opening the doors of culture to the people did not ensure that they would select the culture being offered. Hence the wistful comments in 1938 by the CCEO's Georges Vidalenc: 'it is sad to see the preoccupation of workers with the commercial Tour de France . . . our comrades have better things to do'; he lamented that workers read only *L'Auto*.[42] There was, then, only a limited convergence between the desired democratization of culture, the movement of intellectuals towards the masses and the generalization of leisure. For most people the music of the Popular Front era meant not Koechlin, or even Bizet but Charles Trénet, even Tino Rossi. More importantly, the possibility of such choices was implicit in the Popular Front's very cultural eclecticism. Although Koechlin might agonize over the nature of authentic popular music, had not Aragon himself declared in 1936: 'I greet you my France for this light in your eyes which saw the Bastille fall . . . for Racine and for Diderot . . . for Maurice Chevalier'.[43] Who was to say that Chevalier would not be preferred to Racine?

It may be, paradoxically, that the Popular Front, that supremely political movement, contributed unwittingly in its search for cultural consensus, to a process of depoliticization, or at least that it did not link its conception of leisure clearly enough to the republican vision that was being defended. Apoliticism had been the motto of both the *maisons de culture* and the CLAJ. The rationale of this strategy was political *rassemblement*; perhaps its result was partly depoliticization. *L'Humanité* in November 1938 gave as

---

[42] G. Vidalenc, 'Le problème de l'orientation des loisirs' in *Le droit au savoir* (CCEO publication, Paris, 1938).

[43] Quoted by Vaillant-Couturier in G. Cogniot et al., *L'avenir de la culture* (Paris, 1937), p. 13.

much coverage to boxing as to the general strike of that month.[44] Of all the forces within the Popular Front it was indeed the PCF which most easily accommodated the developments deplored by Vidalenc, perhaps because it was clearest what it wanted from the Popular Front. Denunciations of the Tour de France largely disappeared from *L'Humanité* but continued in the socialist and CGT press, coming especially from CCEO members. They criticized Lagrange's policies for an excessive concentration on the young, and on physical activity – 'the religion of the muscle' – over intellectual pursuits. They worried about a 'certain indifference towards social, economic and political questions'. The youth hostel movement had after all been successful in central Europe. Yet there the physical liberation of the individual had not prevented political servitude: 'perhaps it has to some extent helped it; marching together in joy carries the risk that people will march together joyfully irrespective of the destination'.[45] There was prescience in this: many themes of 1936 recur hauntingly in the politics of Vichy.

As the political hopes of 1936 shaded into disillusion, a retreat occurred from the public into the private domain; this withdrawal was perhaps aided by the new possibilities of leisure. From the beginning of 1938 membership of Popular Front organizations began to decline and it became less easy to assemble workers for union meetings. Leisure and tourism had certainly failed as instruments of political *rassemblement*; perhaps they succeeded partially as alternatives to it.

[44] Depretto and Schweitzer, *Le communisme à l'usine*, p. 225.
[45] G. and E. Lefranc, pp. 38–9; E. Lefranc, *Le Cri des Auberges*, February 1938.

The educational and cultural policy of the Popular Front government in Spain, 1936–9

CHRISTOPHER H. COBB

Time's passage has tended to blur the vision of the Second Spanish Republic and judgements of particular aspects are extended to cover the whole period from 1931 to 1939. Leaving aside the more obvious hiatus of the 1933–5 right-wing governments, many other studies have been allowed to gravitate essentially around the first two years of the new regime. The war period has somehow been set aside as an entirely separate order of things which has made it difficult to contrast the achievements of the social democratic governments of 1931–3 with those of the Popular Front government which assumed power on 16 February 1936. This is particularly evident in the cultural and educational fields. Several of the major studies of the period consciously limit themselves to the era from 14 April 1931 to 18 July 1936.[1] These project an idealized vision of the work of ministers like Fernando de los Ríos and Marcelino Domingo, presenting it as the crowning success of the republican years. The 'teachers' Republic' has become a byword for the period, whilst Claudio Lozano has referred to the drive to curb the power of the Catholic Church, by a close-knit educational elite, as a Spanish *Kulturkampf*.[2]

It is important to appreciate the exact nature of achievements in the educational field, as well as their limitations, in order to evaluate the

[1] See, for example, A. Molero Pintado, *La reforma educativa de la II República Española* (Madrid, 1977); M. Perez Galán, *La enseñanza en la II República Española* (Madrid, 1975); M. Samaniego, *La política educativa de la II Répública* (Madrid, 1977).
[2] *La educación republicana* (Barcelona, 1980), chapter 2.

change of orientation introduced in September 1936. The topic which was to cause most heated debate was essentially political and constitutional: the status of the religious orders, particuarly within the educational system. The objective of replacing their schools by extending the lay network would inevitably place a heavy burden on the state system. Yet this, despite its favoured position in the new government's budget, nonetheless suffered from a long backlog of underprovision. The building programme was consequently a major priority. So too were recruitment, training and the general improvement sought in the status of teachers. A revised curriculum was, at this stage, perhaps less significant than the establishment of the main characteristics of the new unified (or comprehensive) schools. Nor was the social dimension of education forgotten: special provision was made for school canteens and clothing for needy children, educational missions were established to visit and act as a stimulus in the most destitute areas and a broad range of adult extension activities was set in motion with particular emphasis on the literacy campaign. Most of these points had been the object of preoccupation and experimentation amongst liberal educators, many of whom (like Lorenzo Luzurriaga), had for some years been closely associated with the Spanish Socialist Party.

Superficially this would seem more than sufficient to justify the high reputation of the reformers' work. But local realities, as revealed in several recent studies, tell a different story. Ortega Berenguer has examined the educational provision in the province and municipality of Malaga in 1931. There, of the 333 extra classes considered necessary, only thirty-one had been established by the year's end. As regards the extra staff required (who came under a central budget), only twenty new teachers were in post by the end of 1932 in the municipal area.[3] The well-established tradition by which the middle classes sought a socially more prestigious education in the Church's schools continued, as the latter learned how to adapt to changed circumstances by refounding themselves to comply with the letter of the Republic's legislation. Thus, in 1934, the Federation of Friends of Education, a front organization for Catholic schools, was able to list in its annual report several hundred religious schools still operating.[4] At the other end of the social scale a similar discrepancy existed between the reality of rural Spain's deprived areas and the ideals of the educational

---

[3] *La enseñanza pública en la II República, Malaga 1931* (Malaga, 1982). See also the national statistics provided by Lozano, *La educación republicana* pp. 73–98.
[4] Quoted by A. Molero Pintado, 'La educación primaria durante la II República Española' in *Lorenzo Luzurriaga y la política educativa* (Ciudad Real, 1986), p. 87.

missionary movement in sending out actors, musicians and poets to familiarize an illiterate public with the great classics. As the famous playwright Alejandro Casona, himself a 'missionary', later said: 'They needed bread and medicine and we had only songs and poems in our bags.'[5] Despite the reformers' eminently worthy objectives, it is possible to see how they were failing to win a basis of committed support, either amongst the bourgeoisie or working class, a situation all too typical of the history of middle-class reformism in Spain.

As was the case in many other Spanish unions and professional associations, an increasingly radical alternative began capturing support amongst teachers from 1931 onwards. This was a tendency visible not only in articles on the educational ideals of Marx and Engels which appeared in *Trabajadores de la Enseñanza*, the journal of the Federation of Workers in Education (FETE), but also in the conflicts frequently reflected in its pages over the identification of teachers with the working class or the union's membership of the International of Workers in Education. The radical elements in the FETE were led by García Lombardía, who was to become director general of primary education in September 1936.

In many ways this pattern of events reproduced itself in the field of more broadly defined cultural activities.[6] Aware that the arts remained the preserve of a narrowly restricted social group, the proponents of broader popular cultural activities involving mass participation saw equally clearly the role of more combative art in hastening the desired process of social change. In the relationship between the arts and political commitment, the more accommodating attitudes apparent in Russia from 1932 onwards (abandonment of the 'proletkult'; the admission of fellow travellers to the Association of Revolutionary Artists and Writers), were to find their equivalent in Spain. 'Paint, write, publish whatever you think best. Make free use of your own initiative', said José Diaz to José Renau when discussing the Valencian Union of Proletarian Artists and Writers.[7]

From 1933 onwards several experimental proletarian or revolutionary theatre groups began their activities in Madrid, Barcelona and Seville. These were not limited to the representation of an established repertoire: the Madrid group Nosostros carried out a tour of agit-prop theatre in

[5] *Una misión pedagógica social* (Buenos Aires, 1941), p. 13.
[6] For further information on this question see M. Aznar, *Pensamiento literario y compromiso antifascista de la inteligencia española republicana* (Barcelona, 1978), and C. H. Cobb, *La cultura y el pueblo. España, 1930–39* (Barcelona, 1981).
[7] *La batalla per una nova cultura* (Valencia, 1978), p. 67.

Toledo province before the 1933 elections.[8] From then on regular references to an expanding range of groups are to be found in the press. Many of them brought together amateurs and professionals, whilst some obtained the collaboration of well-known authors such as Rafael Alberti and Ramón Sender. In the cinema, apart from the frequent showing of films by the new Russian directors at the meetings of unions, political parties and other local associations, the film critic Juan Piqueras reported to his readers the activities of the French Alliance du Cinéma, and particularly its production of documentaries on strikes and demonstrations.[9] This example was swiftly followed in the filming of the 1936 May Day celebrations in Madrid.[10]

Even more successful was the development of popular sporting activities. This was partly a reaction to the growth of commercialized spectator sports. The campaign was led by the Federation of University Students which was especially keen to promote sports which allowed mass participation. Cross country running was particularly suitable, as were cycling and pelota. These all facilitated not only greater physical fitness but also an element of socialization for marginalized groups. Finally, only days before the outbreak of the Civil War, these activities were brought together and articulated in the association Cultura Popular. This included sections devoted to education and popular universities, popular missions, theatre, cinema clubs and choirs, creative arts, sports, libraries and publications.[11] Such preliminary experiences, together with an organizational framework, provided the basis for the development of these activities in the struggle against Franco.

Despite the severity of the fighting in certain areas and the mood of popular exaltation on the outbreak of war in July 1936, an almost unreal sense of calm prevailed in all the education ministry's documentation for the subsequent weeks, almost as if the uprising was seen as an isolated incident which would be concluded before the commencement of the next school year. The real change in educational and cultural policy occurred with the formation of Largo Caballero's ministry in September 1936. Whilst the communist, Jesús Hernández, was appointed education minister, real power was exercised by the triumvirate of Wenceslao Roces as sub-secretary, Lombardía as director general of primary education and Renau as director general of the Arts. Lombardía's militancy in the FETE

[8] See C. H. Cobb, 'El teatro de agitación y propaganda en España. El grupo teatral "Nosostros" (1932–34)' in *Literatura popular y proletaria* (Seville, 1986).
[9] *Mundo Obrero*, 24 June 1936.   [10] Ibid., 13 May 1936.   [11] Ibid., 7 July 1936.

has already been mentioned. Renau had founded the Valencian Union of Proletarian Artists and Writers, edited the review *Nueva Cultura*, and was an innovative artist who had introduced John Heartfield's techniques of photomontage into Spain. Roces, besides his university post as professor of law, had worked tirelessly to introduce new, radical currents of thought into Spain. He directed the publication of marxist classics (his translation and introduction to the Communist Manifesto being still in print in Spain), the monthly *Bulletin of Political Doctrine* and contributed regularly to the left-wing press. He also translated contemporary German and Russian novelists like Remarque, Glaeser, Belyk and Panteleev. This previous experience and commitment welded Roces, Lombardía and Renau into an extremely cohesive and competent team. The tone to be adopted was quickly apparent in the decree of 16 September 1936 which dissolved the academies as 'outworn, sclerotic institutions, out of touch with the social climate of the present day'.

The problems which confronted the ministry were formidable and must inform any evaluation of its work. Urgent arrangements had to be made for some 50,000 evacuated children. Buildings had to be requisitioned, personnel appointed, basic services organized and clothing provided. The staffing situation was a constant nightmare: their tradition of loyalty to the Republic made primary school teachers obvious choices for command in a volunteer army.[12] In addition to these losses there were those trapped on holiday in the nationalist zone and unable to return, besides a significant number of disaffected teachers who either chose not to rejoin their posts or were later dismissed. No efforts were spared to replace them through crash courses for those with a suitable educational background. Some estimates have put the number of those thus recruited at 60,000.[13]

Such a situation demanded draconian measures. Consequently the ministry lost no time in establishing an almost military system of appointments and transfers, followed by the establishment of double working shifts in all schools.[14] The same austerity was still evident a year later when the summer vacation for staff was abolished.[15] Most of all, Roces's determination to overcome these difficulties and to transform the educational system, putting it at the service of the Republic, can be seen in his drive to

[12] The Felix Barzane battalion, which fought on the Madrid front, was composed almost entirely of volunteers from the ministry's personnel and, at one stage, Lombardía joined them in the front line.
[13] J. M. Fernández Soria, *Educación y cultura en la Guerra Civil (España 1936–1939)* (Valencia, 1984), p. 31.
[14] Decree of 24 September.   [15] *Gaceta de la República*, 9 July 1937.

achieve complete autonomy in the organization of his budget. The rigid headings and compartments, the careful comparisons with previous budgets – part of a well-established practice – hindered innovation. Thus, in presenting his first budget – *in extremis* on 30 December 1936 – Roces requested authority 'to reorganize all the sections of his ministry and to reallocate their budgets whilst remaining within the overall figures'.[16]

This was to acquire particular significance when it came to subsidizing groups and associations collaborating in operations like the cultural and literacy campaigns. The eight budgetary headings previously used were reduced to one. This enabled the ministry to respond speedily in a constantly changing situation.[17] Valuable though the creation of their own programmes was, more important still was the work of Roces and his aides in readily supporting and coordinating the activities of a plethora of groups born in the heavily charged atmosphere of the war's opening months. That this was possible was no small measure due to the existence of an appropriate administrative framework.

Given the context of the war, it would be unrealistic to look for the implementation of major structural reforms of the educational system. The study of governmental decrees and orders provides a guide to ministerial thinking but can be entirely misleading in appraising what was achieved.[18]

This is not to diminish education's priority in the government's overall budget, nor the importance of the work undertaken in such basic areas as school building.[19] However, it is important to appreciate that the achievement has to be sought in a complex skein of activities undertaken at a variety of levels, both official and unofficial. Behind these it is possible to discern certain constant features. Firstly, despite confronting ever-changing circumstances, the ministry revealed remarkable adaptability. Thus it recognized the limitations on control from the capital in the chaotic conditions of communications created by the war. As a result it delegated considerable authority to the provincial directors of primary education and

16 Archive of the Ministry of Education, Alcalá. Legajo 11.415.2.
17 See the preparatory notes for the 1938 budget, Alcalá. Legajo 11.415.2.
18 An example of this approach is contained in M. Vázquez, 'La reforma educativa en la zona republicana durante la Guerra Civil', *Revista de Educación* (September–October 1975). Leaving aside the polemical diatribes of the Franco period such as Iniesta's *La garra marxista en la infancia* (Burgos, 1939), or Castro Marcos's *El Ministerio de Instrucción Pública bajo la dominación roja* (Madrid, 1939), the most complete accounts are those by J. M. Fernández Soria, *Educación y cultura* and E. Fontquerni and M. Ribalta, *L'ensenyament a Catalunya durante la Guerra Civil* (Barcelona, 1982).
19 For information on the ministry's budget see Lozano, *La educación republicana*, pp. 334–6. Cf. Fernández Soria, *Educación y cultura*, pp. 28–9, which offers a figure of 5,413 new schools, but places considerable reservations around this estimate.

created schools' commissions to direct work in those provinces partially occupied by the nationalist forces.[20] In the literacy campaign the ministerial authorities gladly left the FETE to organize a large part of the work of the 'cultural militias' in the army, whilst themselves concentrating on other aspects of the programme such as the flying literacy brigades, where they readily made use of improvised assistance from local women and adolescents.[21]

Roces and his assistants sought to maximize the educational system's contribution to the republican cause. Hence the universities were directed to ensure that adequate numbers of engineers, technicians, doctors and para-medical staff were available to the armed services and war industries. Special short practical courses were organized for final-year students to give them a temporary qualification.[22] This was just one illustration of the PCE's priority of winning the war before conducting the social revolution.

Nevertheless its commitment to the social transformation of Spanish education cannot be doubted. Proof lies in the establishment of the workers' secondary schools, the accelerated *bachillerato* or secondary education examination, the workers' polytechnics, the proposals to reform agricultural education, the development of technical schools at towns like Sabadell, which had centres to train artisans, nurses and workers in textiles and commerce.[23]

Of equal importance as a theme was the continuing debate about the need not only to ensure the loyalty of their personnel but also to cultivate a sense of identity with the anti-fascist cause throughout the population. Thus the short courses to train primary school teachers included classes on socio-political questions, 'the different aspects of the present war, the basis of anti-fascism, the patriotic content of our cause and its reflexion in the school'.[24] The circular from the director general of primary education to training college lecturers indicated how the history teacher was to 'study the path followed by all peoples to free themselves from their oppressors'.[25] The question of including references to the war in primary school teaching provoked a heated discussion in which the idealism of the anarchists was severely criticised in the columns of *Escola Proletaria* and *El Magisteri Catala*, which both expressed the FETE viewpoint.

Yet it is in the field of extra-mural education that the Popular Front

---

[20] Decree of 22 February, 1937.   [21] Ministerial Order, 20 September 1937.
[22] See Fernández Soria, *Educación y cultura*, pp. 36–41.
[23] Ministerial Order, 24 November 1936; decrees of 21 April 1937, 25 February 1938. The *bachillerato* was established on 21 November 1936.
[24] Ministerial circular, 4 October 1937.   [25] *Gaceta*, 15 March 1937.

government's policy and the contemporary social climate both become most obvious. Fernández Soria has noted that 'the 18 July removed restraints on so many revolutionary impulses: all hesitation about innovation was to disappear ..., populist credibility increased'.[26] Similarly Nina Gourfinkel has indicated the catalytic effect of a revolutionary situation on the theatre, quoting the cases of Soviet Russia, Germany in 1919 and Spain in 1936.[27] The overall objectives were clear:

To raise the cultural level of the soldier is to strengthen his political consciousness. It is obvious that our army has to be composed of men conscious of an ideal, for which they are fighting and prepared to die. Down with illiteracy! Bear in mind that illiteracy does not simply mean the inability to read or write, but rather a lack of clear concepts and indifference to the great moral and social conflicts facing us.[28]

The government's strength was its consciousness of the tremendous popular fervour at its disposal, and its concentration on supporting, channelling and coordinating these energies.

Some idea of this widespread, heterogenous movement can be obtained from provisional national committee membership of Cultura Popular: this ranged from student federations through women's groups to workers' sports associations.[29] The dominant note was the enthusiasm and improvisation at all levels which characterized the resistance to the military coup. For Carmen Grimau:

It is necessary to look for the art of the period in the trains, painted by groups of artists and volunteers, transporting militiamen to the front. It is equally to be found in the Madrid underground stations, converted into air-raid shelters. A militant art with popular and spontaneous features which moulded the general feeling of commitment.[30]

Serge Salaün has stressed that it was not a campaign controlled by a professional government minority, but was based on the active participation of large sections of the population. 'The originality of the press between 1931 and 1939 lies in the proliferation of very localized news-

---

[26] 'La educación en la España republicana durante la Guerra Civil. Ideología y praxis' in *Lorenzo Luzurriaga y la política educativa*, p. 59.
[27] 'La politique théâtrale russe et le réalisme' in J. Jacquot (ed.), *Le théâtre moderne. Hommes et tendances* (Paris, 1958), p. 202.
[28] *Cultura Popular*, 2, (June 1937).
[29] Membership comprised: the Working Men's Cultural and Sporting Federation, the Federal Union of Hispanic Students, the Unified Socialist Youth Movement, the Popular Universities, the FETE, the Alliance of Anti-fascist Intellectuals, the Youth Movement of the Republican Union, the Federation of the Left, the Hispanic American University Federation, the Spanish University Federation, the Esperanto Association, the Popular Atheneums, the Federation of Pioneers, and the Anti-fascist Women's Association.
[30] *El cartel republicana en la Guerra Civil* (Madrid, 1979), p. 19.

papers (town, district and firm), always identified with one of the major ideological currents.'[31]

Inevitably the success of many of these organizations depended on their members' pre-war experience. If Cultura Popular was so successful in setting up a system of transportable libraries for military units (781 units just in 1937), it was because it had emerged with clear objectives before the war started and knew how to adapt a long heritage of working men's libraries in Spain.[32] Similarly, César Falcón's earlier experience in the field of agit-prop theatre, allied with his knowledge of the revolutionary tradition in other countries, was crucial to the speed with which Altavoz del Frente set up its 'war theatre', and a cinema unit producing its own documentary films, radio broadcasts and a graphic workshop to make posters.

The distribution of ministerial grants serves to underline the variety of activities undertaken. The 1937 and 1938 accounts show major entities receiving large sums of money. The literacy campaign brigades got 111,490 pesetas for the first nine months of 1938. But these accounts also record the twenty-five pesetas awarded to the agit-prop organizer for north Madrid. In between are amounts allocated for the purchase of books, for concerts, exhibitions, student theatre groups, the establishment of the anti-fascist intellectuals' publishing house, festivals for evacuees, the Red Cross and other movements, meetings of gymnastic, cultural and sporting feder-ations, together with grants to individual writers and artists like Alberti, Léon Felipe, Sender and Luis Quintanilla.[33]

Specific areas of cultural activity illustrate not only the intense creative activity in support of the popular cause, but also the ministry's aims and the sort of modus vivendi achieved with their partners. Book publishing and distribution is an example: predictably it played an important part in official plans and yet the case presents several unusual features. Salaün has analysed the changes occurring in popular reading habits during the war: 'The book, in its traditional form, did not respond to the needs of the moment in the way that the press did ...; books are not so suitable in a rapidly changing period with an uncertain future.'[34] Thus the bibliograph-ies of books of poetry published between 1936 and 1939 show how many of them were edited by entities depending on individual military units such as

[31] *La poesía de la guerra de España* (Madrid, 1985), p. 16.
[32] *La Sección de Bibliotecas de Cultura Popular* (Valencia, 1938).
[33] Alcalá, Legajo 10241–2, 10346.38, 10346.40, and 11.374.
[34] Salaün, *Poesía de la guerra*, p. 80.

Education and cultural policy of Popular Front government in Spain

the famous Fifth Regiment, the commissariat of the International Brigades, or other organizations such as political parties and trade unions. Roces recognized the task of book editing and distribution as an essential part of the campaign, channelling the grants through the well-established committee charged with purchasing and exchanging books and bringing together the Valencian publishing houses and booksellers into a coordinated organization. Nevertheless, the range of publications reflected, in their use as propaganda, the political conflict between anarchists and communists over the fate of the popular revolution. Thus one sees Roces striving to establish the hegemony of the PCE in Aragón, where dispute with the anarchists was particularly sharp. In June 1937 the ministry ordered five hundred copies of *The Communist Party Fights for Liberty*, two hundred copies of *What is the Communist Party and How it Works*, and two hundred copies of *The Youth Movement* by Santiago Carrillo to be sent to the Department of Political Instruction of the Council of Aragón, together with other bulk orders for *The Communist Manifesto, Stalin and the Red Army*, and *The Zinoviev Trial*.[35]

The development of theatrical activities during the war has been comprehensively studied by Robert Marrast and there are several aspects which provide clear indications of the direction of the ministry's cultural policy.[36] Firstly one sees, yet again, willingness to support a wide variety of activities contributing to the morale-building operation, from the highly professional group Nueva Escena led by Rafael Alberti and María Teresa León at the Teatro Español, down to a wide variety of agit-prop groups like Altavoz del Frente performing in the streets and to front-line units. However, the Madrid theatre and cinema programmes for 1937 and 1938 show how, following the heroic defence of the capital in the war's early months, the worst sort of commercial opportunism quickly reappeared. The recent study of the minutes of the Madrid Defence Junta has shown that much of the blame rests with various trade union and political organizations which, behind a facade of workers' management, were not only failing to pay any taxes but also were content to present frivolous, escapist entertainment, provided that it was profitable.[37] Consequently there was a certain inevitability about the establishment of the central

[35] Alcalá, Legajo 10.322.7.
[36] *El teatre durant la Guerra Civil Espanyola* (Barcelona, 1978). See also J. Coca, E. Gallén, A. Vázquez, *La Generalitat Republicana i el teatre (1931–1939)*, (Barcelona, 1982), and M. Bilbatúa, *Teatro de agitación política, 1933–39* (Madrid, 1976).
[37] J. Aróstegui and J. A. Martínez, *La Junta de Defensa de Madrid* (Madrid, 1984).

theatre council to exercise greater vigilance over public entertainment in the besieged capital.[38]

One of the most remarkable campaigns conducted by the ministry was the drive for literacy amongst the republican troops. The full implications of literacy in terms of greater social participation and increased civic consciousness have already been underlined. It was toward this goal that the members of the FETE first undertook the task. Their strong pro-republican convictions and earlier experience of work amongst the illiterate made it natural that they should begin this work without any official prompting. Rafael Guisasola, then secretary of the FETE's Madrid branch, has clearly recalled how those units without a teacher to undertake the task would request the FETE's assistance to fill the gap, something which they were able to do in collaboration with ministerial officials in Madrid.[39] Similar work was carried out in Valencia by Domingo Amo, the FETE's assistant national secretary. The curiously varied pattern of this early cultural work was related in *El Ataque*, the newspaper of El Campesino's brigade. This unit established a library containing a range of socio-political materials. The commissar also obtained for the brigade contemporary revolutionary films, distributed leaflets on sexual hygiene and invited prominent anti-fascist intellectuals to speak or give recitals.[40]

The FETE's Madrid records showed that some two hundred primary school teachers had already begun this work on the Madrid front alone in the war's opening months. Later, *Armas y Letras*, the official review of the 'cultural militiamen', reported that there were six hundred by June, a number which rose to 1,500 under seventeen inspectors by the end of September 1937. Fernández Soria suggests a final total of 2,200 teachers providing classes for between 70,000 and 100,000 adult learners.[41] Estimating the number of troops involved is notoriously difficult. It is probably more meaningful to note the breakdown published by many of the units in their own newspapers. Repeatedly a roughly even distribution emerges amongst three groups: illiterate, semi-literate and literate. In many cases the 'militiamen' would be providing classes for the great majority of the unit.

The ministry officially underwrote the scheme through the decree of 30 January 1937. This not only integrated the 'militiamen' into the army's structure but, more importantly, provided a generous budget. This was

[38] *Gaceta*, 22 August 1937.   [39] Interview with the author, 19 March 1986.
[40] 9 January 1937.
[41] Fernández Soria, *Educación y cultura*, pp. 57–8.

prepared by Lombardía and signed by Roces on 6 June 1937: the total of over 250,000 pesetas allowed for 100,000 possible pupils.[42] Easily the most notable item of equipment was the literacy instructional pamphlet, written by the school inspector Fernando Sainz and the journalist Eusebio Cimorra. Carefully produced and lavishly illustrated, this successfuly combined modern teaching practice with a content adapted to the wartime situation: 'Two field guns multiplied by two make up a battery.'

Placement of the 'cultural militiamen' under the brigade commissar's direct authority frequently led to tensions, raising possible conflicts between educational and political duties. The work of the 'militiamen' was evidently intended to go beyond basic instruction in reading and writing, to consolidate the troops' awareness of the popular cause. This was especially visible in the talks on Spanish history and geography, a regular part of the teaching of the 'militiamen', designed to suggest the continuity of the popular struggle against oppression. The author Ramón Sender, who at the end of 1936 was with a unit on the Madrid front, traced such an outline from the war of the 'Comuneros' onwards.[43] Inevitably such accounts frequently indulged in gross simplifications. In daily work there were probably no clear divisions between particular types of duty for the 'cultural militiaman'. He had to adapt himself to his unit's particular needs. As the war continued he was called increasingly to assist in the technical training of corporals, sergeants and officers.[44] The dominant theme in the instructions given to the 'cultural militiamen' in the military press reflected not so much any political orientation as the traditional vigilance of the school inspectors. Thus *Norte*, the journal of the II Division, included on 15 August 1937 a series of directions on marking registers regularly, sending the attendance lists to the inspectorate three times a month, and keeping materials used in the wall journals at the inspectors' disposal.

The question of the control of the education ministry by a communist triumvirate, and the extent of political exclusivism such as dispatching communist political propaganda to Aragón, merits examination. The single-mindedness of the sub-secretary, Roces, undoubtedly led to a lack of confidence and downright suspicion. Yet, according to Aróstegui and Martínez, the anti-communist thesis (so beloved of Francoist historians like Eduardo Comín Colomer), requires revision.[45] In the analysis of the

[42] Alcalá, Legajo 10241.2.   [43] *Juventud*, 15 December 1936.
[44] See *Superación*, 7 November 1938.
[45] *Junta de Defensa*, p. 136. For an example of Comín Colomer's work see his *El V Regimiento de Milicias Populares* (Madrid, 1973).

former the war provoked the problem of the exercise of power, rendering inevitable a series of conflicts between different political and ideological tendencies. In a wartime situation the ministry was forced to take authoritarian measures to maintain the educational system, to control the use of radios and clandestine transmitters in Madrid, and to promote theatre and cinema programmes more in keeping with the conditions of the siege of the capital. The previous experience of the FETE members, the knowledge of agit-prop techniques possessed by PCE members and sympathisers, naturally brought them to the fore in many of the activities under discussion. Nevertheless, the overall picture was by no means so straightforward: reference has been made to the ministry's need to delegate large areas of its authority, to improvise and to rely on a wide variety of voluntary collaborators.

A final example of the complexity of the relationships between the different ideological tendencies of the left in Spain occurs in the confused situation arising from the change of government in April 1938. Segundo Blanco's arrival at the education ministry favoured anarchist interests and it is revealing to follow their problems in countering communist dominance among the 'cultural militiamen'. The anarchists' major difficulty arose over finding their own candidates to replace the existing 'militiamen'. The proposals from local federations were supposed to indicate candidates' aptitudes, but mostly limited themselves to broad comments of the type, 'good general knowledge', or 'good speaker'.[46] This lack of qualified candidates led one of the inspectors to request the suspension of any further appointments and to complain of how he had been sent a group of hairdressers, basket makers and waiters.[47] The problem was, in fact, broader, as Ribalta and Fontquerni have shown concerning the dilemma facing the anarchists when they had the chance to influence educational development in wartime Barcelona. For them the ideal was rather to preserve their ideological independence at a distance from any official structures. In 1938 they wished to replace the communist 'cultural militiamen' but it was alien to their principles to propose a generalized alternative educational model.[48] The programme of activities, the organization and the materials created by the aides of Roces and Lombardía had proven their efficacy, whilst the situation did not lend itself to a sudden and massive change of personnel.

In conclusion, it is perhaps not surprising that activities in the cultural

---

[46] Archivo Histórico Nacional, Salamanca, Legajo M. 437.   [47] Ibid., Legajo b. 809.
[48] Fontquerni and Ribalta, *L'ensenyament a Catalunya*, pp. 135–6.

and educational sphere should so precisely reflect the broader trend of events during the war. The pattern included the collapse of established institutions and the resultant climate of vigorous improvisation, identified by Aróstegui and Martínez as determinants of the government's response to the military rebellion. Its successful record in culture and education was in part due to the capacity and energy of Roces, Lombardía and Renau – a triumvirate determined to create a clear identity and consciousness for the loyalist troops. However, of equal significance was their avoidance of bureaucratic centralism and their readiness to capitalize on the mood of popular fervour, channelling the efforts of those individuals and groups who had already acquired experience of educational and cultural work. Here the Communists' greater dynamism, coupled with their awareness of the potentialities of this type of action, naturally thrust them to the forefront. Despite the excesses occasionally resulting from misplaced zeal, which provoked the suspicion of other government supporters, the record of their initiatives in the face of increasing difficulty remains one of the most positive achievements of the Second Republic.

French intellectual groups and the Popular Front: traditional and innovative uses of the media

MARTIN STANTON

What is an intellectual? A simple question, but one which has been answered in very different and often complex ways. Intellectuals, according to Karl Mannheim's classic 1936 definition, embody the relative freedom of thought.[1] But this broad definition has suffered increasing criticism, notably on account of its insistence that intellectual thought eludes class definition by means of the magical powers of its relative freedom. Historians have been amongst Mannheim's more severe critics, and have proffered instead more specific definitions, and suggested, for example, that the appearance of intellectuals is not to be explained by some function of thought, but rather by more concrete factors such as the growth of the literary market from 1840 on.[2] The new title of 'intellectual', with all its supposed 'independence', had to be purchased in hard cash, so, like everything else, suffered from market fluctuations.

In the last decade, this notion of the intellectual's 'freedom of thought' has been debunked. It has become clear that the intellectual was neither a trans-national, nor trans-cultural, nor trans-historical phenomenon. In France, the term 'intellectual' (*l'intellectuel*) was said to have come into

[1] Karl Mannheim, *Ideology and Utopia* (London, 1936/1954), pp. 136–46; Karl Mannheim, 'The problem of the intelligentsia' in *Essays in the Sociology of Culture* (London, 1956), pp. 104–6.
[2] For a review of recent studies on the subject, see R. J. Brym, *Intellectuals and Politics* (London, 1980); for a review of recent French studies, see Antoine Spire, 'Les intellectuels, le pouvoir, et les médias', *Raison Présente*, 73 (1985).

common currency in 1898 in conjunction with the campaign to exonerate Dreyfus. French intellectuals, therefore, like Dreyfusards, formed neither a narrow nor homogeneous group. Instead their function was to guard the rights of the individual against the state, and to challenge generally the crude and anonymous operations of all large groups like religious denominations and political parties. French intellectuals were each in their own right outspoken individuals militating for whichever right they themselves felt to be in question at the time. In short, there was no question of a French 'intelligentsia', with common policies and strategies.

To assumptions of intellectuals' idealism, the rider is often added that they were over confident about the influence the written word could exert on the world of politics. Régis Debray, for example, has argued that French intellectuals were often wilfully blind to the opportunities that film, radio and television offered them.[3] Even the more 'enlightened' were at best opportunistic, and remained scornful of the achievements of popular culture. In essence, this criticism re-enacts the primal separation of thought from its context. It suggests that intellectuals' political function *adapted* to the new media, rather than undergoing fundamental transformation. 'Ideas' remained the same, but were just presented in a different way to larger audiences who possessed less evident critical skills, and less evident means of reply. Debray ignores the fact that in the transitional process from the era of written high culture to popular audio-visual culture, the medium itself might have indeed changed the message.[4]

This essay starts from the opposite viewpoint from Debray. It will suggest that French intellectuals, and French Popular Front intellectuals in particular, viewed the new media of film, television, and radio not just as interesting opportunities to preach the same message to a larger audience, but as factors crucial to intellectual involvement in politics, and certain to transform it in fundamental ways. Establishing critical awareness of the new media, *within the technical framework imposed by those media*, was therefore given prominence and often priority amongst intellectual frontist strategies. It involved an exposition of the uses made of these media by fascists, and the development of new creative techniques which would bring new light to old themes, notably the 'freedom' that fascists tried to obscure. Common to the rhetoric of left and right, then, was a specific intellectual need to explore the grounds on which the new media constructed its messages, told its stories, or mixed the colours. This was accompanied by

[3] Régis Debray, *Teachers, Writers, Celebrities*, trans. D. Macey (London, 1979).
[4] Ibid., pp. 141ff.

an equally strong desire to expose the political constraints imposed on that construction by censorship. Ironically, tradition reinforced the point. In 1898, Dreyfusard and anti-Dreyfusard intellectuals had argued through the press about the so-called 'freedom' of the press. In 1936, French Popular Front intellectuals and their opponents used the new media to reflect on and revise the notion they inherited of the 'freedom' of the press.

DEFINITIONS OF FRENCH POPULAR FRONT INTELLECTUALS AND THE DEVELOPMENT OF A MEDIA STRATEGY

Intellectuals are traditionally counted amongst the founders of early French Popular Front movements, and are credited with influencing government policy from 1936 to 1938 in the fields of educational reform, the arts, leisure, and radio, television, and film. It is strange though that they are equally blamed for initiating 'wild hopes', based on a 'generous utopia', that never had any chance of becoming political reality.[5] Concern for the new media was obviously central to this criticism; too many films, records and books could be said to blur distinctions between fact and fantasy. Even so, the thrust of the critical attack on frontist intellectuals seems to be set on demolishing a whole 'theatrical set'. Pascal Ory, for example, has dismissed frontist intellectual involvement as a matter of 'festival', a well-organized party with a good floor show, but destined to die when the food and drink ran out.[6] He portrays the celebrations fading rapidly with the morning light, that is, with the fall of the second Blum government on 8 April 1938.

This criticism suggests that intellectuals might not have been invited to the Popular Front 'party' in the first place. Their presence, their thoughts and gestures, are dismissed as mere *ornaments*. Once the firework colours dimmed in the night, intellectuals tended to appear a bit 'naive', too lost in their creative games to realize that the real world did not centre around them in the broad daylight.[7] To cut a long story short, politics was authored by politicians, or generals, or businessmen. Intellectuals were left traditionally 'free' to find their way back to their desks, their studios or classrooms.

[5] Cf. Henri Noguères, *La vie quotidienne au temps du front populaire* (Paris, 1977), pp. 196ff; and David Caute, *Communism and the French Intellectuals* (London, 1964).
[6] Pascal Ory, 'Front populaire et création artistique', *Bulletin de la Société d'Histoire Moderne*, 8 (1974), 13: 'A generous utopia, soon to be belied by the facts, without much echo today, but whose optimistic and popular style – a festival in a word – is representative of the hopes and limits of the Popular Front as a whole.'
[7] Cf. Caute, 'Principles of utility', *Communism and the French Intellectuals*, pp. 34ff.

French intellectual groups and the Popular Front

This extended party analogy adds a new dimension to the distortions imposed by the 'freedom of thought' definition of intellectuals. It suggests that French intellectual involvement in the new media was more theoretical than practical; French intellectuals might have *discussed* changes in forms of communication, but rarely participated in film, radio and television. Moreover, it is often claimed that they ignored the more flexible narrative styles operative in such media, and clung stubbornly to the classic format of the literary review. Obviously, there are cases of such reactionary sentiment, but it is hardly typical. This essay will argue rather that intellectuals tended to relate to these media changes in different ways from politicians, who evidently had more to gain from trying to magnify the effects than studying the small detail of the causes.

One factor is central: French intellectual discourse in the 1930s was preoccupied with intense questioning of the effect of media changes on traditional narrative forms.[8] All the 'new' intellectual movements that incorporated political involvement in the Popular Front were equally concerned to question perceived reality. Existentialist, surrealist, and personalist views of intellectual strategy during this period all equated the struggle against fascism with that of finding adequate analytical tools to expose the fascination fascist groups exerted. Frontist intellectuals therefore found some common ground amongst themselves in 'the defence of culture', that is, a general concern with *the power behind those narrative forms that seemed able to mobilize a mass audience.*

Intellectual awareness of and involvement in radical changes in the media context in which this 'defence of culture' took form only served to heighten their own sense of power and importance. Quite rightly, because over the years they had constructed a unique position from which to overview such changes in the form in which information was presented to the public. The precedent, and, in fact, the first coherent political usage of the French noun *intellectuel*, was set in 1894 by a group of anarchist writers and creative artists who used their creative skills to evade the particularly stringent censorship laws of that year, and discovered spaces within the media that both favoured experiment and were hard to attack because of the difficulty of establishing effective legal distinctions between political and aesthetic factors.[9] Their innovative incorporation of new photo and graphic techniques in the political–literary review established a precedent

[8] Cf. Michel Winock, *Histoire politique de la revue 'Esprit' 1930–1950* (Paris, 1975), p. 14.
[9] P. Fabreguettes, *Traité des délits politiques et des infractions par la parole, l'écriture, et la presse* (Paris, 1901), vol. I., pp. 53ff.

that typified intellectual involvement from 1894 to the French Popular Front.[10] Especially important was the status given to *caricature*, where fine lines between humour and defamation operated, *photographs* whose relationship to social reality was hard to contest – the camera never lies – and the encouragement of *street art*, where theatre and poster 'events' proved too spontaneous and flexible to be effectively policed. Popular Front intellectuals not only worked within this tradition, but seized the opportunity of the Blum cabinet's tacit support to transform radically their own position and sense of creative freedom within the new audio-visual context. The oft-cited 'popular cultural revolution', then, was not simply the rapid increase in expenditure on the arts and sciences, the Zay educational reforms, the *bibliobus* and the promotion of higher literacy, but the creation of new *audio-visual forms* of intellectual expression.[11] These promoted a new format for daily and weekly newspapers, a significant upgrading in the use of caricature and photograph, experimental exploitation of collage and photomontage, and the adaptation of film and theatre technique to the production of significant political 'events'.

Clearly the limited format of this essay precludes any detailed consideration of the political involvement of specific intellectuals, how they assumed power and prestige, utilized traditional media spaces, or innovated. What it can do, though, is to examine the way in which media considerations were formative and transformative in French intellectual history during this period; the way in which critical consideration of new narrative possibilities offered within the media constituted frontist intellectual strategies 'in the defence of culture'.

ORGANIZATIONAL LEVELS OF INTELLECTUAL INVOLVEMENT IN THE FRENCH POPULAR FRONT

'Literary France means a few hundred writers, critics, and chroniclers, backed by thousands of snobs and cruisers [*badauds*].'[12] This comment of Marcel Martinet expressed a common impression of the organizational nature of the French intellectual front: large amorphous groups that held high profile conferences and bombarded the daily press with manifestos denouncing fascist encroachment of civil liberties, but which, in reality,

[10] Cf. Pascal Ory, 'La politique culturelle du premier gouvernement Blum', *La Nouvelle Revue Socialiste*, 10–11 (1975).
[11] Nicolas Berdiaev, *Destin de l'homme dans le monde actuel: pour comprendre notre temps* (Paris, 1936).
[12] Marcel Martinet, *Le Populaire*, 4 December 1937.

had little credibility beyond the fame or notoriety of the few. Such an impression derived from media coverage of the great 'events' associated with the intellectual front, rather than the administrative structures set up to channel the effort and enthusiasm of some five to fifty thousand people, depending on your method of calculation.[13] The coming of the Popular Front did not affect the media's tendency to construct its feature stories around the traditional appeal of powerful, wise or glamorous individuals. The only difference was that the individuals featured were often intellectuals rather than the aristocracy or film stars. In contrast, little or nothing was reported on the lengthy debates on pacifism that shook many emergent frontist intellectual groups.[14]

Ironically, the evident distortions engendered by this emphasis on heroic individuality fed back into the intellectual groups themselves, who made it a prime subject of debate and a means of defining alternative strategies. The debate was generally entitled 'the unhappy consciousness' (*la conscience malheureuse*). The term was originally borrowed from the German philosopher Hegel, who used it in the *Phenomenology of Mind* to describe the process of thought endlessly generating its own divisions. Hegel believed that any attempt to overcome these divisions would simply be fictional, and add new dimensions to the original 'unhappy' predicament.

As abstruse and complex as Hegel's meditations were, they informed nonetheless French Popular Front intellectuals' conceptions of the violence that fascist propaganda performed on 'reality'. In a more abstract vein, commentaries on Hegel's notion by Benjamin Fondane, Jean Hyppolite, Emmanuel Mounier, Jean-Paul Sartre and Jean Wahl, set out to illustrate the dire consequences of assuming that logic, and 'history' for that matter, would automatically regulate the excesses of fascist 'dynamic' philosophy.[15] Fondane and Sartre, especially, argued for new, mass-oriented

---

[13] On establishment, the CVIA had some 3,500 members, for example, and the AEAR 1,200, but by 1937 the Association of the Maisons de la Culture claimed 70,000 members; see Georges Cogniot, *L'avenir de la culture* (Paris, 1937), pp. 7–8; 'La Maison de la Culture et ses amis', *Commune*, November 1938, pp. 1944ff.; Noguères *La vie quotidienne*, p. 198, and Ory, 'Front populaire et création artistique', p. 7. Joint membership has not been calculated.

[14] Jean-Pierre Maxence, *Histoire de 10 ans (1927–1937)* (Paris, 1939); Romain Rolland, *Par la révolution la paix* (Paris, 1935).

[15] Benjamin Fondane, *La conscience malheureuse* (Paris, 1936) (Cf. note 40); Jean Wahl, *La conscience malheureuse dans la philosophie de Hégel* (Paris, 1937); Jean-Paul Sartre, *L'être et le néant* (Paris, 1943); Emmanuel Mounier, 'La conscience malheureuse', *Oeuvres* (Paris, 1961), vol. 4, pp. 852ff. The term was also used by Bukharin during his trial: 'Compte rendu du matin du 7 mars 1938', *Procès du Bloc des droitiers et Trotskistes antisoviétique*. (Moscow, 1939), pp. 499ff., and comments by Georges Sadoul, 'Le procès de Boukharine', *Commune*, June 1938, pp. 250ff. General interest in Hegel in Paris was stimulated by the work of Alexandre Kojève (formerly Kojevnikoff).

excursions into the contradictions of 'Western subjectivity'. Fondane began to produce films and Sartre wrote novels, each in their own way hoping to introduce critical dimensions in the fields they felt the fascists had colonized. In a similar manner, André Malraux travelled to the Soviet Union in 1934 to defend the 'revolutionary' nature of James Joyce's novelistic explorations of 'Western subjectivity', and committed himself to documentary accounts of his own political position that ranged from novels and films to designs for new 'cultural centres' (*maisons de la culture*) which would exhibit paintings and screen films that were hitherto confined to relatively affluent middle-class audiences.

From the headier heights of these global projects, a few basic features emerged that served as focal points for intellectual Popular Front programmes, and helped mould the general style of intellectual involvement in this period. To list them briefly: first, to discredit prevalent assumptions that *extraordinary* subjectivity, or 'genius', and the people it inhabits, somehow miraculously escape the division and damage from the social contradictions of the time; secondly to elaborate an alternative notion of 'culture', to be defended in the context of such contradictions, rather than by some vague appeal to its immutability or Mannheimian 'relative freedom';[16] thirdly, the exposure of the hierarchical, authoritarian and essentially imaginary features of intellectual pretensions to 'objectivity', by reference to fascist manipulation through propaganda, that is, the appeal to the so-called 'power' of words and images over reality;[17] finally, the call for an incorporation of a conscious authorial awareness, that is, constant reminders to the audience that works are produced, and not inspired from on high as a direct reprint of 'reality'. So a new popular, critical, cultural style should introduce the clatter of printing machines into the written text, and the camera and crew into films. In theory, at least, this aimed to destroy unconscious identifications with all the dangerous myths of heroics and omnipotence that fascists supposedly liked to create, but even the most ardent frontist avant-gardist had doubts that renouncing 'bourgeois lyricism' might amount to losing both an audience and a market.[18]

In practice, such critical ventures reached no further than the higher

---

16 See the declaration by frontist intellectuals in *L'Oeuvre*, 5 October 1935; see also *Union pour la vérité. Bulletin*, December 1935–January 1936.
17 One of the many major achievements of Willi Münzenberg, whose initiative was central to the founding of the Institut pour l'Etude du Fascisme. See W. Münzenberg, *Propaganda als Waffe* (Paris/Basel, 1937), and Babette Gross, *Willi Münzenberg* (Stuttgart, 1967).
18 Jean-Richard Bloch, 'Paroles à un congrès soviétique', *Europe*, 15 September 1934, p. 105; and André Malraux, 'L'attitude de l'artiste', *Commune*, November 1934.

echelons of their own group diffusion networks, with the exception, perhaps, of the odd notorious 'anti-autobiography', or 'antimémoires'.[19] On the whole, manifestos represented the tip rather than the base of the iceberg, as review groups reached their maximum audience in that context. Indeed, it was an oft-expressed aspiration of review groups to get manifestos placed in the daily press to draw attention to the originality and ever-changing nature of their views.[20]

Sadly, though, many of them never made it that far, and were condemned to bear the brunt of their intellectual wranglings in their own columns. Even those that made the heady heights felt under considerable pressure to display tight solidarity in the dailies, and refer difficulties to more elitist fora. Review groups therefore tended to divide like amoebas without the slightest awareness of the wider audience, unless this wider audience happened to notice that the same names were slightly differently arranged behind a broad general manifesto.

In this context, the broad intellectual organizations founded between 1932 and 1934 to support a united front against fascism seemed almost predestined to be insensitive to the finer philosophical nuances produced in debates on the media and political commitment. To illustrate with the four main large groupings: the Front Commun contre le Fascisme (FC), created by Gaston Bergéry after his resignation from the Radical Party on 10 March 1932; the Association des Ecrivains et Artistes Révolutionnaires (AEAR), founded on 17 March 1932 as the French section of the International Union of Revolutionary Writers, established in Moscow in November 1927; the Mouvement Amsterdam–Pleyel contre la Guerre et le Fascisme (MAP), named after the sites of its founding congresses in June 1932 and 1933; and the Comité de Vigilance des Intellectuels Antifascistes (CVIA), established in Paris on 12 February 1934. First of all, these shared the same stars, most of whom developed considerable skills in the strategies derived from Hegel's 'unhappy consciousness' mentioned above. Romain Rolland and Henri Barbusse brought their differences on Gandhi's 'active non-violence' to the early days of the AEAR; then the French Communist Party militants, the prominent novelist, playwright and editor, Jean-Richard Bloch, and the Nobel Prize physicist, Professor Paul Langevin, supposedly put an undue marxist gloss on the joint declaration of the FC at its first executive meeting at the Palais de la Mutualité on the 26 May 1933,

[19] A fashion of this time associated with stars like Emmanuel Berl, Nicholas Berdiaev, Denis de Rougemont, André Gide, and Simone Weil; retrospectively, amongst others, with André Malraux, Jean-Paul Sartre and Simone de Beauvoir.
[20] Cf. Denis de Rougemont, *Journal d'une époque 1926–1946* (Paris, 1968), pp. 100ff.

with the effect that Gaston Bergéry needed a dozen feature articles to explain his sources of disagreement;[21] a similar case is contained in the 'horror' that AEAR representative, novelist, philosopher, and critic, Paul Nizan, expressed at the 'distortion' his views underwent in a joint *Cahier de revendications* published by the *Nouvelle Revue Française* in December 1932.[22] Furthermore, the media attention – supposedly the 'positive' side of such ventures – was far from approved by the organizations' joint political sponsors. The Socialist, Radical, and Communist Parties, and the major trade union, the CGT, became increasingly concerned by what they saw as a 'bizarre use of funds'.[23] The Communists, especially, became locked in a bitter dispute over the matter. The official Comintern report of the 1932 and 1933 congresses of the MAP expressed dismay that Moscow should be subsidizing events at which only 830 of the 2,195 members present were Communists.[24]

Manuilsky, a senior Comintern official in Paris, even reported back to Moscow in June 1934 that he saw no hope for the French Party which he regarded as too obsessed with its own 'philosophical crises' to be able to respond to the political realities of the day.[25]

French intellectuals' debates on the media therefore generally took place within their traditional forum since 1894, namely the review group. The pressure generated through shifts of political opinion had the most devastating effects on this level, as reviews quickly disappeared when principal participants resigned, and disputes tended to lose the groups the accreditation they needed from more powerful bodies like the Church or a political party. In contrast, the broader groupings of French intellectuals were constructed from these review groups with precisely the new popular media in mind; their promotion of 'key' events and gatherings of 'stars' aimed at maximum media coverage. This also had the unfortunate consequence of highlighting the personal differences, and personal 'crises' that the review groups were trying to expose as 'media constructed'. Intellectual involvement in the media thus seemed to feed the very

---

[21] Cf. Romain Rolland, 'Déclaration lue à la première séance du Congrès mondial de tous les partis contre la guerre', reprinted in *Par la révolution la paix*, pp. 45–6; 'Manifeste du Front Commun', *Mantes-Républicain*, 5 April 1933; Gaston Bergéry, 'Le Mouvement Amsterdam-Pleyel et le Front Commun', *Le Monde*, 10 June 1933.

[22] Paul Nizan, 'Les conséquences du refus', *Nouvelle Revue Française*, December 1932.

[23] Dominique Desanti, *L'internationale communiste* (Paris 1970), p. 200.

[24] *The Communist International 1919–1943 Selected Documents*, ed. J. Degras (London, 1965), vol. 3, p. 239.

[25] Desanti, *L'internationale communiste*, p. 198; Kermit E. McKenzie, 'The messianic concept in the Third International 1935–1939' in *Continuity and Change in Russian and Soviet Thought*, ed. E. J. Simmons (Harvard, 1955), p. 523.

contradiction it set out to analyse. This, in turn, was reflected in intellectuals' creative work, notably forcing some to reconsider Hegelian philosophy, and others to move into new genres, and rehearse their 'defence of culture' in front of the mass they assumed to be structurally exposed to propaganda through the daily words, sounds and images they had become accustomed to consume.

THE PRODUCTION DYNAMICS OF FRENCH POPULAR FRONT INTELLECTUAL GROUPS

The words 'Loi du 29 juillet 1881 – défense d'afficher' (Law of 29 July 1881 – posters forbidden), impressively engraved on most prominent French walls, attest to the durability of the Third Republic's censorship regulations. The law is entitled 'Freedom of the press, printing, book sales, periodical press, posters, retailing, street sales, crimes, offences, prosecutions, punishment, and temporary provisions', and differed from its predecessors by limiting the jurisdiction of 'special correctional tribunals' to cases of damages and insult against individuals. Press matters were left to a public jury system under common law. Although superficially this seemed liberal, in so far as the corrective tribunals had previously proved overzealous in their 'control' of the press, in practice the new laws reinforced the reactionary powers of local authorities under common law, and encouraged the legal profession to earn considerable sums in providing officially approved definitions of how to constitute a jury. Not only were government officials, the police, the army, teachers, and religious ministers debarred from service, but also telegraph operators, domestic servants, those who fail to meet established standards of reading and writing French, all those who need to work to live, and anyone over seventy: in short the vast majority of people.[26]

These laws set precedents which survived essentially unchanged up to the triumph of the Popular Front, and, indeed, in important ways, up to the present day. First, they established a detailed legal context in which 'offence to public morals', 'provocation to civil disobedience or riot', or 'defamation of character' could be processed. Formative, of course, in this respect, was the novelist Emile Zola's famous article *J'accuse*, in which he *chose* to accuse the president of the Republic of concealing evidence in the Dreyfus Affair, hence focussing on the whole debate about public 'con-

[26] Fabreguettes, *Traité des délits*, p. cxc and L. Gabriel-Robinet, *La censure* (Paris, 1965), section 2, part 1.

fidence' in the jurisdiction of the tribunal, as well as drawing attention to the special protection given by law to the Church, army and republican institutions of order. Henceforth, intellectual causes knew precisely which legal avenues to follow to gain maximum publicity. Secondly, the 1881 regulations made it extremely difficult for any government to intrude in common law on the jurisdiction of local authorities in matters of censorship. Instead, tacit manipulation of public opinion at local level was engaged in by governments of varying shades by use of confidential 'instructions' communicated when necessary to mayors. Intellectuals, then, might be able to cause a minor stir amongst the informed few in Paris, but were unlikely to reach audiences in Lyon, Toulouse, Nantes or Marseille.

In a very real sense, these two lines of precedent circumscribed French intellectual groups' frontist activity. It has often been noted that their intense critical attack on censorship laws within their own publications made no impact at all on government policy. The most notable case of this was in film. Review groups' obvious enthusiasm for the theoretical 'enlightenment' that avant-garde documentaries could bring to the general public was matched by the recalcitrance of local censors. Despite the first Blum government's hesitant 'liberalization' proposed to the film censorship board (the Commission du Péristyle Montpensier), especially concerning the screening of Soviet avant-garde films, mayors and distributors effectively blocked distribution.[27] Even French films declared with hindsight to be 'formative' or 'classics' of frontist film style never actually reached the public they were supposed to revolutionize. The anarchist film director Jean Vigo's *Zéro de conduite* did not pass the censor during the Blum government's period, as it was deemed to 'corrupt youth' about the values of public education. Jean Renoir's *La vie est à nous*, fared little better. It only made limited and private PCF circuits in France, whereas it was a box-office hit and pronounced a masterpiece in New York.[28] Neither did the Blum government renounce the manipulation of public opinion through 'instructions'. Two sets of instructions addressed to the Péristyle Montpensier in March and October 1937 reinforced the old values of 1881 and 1894 by condemning 'films that ridicule the army or lessen its prestige', or that 'undermine national feeling or the image of France

---

[27] The classic example was the prefectorial order banning the screening of *Kronstadt* in Toulon in October 1936.
[28] See Keith Reader, 'Renoir's Popular Front films in context' in Keith Reader and Ginette Vincendeau, *La vie est à nous: French Cinema of the Popular Front 1935–1938* (London, 1986), pp. 48ff.

abroad', or that 'encourage civil disobedience, or undermine public morals'.[29]

This situation served to cement the division between critical debate on avant-garde film strategies and the 'popular' cinema that toured the local circuit. Indeed, this is sometimes cited to illustrate the unavowed preference of frontist intellectual groups for high rather than low cultural products, and written rather than verbal means of communication.[30] This not only fails to appreciate the crucial role of censorship, but misses the importance of the central example around which most alternative cultural strategies were based – the Soviet Union in the 1920s. From a distance, at least, Soviet art seemed to have government support in its most avant-garde projects. Its graphic designers transformed the press with new photographic techniques, its film school pioneered whole new approaches to camera angle and cutting room skills, and its modernist writers, Mayakowsky foremost, seemed to have won official approval and popular success from texts that were considered 'daring' in the West.[31] Of course, for many, the glitter from afar proved too good to be true, but it took them some time to discover that the Soviet government might have changed tack. The new policy of socialist realism introduced stringent definitions of what constituted 'proper' subjects for true revolutionary artists; namely insisting on themes that directly concerned the working classes, which had to be expressed in a manner that was accessible to them, which would not promote a depressive or morbid view of the world. Nonetheless, socialist realism took a long time to reach France in a clear and unadulterated form. French cultural representatives sent to the Soviet Union in the early 1930s returned with very different impressions. It is often forgotten, for example, that André Gide's famous hatchet job, *Return from the USSR*, executed after his visit in 1936, was neither taken as gospel, nor as illustrative of a general trend in intellectual fashion.[32] Louis Aragon and Georges Sadoul, in contrast, both surrealists who broke with Breton, came back from the 1932 Kharkov Congress with renewed enthusiasm, which surprised even the most sceptical of their colleagues who had previously felt certain they had been set up as indicative of Manuilsky's 'French disease', that is, the unashamed and expensive cultivation of the bizarre.[33] Similarly, André

---

[29] Cf. Ginette Vincendeau, 'The popular cinema of the Popular Front', ibid., p. 87.

[30] Cf. Debray, *Teachers, Writers, Celebrities*, pp. 141ff.

[31] Szymon Bojko, *New Graphic Design in Revolutionary Russia* (London, 1972).

[32] Cf. letter from André Wurmser to Jean Guéhenno which appeared in *L'Humanité*, 13 February 1937; also Paul Nizan on the subject in *Commune*, May 1938, pp. 1,123–5.

[33] J. P. A. Bernard, *Le PCF et la question littéraire 1921–1939* (Grenoble, 1972), p. 22.

Malraux and Jean-Richard Bloch, both viewed as more independent and 'tough-minded' French representatives at the 1934 Soviet Writers Congress, returned with a real sense of the debate governing Soviet cultural policy, even though they had to defend, with a little help from Bukharin, the 'bourgeois lyricism' of James Joyce against strident 'socialist realist' critique.[34] Ironically, even when more serious doubts about the 'durability' of Soviet cultural experiments began in March 1936, with the Moscow trials, the notion of Soviet cultural experimentation seemed so central and well-entrenched that stalwarts still argued that the Blum government should finance projects in Paris that Stalin axed in Moscow.[35]

The most obvious effect that Soviet precedents had on French intellectual frontist strategies was the concern for media *format*. Central to this was the notion of *montage*, or the process of cutting and assembling film to design meaning. The AEAR's review, *Commune*, played a seminal role in this area; first, largely through the pen of Georges Sadoul, in introducing Soviet film-school montage techniques, especially those of Eisenstein and Vertov; then, in more general terms, principally through contributions by fellow ex-surrealist Pierre Unik, by questioning the assumptions behind the construction of film events.[36] The main political aim of such critical ventures was to expose how a so-called Hollywood approach tried to hide the cuts that literally made up the smooth story line, so that a Ginger Rogers and Fred Astaire movie, a Pathé news clip, or a Nazi propaganda film could be subjected to the same unmasking to reveal 'true', that is, exploitative, motives.[37] The interest, though, actually spread wider than that, and involved play with technical sophistications that derived from such discoveries as collage and décollage (*affiches lacérées*), that is, the tearing or amendment of wall posters to suitable effect. Collage had in fact been used by the early Soviet design school to decorate sports magazines, and many French surrealists used it to similar effect, but décollage gained more power in the French context, given the special place accorded posters in the 1881 law.[38] Camille Bryen turned it into a 'crisis of reality' in its own right, a 'desecration of sacred objects', in the festive days of

[34] See *Commune*, September/October 1934.
[35] See some of the Discours at the second Congrès d'Ecrivains, held in Spain in June 1937 (*Commune*, September 1937); especially Claude Aveline, reprinted in *Les devoirs de l'esprit* (Paris, 1945), pp. 273ff.
[36] Georges Sadoul, *Dziga Vertov* (reprinted Paris, 1985); Pierre Unik, 'Le roman, le documentaire, la haine' *Commune*, January 1938.
[37] Cf. Dziga Vertov, *Articles, journaux, projets* (Paris, 1972), and Jean Vigo, *Etudes cinématographiques* (Paris, 1962).
[38] Roland Gagey, *Interdit à l' affichage*, (Paris, 1965).

May 1936.[39] In a similar vein, play between written and visual media conventions provoked powerful effects, both amongst the general public and within intellectual debate. Prominent, in hindsight, is probably André Malraux's *Espoir* (Days of Hope), conceived as a 'dialogue' between novelistic and film form, although many so-called *existentialist* projects at this time followed this path; the 'novels' of Nizan or Sartre, for example, or the amazing ciné-poems of Benjamin Fondane (surely the most underestimated intellectual of the 1930s).[40]

Perhaps the most important transformation of media format took place in the new frontist weekly press, the main examples of which were *Marianne, La Flèche, La Lumière, Vendredi,* and *Regards.* Although different in scope and scale, they were united in their aim of reaching a wider audience through modern photo and graphical techniques of presenting an attractive mix of political comment, news of the cultural scene, fashion, gastronomy, and humour. The effect is quite easy to illustrate. *La Flèche,* for example, had to content itself with an impressive arrow logo, that adorned hundreds of flags at FC meetings, and special effects, bold type, photos and cartoons to promote its star editorial committee, notably Gaston Bergéry and Paul Langevin. *Marianne* could afford much more space to make its point, so left political comment to page 2, and featured a photomontage or cartoon on page 1. It also could afford to use many more photographs, and consequently could organize its space in more exotic ways. It is interesting that though both drew on the same sources, notably the amazing and prodigious work of the cartoonist Jean Effel, they represented their political position in very different ways.[41] *La Flèche,* as a forum for the FC, was much more drawn to feature the political above the cultural, whereas *Marianne* tended towards the opposite, and feigned a frontist neutrality, which worked very much in its favour when the political – and funding – components of the Popular Front fell apart in 1937. *La Flèche* – and even more spectacularly *Vendredi* – could claim that the PCF had destroyed their viability, whereas *Marianne* continued to inspire a peculiar *genre* in French politics, as illustrated by *Le Nouvel Observateur* or *L'Express.*[42]

French Popular Front intellectual groups were thus not only bound by

---

39 Camille Bryen, *L'aventure des objets* (Paris, 1937); and *Bryen,* Exhibition Catalogue from Musée National d'Art Moderne, 1973.

40 Benjamin Fondane, *Ecrits pour le cinéma* (Paris, 1984).

41 Jean Effel (pseud. of François Lejeune), was the most prodigious of frontist cartoonists, contributing to all of the papers mentioned here; cf. *Jean Effel, Exposition du 15 Octobre au 26 Novembre 1983,* Galerie du Messager.

42 Cf. Jean Daniel (*L'Express*), François Bizot (*L'Actuel*), and Serge Richard (*L'Unité*).

their organizational structure, but also by the censorship laws which confined both the media and strategies open to them. Far from revoking these laws, the Blum government actually reinforced them. This generated a situation in which intellectuals naturally looked to narrative forms and media that were less open to censorship. Even so, the prominence given to local authorities in censorship matters meant that many important intellectual innovations during this period reached only a narrow audience. It followed then that the techniques they pioneered were often more appreciated and utilized abroad rather than in France, although this of course should not diminish their value. Finally, following the early Soviet example, French Popular Front intellectuals did manage to incorporate avant-garde graphic techniques in the publications they aimed at the wider audience. These pioneered a new 'style' of magazine which mixed cultural, political, entertainment, and leisure features, and captured a considerable market. Ironically, the magazines less bound by set frontist groups, or specific sponsors, proved more durable, though, again, the impact that more ephemeral productions like *Vendredi* had abroad, and on later French generations, should not be underestimated.

CONCLUSION

To return to the 'festival', or party analogy mentioned earlier: the rather stark separation between night and day, fantasy and reality, and intellectuals and politics, clearly collapses when placed in the frontist media context outlined above. The 'reality' of war in Abyssinia or Spain, for example, was neither simply produced by those that fought it, nor the politicians who negotiated around the *fait accompli*, but also by the film crews, radio journalists, photographers, *afficheurs*, and writers, who carefully constructed their accounts for a mass audience. The fact that intellectuals often, or even in the main, failed to reach that audience, is less a reflection of 'naivety' than of the tight restrictions on the space open to them to express themselves. Even if it is admitted that the broader intellectual organizations, the FC, AEAR, MAP and CVIA, could be judged inadequate to negotiate a realistic position with the political parties that formed the Popular Front, this still does not condemn their political objectives as a whole. On the contrary, the embarrassment value of some of the issues they proposed has remained remarkably durable – the 'peace front', for example, or freedom of information and rights to express opinion on military, police, or Church matters, have proved hard to integrate into political party programmes, precisely because of the radical critique of power involved. This embarrassment might just be why intellectuals were invited to the 'festival' in the first place, presuming, of course, that the guest list was drawn up democratically.[43]

Furthermore, it would be wrong to regard these four organizations as *the* intellectual front, as most of the strategy formulation took place on a totally different level, that of the review groups. Unlike the famous four, the review groups handled the vicissitudes of the frontist period with varying degrees of subtlety, even if they reached a much smaller audience. The smaller forum also favoured keen experimentation with media form, as we have seen. In this respect, it is important to recall too that both radio and television, though fêted at the 'Expo 37', were in early growth at this time.[44] Intellectuals' critical efforts to draw attention to them were of great political importance, given the particular, all-embracing nature of French censorship at the time, and the integral role which propaganda played in the fascist programmes that the Popular Front was supposed to attack.[45] Last, but not least, considerable cooperative creative effort was made to break the narrow boundaries of high culture and reach a mass audience, if not in the home, library, museum, or cinema, then in the streets. However pretentious some of the rhetoric, the festive variety and odd open-air theatrical display at least raised a few smiles amidst the gloomy news of the day.

[43] One of the presuppositions consistently questioned by Jean-Paul Sartre: cf. *Plaidoyer pour les intellectuels* (Paris, 1972), pp. 43ff.

[44] Cf. Noguères, *La vie quotidienne*, pp. 280ff. Television, for example, could only reach some 30–40 kilometres from the Eiffel Tower.

[45] See notes 8 and 16.

Index

Note: Organizations are listed under their initials
where this is the principal form used in the text

271

INDEX